THE NATURAL SUPERIORITY
OF SOUTHERN POLITICIANS

A Revisionist History

Also by David Leon Chandler
BROTHERS IN BLOOD

David Leon Chandler

THE
NATURAL
SUPERIORITY
OF
SOUTHERN
POLITICIANS

A Revisionist History

DOUBLEDAY & COMPANY, INC., GARDEN CITY, NEW YORK 1977

Library of Congress Cataloging in Publication Data

Chandler, David Leon.
The natural superiority of Southern politicians.

Includes index.
1. United States—Politics and government.
2. Statesmen—Southern States—Biography. 3. Southern
States—Politics and government. I. Title.
E183.C46   975′.00992 [B]
ISBN 0-385-03526-8
Library of Congress Catalog Card Number 75–21219

to Patricia

ACKNOWLEDGMENTS

For assistance and guidance in preparing this book, I am very much indebted to Jack Kneece; and to Danny Barbarin Barker, Richard Batt, Lindy Boggs, Philip Carter, Justice Tom Clark, Walter Clawson, Jesse Core, Mimi Crossley, Diane Hamilton, Bennett Johnston, Iris Turner Kelso, Charles McBride, Steve Mitchell, Fred Pauls of the Library of Congress, Al Rubin, Marty Schramm, Russell Sackett, Sarah Simon, Hoke Smith, John Stennis, T. Harry Williams, Peter Wolfe; and finally to my editor John Ware and to that astute counselor on political matters, Lawrence Chehardy.

ILLUSTRATIONS

Follows page 60

1. Captain John Smith
2. John Randolph of Roanoke
3. Senator Richard Henry Lee
4. Thomas Jefferson
5. James Madison
6. Charles Pinckney of South Carolina
7. Alexander Hamilton
8. William Blount
9. James Monroe

Follows page 132

10. Andrew Jackson
11. John Calhoun of South Carolina
12. Jefferson Davis
13. Hiram Revels of Mississippi
14. Joseph Rainey
15. Senator Blanche Bruce of Mississippi
16. Woodrow Wilson

17. Franklin Roosevelt and John Nance Garner, Hyde Park
18. Sam Rayburn and Warren Atherton

Follows page 252

19. Congressman and Mrs. William B. Bankhead
20. Senator Huey Long
21. Senator Tom Watson of Georgia
22. Senator Rebecca Latimer Felton
23. Senator Hattie Caraway of Arkansas
24. Senate Foreign Relations Committee, 1944
25. Senators Richard Russell of Georgia and A. B. Chandler of
      Kentucky
26. President Harry Truman

Follows page 324

27. Senator Leroy Percy of Mississippi
28. Senator Theodore Bilbo of Mississippi
29. Senator John Stennis of Mississippi
30. Senator James Eastland of Mississippi
31. Senator Sam Ervin of North Carolina
32. Senator Herman Talmadge of Georgia
33. Martin Luther King, Jr.
34. Lyndon Johnson

CONTENTS

Acknowledgments   vii
Illustrations   ix
Introduction   History Is a Chronicle of Winners   1

Book One   THE EARLY SOUTHERNERS

1 John Randolph of Roanoke   17
2 Three Peoples   36
3 Virginia in the Lead   55
4 The Constitution, The Bill of Rights   72
5 The Democrats   87
6 North versus South, 1790s   98
7 Two Styles, Aristocrat and Demagogue   117

Book Two   THE MEANS OF POWER

8 "The Most Remarkable Invention of Modern Politics"   127
9 The Forgotten Man   133
10 The Black Breakout   150
11 Seniority   173
12 New Freedom   185
13 New Deal   199

14   Huey Long   207
15   Protégés   240
16   The Club   253

Book Three   THE USE OF POWER

17   The Republic   277
18   The Mississippian   281
19   The Chairman   298
20   The Constitutionalist   306
21   Leaders I   319
22   Leaders II   338
23   Power   356

Epilogue   Populist   370
Index   374

Introduction
HISTORY IS A CHRONICLE OF WINNERS

This book was originally intended to be a history of Southern congressmen, those who served from the 1920s to the present. But the research for that book led to an inescapable conclusion, a fact that dominated all others in the landscape.

It is that the South has produced the pre-eminent geniuses of all American political history.

Another discovery of the research was that the role of Southerners in designing the American political system has gone unrecognized in histories and textbooks, whether written in America or written abroad.

Accordingly, the original idea was scrapped and there emerged this book which reviews the Southern contribution to the national political system.

During the past two hundred years, Southerners have invented the Declaration of Independence; the world's first written national Constitution; the balancing of governmental powers between three equal houses—the legislative, executive, and judiciary; the Bill of Rights; the concept of judicial review of legislative and executive acts; and that unique body, the United States Senate, with its powers of investigation and appointment extending into the executive and the judiciary, and into foreign affairs.

Southerners also invented lesser but equally distinct American political institutions such as the two-party system, the filibuster, and the seniority-committee system which allows the Congress independence from the President and from party bosses. And it was Southerners who provided the legislation and leadership for such phenomenon as Woodrow Wilson's New Freedom, Franklin Roosevelt's New Deal, the creation of the United Nations, and Lyndon Johnson's Great Society.

Indeed, in reviewing the history it appears that only one major American political invention did not originate in the South. That was the doctrine of Secession, which was created in New England universities and law schools.

Southerners have been the architects of the American political system and during the two centuries have functioned as its caretakers, working to keep the system close to the original design.

The world has rarely seen such an outpouring of political creativity as has issued from the South. And yet this staggering array of accomplishment has gone without credit. The Southern mind and culture, the Southern "civilization," has instead been given the image of an outlaw camp; impoverished in goods and ideas, mistrustful of strangers, quick to shoot, quick with the rope, having no principle other than its own miserable survival.

The image of the South is that of the land which produced the Jukes and the Kallikaks, which has castrated blacks and ambushed civil rights dissenters. It is the South of the Ku Klux Klan and the South which murdered and rioted to prevent equal rights for the 40 per cent of its population which was black. It is the South portrayed by Caldwell and Faulkner.

This image sustains because it is a true one, as far as it goes.

While it is nowhere the purpose of this book to refight the Civil War, for a more complete picture of the South, and of America, it is worth while to look at that unique time when the North and the South functioned under separate governments.

That war was an empirical example of the differences between two political philosophies. Two of these differences, of course, were the right of secession, the cause of the war; and slavery, an underlying cause surfaced reluctantly by Lincoln during the war.

A far less advertised difference was the North-South position on the Bill of Rights. Fighting for conquest, the North by military and presidential edict effectively suspended the Bill of Rights for five years. Fighting for survival, the South adhered to the Bill of Rights through most of the war.

The North, for example, conducted a war against the whole population of the South, combatant and noncombatant alike. Plantations, farmhouses, and industries were systematically destroyed. Entire towns were burned and ransacked. Clothing of women and infants were stripped from their persons. All this done without a semblance of military or civil trial.

In addition, for its own loyal Union states, the Washington government formed a special bureau of the War Department which established provost marshals for each congressional district. These marshals, having the full service of Union troops at their call, were charged with the maintenance of internal security for their areas. Through them, the arm of the national government reached into every Northern home. The marshals were not idle.

More than three hundred Northern newspapers, large and small, were suppressed or suspended for a variety of charges.

A minimum of 13,535 Northern civilians were arrested and confined in military prisons without trial.[1]

In contrast, the South, at much cost to its military performance, adhered strictly to the law. Early in the war, Confederate President Jefferson Davis made notice of the differing philosophies:

"There is indeed a difference between the two peoples . . . Our enemies are a traditionless and homeless race. From the time of Cromwell to the present moment they have been disturbers of the peace of the world . . .

"They have destroyed the freedom of the press; they have seized upon and imprisoned members of state legislatures and of municipal councils, who were suspected of sympathy with the South; men have been carried off into captivity in distant states without indictment, without a knowledge of the accusations brought against them, in utter defiance of all rights guaranteed by the institutions under which they live.

"These people, when separated from the South, and left entirely

[1] The minimum figure comes from a postwar search of War Department records. Other surveys placed the total as high as thirty-eight thousand. The exact number can never be known because not one of the prisoners ever appeared before a civil court. A few were sentenced by military tribunal.

to themselves, have in six months demonstrated their utter incapacity for self-government . . ."

The dominant North continued its casual attitude toward the
Constitution until the disputed election of 1876 when the South,
through its political skills, achieved a partial return to its place in
the national union.

During our two-hundred-year history, the North has behaved
villainously toward its primary economic and political competitor
—the white South; just as the white South has behaved villainously toward the people it viewed as a threat—the black South.
Such conduct, unfortunately, is common to and characteristic of
the human species.

Neither North nor South is unique in its crimes. Each, however,
is close to unique in other aspects. The North, with its commercial
and industrial genius, has created a society of great social and
economic mobility. The South, with its political genius, has
created a government so far unexcelled in institutions favoring individual liberties. Together they make up the American phenomenon.

This book will address itself to the Southern contribution, the
evidence of which can be seen all around us, once the eye is
focused to perceive. Southerners have set the pace of American
government from the beginning, producing quality leaders.

The source which has produced these leaders is the small towns.
These are communities large enough to be connected into the
American information network, but small enough to be bypassed
by urbanization and industrialization. As a consequence, they
have remained informed but socially stable communities. They
tend to act as sanctuaries for the eighteenth-century ideals.

Children who grow up in such towns have a large personality
advantage. They are exposed to a set of community values in their
formative years which seem to them to be universal values. They
arrive into adolescence armed with firm concepts of family, work,
religion, liberty—values present when the nation was born.

Those who enter the mainstream of American life find, and
have always found, such ideals to be quickly challenged by the
pressures and needs of a city-based industrial society. If they have
a weak hold on their formative rural ideals, they will succumb.

But the ones whose early American values survive the test of challenge will find they have a strength to fall back upon in moments of stress. It will be the basis for their judgments, the basis of their courage. From this class have come nearly all of the American political statesmen.

Such seedbed towns exist everywhere in the nation, from coast to coast, and border to border. A sprinkling of them are found in the Northeast, fewer in the Far West. A large number are in the Midwest, but by far the greatest number of them are in the eleven states of the Confederacy and the border states of Oklahoma and Kentucky.

This advantage in stable small towns may be the reason the South has produced such a preponderance of leaders, men who zealously guard the original principles of the nation, as embodied in the Constitution, as taught in their towns. Their principal philosophy has been not to let history happen too fast, and in the course of it their political expertise has become legendary.

Richard Nixon, when he learned Senator Sam Ervin of North Carolina would chair the Watergate investigation, moaned on tape: "Goddamn it . . . Ervin works even harder than most of our Southern gentlemen. They are great politicians. They are just more clever than the others. Just more clever."[2]

An obvious question is this: If the Southern contribution is so large, then why has it gone unrecognized?

The answers are several, but they can be summarized in the axiom that conquerers, not losers, write history. The South and the North have been in conflict since the nearly concurrent foundings of the Virginia and the Massachusetts colonies. The South has lost the contest in terms of economics, population, and military force. As a consequence, the major universities are in the North, the major newspapers, magazines, and broadcasting media are in the North. The North, for most of our history, has had a near monopoly of the people who shape opinion. And they have written and lectured and preached for Northern audiences.

This is not to say they all have deliberately lied about the South.

[2] Transcript of meeting between President Nixon and White House counsel John Dean, February 28, 1973.

It is to say that they have been motivated to write from a Northern point of view. Harvard University traditionally focuses on the New England contribution to the American Revolution and pays relatively little attention to the contributions that welled up from the South. The Southerners are treated more or less as footnotes.

The South, on the other hand, since the early nineteenth century has not had a university comparable to the weight of Harvard, Yale, Dartmouth, or the later institutions in the Midwest and Far West.

In addition, a very large number of Northern opinion-shapers, from the beginning to the present, have deliberately distorted the realities of the South. They have usually done this for ideological reasons, a primary example being Harriet Beecher Stowe. Her epochal work, *Uncle Tom's Cabin,* was based on a North Louisiana slaveowner she was acquainted with. The owner did indeed commit the atrocities described in the book. But, as Stowe well knew, the man was a Northerner, only recently arrived in the South. And though she portrayed him as typical of Southern slaveowners, he in fact was rigorously ostracized by his neighbors for the very mistreatments she represented as commonplace.

The South has been a victim of propaganda and a victim of reverse prejudice. Furthermore, from the Civil War to the 1970s, the Northern-connected historians and journalists who might be inclined to defend the South have faced the risk of being identified with Southern racial policies.

Another part of the image problem has been the Southerners' internal contentiousness. When John Marshall invincibly expanded the power of the Supreme Court, he locked into battle with Thomas Jefferson, a battle and a hatred that went on for a quarter of a century. In the process it was forgotten that Marshall, too, was a product of Virginia. It came across to the generations that he was a "positive-thinking" man, out of step with the Southern establishment.

This Southern establishment has been viewed as negativist. And while it is true that the characteristic of the South has been to slow down history, it is not true that the South lacks radicals or innovators of social change. The first black senators were Southerners and they were not kept in by Northern bayonets. The first women senators were Southerners. A handful of Southern Presidents, Jefferson, Jackson, James Polk, Woodrow Wilson, and Lyndon Johnson, gave the nation large forward thrusts.

The Civil Rights movement was born and raised in the South under Southern leadership, and Franklin Roosevelt's New Deal administration was heavily influenced, "pushed to the left" according to Roosevelt's campaign manager James Farley, by Southerner Huey Long.

Some of the negativist political doctrine which has come to be identified with the South is of Northern origin. The doctrine of Secession, for instance, evolved in the North and was first used by the New England states chafing under the administration of Thomas Jefferson. (Jefferson and Madison were the first to write reasons why the doctrine was illegal, unworkable, and destructive.)

North or South, states and politicians are negative if they *believe* their interests are threatened, which often means whenever the status quo is threatened. For instance, beginning about 1945, the United States, itself created by revolution and democratic ideas, became negative and obstructionist toward social revolution in China, eastern Europe, and in the former colonies of the Great Powers. U.S. leadership believed the revolutions threatened American interests, although whether that were truly the case is highly debatable. No positive alternatives were offered by America, she simply became hard-line negativist to protect the status quo.

So it has been with the South, and the reason that Southerners have been negative so often is that their status quo has been threatened so frequently.

The South, as a political, social, and economic subnation, has been battling against Northern domination for nearly two hundred years. It has had its back to the wall since at least the Constitutional Convention of 1789. In the beginning, from the convening of the First Congress to about 1830, the attacks on the South ranged over a wide variety of issues, including taxes, fiscal policies, states' rights, and foreign relations. Slavery and oppression of blacks was one of the major issues prior to the 1830s.

After that time it was *the* major issue, the battleground upon which the South chose to make its stand and retreat no further.

This was not because the South truly perceived unique merits in slavery; individual Southerners such as Jefferson were in the forefront of the eighteenth-century movement to abolish the institution. It was because the structure of the South's culture, its identity, rested on a foundation of two races, nearly equal in number, inhabiting the same land. Corollary with this was the belief that one or the other of the two races *must* be dominant and the reigning whites were determined it would be themselves. That was the status quo they were hell-bound to defend.

The coexistence of two races was a huge obelisk, miles high, the central point of reference to which all else was oriented. The Northerners concentrated their attack on this monolith, too large to be removed, and the Southerners had a choice to abandon it, and their communal identity, or defend it. They chose the latter and defended with every political art they could conjure.

The South made a moral and strategic mistake in letting the North choose race as the battle issue. Ironically, it was the black population of America who suffered the most from this battle.

Race was settled upon as *the* issue in the 1830s. Prior to then, blacks were merging into the general economic and political life of the nation at a rate which would not be matched until the 1950s. This setback of a full century was caused by the economic-political struggle between North and South. The blacks themselves were pawns in a continental conflict.

Racial policy was simply an objective in the overall battle, not a cause of the war itself. The struggle between North and South was a struggle over who would control the country. For those who doubt it, consider the following argument.

Race has been the one consistent issue in American politics since the writing of the Constitution in 1789. It has not always been the dominant issue but has always been present. It has played a role in every single national election for two hundred years and has occupied a great deal of the time of the Congress and of the federal courts from John Marshall to the present. For two centuries, much of American politics has centered around a single question: What to do about black Americans.

How do we explain such longevity?

It is obvious that blacks would have a keen interest in this quarrel. They want to get out from under the weight of the other 90 per cent of the continent's inhabitants. But the black people have had a direct influence, being one of the contestants, so to speak, in the quarrel for just the past thirty years or so. It is the whites who have made the quarrel.

Why?

Why have the whites shown such keen interest in racial policy and racial justice? The Southern interest, like that of blacks, is obvious. A change in policy meant change in their social and economic system. But why the Northern interest? Is it morality?

Is it possible that one faction of our white population, the North, is inspired to unshackle their black brothers, while the other faction, the South, is equally bent on keeping them in chains, and whipping them when possible? Not likely, not on the basis of morality. Morality comes to individuals, but it does not motivate two centuries of social struggle.

The truth is that whites, North or South, are just not that keen on the welfare of blacks. Indeed, the whites in the North, if anything, seem to care less on a personal level about the blacks than do the whites in the South.

What is at work here, instead, is the power of ideas, not their morality. The idea that blacks should be as free as other Americans has power. And while it is a cliché that ideas have more power than armies, it is also truth. Jefferson's idea of "all men" created free and equal has changed the world more than anything since the birth of the great religious ideas.

For more than a century prior to the Revolutionary War, the fishing, commercial, and manufacturing colonies of New England were in contest with the agricultural colonies of the South. The contest grew more intense when the colonies joined together to form a single nation. One side seized an advantage in the 1789 Constitutional Convention when slavery emerged as a major issue in the convention. Northern politicians, writers, and churchmen moved firmly behind the issue. It became their ideal, and with it the power of the idea became their power.

Over this issue, the two societies, North and South, locked into combat—one middle-class, industrialist, and mercantile, the other, feudal and agricultural. The welfare of the blacks was the objective of the battle, not the cause of the war. The cause was the natural collision between two differing economic and social systems sharing the same continent.

The Southerner has been inclined to slow down the process of history to protect what he considers his civilization.

It is the civilization of the Randolphs and the Lees, men later described by Alexis de Tocqueville as constituting "a superior class, having ideas and tastes of their own, and forming the center of political action . . . The class which headed the [American Revolution] in the South, and furnished the best leaders of the American revolution."

It is the civilization of John Calhoun and Jefferson Davis, hostile to the North. "The South," General Tecumseh Sherman would write Lincoln, "must be ruled by us, or she will rule us. They hate Yankees *per se* and don't bother their brains about the past, present or future . . . They are the most dangerous set of men turned loose upon the world."[3]

It is the civilization of the sharecropper and tenant farmer, the black slave and the indentured white. The civilization which degenerated into the barbarism of long-coated Methodists and Baptist snake-handlers, the civilization of the Snopeses and Tobacco Road. A civilization which imported the worst and trashiest aspects of Northern commercialism and set it atop a social structure that was never far removed from savagery. A civilization which became mediocre, and caused H. L. Mencken to write, "There are single acres in Europe that house more first rate men than all the states south of the Potomac." The South of that time, 1917, found itself incapable of challenging the sharp, stabbing accuracy of his impudence.

This South "civilization" has been in conflict for two hundred years with the industrial North. It is the South of Lyndon Johnson, brooding in retirement on the Pedernales, brooding on "the

---

[3] *Abraham Lincoln: The War Years* by Carl Sandburg (New York: Harcourt, Brace & Co., 1939), vol. 2, pages 390–91.

disdain for the South that seems to be woven into the fabric of Northern experience."[4]

It is a South in conflict with itself, a South of black men, women, and children in overalls and bandannas and gunny-sack dresses trudging barefoot into country churches to hear Martin Luther King's dream of freedom from "Stone Mountain, Georgia, to the low hills of Mississippi."

It is a South which has survived external attacks and internal explosions for two hundred years by developing uncommon political skills. The skills of Jefferson and Madison; of Joseph Rainey, Hiram Revels, and Blanche Bruce; of Sam Rayburn, Sam Ervin, and John Stennis.

Looking at the Congresses of Rayburn and Johnson, Stennis and Ervin, the historian James MacGregor Burns would conclude: "If a test of political expertness is the capacity to convert limited political resources into maximum governmental power, the most expert of the politicians in Washington today are the leaders of the Congressional Democratic party."

The leaders Burns referred to were Democrats from the eleven states of the Confederacy—Texas, Louisiana, Arkansas, Mississippi, Tennessee, Alabama, Georgia, Florida, Virginia, North Carolina, and South Carolina.

The Southerners, said Burns, "represent a tiny fraction of the nation's electorate; the approximately ninety [Southern House] members are elected by about two million of the nation's sixty million voters. Those ninety members make up less than one-fourth of the House; they cannot by themselves muster enough votes even for a veto when a two-thirds vote is required. But they make up for their lack of numbers in the quality of their political craftsmanship, their grasp of the relation of policy goals and political means, and of course their control of congressional machinery."

Southern craftsmanship has been a fact of American politics since the beginning. And whether the issue has been a new Constitution, the Jay treaty, slaves, tariffs, the Boulder Dam, the Louisi-

[4] *The Vantage Point* by Lyndon B. Johnson (New York: Holt, Rinehart & Winston, 1971), page 95.

ana Purchase, social security, cabinet appointments, income tax, civil rights, or military and foreign aid, the South has had an influence far greater than its weight of population.

The presidency itself, where the weight of population prevails, has been beyond Southern abilities. Since Zachary Taylor's inauguration in 1849 only two Southerners have been elected President—the Virginian Woodrow Wilson in 1912 and the Texan Lyndon Johnson in 1964. During that 127 years the only other Southerner to serve as President was Andrew Johnson of Tennessee who was not elected but filled out the unexpired term of Abraham Lincoln.

Meanwhile, Southern control of congressional machinery has slipped. It is now apparent that the decline began in 1932 when the Democratic party, under Roosevelt, entered its long era as the dominant American political party. As a majority party, the Democrats broadened their base and began programs designed to appeal to an oppressed black minority and to give them relief. The Southerners, who previously had been the majority wing of the Democrats, now found themselves in a minority and their party power diluted. They began to drift from the solid Democratic South concept, flirted with third parties and increased alliances with the Republicans.

The story of Southern congressional politics since 1932 has been that of a skillful rear-guard action, fighting to hold on through seniority, key committee appointments, and other devices.

That the South made the mistake of defending its racial policies should not blind the world to its many worthwhile and unique historical accomplishments. Nor should it blind us to the continuing national service of the modern Southerners, men like Huey Long who wanted to redistribute the national wealth, or Tom Connally of Texas, the American most responsible for creating the United Nations, or Richard Russell of Georgia who, in 1951, defused a situation which could very well have led to an immediate World War III with atomic weapons.

There are not many of these Southerners left. Bearing the weight of a national prejudice, a shrinking loyalty to and from national Democrats, their strength has steadily dwindled in the

Congress, even in their traditional stronghold of the U. S. Senate. Yet a few of them remain, men such as John Stennis and James Allen and Herman Talmadge.

The nation saw them closeup during the summer of 1973, during the time of the Senate Watergate hearings, and it seemed that these men had a strength of conviction and a power of speech that belonged to an earlier period. It seemed, too, that we were seeing the last of a breed. That such men wouldn't come this way again. Questions arose: Where, in our history, did they come from? And how did they get to be the way they are?

And there are some questions about the future. In modern Southern politics, race has virtually disappeared as an issue. It is being replaced by an equally traditional Southern issue of economic class against economic class, the politics dramatized by Huey Long.

When Long lay dying of an assassin's bullet on September 10, 1935, his last words were, "God, don't let me die. I have so much to do." It appears possible that a new Southern politics, an evolving populism, will pick up that work.

David Leon Chandler
New Orleans, December 1975

Book One
THE EARLY SOUTHERNERS

Chapter 1
JOHN RANDOLPH OF ROANOKE

The date was March 4, 1789.

The day, being the first Wednesday of March, had been the time set aside by the Continental Congress to commence proceedings of the new Constitution. The night before, at sunset, the guns of the battery had been fired to bid farewell to the old Confederation. At noon on this day, the cannons had boomed again. Red, white, and blue bunting was hung and there was the ringing of bells. A general joy pervaded the whole city in tune with the important and memorable event. It was cold, but the scarcity and dearness of fuel seemed not to be noticed. (The city had been virtually without wood since the winter of 1779 when all the trees of Manhattan Island had been cut down.)

Now, ten years later, fuel still had to be hauled from great distances and was expensive. This, in turn, made lodgings and food and manufacture rise in price, and everything else that needed heat for workers or preparation.

The unavoidable increase had added to New York's already evil and deserved reputation for gouging. But today all was overlooked. Parties were everywhere and houses open to guests. Boards were piled with venison, bear, and fish of every kind; with

wild turkeys, partridges, grouse, and quail in abundance. Tank-
ards were lavishly laid full with Madeira, with ale, strong beer,
cider, and punch. One could eat and drink as one pleased, to
stupefaction if that were his style.

In front of Federal Hall, on Wall Street, a huge crowd had been
gathered since dawn, waiting for the first Congress to take its seat,
waiting for the appearance of the famous. There was a rumor that
George Washington had arrived yesterday, but this was untrue.
He was waiting at Mount Vernon in Virginia, impatient for the
Congress to meet and certify his presidency.

There was widespread optimism that this day would truly begin
the United States of America. The old Confederation of American
States had floundered greatly after the Declaration of Independence in 1776. The war was won but peace and prosperity
were not gained. The former colonies proved unable to pull together under the old Articles. The new Constitution, proposed by
Southern states and worked out in Philadelphia barely a year
earlier, was innovative, providing a two-house legislature, a chief
executive, and a supreme court. It promised a new era for all people, not only in America but in the world. Such was the feeling of
the day.

The cannons boomed anew. Noon had come. On the balcony of
Federal Hall stood a dozen representatives—among them, Fisher
Ames and Elbridge Gerry from Massachusetts, John Gilman of
New Hampshire, Samuel Huntington of Connecticut. There were
a number of senators, too: Caleb Strong, Paine Wingate, Oliver
Ellsworth, all from New England. Robert Morris and William
Maclay, both of Pennsylvania, were there. The only Southerner
present, however, was William Few of Georgia. And there were
no New Yorkers. The voting for congressional seats was not yet
completed in New York; the polls were open on the day the new
government was making ready to convene.

It is a coincidence of history that among those pushing, shoving
people in front of Federal Hall was the fifteen-year-old Virginian,
John Randolph, then a student at New York's Columbia College.
He heard a commotion: the shouts and laughter of the crowd

growing into hurrahs; the bellowing and cursing of harassed coachmen, the clattering of iron-shod hooves on cobblestones.

A fine carriage had arrived, a coat of arms emblazoned on its sides. It was a regal carriage, that of John Adams, presiding officer of the United States Senate and Vice President of the nation.

John Randolph and his older brother Richard moved toward the coach. They had once been introduced to the Vice President by their uncle, Edmund Randolph, Attorney General-designate of the United States.

"Sir!" they shouted to Adams. "Oh, sir! Sir!" And they pressed closer to the carriage.

Two cracks of the coachman's whip drove them back. Sharp cracks. Frightening. Insulting. Not touching the face of either boy, but close. They retreated.

John Randolph of Roanoke would someday become powerful chairman of the House Ways and Means Committee and, after that, a wicked, filibustering senator. He would revenge himself mightily time and time again on the Adams presidencies.

Not at all noticing the incident, the Vice President left his carriage and entered Federal Hall. He was all smiles, waving at the people, shaking hands with old acquaintances from the Revolution. This was exceptionally happy behavior, for Adams was a long-faced and sober man. Randolph would later call him "mean-faced and sour."

Adams was inside the Capitol but a short time. When he returned to his carriage, his mood had changed to annoyance and frustration.

An hour more passed, then two hours. A chant began in the crowd, a restless tension hung in the air.

On the balcony, no official, no senator or congressman or clerk had come forward with an explanation or an announcement of why the new nation hadn't begun.

More time passed. The crowd began to drift apart and thin. By night only a few people were at hand when a clerk came out with the announcement. There was an insufficient number of representatives and senators present to begin the Congress. The people were advised to go home. The United States of America was delayed. And the word passed quickly through the city:

"The Southerners are missing."

Days of waiting ensued. Many members of the new government, those who had arrived, were repulsed by the friendly attention of the city. New York had been whorishly accommodating to George III and it was suspected the hospitalities extended to the American Congress were equally cynical and self-serving.

New York had been chosen as the capital of the new United States out of convenience. Since 1785, the Continental Congress had been meeting in the old City Hall, now called Federal Hall.[1] It was figured, when the Constitution was written up in 1787, that it was easiest to keep the new government at the site of the records and clerks of the old. This may be viewed as an augury of gathering ominous clouds, a prescient tip-off on where true power would someday lie in American government—which is to say with the bureaucracy.

In view of weather and road conditions, the date of convening the government, March 4, was unseasonable. Traveling would have been easier and surer had the birthdate been postponed until early summer. But foreign ships with goods were due to arrive in American harbors beginning in April and the new Congress wanted to pass a quick customs tax before the ships arrived. The nation wanted to get its hands on some money, thus establishing early-on its practical aspirations.

Meanwhile, George Washington was at Mount Vernon, four to six days' journey, awaiting the call. He had been elected President by the Electoral College which had met a month earlier, on February 4, 1789. It was the first time the college had been used and it worked, this first time around, as the Constitution intended it to:

"Each state shall appoint . . . a number of electors, equal to the whole number of senators and representatives to which the state may be entitled in the Congress . . . The electors shall meet in their respective states, and vote by ballot for two persons . . .

[1] At Wall and Nassau streets, the site of the present Subtreasury Building.

The president of the Senate shall, in the presence of the Senate and House of Representatives, open all the certificates and the votes shall then be counted. The person having the greatest number of votes shall be the President . . ."

The gentlemen electors, this first time around, were not pledged to a particular candidate. There had been no general election for President and Washington had not campaigned, publicly or privately. He had been chosen by the electors, unanimously.

It could not become official, however, until a president of the Senate, temporarily elected for the purpose, opened the ballots in the presence of a quorum in both houses.

The days passed, and then weeks. One or two representatives came into town but still there was no quorum. The nation was adrift. There was no authority to transact any business in behalf of the new government. March 31 came and went. Foreign ships arrived and offloaded their duty-free goods and hauled return cargo back to England and France. The nation lost an estimated three hundred thousand pounds in taxes.[2]

There was resentment about all this. Listen to Fisher Ames, thirty-year-old representative from Dedham, Massachusetts, Harvard graduate, son of astronomer Nathaniel Ames, a famed orator and a revolutionary pamphleteer. (He wrote under the names "Lucius Junius Brutus" and "Camillus.") He would later give Congress' eulogy on George Washington. Now, waiting for the Southerners to arrive, he complained that "the languor of the old Confederation is transferred to the members of the new Congress . . . We lose one thousand pounds a day revenue. We lose credit, spirit, everything. The public will forget the government before it is born."[3] There was confusion about the turnover from the old government to the new, Ames wrote. "The old Congress still continues to meet, and it seems to be doubtful whether the old government is dead, or the new one alive." These words came on March 31, nearly one month after the new government was supposed to begin.

Down in Mount Vernon, Washington had begun the month with enthusiasm. It had rapidly degenerated into gloom. He re-

[2] Approximately $9 million in U.S. currency.
[3] *Works of Fisher Ames* (Boston: Little, Brown and Co., 1854).

gretted the "stupor or listlessness" of the absent members of the
new Congress. His own confidence was sapped. "My movements
to the chair of government will be accompanied by feelings not
unlike those of a culprit who is going to the place of his execution
. . ." He felt he lacked the "political skill, abilities and inclination
which is necessary to manage the helm." Inaction had turned his
thoughts inward, to self-contemplation, where he discovered feelings of inadequacy and doubt.

He had had to borrow five hundred pounds at 6 per cent interest to settle immediate debts and keep Mount Vernon going.[4]
(When the election is certified, he will borrow another one hundred pounds to pay travel expenses and to set himself up in New
York, where there is no presidential residence. Washington expects, "I would take rooms in the most decent tavern.")

By April 1, enough members had arrived to make up a quorum
in the House. The Senate, however, was still unable to convene
and the House members turned their anger onto the absent senators. Their conduct, said Representative Henry Wynkoop of Pennsylvania, savored "too much of the remains of Monarchial Government, where those promoted to public office consider themselves as clothed with Majesterial Dignity instead of confidential
servants of the people."[5]

The democratic House for all its history would be annoyed by,
and jealous of, the airs and prerogatives of the Senate.

Five days later, on April 6, 1789, Richard Henry Lee rode into
the city. Tall, with large, strong hands capable of controlling the
most spirited of horses, he has the bearing of a king and a face
striking in its show of strength and intelligence. He is descended
from one of the oldest and most noble families in England. (The
Norman founder, Launcelot Lee, went to England with William
the Conqueror.) The American Lees are literally older than Virginia, the first Lee having landed on those shores in 1600—seven
years before the Virginia charter and the founding of Jamestown.[6]

[4] Approximately $15,000 in 1975 currency.
[5] "United States Senate, 1787–1801" by Roy Swanstrom in Senate Document 64, 87th Congress, page 35.
[6] *Memoirs of the War in the Southern Department of the United States* by
Henry Lee (New York: Arno Press, 1969).

His first cousin is "Light Horse" Harry Lee, one of the most daring of the Revolutionary generals.[7] As for Richard Henry Lee, senator, he is the man who, as delegate to the Continental Congress on June 7, 1776, made the original motion in Congress that the colonies were "free and independent states." It was the original declaration of independence.

Now, Richard Henry Lee ascends the stairs of Federal Hall and presents his credentials, the twelfth senator to do so. A quorum is present in both houses. Congress is convened, Washington is certified, and the government of the "United States of America" begins, a month and two days late.

With the perspective of history, there is a certain poetic symmetry in the government being delayed until the arrival of Richard Henry Lee, the man who first officially proposed the creation of the new nation.

At the time, however, it was viewed as arrogance, Southern arrogance, and was the source of fierce and bitter resentments in the North.

There is general agreement among historians that the phenomenon we know as the South, a feeling of the South as community, took shape in the 1830s. The date, however, seems to be picked too casually. It is a shortsighted assumption based on the fact that the 1830s saw a sudden growth in the emancipation movement, and the Southerners reacted by binding themselves together, mostly behind the leadership of John C. Calhoun.

There is considerable evidence that sectionalism, North versus South, a sense of community, existed much earlier, being older than the nation itself.

In 1775, John Adams had written home from the Continental Congress that "the characters of gentlemen in the four New England colonies differ from those in the others . . . as much as several distinct nations almost." He feared the colonies might not be able to come together because of the differences.

A few years later, Thomas Jefferson wrote:

[7] "Light Horse" Harry Lee was the father of Confederate General Robert E. Lee.

In the North, they are:	In the South they are:
Cool	Fiery
Sober	Voluptuary
Laborious	Indolent
Persevering	Unsteady
Independent	Independent
Jealous of their liberties and those of others	Zealous for their own liberties but trampling on those of others
Chicaning	Candid
Superstitious and hypocritical in their religion.	Without attachment or pretensions to any religion but that of the heart.

At the Constitutional Convention of 1787, the "crabbed, foxy . . . raspy whine [of Northern] speech was a continual irritant to anyone from below the Pennsylvania line. A South Carolinian . . . was heard to say that before he really knew them he had disliked all New Englandmen because they wore black woolen stockings. These were the damned Yankees."[8]

The external threat of Northern hostility to the Southern white has existed since at least 1776. The internal threat, the high number of blacks, is almost but not quite as ancient, the critical mass in black population being reached in the first few decades after the Revolutionary War when the Northern states began selling slaves southward.

Once the races became nearly equal in number in the south, it was feared there would be race war. To avert this and to give justice to the blacks, many eighteenth-century intellectuals, North and South, American and foreign, favored freedom and transportation of the ex-slaves to Africa or to some wilderness colony in America.

Thomas Jefferson, who had written into the Declaration of Independence a stinging attack against slavery only to have it struck out by the Continental Congress, believed the races could not live

[8] *Miracle at Philadelphia* by Catherine Drinker Bowen (Boston: Little, Brown and Co., 1966), page 91. The term "damned Yankees" dates from at least 1776, according to Bowen.

peaceably together in the same land. While governor of Virginia, in 1779, he had proposed a law which would free children born of slaves. They would remain with their parents but would be supported and schooled by the state and upon reaching majority would be deported to a suitable colony along with tools and supplies.

It was rejected by the Virginia legislature and Jefferson rebutted forcefully: "Nothing is more certainly written in the book of fate that these people are to be free. Nor is it less certain that the two races, equally free, cannot live in the same government. Nature, habit, opinion has drawn indelible lines of distinction between them.

"It is still in our power to direct the process of emancipation and deportation peaceably and in such slow degree as that the evil will wear off insensibly, and their place be *pari passu* filled up by free white laborers. If on the contrary it is left to force itself on, human nature must shudder at the prospect held up."[9]

This *prospect,* what to do about the slaves, was peculiar to the South at the end of the eighteenth century. The North had solved the problem. The South hadn't and this contributed heavily to the Southern sense of community.

There were, in addition, many other aspects to the Southern community and among these was the aristocratic tradition embodied in such people as John Randolph.

The political arts of the South appeared early, as seen in the Virginia dynasty of Richard Henry Lee, the Randolphs, Patrick Henry, James Madison, Jefferson, and Washington. The Virginians represented the left wing of the early Southern tradition, a wing which developed prior to the critical mass in black population.

The right wing, led by an almost equally skillful though less innovative South Carolina dynasty under John C. Calhoun, developed during the rise of black population.

A man who, in terms of time and philosophy, came between the two eras and overlapped both was John Randolph. He was a kins-

[9] *The Living Jefferson* by James Truslow Adams (New York: Charles Scribner's Sons, 1936), page 117.

man and protégé of Jefferson, an ally and mentor of Calhoun, and somewhat patronizing toward both.

(Shortly after entering the Senate in 1825, Randolph addressed the chair occupied by Vice President Calhoun, who had ambitions to be elected President. Randolph, accustomed to the procedures of the House where he had spent twenty-two years, said, "Mr. Speaker! I mean Mr. President of the Senate and would-be President of the United States, which God in his infinite mercy avert."[10])

The style, the philosophy, and the tactics of mainstream Southern politics were set by four men: Thomas Jefferson, Jefferson Davis, John C. Calhoun, and John Randolph of Roanoke, Virginia. John Randolph is the least known and least remembered of the four, but he most completely fits the mold of the classic Southerner. Jefferson was too liberal, Davis too humorless, Calhoun too fanatic. Randolph was the profile of the Southern ideal. He was a gentleman farmer with strong family roots, well versed in law and the humanities, strong on the Constitution, eloquent, severe, and eccentric. In debate, he frequently would wander from the subject, seemingly as an entertainment. But these meanderings were loaded like a shotgun with wit and wisdom and almost always had a purpose. He was the first of the Senate filibusterers and Henry Adams regarded him, sullenly, as the spiritual father of the Southern consciousness.

John Randolph was a direct descendant of Pocahontas and John Rolfe, married in 1614.[11]

[10] *Perley's Reminiscences of Sixty Years in the National Metropolis* (Philadelphia: Poore, 1886), vol. i, page 64.
[11] Rolfe arrived in Jamestown in 1610 and two years later became the first colonist to plant tobacco. Pocahontas, whose real name was Matoaka (Pocahontas was a nickname meaning "playful one"), was the daughter of Powhatan, whom the English described as "Emperor" of all the tribes (or villages?) along the "Appamatuck." According to Captain John Smith's *Generall Historie of Virginia*, written in 1624, and a Smith letter to Queen Anne in 1616, Pocahontas saved his life. Powhatan had caused his warriors to seize Smith and they laid his head on two great stones to beat out his brains. "At the minute of my execution, she hazarded the beating out of her owne braines to save mine, and not only that, but so prevailed with her father that I was safely conducted to James towne." Thereafter, she was "many times a preserver of (myself) and the whole Colonie." Because Smith had omitted mention of the incident in some earlier letters, the story was suspected of being fictitious. Modern examinations, however, support

Randolph, born in 1773, received an irregular schooling in Virginia and studied law with his renowned uncle, Edmund Randolph.[12] Elected to the House of Representatives in 1799 as one of the earliest members of the Democratic Party, he was a prominent and leading figure until he fell out with Jefferson over the acquisition of Florida and lost his leadership. He was a man of bewildering contradictions. Recognized, deservedly, as the most outspoken champion of individual liberty in his day, he ultimately defended slavery and, yet, at his death freed his own slaves, numbering more than three hundred. And it is this contradiction that makes him worth attention, for it is a contradiction endemic to Southerners. It is the same contradiction described by Jefferson: "Zealous of their own liberties but trampling upon those of others."

Randolph held a typically contradictory political philosophy:

"I am an aristocrat. I love liberty; I hate equality."

He served in the Senate only two years, 1825–27, but it was enough to make his mark, for in that time he staged the first major filibuster, fought or, more precisely, performed in a duel with Henry Clay, then Secretary of State, and conducted himself with such cool confidence, and with such devastating sarcasm, on the Senate floor that his appearance was a general entertainment, drawing crowds of colleagues, clerks, and press.

His major program during the two Senate years was to defeat a series of fiscal bills proposed by President John Quincy Adams, bills which Randolph believed were aimed to assist New England industry at the cost of the agrarian South. His method was to talk the bills to death in a series of rambling discourses, holding the floor day after day, talking for hours at a time without the slightest reference to the business at hand.

---

its validity. Pocahontas and John Rolfe met while she was a prisoner of the English colonists and their marriage began a long peace with Powhatan. Visiting England in 1616, she was received as a princess and presented to the King and Queen as Lady Rebecca, her baptismal name.

[12] An aide-de-camp to George Washington in the war, Edmund Randolph was a delegate to the Continental Congress, governor of Virginia (1786–88), and delegate to the Constitutional Convention. He was architect and introducer of the "Virginia Resolves," also called the "Randolph Plan," which was a working paper from which the Constitution was drawn. He was Attorney General in Washington's first administration and Secretary of State in Washington's second administration.

Leaning or lolling against the railing "which in the old Senate chamber surrounded the outer row of desks, he would talk two or three hours at a time . . . while Mr. Calhoun sat like a statue in the Vice President's chair, until the senators one by one retired, leaving the Senate to adjourn without a quorum, a thing till then unknown to its courteous habits."[13] The gallery responded with open delight at his witty thrusts into the bowels of opponents, his learned discourses on a thousand and one subjects.

Hezekiah Niles, a prominent editor, attended one of these filibusters on May 2, 1826, and—though he listened but thirty-five minutes—printed what is probably the first recorded one. (Randolph's earlier filibusters had been given passing reference, but not reported.)

The editor wrote:

"I had been told that the bankrupt bill was before the Senate— but, during the time stated, [Randolph] never, to the best of my recollection, mentioned, or even remotely alluded to it, or any of its parts, in any manner whatsoever.

"The chamber was nearly empty, the gallery nearly full, and the stolid Calhoun patiently listened from his throne as Randolph rambled on with careless ease. He gave out a plan for the national bank. It would not need an iron chest for 'who would steal our paper, sir?' He then said something about Unitarians and made a dash at the administration.

"He spoke of the Bible, and expressed his disgust at what are called 'family Bibles,' though he thought no family safe without a Bible—but not an American edition. Those published by the Stationers Company of London ought only or chiefly to have authority, except those from the presses of the Universities of Oxford and Cambridge. He said those corporations would be fined ten thousand pounds sterling should they leave the word *not* out of the seventh commandment [adultery], 'however convenient it might be to some or agreeable to others.' Randolph looked directly at certain members and half-turned himself around to the ladies in the gallery.

"He said he never bought an American edition of any book—

13 *John Randolph* by Henry Adams (New York: Fawcett Publications, 1961), page 194.

he had no faith in their accuracy. From the Bible he passed to Shakespeare, drubbing someone soundly for publishing a 'family Shakespeare': He next jumped to the American 'Protestant Episcopal Church,' and disavowed all connection with it, declaring that he belonged to the Church of Old England; he had been baptized 'by a man regularly authorized by the bishop of London who had laid his hands upon him' (laying his own hands on the head of the gentleman next to him). Then he quoted from the service.

"He spoke about wine—it was often mentioned in the Bible and he approved of drinking it—if in a gentlemanly way—at the table —'not in the closet—not in the closet, sir; but as to whiskey' he demanded that anyone show him the word in the Bible. 'It was not there—no, sir, you can't find it in the whole book.' Then he spoke of his land at Roanoke, saying he had it by a *royal* grant. He then spoke of a song about the men of Kent, saying Kent had never been conquered by William the Norman." He was about to sing it when the editor Niles left.[14]

Randolph's style in Congress appalled Northerners. Listen to Henry Adams, whose grandfather and great-grandfather, both presidents, had been lashed and scored by Randolph. Adams' words, from an 1882 biography, still tingle with electric animosity:

"Neither his oratory nor his wit would have been tolerated in a Northern state. To the cold-blooded New Englander who did not love extravagance or eccentricity, and had no fancy for plantation manners, Randolph was an obnoxious being . . . (but) there is no question that such an antagonist was formidable . . ."

Adams made a disgusted reference to the style of Southern politics: "He began by completely mastering his congressional district. At best, it is not easy for remote, sparsely settled communities to shake off a political leader who has no prominent rival in his own party, and no strong outside opposition, but when that leader has Randolph's advantages it becomes impossible to contest the field. His constituents revolted once, but never again. His peculiarities were too well known and too much in the natural order of things to excite surprise or scandal among them. They liked his long stump speeches and sharp, epigrammatic phrases,

[14] *Niles Weekly Register*, May 13, 1826, vol. 30, page 1867.

desultory style and melodramatic affections of manner, and they were used to coarseness that would have sickened a Connecticut peddler. They liked to be flattered by him, for flattery was one of the instruments he used with most lavishness."[15]

The style of Southern electioneering would hold through the centuries, whether it be in the Virginia of Randolph, the Louisiana of Huey Long, or the Texas of Sam Rayburn and Lyndon Johnson. The very excesses of language and emotion that would astonish and appall the North would delight the South.

Biographer Adams viewed Randolph as the spiritual father of the Civil War. "John Randolph stands in history as the legitimate and natural precursor of Calhoun. Randolph sketched out and partly filled in the outlines of that political scheme over which Calhoun labored so long . . . the identification of slavery with states' rights. All that was ablest and most masterly . . . in Calhoun's statesmanship had been suggested by Randolph years before Calhoun began his states' rights career."[16]

John Randolph's stand on states' rights derived from one of the foundations of Southern political philosophy: strict interpretation of the Constitution.

Opposing an 1806 expansion of the Army and Navy, Randolph objected, and the italicized emphasis is his, that the Constitution empowers Congress "to provide for the common *defence* and general welfare of the *United States.*" It grants no power whatsoever for offensive attack upon other countries. "I declare in the face of day," said Randolph, "that this government was not instituted for the purposes of foreign war . . . I call that offensive war, which goest out of our jurisdiction and limits for the attainment or protection of objects . . . I fear if you go into a foreign war . . . you will come out without your Constitution."[17]

He did not believe that humanitarian ideals *per se* could motivate governments. Said Randolph in an early speech: Could there be any man "so weak, or so wicked, as to pretend that there is any

---

[15] *John Randolph* by Henry Adams (New York: Fawcett Publications, 1961), pages 168–69.
[16] Adams, pages 178–79.
[17] *John Randolph* by Richard Dabney (Chicago: Union School Furnishing Company, 1898), page 15.

principle of action between nations except interest? . . . Sir, we are not theo-philanthropists, but politicians; not dreamers and soothsayers, but men of flesh and blood. It is idle to talk of a sense of justice in any nation. Each pursues its sense of interest, and if you calculate on their acting upon any other principle, you may be very amiable, but you will prove a cully."[18]

This was a cynical and practical perspective to put on politics and, when the early abolition movement began in England and spread to America, he viewed it as a hypocritical meddling, a scheme of politicians and churchmen to use the plight of blacks as stepping stones to power. This, too, would become part of the Southern perspective.

Randolph, like his brother Richard, had made provision in his will to free his own three hundred slaves and felt slavery could peaceably be eradicated.

"It must not be tampered with by quacks, who never saw the disease or the patient. The disease will run its course—it has run its course in the Northern States; it is beginning to run its course in Maryland.

"The natural death of slavery is the unprofitableness of its most expensive labor—it is also beginning in the meadow and grain country of Virginia . . . The moment the labor of the slave ceases to be profitable to the master, or very soon after it has reached that stage—if the slave will not run away from the master, the master will run away from the slave; and this is the history of the passage from slavery to freedom of the villenage of England . . ." Meanwhile, he was tired of interference.

"Sir, there has a spirit gone abroad—both in England and here . . . it is raging here, and I wish I could say that it does not exist even in Virginia. It is the spirit of neglecting our own affairs for the purpose of regulating the affairs of our neighbors."[19]

This was the healthy Randolph speaking, a man who had his powers intact. After he left the Senate in 1827, his mind would come unhinged from brandy and opium, from fear and hatred of Northern domination.

[18] Dabney, page 62.
[19] Dabney, pages 63–64.

Even in that state, he was appreciative of black suffering.

Josiah Quincy IV, mayor of Boston from 1845 to 1849, visited Randolph, after the latter had retired, to inquire about Randolph's views on oratory.

"I was admitted to his bedchamber," wrote Quincy. "He was sitting in flannel dressing-gown and slippers, looking very thin, but with a strange fire in his swarthy face . . . I had listened with admiration to his wonderful improvisations in the Senate, and had determined to get at his views about the oratory of Patrick Henry, of which I had heard John Adams speak in terms of some disparagement . . .

"I asked who was the greatest orator he had ever heard. The reply was startling, from its unexpectedness. 'The greatest orator I ever heard,' said Randolph, 'was a woman. She was a slave. She was a mother, and her rostrum was the auction-block.'

"He then rose and imitated with thrilling pathos the tones with which this woman had appealed to the sympathy and justice of the bystanders, and finally the indignation with which she denounced them. 'There was eloquence!' he said. 'I have heard no *man* speak like that. It was overpowering!'

"He sat down and paused for some moments; then, evidently feeling that he had been imprudent in expressing himself so warmly before a visitor from the North, he entered upon a defence of the policy of Southern statesmen in regard to slavery. 'We must concern ourselves with what is,' he said, 'and slavery exists. We must preserve the rights of the States, as guaranteed by the Constitution, or the negroes are at our throats. The question of slavery, as it is called, is to us a question of life and death. Remember, it is a necessity imposed on the South; not a Utopia of our own seeking. You will find no instance in history where two distinct races have occupied the soil except in the relation of master and slave.'"

The interview was conducted in 1831. Randolph—his failing health having been observed by Quincy—died two years later.

If one searches through the available writings, evidences of Randolph's humanity frequently peer through, as in the above story about the woman orator. And in these writings, as above, there is seen the educated white Southerner's prejudice against the black. The prejudice is not racism per se, a belief that blacks are an inferior species or race. The preponderance of pre-Civil War Southern writings show a common agreement that the black race through education can and should become equal to the white. Randolph cites the black woman as a superior individual.

It is not race prejudice at work with Randolph and his class but class prejudice. Randolph fears and loathes the class of poor blacks, which he views as indolent, ignorant, and dangerous.

Another example of this Southern class prejudice can be seen in an 1806 letter written by Randolph to his young nephew away at school. The nephew has complained of being too closely supervised at school and that students should have more freedom. Randolph replies that freedom carries responsibilities:

"Independence, which is so much vaunted, and which young people think consists in doing what they please (with as much justice as the poor negro thinks liberty consists in being supported in idleness by other people's labor)—this independence is but a name . . . The more exalted the station, the more arduous are the duties . . ."

Following the Revolutionary War, the Northern states, through a skillful phasing out of slavery, had caused the Northern slaves to be sold South, the only states where they could legally be bought after about 1790. Once rid of its own slaves, the Northern states called upon the South to free its slaves, including the newly purchased ones. The financial problem for Southern owners was that they had no place else to sell them.

Randolph felt the agitation for emancipation was a Northern hypocrisy and one which did a disservice to blacks. He accused the antislavery societies of stirring up mischief among a people who, at this stage in their skills, if made free could not fend for themselves:

"You have deprived him of all moral restraint; you have tempted him to eat of the fruit of the tree of knowledge, just enough to perfect him in wickedness; you have armed his nature against the hand that has fed, that has clothed him, that has cherished him in sickness; that hand which before he became a pupil of your school, he had been accustomed to press with respectful affection."

He feared that the awakening of the slaves to liberty would bring a slaughter of the whites: "I speak from facts, when I say, that the night-bell never tolls for fire in Richmond, that the mother does not hug her infant more closely to her bosom. I have been a witness of some of the alarms in the capital of Virginia."

Randolph embodies one half of the fear of the Southern white toward the black. The class fear of being physically overwhelmed by another class.

The other half of the fear is miscegenation. This fear, not at all peculiar to the South, seems common to most cultures of the world, whether European, African, Slavic, Arabic, or Oriental. Social punishments for miscegenation vary from mild to severe. In the South, it became particularly intense because of the concurrent class struggle between black and white. John Randolph, member of the Southern community, loathed miscegenation.

In 1831, in the last two years of his life, weak and dying as he was, John Randolph went round Virginia making speeches for the South to hold fast against the federal government's tariffs, against its "encroachments" on states' rights and slavery. And in one of these speeches, he let the creature fly.

"There is a meeting-house in this village, built by a respectable denomination. I never was in it, though, like myself, it is mouldering away. The pulpit of that meeting-house was polluted by permitting a black African to preach in it. If I had been there, I would have taken the uncircumcised dog by the throat, led him before a magistrate, and committed him to jail. I told the ladies, they, sweet souls, who dressed their beds with the whitest sheets and uncorked for him their best wine, were not far from having Negro children."[20]

He made few such speeches. And when he had his powers together he kept the creature suppressed. In 1821 he wrote in the very first paragraph of his will:

"I give my slaves their freedom, to which my conscience tells me they are justly entitled. It has a long time been a matter of the

[20] Adams, page 198.

deepest regret to me, that the circumstances under which I inherited them and the obstacles thrown in the way by the laws of the land, have prevented my emancipating them in my lifetime, which it is my full intention to do, in case I can accomplish it." Other paragraphs provided for the purchase of land outside Virginia, in a free state, on which to settle the freed slaves and for defraying their initial outlay. He knew in "my conscience" that slavery was wrong. Morally wrong.

When he died, farms were purchased in Ohio, the blacks were freed and given funds to establish themselves. Shortly afterward, Ohioans burned out the entire community and the ex-Randolph slaves were scattered to no one knows where. The Ohioans, too, had the demon.

There is a contradiction in John Randolph, as there is in modern Southerners. They are libertarian and law-abiding on the one hand, oppressive and criminal on the other. Jefferson summed it up when he said they were "zealous" in the protection of their own liberties, "careless" about the liberties of others.

Chapter 2
THREE PEOPLES

The culture and politics of the white South were formed by a powerful and competitive interaction between three peoples, the New Englander, the Southern black, and the Southern white.

Each of these people was an intruder on the continent and each arrived in the early seventeenth century. The first of the arrivals, by a few years, was the Southern white, and among the earliest of the colonizers were the aristocratic Randolphs.

The Randolph name had been a distinguished one in England for centuries. The American Line was founded in 1674 when William Randolph settled at Turkey Island on the James River. There he married Mary Isham and from the Randolph-Isham union the direct descendants included Peyton Randolph, the first president of the first Continental Congress; Edmund Randolph, George Washington's first Attorney General and his third Secretary of State; Thomas Jefferson; Chief Justice John Marshall; Light-Horse Harry Lee; and Robert E. Lee.

By the time John Randolph was born in 1773, Virginia had become the most populous colony on the continent but, unlike the Northern colonies, it had not developed cities and its population was spread among plantations, farms, and villages. It was an agrarian Eden and one which worked at that time in that place. Virginia's success caused Jefferson, Madison, Randolph, and others to believe the agrarian democracy formula could be applied to the nation as a whole. It never could, it never did, but the myth that it had worked, and that it should continue to work entered the Southern tradition. And it shaped character.

"The life of boyhood in Virginia," wrote Henry Adams, "was not well fitted for teaching self-control or mental discipline, qualities which John Randolph never gained; but in return for these the Virginian found other advantages which made up for the loss of methodical training. Many a Virginian lad, especially on such a remote plantation as Bizarre, lived in a boy's paradise of indulgence, fished and shot, rode like a young monkey, and had his memory crammed with the genealogy of every well-bred horse in the state, grew up among dogs and Negroes, master equally of both, and knew all about the prices of wheat, tobacco, and slaves. He might pick up much that was high and noble from his elders and betters, or much that was bad and brutal from his inferiors, might, as he grew older, back his favorite bird at a cocking-main, or haunt stables and race-courses, or look on, with as much interest as an English nobleman felt at a prize-ring, when, after the race was over, there occurred an old-fashioned rough-and-tumble fight, where the champions fixed their thumbs in each other's eyesockets and bit off each other's noses and ears; he might, even more easily than in England, get habits of drinking as freely as he talked, and of talking as freely as the utmost license of the English language would allow. The climate was genial, the soil generous, the life easy, the temptations strong. Everything encouraged individuality, and if by accident any mind had a natural bent towards what was coarse or brutal, there was little to prevent it from following its instinct."[1]

Adams, raised in the tight grip of New England tradition, seems to write with an envy which is nostalgic and revealing.

An interesting comparison between the late eighteenth-century life-styles of New England and Virginia was written by Joseph

[1] *John Randolph* by Henry Adams (New York: Fawcett Publications, 1961), page 22.

Baldwin, a native Alabamian, a judge, historian, and from 1863 to 1864 chief justice of the California Supreme Court. In his description, Baldwin reiterates a theme that appears time and again throughout Southern literature prior to the Civil War. It is a belief that the North-South conflict in America was carried over from England, where two separate types of peoples had long been in competition:

"The population of Virginia was very different from that of Massachusetts and of the other New England states. The difference between the Yankee and the Virginian was as marked as that between the Roundhead and the Cavalier, or that between the Churchman and the Puritan in the mother country; or rather, the difference was the same. The iron men of New England came from old England as from the house of bondage. They fled from persecution, leaving behind neither attachments nor regrets. They were strongly touched with Republicanism in England. They soon became full-grown Republicans in their forest homes, which were, indeed, the *only* homes they had ever known. They were a race of men stern, practical, ascetic, serious, devout, prejudiced, fanatical, fearing God, and without other fear; scorning the tendernesses and humanities, the elegant arts, embellishments, and refinements of polished and cultivated life as weaknesses, if not denouncing them as sins; magnifying small frailties into huge crimes; carrying religion into government, and seeking to enforce religious duties and observances by the arm of temporal authority; pushing an inquisitorial spirit of tyranny and *espionage* into the families and affairs of the members of the community; harsh to visit punishment, and ruling in state and household by fear more than by kindness and love; men of large reverence, and high and conscientious, though often mistaken, sense of duty; of strong passions, the instruments of stronger wills; of fixed purposes, and of an energy and faith that never fainted in adversity, or quailed before danger and difficulty; obeying law with a prompt and reverential obedience; administering it usually with justice, and executing it always without mercy. Probably the world has never seen so efficient a breed of men; for the men of Lexington and Bunker Hill were of the same strain with the men before whose unpractised valor, under Cromwell and Fairfax, the trained chivalry and fiery courage of Prince Rupert and his cavaliers went down at Naseby and on Marston Moor."

The New Englanders had settled on barren rocks and on arid, stony hills. They crowned the hills with villages, made the long coast gleam with streets. They brought little outward wealth save their untiring labor. They sent out their mariners to strike the whale in the Arctic zone, and to vex with their prows the water of unknown seas. They soon laid the foundation of the largest marine in the world; and almost before they were known to England, as worth either taxing or governing, they were competing with her for the trade of the Asiatic and African coasts.

"They turned," said Baldwin, "every thing to account, even the seeming disadvantages of soil and climate, of poverty and weakness. The sterility of the land drove them to the sea; their weakness to union; their poverty to greater labor. The rigorous climate hardened them to endure the added toil it required to afford them food and shelter.

"Such were the mighty race of men, who were the founders of empire, and builders of states and cities in the northern portion of the Union."

As for the Southerners, they were, in Baldwin's view, more careless, more attractive, and more fun.

"Very different were the settlers in the Southern Colonies, especially in Virginia. This colony was settled by Englishmen, proud of their country, loyal to the crown and the bigoted King who wore it; loyal to the successor, who lost it with his life; and, on the change of dynasty, after the head of the first Stuart had rolled down the steps of Whitehall, keeping their faith, as long as they could, to the heir of his follies and his sceptre. The soil was grateful, and the climate genial; and the woods and fields abounded with easily acquired means of sustaining life. Large grants of fertile lands were made to favored subjects and colonists."

The principal interest was agricultural; and tobacco, coming into general use, and bearing a high price, became the staple which, for a time, yielded a large revenue. The labor on the estates was cheap; being that of servants, transported from the mother country, or that of slaves.

The slaves that stocked the new plantations were sold cheap—

indeed, those engaged in the traffic could well afford to sell them at low prices, as they cost nothing but the trouble of stealing and transporting; or, at most, were bought at the coast, for a jackknife or a yard of calico per dozen; and allowing for a loss of one half by death on the middle passage, the remainder would bear a handsome profit at 150 pounds of tobacco apiece. Persons of family and wealth came out from England. Much wealth was thus brought into the colony, and much more was afterward made. There were no large towns. Williamsburg, the seat of government, with a population of two thousand souls, was the largest. The planters traded directly with Scotch and English merchants, who supplied them with merchandise, and took their crops, advancing them money as they needed it, and taking mortgages, as the debts begun to grow large, upon their estates. The Vice-Regal Court, with its elegance, and mimic forms of royalty on a small scale, infected the manners of the gentry, and kept up social distinctions among the different classes of the colonists. Baldwin continues: "The insular situation and retired habits of the planters on their estates, who made large quantities of provisions for which there was no market, made the rites of hospitality a grateful and inexpensive exercise. The planter had leisure, ease, money; and in the absence of other excitements or occupations, amused himself with company, horse-racing, gaming, drinking, and such other modes of recreation as opportunity allowed." Literature was not much cultivated, except among a few, and even by them more as an accomplishment or a means of diversion than as a profession.

"The established religion was the Church of England; and the ministers of it, selected more from regard to their own convenience than to the interests of religion, and from the orthodoxy of their profession than the piety of their practice, conformed, as much, at least, to the tone of society around them, as to the injunctions of their faith."

The colony was essentially English—Cavalier English.

"Gay, dashing, hospitable, careless, proud, high-spirited and gallant, loving pleasure and excitement, unused to labor or self-denial, there was but little sympathy between the Virginia planter and his more sour, thrifty, practical, shrewd and calculating neighbor of the North. They belonged to essentially different classes of men."[2]

Massachusetts was founded in 1620 by Pilgrims, a group of separatists who had migrated from England to Holland and thence to Cape Cod. Opposed to the Church of England, these righteous, self-exiled, puritanical, and rather oafish people were the opposites of Elizabethan or Stuart Cavaliers. Clever at mechanical things, hard-working, stoical, they were a fit group to populate the New England rocks. Cold and hard and gray, unimpressed by the warmth of the sun. They were as Baldwin described them. Cromwell's Roundheads.

Virginia was founded in 1607 but the colonists there were Elizabethans, people raised during the reign of England's most glorious and successful monarchy.

It was Elizabethan Englishmen who planned and undertook the early settlements in America. They began in the South and affected it greatly. Even today, in isolated sections of Georgia, Alabama, the Carolinas, Tennessee, Mississippi, and Arkansas, one can hear the grammar, the vocabulary and imagery of the Elizabethan tongue used by Spenser, Marlowe, and Shakespeare. Throughout the United States, Elizabethan political institutions likewise survive. Sheriffs, coroner, constables, justices of the peace, county clerks, juries, and representative assemblies, though ancient parts of the English scene, took their modern place and function under Elizabeth.

By 1610, Jamestown had seven hundred English inhabitants of which about thirty were women. There were one hundred wooden houses, a wharf off which rode the great ships from London, shelters for horses and cattle, streets used at times for bowling, a market place, a storehouse, and a church.

By the end of 1618, the Virginia population was slightly more than a thousand. During the next five years, another forty-five hundred persons emigrated from England. In 1619 there convened the first representative assembly in the English colonies— the first American home government. And in that same year,

[2] *Party Leaders* by Joseph G. Baldwin (New York: D. Appleton & Company, 1855), pages 149–53.

Dutch ships brought black slaves to Jamestown and sold them, the first such event recorded in what is now the United States.[3]

By 1640, Virginia's total population numbered eight thousand. But meanwhile, in a pattern that was to characterize future North-South relationships, the New England colonies were rapidly outstripping the Southerners in population and economic growth. Ironically, the earliest exploration of Massachusetts was by "Southerner" John Smith. Coming up from Virginia, in 1614, he sailed an open boat from Penobscot to Cape Cod, making maps. He described it as a place where "a hundred men may, in one houre or two, make their provisions for a day . . . He is a very bad fisher (who) cannot kill in one day with his hooke and line, one, two, or three hundred Cods . . . If a man worke but three dayes in seaven, he may get more than he can spend . . . fish but an houre to take more than they eate in a weeke."

The Pilgrims arrived at Cape Cod in 1620 and began Plymouth. By 1640, New England's population outnumbered Virginia three to one. Expanding at a rate beyond her capacity to produce food, despite Smith's enthusiastic estimates, New England developed manufacturing and trading abilities and turned to Virginia for her agricultural goods. Thus, very early, forty years after the founding of Jamestown, the character of an industrial North and an agricultural South was established. The Yankee trader, in the dawn of America, was a familiar figure in the South.

The Southern colonies, which by the mid-1600s included Maryland, formed a small and scattered community remote from all other European settlements in America. Generating their own energies, they spread out in the Chesapeake area and south to what would become the Carolina colony. The impetus into Carolina was largely from Scotsmen who felt uncomfortable with their English cousins in Virginia. A prominent Virginia Scot, Alexander Moray, wrote, "I should think myself very happy in living in this Country, but that the emulations, and differences betwixt us and the English not only give discouragement but that when we have

[3] Slaves already had been heavily introduced into the West Indies. The trade multiplied greatly toward the end of the century. Between 1680 and 1786, British flags alone would ship two million West Africans to the Caribbean colonies. Every European power except Italy engaged in the trade.

occasion, we meet many disappointments in justice." Moray and other Scottish associates began mapping sites in the Carolinas.

Settlement began in 1656 and spread into present-day South Carolina, Charleston being founded in 1670 under a land grant which gave feudal rights to a group called the "Lords Proprietors" and which provided for three orders of nobility to rule the region.[4] Here again we see the aristocratic tradition entering Southern mythology.

As Virginia, Maryland, and the Carolinas began to fill, ever so slightly, with people, Georgia was opened up by a land grant from George II signed in 1732. The first colonists, headed by James Oglethorpe, arrived the following year. Georgia was the last of the original thirteen colonies to be settled.

Everywhere—Virginia, Carolina, Georgia—slaves were a vital part of the economy, an important source of labor and wealth. Southerners measured, to a certain extent, their rank in society by the number of slaves they held.

The result was a tripartite social structure. At the top was the aristocracy. Beneath them were two distinct classes: the poor whites, who by the 1830s were being called "red-necks" and "crackers," and the blacks.[5]

All three of these classes were prone to violence and as a defense measure the aristocrats developed a special manner of pater-

---

[4] The charter was drawn up by the philosopher John Locke and, to "avoid a too numerous democracy," restricted political rights to three orders of nobility: barons, caciques, and landgraves.

[5] The "tripartite structure" is of course an oversimplification. The Southern social makeup was far more complex, but it was essentially the three classes that gave the South its cultural personality. Federal censuses taken prior to 1861 show that the three groups—planters, slaves, and dependent whites—made up slightly less than half the total Southern population. Of the remainder, the largest single group was the independent farmer, of varying degrees of affluence, who seldom owned slaves. Smaller groups included businessmen, professional men, artisans, and tenant farmers.

The South as a whole, however, took its politics, laws, and social roles from the social pattern imposed by the dominant minority of aristocrats. The more numerous yeomen and middle class had little solidarity or self-awareness and the individuals tended to take their place in the pecking order as their abilities and temperament allowed.

[6] Statistics on crime traditionally show Southern communities to be low in overall crime but high in violent crime. The 1975 statistics of the FBI showed only three Southern communities among the top fifty U.S. crime centers (Baton Rouge ranked twenty-fifth; Little Rock, forty-first; and Memphis, forty-seventh). In the category of rape, however, three of the top

nalism and courtesy,[6] forms which continue today. When a poor
white attends a public gathering he is received as a fine gentleman.
A familiar hand is laid on his shoulder. His first name is used and
members of his family are asked about. Forms of address identify
class status. The lower castes, black or white, are called by first
names. It is "Bill" or "Mary." The upper-class whites are
addressed as "Mister Sam" or "Miss Sarah." Maybe "Mister Sam"
offers his man a drink. Usually some treasured misadventure or
boasted weakness of "Bill" is recalled with indulgent good humor.
In short, Bill is patronized, and he loves it. He does not regard
such deference to the "quality" as an acknowledgment of intrinsic
inferiority. He is, instead, showing good manners by recognizing
power and status and property. He feels that should *he* obtain
"quality" then he too will be addressed as "Mister" and woe to
those who fail to do so. Particularly if they happen to be black.

The black African came into this country in 1619, a bare twelve
years after Jamestown was founded. He preceded the settlement
of Manhattan in 1623 and he preceded by seventy years the
French and the Spanish entry into the Mississippi valley. He came
ahead, too, of the Germans, the Scots, the Irish, the Pilgrims, and
the Quakers.

Each of the early inhabitants of the country grew up to regard
the other with painful suspicion (an indulgence they would never
entirely surrender). But by the time the first U. S. Congress sat
down, all were citizens, save for the black African. Resident
blacks, free or slave, were not eligible for citizenship in 1789 and,
indeed, one of the early acts of the new Congress was a law that
only a free white person could be naturalized. Implicit was the in-
tent to maintain an inferior status for the black.

Southern whites have long recognized their community ties with
blacks. And they maintain that these ties cross color lines, that
relations are better among Southerners black or white than between Northern whites and blacks or between Northern city

---

four cities were Southern. In aggravated assault, the first six cities were
Southern. And in murder, eight of the first nine cities were Southern
(Atlanta; New Orleans; Waco, Texas; and Jackson, Mississippi, led the list.
Detroit, called "Murder City" in the press, ranked tenth and New York
City sixteenth).

blacks and Southern farm blacks. The traveler in the South can find considerable firsthand evidence to support the view.

However, a secondary and corollary Southern white belief seems demonstrably untrue. Southerners believe, or *did* believe, that blacks prefer the stable, biracial arrangements of the segregated South. "They like it that way," is a Southern cliché when talking of the segregation system.

If Southern whites have grossly underestimated the aspirations of the blacks, Northern scholars have made equally large mistakes in drawing their histories of black suffering in the South. Most historians of the North have accepted wholesale the Abolitionist propaganda and have painted a South built around Eliza on the ice floe, families torn from their parents' arms at slave auctions, casual rapes—all played to the rhythmic background of the lash, laid across the backs of blacks strapped to the whipping post.

It was until publication in 1974 of *Time on the Cross*[7] that a truer picture of the physical conditions began to emerge. Applying reams of fresh data and computer analysis of economics, the authors demonstrated that slavery rarely meant a life of terror or malnutrition. As property, slaves were too valuable for such treatment. Rapes were probably of much lower incidence than in big cities today. And there was a strong South-wide ethic against breaking up families at sales. (A visitor to the Richmond, Virginia, slave market in 1840 noted that in a two-week observation he saw only one family put up for individual sale. The original owner had gone bankrupt and had no control over the division of

[7] By Robert William Fogel and Stanley L. Engerman (Boston: Little, Brown and Co.). The statistical methods and interpretations of Fogel and Engerman came under vigorous academic attack following publication. By coincidence, I had researched the same subject, the living condition of slaves, in 1973–74. I did not use statistical methods but instead relied exclusively on the journals of English and French travelers in the South during 1830–60. Virtually to a man, these eyewitnesses present a picture nearly identical to the conclusions reached by *Time on the Cross*, except for one important area: Unlike Fogel and Engerman, the foreigners did not perceive slave labor to be as efficient as free labor. To the contrary, there are numerous comments on its inefficiency. In addition to its revisionist conclusions, *Time on the Cross* was a jarring attack on the methods of traditional historical scholarship. Though economists were generally pleased with the book, many historians claimed to have found discrepancies in the statistical base upon which the authors had based their arguments and conclusions.

the family. He wept and the crowd reacted by taking up a collection to buy and then free the parents and their four children.)

Slave diet was above modern recommended nutrient levels and on a par with, or superior to, the diet of free labor in Northern cities. Luxury food, meat, milk, wheat, was not available daily, but was usually given in abundance on holidays—and nearly every month there were two or more holidays. In addition, slaves were encouraged to raise their own protein, particularly poultry, to sell or consume as they desired.

Miscegenation was rare and the authors use a remarkable calculation to show that not more than 8 per cent—and probably far less—of the black population was parented by whites. Other statistics, compiled from surveys of ex-slaves early in the twentieth century, put the figure even lower, at 4½ per cent or less.

Slaves, Fogel and Engerman concluded, seem in terms of health and nutrition to have fared roughly as well as the general population. In some aspects they fared better. For instance, fewer slave women died in childbirth, though the infant mortality rate among slaves was higher.

Black life expectancy overall was shorter than that of white Americans in 1850 but black deaths were pushed up by the higher infant mortality rate. Both the slave and the rural white, however, had longer life spans than the American city dweller and equal to the average northern European of the era.

The authors even contested the long-spread belief that slavery was inefficient. In estimating the relative efficiency of Southern and Northern agriculture, they showed that Southern farms (west of the Appalachians) got 50 per cent more output from the same inputs of land and labor than the comparable Northern farms. And Southern farms with slaves did better than those without. (That conclusion, however, is disputed by the bulk of writings contemporary to the 1776–1860 period. There is a vast amount of letters, diaries, and published works by native Southerners and visiting Englishmen and Frenchmen all pointing out the inefficiency of slave labor compared to free labor, and using statistics to prove it. An unscientific example was given by an Englishman who visited New Orleans in 1837. There was an old slave, at the house in which he stayed, whose sole job each day and every day, after breakfast, was to wheel an empty barrel five blocks down the street to the Mississippi River. There he passed the hours with friends, leisurely ate his lunch, which had been packed for him at the house, and took a nap in the cool shade of some warehouse. Around 4 P.M., he would fill the barrel with river water and truck it back to the house for his master's bath. And that was his day. He was free for the rest of the evening and night to go about the city and do as he wished.)

More than a century ago Sir Charles Lyell, in his book *A Second Visit to the United States* published in 1849, said he had believed the propaganda about widespread slave mistreatment until he arrived in the South and found it—to his surprise—to be untrue. And he was impressed with how slaves dominated the skilled labor market. "I was agreeably surprised to see the rank held here by the black mechanics. One day I observed a set of carpenters putting up sluices, and a lock in a canal of a kind unknown in this part of the world. The black foreman was carrying into execution a plan laid down for him on paper by Mr. Couper, who had observed it himself many years ago in Holland. I also saw a steam-engine, of fifteen horse power, made in England by Bolton and Watt, and used in a mill for threshing rice, which had been managed by a negro for more than twelve years without an accident. When these mechanics came to consult Mr. Couper on business, their manner of speaking to him is quite as independent as that of English artisans to their employers. Their aptitude for the practice of such mechanical arts may encourage every philanthropist who has had misgivings in regard to the progressive powers of the race, although much time will be required to improve the whole body of negroes, and the movement must be general."

Lyell noted that a Southern movement to educate blacks had been reversed by reaction to the Abolitionists. "One planter can do little by himself, so long as education is forbidden by law. I am told that the old colonial statutes against teaching the slaves to read were almost in abeyance, and had become a dead letter, until revived by the reaction against the Abolition agitation, since which they have been rigorously enforced and made more stringent. Nevertheless, the negroes are often taught to read, and they

learn much in Sunday schools, and for the most part are desirous
of instruction."

Lyell also was surprised by the low incidence of illegitimate
children. "The female slave is proud of her connection with a
white man, and thinks it an honor to have a mulatto child, hoping
that it will be better provided for than a black child. Yet the
mixed offspring is not very numerous. The mulattoes alone represent nearly all the illicit intercourse between the white man and
negro of the living generation. I am told that they do not constitute more than 2½ per cent of the whole population. If the statistics of the illegitimate children of the whites born here could be
compared with those in Great Britain, it might lead to conclusions
by no means favorable" to the English.

"There are scarcely any instances of mulattoes born of a black
father and a white mother. The colored women who become the
mistresses of the white men are neither rendered miserable nor
degraded, as are the white women who are seduced in Europe,
and who are usually abandoned in the end, and left to be the victims of want and disease. In the northern states of America there
is so little profligacy of this kind, that their philanthropists may
perhaps be usefully occupied in considering how the mischief may
be alleviated south of the Potomac . . ."

On the other hand, says Lyell, if sexual relations between the
races were allowed to increase the color problem would vanish.
"Almalgamation would proceed very rapidly, if marriages between
the races were once legalized; for we see in England that black
men can persuade very respectable white women to marry them,
[if] all idea of the illegality and degradation of such unions is
foreign to their thoughts."

Breeding between the races was, of course, what the Southern
white feared most. It was the most obvious and direct threat to
their communal identity. Yet it also was a solution to the problem
of how to eventually achieve peace among two races inhabiting
the same land. In fact, an experiment in miscegenation on a wide
basis was begun in Louisiana, and seemed to be working well until
it was derailed by economic factors. We will look at that experiment shortly.

When Lyell arrived in 1849, he found the American South had

already become the international symbol of slavery, although, as apologists were fond to point out, slavery was as old as history. (And, it may be added, as modern as the space age. Some nations have only recently abolished slavery, such as Saudi Arabia in 1964, and the United Nations as late as 1975 was still reporting an active slave trade in some of the Arab countries.)

On the North American mainland the initial source of cheap labor was indentured whites from England and Europe. Black slaves did not become numerous or commercially important until about 1700.

The first blacks brought to American colonies arrived in Virginia as indentured servants. (They were indentured to John Rolfe, husband of Pocahontas and ancestor of all the Randolphs.) By 1650 there were only an estimated three hundred blacks in the colonies, compared to fifteen hundred indentured whites. It wasn't until 1661 that Virginia passed the first law making Negroes slaves, and thereafter slave laws were adopted in the other colonies. By 1681 the black slave population had risen to three thousand.

By 1776 there were 530,000 black people in the colonies. The Negro population had more than doubled since 1750 and constituted 20 per cent of the total population.[8] When the Declaration of Independence was signed, slaves existed in all colonies of the confederation.

(In French America, the area embodying the Gulf coast and the Mississippi River basin, slaves were introduced in 1712 when King Louis XV granted a license to a merchant named Crozat to import them into the then French colonial capital at Biloxi [Mississippi]. Under this license about twenty blacks were imported.)

In the next twenty-five years, slavery was phased out of the Northern colonies.

In 1831, Alexis de Tocqueville, a twenty-six-year-old French

[8] Black population held at about the 20 per cent ratio until, beginning in the 1830s, the white population was swelled by European immigrants. In the 1970 census, Negroes constituted 11 per cent of the total population. In 1776, 90 per cent of blacks lived in the South. Two hundred years later less than half lived in the South. The Northern migration was historically recent, the bulk of it coming after 1950.

magistrate, visited the United States to study the penal system. He would return to France to write *Democracy in America,* the classic examination of American institutions. And he observed that the South seemed saddled with an unremovable problem.

His visit occurred at a time when it appeared that slavery might be peaceably eradicated throughout the United States. The Abolitionist movement had not yet become offensive in the South and was, in these early days, aimed at eliminating slavery by national legislation. To intellectual Southerners, where the blacks' near-monopoly on the skilled trades was well known, it appeared that slaves might buy freedom with their own labors, talents, and initiative. Southern owners, in general, said they would be glad to be rid of the obligations of slavery and wanted only just compensation for their investment.

Tocqueville did not believe such peaceful transitions would occur. He viewed slavery not as an economic problem but as a race problem imposed upon the South by the North. The Southern whites could not get rid of it.

Tocqueville began his argument with the premise: "Wherever the whites have been the most powerful, they have maintained the blacks in a subordinate or a servile position; wherever the Negroes have been strongest they have destroyed the whites.[9] Such has been the only retribution which has ever taken place between the two races."

The free states of the North, he observed, are more prejudiced against blacks than the slave states. "The prejudice of the race appears to be stronger in the states which have abolished slavery than in those where it still exists; and nowhere is it so intolerant as in those states where servitude has never been known." (Ohio and Illinois, for example.)

"It is true, that in the North marriages may be legally contracted between Negroes and whites; but public opinion would stigmatize a man who should connect himself with a Negress as infamous, and it would be difficult to meet with a single instance

[9] Like many whites, European and American, Tocqueville had been impressed by Christophe's racial war in Haiti. The Tocqueville quotations come from *Democracy in America,* Henry Reeve translation (New York: Shocken Books, 1961), Volume 1.

of such a union. The electoral franchise has been conferred upon the Negroes in almost all the states in which slavery has been abolished, but if they come forward to vote, their lives are in danger. If oppressed, they may bring an action at law; but they will find none but whites amongst their judges. And although they may legally serve as jurors, prejudice repulses them from that office. The same schools do not receive the child of the black and of the European. In the theatres . . ."

The black is free, said Tocqueville, but cannot share the rights or pleasures or labor or afflictions of the free, "not even the tomb of him whose equal he has been declared to be."

"In the South, the Negroes are less carefully kept apart; they sometimes share the labor and the recreations of the whites; the whites consent to intermix with them to a certain extent, and although the legislation treats them more harshly, the habits of the people are more tolerant and compassionate. In the South the master is not afraid to raise his slave to his own standing, because he knows that he can in a moment reduce him to the dust, at pleasure."

If, asks Tocqueville, the North and the South are equally prejudiced then why has the North abolished slavery and the South maintained it?

"The answer is easily given. It is not for the good of the Negroes, but for that of the whites, that measures are taken to abolish slavery in the United States."

In most Northern states, slavery had once been as economically desirable as in the South. William Smith in 1757 published the *History of the Province of New York* and noted, "The province being poorly inhabited, the price of labor became so enormously enhanced, that we have been combined to import Negroes from Africa, who are employed in all kinds of servitude and trades."

Just prior to the Declaration of Independence, the Boston slave Phillis Wheatley Peters published a popular book of poems in which she compared the "Fair Freedom" of white New England with her own condition, "young in life . . . snatched from Africa," seized from her father. "Such, such my case. And can I then but pray others may never feel tyrranic sway."

Mrs. Peters, born about 1754, had been brought from Africa as a seven-year-old girl and sold in the Boston slave market.

The New Yorker John Jay, a leading abolitionist, wrote to an English abolition society in 1788 that slavery was so entrenched *North* and *South* that it took time, much time, to change it:

"Prior to the late revolution, the great majority, or rather the great body, of our people had been so long accustomed to the practice and convenience of having slaves, that very few among them even doubted the propriety and rectitude of it. Some liberal and conscientious men had, indeed, by their conduct and writings, drawn the lawfulness of slavery into question, and they made converts to that opinion; but the number of these converts compared with the people at large was then very inconsiderable. Their doctrines prevailed by almost insensible degrees, and was like the little lump of leaven which was put into three measures of meal; even at this day, the whole mass is far from being leavened, though we have good reason to hope and to believe that if the natural operations of truth are constantly watched and assisted, but not forced and precipitated, that end we all aim at will finally be attained in this country."[10]

Jay was in fact defending the recognition of slavery in the new Constitution which was then going round for approval.

Tocqueville notes that the Northern states abolished slavery soon after the rise of industry made free labor more profitable. The South, however, with its reliance on tobacco, sugar, and cotton and the absence of industry, held on to it. Indeed, in 1793 the South's need for slavery was accelerated by the invention of the cotton gin which spurred large-scale production of cotton.

Meanwhile, the Northern states phased out the use of slaves in a manner to protect their masters. John Jay's own New York State abolished the *sale* of slaves within its borders in 1788 and eight years later decreed that children born to slave parents after July 4, 1799, were free. The message for owners was easy to read: Your slaves will not beget new slaves, so sell them. And since the law forbids sale within New York State, you must sell them elsewhere. Therefore over a period of eleven years the slave trade was

[10] *Library of American Literature* (New York: Charles Webster Co., 1896), Vol. 3, page 325.

abolished in New York while the owners, having ample notice, were able to sell them off in the market place.

"From the time at which a Northern state prohibited the importation of slaves," wrote Tocqueville, "no slaves were brought from the South to be sold in its markets. On the other hand, as the sale of slaves was forbidden in that state, an owner was no longer able to get rid of his slave otherwise than by transporting him to the South . . . Thus the same law prevents the slaves of the South from coming to the North and drives those of the North to the South."

Using the census of 1830, Tocqueville demonstrated that the farther south one goes the thicker the black population, caused, he said, by "compulsory emigration of the Negroes from the North . . . In the state of Maine there is one Negro in three hundred inhabitants; in Massachusetts one in one hundred; in New York, two in one hundred; in Pennsylvania, three in the same number; in Maryland, thirty-four; in Virginia, forty-two; and lastly, in South Carolina, fifty-five per cent." By 1830 the nonslave states had 6.6 million whites and 121,000 blacks, whereas slave states had 3.9 million whites and 2.2 million blacks. This numerical relationship, said Tocqueville, forced the South to continue slavery.

The determinant question, said Tocqueville, was this: If the South rigorously abolishes slavery, "how should it rid its territory of the black population?

". . . The inhabitants of the South would not be able, like their Northern countrymen, to initiate the slaves gradually into a state of freedom. They have no means of perceptibly diminishing the black population and they would remain unsupported [militarily] to repress its excesses . . ."

The one alternative, he wrote, to racial war was that "Negroes and whites must either wholly [separate] or wholly mingle." But mingling, he argued, was rejected by the whites. And as for separation, it had been tried with the Liberian experiment beginning in 1820 and was proving insufficient.

"A certain number of American citizens have formed a society for the purpose of exporting to the coast of Guinea, at their own expense, such free Negroes as may be willing to escape from the oppression to which they are subject . . . In twelve years the Colonization Society has transported 2,500 Negroes to Africa; in the same space of time about 700,000 blacks were born in the United States. [Even] if the Union were to supply the society with annual subsidies and to transport the Negroes to Africa in the vessels of the state, it would still be unable to counterpoise the natural increase of population amongst the black."

With two huge populations vying for supremacy in the same land, he said, "The danger of a conflict between the white and the black inhabitants of the Southern states . . . is inevitable."

Emancipation, said Tocqueville, "will not ward off the struggle of the two races in the United States. The Negroes may long remain slaves without complaining; but if they are once raised to the level of free men, they will soon revolt of being deprived of all their civil rights; and as they cannot become the equals of the whites, they will speedily declare themselves as enemies."

By the 1830s, neither the white South nor the black South had other options. They were locked into the historical roles they would play over the next century.

The South had missed its chances in the late eighteenth century. When the Northern states unloaded their slaves—with no economic penalty to the owners—the South could have done the same. Had they done so, had the North not been able to sell their slaves South, the black population would have been stabilized across all the United States. There would have been no "black problem" peculiar to the South. There would have been a peaceful amalgamation, in Virginia as in New York.

But even if "the black problem" had been removed, there would still have been a sectional division between the industrial North and the agrarian South. The contest between Northern white and Southern white was taut and carefully played. Consider the matter of letting Virginia take the lead in establishing a new nation. It was a finely calculated Northern game.

Chapter 3
VIRGINIA IN THE LEAD

Virginia's role in the American Revolution has usually been shown out of focus. The standard texts make it seem that Virginia was a follower of Massachusetts, and a somewhat reluctant one, in promoting American independence. It is acknowledged that a few Virginians, because of individual brilliance, rose to leadership. But one must look close and long to learn that the American form of government was a product of the Virginia society. Instead, it is Boston which is called "the cradle of liberty."

It is a case of history being written by the conquerors. Early in the game, the writers of New England—particularly men of the Adams family—minimized the Southern contribution and what glory they subtracted from Virginia they added to their own.

The facts, however, are inarguable. Virginia was the *political* leader of the revolution. New England, and specifically the men of Massachusetts, had taken the initiative in *guerrilla* and *military* matters, the Tea Party, the battles of Lexington and Concord. But it was Virginia which organized the Continental Congress. It was Virginia which declared the independence. And it was Virginia which designed, not the Articles of Confederation, but the present Constitution.

While still a colony, Virginia provided the world's first fully developed written Constitution and America's first Bill of Rights.[1]

The Virginia Constitution was written in May 1776 by a crotchety plantation aristocrat, George Mason. It contained the then very liberal statement, "all men are by nature equally free and independent." This "free and equal" doctrine was discussed among liberals in England and America at the time, but in Virginia it had become a currency of the people. (*Some* of the people. In the state constitutional convention, Mason had been quizzed closely on the point. Did he mean to include slaves? After four days of debate, a sufficiently specious reply was evolved. Men have such rights only "when they enter into a state of society." Slaves had not entered society, and thus did not have its natural rights.)

In the Virginia Bill of Rights, Mason wrote down the basics of the English bill and added new notions, for instance that "the freedom of the press is one of the great bulwarks of liberty, and can never be restrained by despotic governments; and that "all men are equally entitled to the free exercise of religion."

In the Continental Congress, it was a Virginian, George Washington, who was named to head the Army. It was a Virginian, Richard Henry Lee, who officially proposed severance from Great Britain. And it was a Virginian, Jefferson, who drafted the Declaration of Independence.

Virginia did not take the lead in all these matters out of a monopoly on political brilliance. Massachusetts had its Adamses and its Hancock. Pennsylvania had Benjamin Franklin. And there was Samuel Chase of Maryland, Edward Rutledge of South Carolina, Caesar Rodney of Delaware, Roger Sherman of Connecticut, and Robert Livingston of New York.

---

[1] The Hittite civilization, according to C. W. Ceram, had a crude constitution, i.e., a statement of fundamental principles according to which a nation is formed. It was written in cuneiform around 1700 B.C. The idea of a constitution, however, vanished with the Hittites and did not reappear until something approaching a constitution was signed by the Dutch provinces of the Netherlands in A.D. 1579. It was in fact a defense treaty which had a few articles describing centralized functions of government, but these were never put into effect. The first "Bill of Rights" was published by the British Parliament in 1689 and listed specific rights possessed by Englishmen that were inviolable.

According to John Adams, the decision to put Virginia at the head of the Continental Congress was made by Northerners at a meeting in Frankfort, Pennsylvania.[2] The Northern purpose was, first, to take British military pressure off New England and, second, to let Virginia pull in the other Southern colonies by giving it leadership.

Perhaps Virginia succeeded too well and took all the leadership out of Northern hands. In Adams' later writings, hints of jealousy can be detected. But Adams never backed away from his statement that Virginia leadership was promoted, at a secret meeting, to take the military pressure off the North.

The Frankfort meeting was one of the most pivotal in American history, although it has been ignored by most historians. No Virginian was present at the meeting, nor, as far as can be determined, did any Virginian know of it at the time. Little is known of the Frankfort meeting to this day. But John Adams, who was present, wrote that without the Frankfort discussion, "Mr. Washington would never have commanded our armies; nor Mr. Jefferson have been the author of the Declaration of Independence; nor Mr. Richard Henry Lee the mover of it . . ."

The meeting demonstrates that North-South sectionalism was a very real factor in the very beginnings of American history.

The meeting was held on August 29, 1774. John Adams, who has written the only known account of the event, was then a thirty-nine-year-old Boston lawyer, a leader of the American revolutionary movement (and later second President of the United States).

Less than two years earlier, Boston rebels had boarded British ships and thrown tea overboard. King George III had ordered reprisals and in May 1774, Rhode Island, followed by Pennsylvania and New York had issued a call for a colonial Congress. The battles of Lexington and Concord, the beginning of the war, would not occur until the following year.

In August 1774, John Adams, delegate from Boston, was en route to the first Continental Congress, which would convene in Philadelphia September 5. As a leading revolutionary, his life was very much on the line and he was anxious for success, anxious to

[2] Now part of the city of Philadelphia.

know the character of the men with whom he'd be dealing. He
relates that en route to Trenton:

"We sent a card to Mr. Sergeant, a lawyer; he dined, drank
coffee, and spent the evening with us. He is a young gentleman of
about twenty-five perhaps; very sociable. He gave us much light
concerning the characters of the delegates from New York, Philadelphia, Virginia, &c., and concerning the characters of the principal lawyers in all these Provinces . . .

"He says the Virginians speak in raptures about Richard Henry
Lee and Patrick Henry; one the Cicero and the other the
Demosthenes of the age."

After leaving Trenton, Adams and his party crossed the Delaware, "a beautiful river," and admired the broad stands of black-
walnut timber. They entered Pennsylvania.

"We arrived at Bristol about eleven o'clock—a village on the
Delaware, opposite to which is Burlington. The scenes of nature
are delightful here. This is twenty miles from Philadelphia. Here
we saw two or three passage wagons, a vehicle with four wheels,
contrived to carry many passengers and much baggages. We then
rode to the Red Lion and dined.

"After dinner we stopped at Frankfort, about five miles out of
town. A number of carriages and gentlemen came out of Philadelphia to meet us—Mr. Thomas Mifflin, Mr. McKean, of the
lower counties, one of their delegates, Mr. Rutledge of Carolina,
and a number of gentlemen from Philadelphia, Mr. Folsom and
Mr. Sullivan, the New Hampshire delegates. We were introduced
to all these gentlemen, and most cordially welcomed to Philadelphia. We then rode into town."[3]

That was all that was written at the time. Adams will make an
oblique reference to the meeting when writing his autobiography
in 1805. But forty-eight years will pass before we hear any actual
details. They come in a letter by Adams, dated August 6, 1822.
Adams was then eighty-eight years of age and he was writing to
his friend Timothy Pickering, aged seventy-eight.[4] Pickering had

---

[3] Entry of August 29, 1774, *Diary of John Adams.*
[4] Pickering, of Salem, Massachusetts, had been Quartermaster General of
the Continental Army, Secretary of War under George Washington, Secretary of State under Washington and Adams, and a U.S. senator and congressman.

solicited Adams to set down the origin of the Declaration of Independence. Adams' reply contains many interesting particulars about the political beginnings of the United States.

The Massachusetts delegation to Congress included John Adams and Samuel Adams, who, "all destitute of fortune, poor pilgrims, proceeded in one coach, were escorted through Massachusetts, Connecticut, New York, and New Jersey, into Pennsylvania. We were met at Frankfort," said John Adams, "by Dr. Rush, Mr. Mifflin, Mr. Bayard, and several other of the most active sons of liberty in Philadelphia, who desired a conference with us. We invited them to take tea with us in a private apartment . . .

"They represented to us that the friends of government in Boston and in the Eastern States, in their correspondence with their friends in Pennsylvania and all the Southern States, had represented us as . . . desperate adventurers . . .

"We were all suspected of having independence in view. 'Now,' said they, 'you must not utter the word independence, nor give the least hint or insinuation of the idea, either in Congress or any private conversation; if you do, you are undone; for the idea of independence is as unpopular in Pennsylvania, and in all the Middle and Southern States, as the Stamp Act itself. No man dares to speak of it. Moreover, you are the representatives of the suffering State. Boston and Massachusetts are under a rod of iron. British fleets and armies are tyrannizing over you; you yourselves are personally obnoxious to them and all the friends of government . . . You must be, therefore, very cautious; you must not come forward with any bold measures, you must not pretend to take the lead. You know Virginia is the most populous State in the Union. They are very proud of their ancient dominion, as they call it; they think they have a right to take the lead, and the Southern States, and Middle States too, are too much disposed to yield it to them.'

"This was plain dealing, Mr. Pickering; and I must confess that there appeared so much wisdom and good sense in it, that it made a deep impression on my mind, and it had an equal effect on all my colleagues.

"This conversation, and the principles, facts, and motives

suggested in it, have given a color, complexion, and character, to the whole policy of the United States, from that day to this.

"Without it, Mr. Washington would never have commanded our armies; nor Mr. Jefferson have been the author of the Declaration of Independence; nor Mr. Richard Henry Lee the mover of it; nor Mr. Chase the mover of foreign connections. If I have ever had cause to repent of any part of this policy, that repentance, ever has been, and ever will be, unavailing. I had forgot to say, nor had Mr. Johnson ever been the nominator of Washington for General . . .

"You inquire why so young a man as Mr. Jefferson was placed at the head of the Committee for preparing a Declaration of Independence? I answer: it was the Frankfort advice, to place Virginia at the head of everything . . .

"Mr. Jefferson came into Congress, in June, 1775, and brought with him a reputation for literature, science, and a happy talent of composition. Writings of his were handed about, remarkable for the peculiar felicity of expression. Though a silent member in Congress, he was so prompt, frank, explicit, and decisive upon committees and in conversation, not even Samuel Adams was more so, that he soon seized upon my heart; and upon this occasion I gave him my vote, and did all in my power to procure the votes of others. I think he had one more vote than any other, and that placed him at the head of the committee. I had the next highest number, and that placed me the second. The committee met, discussed the subject, and then appointed Mr. Jefferson and me to make the draught, I suppose because we were the two first on the list.

"The subcommittee met. Jefferson proposed to me to make the draught. I said, 'I will not.' 'You should do it.' 'Oh! no.' 'Why will you not?' 'You ought to do it.' 'I will not.' 'Why?' 'Reason's enough.' 'What can be your reasons?' 'Reason first—you are a Virginian, and a Virginian ought to appear at the head of this business. Reason second—I am obnoxious, suspected, and unpopular. You are very much otherwise. Reason third—You can write ten times better than I can.' 'Well,' said Jefferson, 'if you are decided, I will do as well as I can.' 'Very well. When you have drawn it up, we will have a meeting.'

Captain John Smith: An Elizabethan, founder of the Virginia Colony, first explorer of Massachusetts. *(Library of Congress)*

John Randolph of Roanoke: He was one of four who set the style, the philosophy, and the tactics of Southern politics. *(Library of Congress)*

Senator Richard Henry Lee: When [he] took his seat, the United States of Am[er]ica was able to begin—a month and t[en] days late. *(Library of Congress)*

Thomas Jefferson: His words have shaken the world order for two hundred years. *(Library of Congress)*

James Madison: Creator of the Democratic party, which began as a small organization in Virginia. *(Library of Congress)*

...rles Pinckney of South Carolina: He ...ented a design for a nation governed ...a congress, a supreme court, and a ...f executive. *(Library of Congress)*

Alexander Hamilton: His perception of the national interests, though not charming, proved accurate. *(Library of Congress)*

William Blount: The first man impeached by Congress and a hero in frontier Tennessee. *(North Carolina Division of Archives and History, the Albert Barden Collection)*

James Monroe: The last of the Virgi gentlemen Presidents. Next came demagogues. *(Library of Congress)*

"A meeting we accordingly had, and conned the paper over. I was delighted with its high tone and the flights of oratory with which it abounded, especially that concerning negro slavery, which, though I knew his Southern brethren would never suffer to pass in Congress, I certainly never would oppose. There were other expressions which I would not have inserted, if I had drawn it up, particularly that which called the King tyrant. I thought this too personal; for I never believed George to be a tyrant in disposition and in nature; I always believed him to be deceived by his courtiers on both sides of the Atlantic, and in his official capacity only, cruel . . .

"We reported it to the committee of five. It was read, and I do not remember that Franklin or Sherman criticized anything. We were all in haste. Congress was impatient, and the instrument was reported, as I believe, in Jefferson's handwriting, as he first drew it. Congress cut off about a quarter of it, as I expected they would; but they obliterated some of the best of it, and left all that was exceptionable, if anything in it was. I have long wondered that the original draught has not been published. I suppose the reason is, the vehement philippic against negro slavery.[5]

"As you justly observe, there is not an idea in it but what had been hackneyed in Congress for two years before. The substance of it is contained in the declaration of rights and the violation of those rights, in the Journals of Congress, in 1774. Indeed, the essence of it is contained in a pamphlet, voted and printed by the town of Boston, before the first Congress met, composed by James Otis, as I suppose, in one of his lucid intervals, and pruned and polished by Samuel Adams."[6]

[5] The censored clause read: the "King of Great Britain kept open a market where *men* were bought and sold, and prostituted his negative by suppressing Virginia's legislative attempts to restrain this execrable commerce."
[6] *The Autobiography of John Adams*, pages 512–15. The Otis reference apparently is to a pamphlet, "The Rights of the British Colonies," published by Otis, a Boston lawyer, in 1764. The pamphlet argues that colonists are entitled to the same rights as citizens living in England. An important document, it nevertheless falls far short of being the equal or even an immediate forerunner of the Declaration of Independence. Adams, however, always had a high opinion of it and once declared of its publication: "Then and there, the child Independence was born."

We are arriving now at the drama embodying the political birth of the nation. North and South will come together as partners on the same stage. Virginians, because of the reasons cited by Adams, will be handed the leading roles. The central character, the protagonist around whose head events swirl, is not the aloof George Washington. His eminence comes during the war. The star is young Thomas Jefferson. Formed during his political career will be the foundation institutions of the United States. Most of these institutions, it will be seen, were a product of Southern culture, forged to accommodate the conflicting interests of the nation's three main people.

The Jefferson family was one of the oldest, though not among the most socially prominent, in Virginia. His father Peter was self-taught and in 1737 surveyed and patented a thousand acres in Albemarle County, then the western frontier of Virginia and occupied by only three or four other white families. (Among the neighbors was that of John Henry, father of Patrick Henry.)

The elder Jefferson had been a friend of the Randolphs and in 1739 he married Jane Randolph. The boy Thomas was born in 1743.

Tom Jefferson's education was picked up mostly at home, more formal education being added on by two years at William and Mary College in the provincial capital of Williamsburg. This town, never numbering more than two thousand population, was Virginia's cultural and political center for one century. It was the seedbed of Jeffersonian Democracy, a doctrine advocating minimal central government, maximum individual rights, and the superiority of an agrarian economy and society.

Williamsburg had taverns and public houses in great number; elegant balls and banquets; the legislature and courts; and William and Mary College, the nation's first law school and second oldest institution of higher learning. It numbered among its students Jefferson, Benjamin Harrison, George Wythe, George Washington, James Monroe, and John Marshall. Yet, Williamsburg was a village, hardly large enough to be called a town.

Here, at Williamsburg, was the embodiment of the Virginia civilization. It was a Midsummer Night's Dream, Puck's magic forest, the likes of which the nation would not see again. The land was bountiful, opportunities maximum, and social, political, and economic problems minimal. It was from this idyllic freak of nature that the Virginia leaders gathered their knowledge of the world and shaped the philosophies which they believed could be applied to America. This would prove impractical, for the Northern colonies had already slipped quietly into the Industrial Age, into an economy fundamentally at war with the manorial system of Virginia and the South. That the Southerners, obdurate and romantic, would cling stubbornly to the Virginia agrarian democracy dream for two centuries is not an evil thing. They were held fast in an enchantment.

Williamsburg had been settled as early as 1632 but did not become important until sixty years later, when William and Mary College was founded. A few years later, Francis Nicholson, a newly appointed Royal governor, chose it as his capital hoping— said a wicked-tongued critic—to gain by the association with learning. "He gave himself airs of encouraging the college . . . in truth he has been so far from advancing it, that now after the six years of his government, the scholars are fewer than at his arrival.

"Soon after his accession to the government, he caused the assembly and courts of judicature to be removed from Jamestown, where there were good accommodations for people, to Middle Plantation [i.e., Williamsburg], where there were none. There he flattered himself with the fond imagination of being the founder of a new city . . . He procured a stately fabric to be erected, which he placed opposite to the college, and graced it with the magnificent name of the 'Capitol.'

"This imaginary city is yet [in 1705] advanced no further than only to have a few public houses, and a store-house, more than were built upon the place before."[7]

By 1760, when Jefferson arrived, Williamsburg contained slightly over two hundred houses on unpaved streets. Boston and New York in that year had approximately fifteen thousand inhabitants; Philadelphia twenty thousand. Williamsburg was a small marketing village but certainly no village in history has ever seen

[7] *The History and Present State of Virginia* by Robert Beverly (1705). Beverly was clerk of the House of Burgesses.

such men as the place was to know between Jefferson's arrival and the change of the capital to Richmond in 1779. Monroe, Marshall, Madison, Washington, Henry, George Mason, George Wythe, all the Lees, and all the Randolphs, all acquainted and associating with one another. All were agrarians, and all were versed in law and government.

After graduating in 1672, Jefferson took up the study of law under George Wythe, the most able lawyer in the colony, and probably on the continent. (Wythe had great influence on the evolving nation, being also the teacher of Monroe, Marshall, and Henry Clay.)

Jefferson, at age twenty-two, stood six feet, two inches tall, was red-haired and freckled, read easily in Greek, Latin, French, and Italian, was an accomplished violinist, appreciated good food, good wine, and fast horses, and was experienced in romance, having had at least two meaningful affairs. He also had a reputation for shyness, but the truth of this is uncertain. He had a frail voice and occasionally stammered and was therefore restrained in talking, a condition often confused with shyness.

It was at this age, on May 29, 1765, that he had his first exposure to world affairs. He attended a speech in the House of Burgesses to hear the Honorable Member Patrick Henry, seven years Jefferson's senior, talk about the Stamp Act which had been passed by the British Parliament. It required all publications and legal documents in America to bear a stamp purchased from the government. Patrick Henry objected on the grounds that not being represented in the Parliament, the colonies could not be taxed by the Parliament.

Henry offered six resolutions and at the end of a fierce speech, in a scene of confusion, said: "Caesar had his Brutus, Charles the First his Cromwell, and George the Third . . ."

He was interrupted by a cry of "Treason!" from the seated members.

And Henry answered: ". . . may profit by their example. If *this* be treason, make the most of it."

At that juncture the Stamp Act, the first direct tax imposed by Parliament on America, had not aroused much interest, let alone outrage. Henry's remarks set the colonies afire. Within five months, nine colonies convened the first American Congress, the Stamp Act Congress, which made a declaration of rights and shortly afterward repealed, however illegally, the act. It was the first unified action among the colonies.

Jefferson favored the resolutions of Henry, although he had ambivalent feelings toward the man, regarding him as a friend but somewhat lacking in education and substance. He would later say, "I have frequently shut my eyes while he spoke and when he was done asked myself what he said, without being able to recollect a word of it. He was no logician. But he was eloquent as Homer."

Four years later, in 1769, Jefferson was elected to the House of Burgesses, where he remained until 1775. In his first session in the House, in 1769, he helped pass several resolutions asserting the right of self-taxation, the right of petition for redress of grievances, and the right of *all* the colonies to unite in such petitions. It was another step toward nationhood.

In the same session, he introduced a bill giving to slaveowners the power to free them. It failed to pass but demonstrated his early feelings on the subject.

In those legislative years, Tom Jefferson became a power among Virginia liberals, a group which included Washington, Henry, and the Lees. By the spring of 1774, when news was received of the Boston Tea Party, power had passed into their hands. The Virginians commenced to move cautiously but surely to a complete break with Great Britain.

They first organized an intercolonial Congress (the First Continental Congress) to meet in Philadelphia and discuss common problems. Delegates were chosen and Jefferson drafted a list of instructions for the Virginians. These were rejected as too liberal, but Jefferson had them published in a pamphlet which had large influence on the Continental Congress. Entitled "A Summary View of the Rights of British America," the pamphlet asked, "Can any reason be assigned why 160,000 electors [the number of Englishmen eligible to vote] in the island of Great Britain should give law to four millions in the states of America . . . ?" It will be noticed that Jefferson refers to *states* of America, not colonies.

After implying that not only was the role of colony illogical and contrary to British democracy, Jefferson went on to complain that the states were being exploited by British financial houses in a manner to cause permanent damage. In permitting the African slave trade, he felt, Great Britain had particularly caused a "lasting" problem.

"The abolition of domestic slavery," Jefferson wrote, "is the great object of desire in those colonies, where it was unhappily introduced in their infant state. But previous to the enfranchisement of the slaves we have, it is necessary to exclude all further importations from Africa; yet our repeated efforts to effect this by prohibition, have been hitherto defeated by his majesty's negative; thus preferring the immediate advantages of a few African corsairs to the lasting interests of the American states, and to the rights of human nature."

(In other documents, the slave-owning Jefferson would advocate freedom for blacks and full citizenship, including the right to vote. In this latter guarantee, he was nearly a century ahead of his time for it would not be until the Civil War that even liberals such as Harriet Beecher Stowe would accept Negro enfranchisement.)

Events moved quickly. In the spring of 1775, the battles of Lexington and Concord were fought. Jefferson departed for Philadelphia as delegate to the Second Continental Congress, the Congress which elected George Washington as commander of all American forces (apparently, according to John Adams, as part of the policy derived from the Frankfort meeting). In 1776, Congress requested all colonies to draft new constitutions.

The first of these was the Virginia constitution, drafted in May 1776. It would become the model for the American Constitution, not the Articles of Confederation passed in 1777 but the document of 1787, the one used today.

The Virginia document provided for separation of three governmental branches, executive, judiciary, and legislative. The last consisted of a House of Representatives and a Senate. The House was elected by all male property owners, over twenty-one years of age. The House in turn would elect the Senate. Both houses would elect a governor of strictly limited power.

Attached was a Bill of Rights, providing for trial by jury, security from unreasonable search and seizure, and the aforementioned freedoms of religion, speech, and press. Jefferson, anchored in Philadelphia by his Continental Congress duties, had sent down suggestions to include rights of property ownership and inheritance for women, abolition of the slave trade, and free public schools. These were rejected.

Meanwhile, the constitutional convention of Virginia instructed its delegates to the Continental Congress to formally propose independence from Great Britain.

On June 7, 1776, Richard Henry Lee, speaking for the entire Virginia delegation, arose and submitted sensational resolutions to the Congress. The Virginia resolutions put Congress on the spot.

Although the war was a year old, this was the first time that the colonies were officially asked to declare themselves "free and independent states." Virginia offered a very practical plan on how to do it.

The first of the Lee resolutions, the first step to independence, declared that "these United Colonies are, and of right ought to be, free and independent States, that they are absolved from all allegiance to the British Crown and that all political connection between them and the State of Great Britian is, and ought to be, totally dissolved."

The second resolution, the second step, which in its way was even more prejudicial to British interests, stated that it would be expedient to make allegiances with foreign nations.

The third resolution said a plan should be drawn for a confederated government and submitted to the colonies for agreement.

Declare independence, and what could Britain do about it? asked the Virginians. Very little. "Your fleet," they told the King, could destroy our towns, and ravage our sea-coasts; these are inconsiderable objects, things of no moment to men whose bosoms glow with the ardor of liberty. We can retire beyond the reach of your navy, and without any sensible diminution of the necessaries of life, enjoy a luxury, which from that period [the English themselves] will want—the luxury of being free."

The resolutions were taken up for debate. Three days later, Congress appointed a committee headed by Jefferson to "prepare a declaration to the effect of the said first resolution."[8]

8 Other members of the committee were John Adams, Benjamin Franklin, Roger Sherman, and Robert Livingston.

We have seen earlier that, according to John Adams' letter to Timothy Pickering, Jefferson was selected because of sectional considerations. Adams confirmed this several times. For instance, in the Adams autobiography written in 1805, Adams again stressed the sectional consideration: "Mr. Jefferson desired me to . . . make the draught. This I declined and gave several reasons for declining. 1. That he was a Virginian, and I a Massachusettensian. 2. That he was a southern man, and I a northern one . . ."

Jefferson did not record such a conversation, but said only: "The committee for drawing the Declaration of Independence desired me to do it."

His final draft was somewhat gutted by the politics of the Congress, an editing which Jefferson regretted, saying, "The pusillanimous idea that we had friends in England worth keeping terms with, still haunted the minds of many. For this reason, those passages which conveyed censures on the people of England were struck out, lest they should give them offence. The clause, too, reprobating the enslaving the inhabitants of Africa was struck out, in complaisance to South Carolina and Georgia, who had never attempted to restrain the importation of slaves and who, on the contrary, still wished to continue it."

And he added a slight thrust at Northern hypocrisy: "Our northern brethren also, I believe, felt a little tender under those censures; for though their people had very few slaves themselves, yet they had been pretty considerable carriers of them to others."

The Declaration was presented and Jefferson had succeeded perfectly in making it as he said "it was intended to be, an expression of the American mind."

Laying aside the long indictment of George III and other matters, the core of Jefferson's Americanism was captured in eleven familiar lines:

"We hold these truths to be self-evident: that all men are created equal; that they are endowed by their Creator with certain unalienable rights; that among these are life, liberty, and the pursuit of happiness. That, to secure these rights, governments are instituted among men, deriving their just powers from the consent of the governed; that, whenever any form of government becomes destructive of these ends, it is the right of the people to alter or abolish it, and to institute a new government, laying its foundations on such principles, and organizing its powers in such form, as to them shall seem most likely to effect their safety and happiness."

That paragraph was the birth announcement of a new social and political philosophy, an affirmation that power resided in the people, people who had unassailable basic rights.

For the next two hundred years, these words would shake the world order. From the Himalayas to the Amazon, from the icy rivers of Siberia to the jungles of Malaya, people of all classes, all religions, and all colors in the two centuries since would strive for that promise. Once uttered, the words could not be destroyed; once heard, the words could not be forgotten.

Previous forms of government became, in a quantum flash, obsolete. Forms of government by the elite—tribal councils, theocracies, oligarchies, monarchies—would be replaced by government of the masses: "popular government." America began it, then came the French revolution, the evolvement of socialism and communism, and two centuries of national revolutions sweeping the world.

With his words, Thomas Jefferson had invented a form of government more efficient and symmetrically balanced than previous forms.

All governments depend upon consent of the governed, whether the consent be gained through fear, logical persuasion, or other means. Upon the publication of Jefferson's words, that men were "created equal" and had "unalienable rights," the cost of gaining that consent went up.

Jefferson's government was more efficient than previous forms because it had less friction between the governed and the governors. It was efficient because it was installed by popularity and popularly abided by. It was symmetrical because to run at all it needed to strike a balance between the ambitions of the rulers and the ruled. It ran smoothly or not at all in direct relation to how well that balance was struck.

That is the sociological phenomenon that began when Jefferson proclaimed citizens' rights. He was not the first to do so. The idea of human rights was articulated by European philosophers in the seventeenth century when they began to argue that man's existence was independent of the state, that the relationship between the two was a contract.

Jefferson took the concept and carried it a large distance further. He made it real. He made the theory into a government. Whether or not those human rights did exist truly in nature didn't matter. People, from the time of Jefferson onward, *believed* they did.

Eleven lines embodying six articles of faith. They made a powerful rallying call when taken up by Robespierre and Napoleon; by José San Martín; by Marx, Lenin, and Jomo Kenyatta; by the Garibaldis and the Masaryks. Dangerous and hopeful words which would set the next two centuries aflame with revolution.

The impact and worth of Jefferson's words were not immediately recognized. While Jefferson's draft was being debated, Lee's original resolution was adopted on July 2, 1776, and it was the Lee document that grabbed attention. Independence was officially declared on that day—not July 4—with the colonies, now become "states," voting 12–0. (New York, with probably a majority of its population loyal to King George, abstained.)

The day of July 2 would be the most memorable in American history, said John Adams, thrilled with the boldness of the event. That very night he wrote his wife in great excitement:

"Yesterday, the greatest question was decided, which ever was debated in America, and a greater, perhaps, never was nor will be decided among men. A resolution was passed without one dissenting colony, 'that these United Colonies are, and of right ought to be, free and independent States, and as such they have, and of right ought to have, full power to make war, conclude peace, establish commerce, and to do all other acts and things which other States may rightfully do.'

"You will see in a few days a Declaration setting forth the causes which have impelled us to this mighty revolution, and the reasons which will justify it in the sight of God and Man. A plan of Confederation will be taken up in a few days . . .

"The second day of July, 1776, will be the most memorable

epocha in the history of America. I am apt to believe that it will be celebrated by succeeding generations as the great anniversary festival. It ought to be commemorated, as the day of deliverance, by solemn acts of devotion to God Almighty. It ought to be solemnized with pomp and parade, with shows, games, sports, guns, bells, bonfires, and illuminations, from one end of this continent to the other, from this time forward, forevermore."

However you look at it, the Second of July or the Fourth, the Lee resolutions or the Jefferson document, Virginia laid the foundation of the new nation. The Virginians' next service was to deliver a national constitution.

Chapter 4
THE CONSTITUTION, THE BILL OF RIGHTS

On June 12, 1776, the Continental Congress appointed a committee to take up Richard Henry Lee's motion that "a plan of confederation be prepared and transmitted to the respective colonies for their consideration and approbation . . ." This would become the Articles of Confederation.

The next twenty years would see dizzying political changes. The nation would invent two constitutions and a national Bill of Rights; implement the doctrine of separation of powers between the legislative, judicial, and executive branches; create its first political parties; and watch a partisan congressional committee system evolve, a tool of power unique among national legislatures.

These triumphs of political creativity were initiated by Virginia, often in collaboration with other Southern states. Virginia proposed the Articles of Confederation (although Virginians had little to do with designing the finished product). When the Articles failed, mostly because of economic disorders, Virginia proposed a national convention to draw a new constitution. Virginia then submitted the blueprint (called "the Virginia Plan") for the new government. And the Virginian James Madison, "the father of the Constitution," argued successfully for the separation of powers doctrine. When all that was done, it was Virginia at the head of the Southern bloc which led the fight for a Bill of Rights. Then followed the creation of the Democratic party, by Madison and Jefferson, and the congressional committee system.[1] Although the South could claim no patent on the invention of the committees, the first powerful chairman would be John Randolph of the House Ways and Means Committee.

The first of the Virginia initiatives was the Articles of Confederation which created a unicameral government. In the one House, each state, whatever its population, had one vote. Congress had no power to levy any tax whatsoever. It could only requisition funds from the states, which the states paid if they were so inclined.

The articles have been scorned as weak and ineffective. They were weak, but they were far from ineffective, for they bound together the various states and often hostile economic interests for eight crucial years. They established a perpetual union of the thirteen states where the citizen of one state had the rights of those in all the states. The Articles made a nation of thirteen separate, jealous, chauvinistic, and suspicious colonies.

John Dickinson of Pennsylvania was chosen to write the Articles and submitted his draft to the Congress on July 4, 1776.[2] He resigned from Congress that day, saying he opposed independence from Britain and had no desire to sign the declaration. He went out in magnificent style, for the draft began, "The Name of this Confederacy shall be 'THE UNITED STATES OF AMERICA.'" Dickinson can claim copyright to the title, for it apparently had not been used before.[3]

[1] The modern Democratic party was first called the "anti-Federalists." It was next known as the "Republicans," then as the "Democratic Republicans." The name of the "Democratic party" was not formally affixed until 1828. As a convenience, it is referred to herein as the "Democratic party."
[2] The committee consisted of one member from each of the thirteen colonies. The delegates were Sam Adams of Massachusetts, Josiah Bartlett of New Hampshire, John Dickinson of Pennsylvania, Button Gwinnett of Georgia, Joseph Hewes of North Carolina, Stephen Hopkins of Rhode Island, Francis Hopkinson of New Jersey, Robert Livingston of New York, Thomas McKean of Delaware, Thomas Nelson of Virginia, Rutledge of South Carolina, Sherman of Connecticut, Thomas Stone of Maryland.
[3] When the Dutch provinces declared independence from Spain in 1581 they called themselves alternately the "United Provinces" or the "United States" and were commonly referred to by English writers for the next two centuries as the "United States." (See the *Oxford English Dictionary*.)

The Congress debated the Articles throughout the summer of 1776. There were three main arguments. One was on whether each colony should have a single vote, an issue of large states versus small states. Second was states' rights, whether the confederation had authority to limit territorial expansion of individual states. Third was the method of apportioning taxation. The North wanted to tax according to total population. The South was opposed to taxing slaves.

The latter issue began one of the enduring sectional debates of the first American century. Were slaves part of the general population? Or were they property? The South held for property and Rutledge of South Carolina said that if ownership of slaves was to be taxed, then so should the ownership of the Northern ships that carried the slaves. There were several strictly sectional votes on the subject with the bloc of seven Northern states lining up against the six-state South bloc. It was finally compromised that taxes would be apportioned according to the private ownership of land and the improvements thereon. (The other issues were decided on a nonsectional basis. The small states, having a majority in the Continental Congress, after granting numerous concessions carried their position that each state would have a single vote and that there would be a limit on territorial expansion.)

In November 1776 the Articles were sent to the states for ratification.

The hottest opposition came from the Southern states (with the exception of Virginia, which ratified wthout qualification or criticism). The reaction of William Henry Drayton, chief justice of South Carolina, was typical of the eighteenth-century South and would remain typical in the twentieth-century South. Drayton felt the Articles gave too much power to the central government and states' rights would be run over roughshod. He observed that there was a natural North-South division among the states, arising "from the nature of the climate, soil and produce." He felt the South's opportunities for growth would be crippled by the Articles because "the honor, interest and sovereignty of the South, are in effect delivered up to the care of the North."

To remedy this, he proposed that important decisions should require the affirmative vote of eleven states, in effect giving the

South a veto. And Virginia's uncritical acceptance of the Articles received sneers from other Southerners. A Maryland delegate wrote with venom that Virginia had become complacent and proud, enjoying "a secret pride in having laid the corner stone of a confederated World."[4]

The debates, quarrels, and compromises delayed ratification until the spring of 1781 when Maryland, the last holdout, signed the Articles. In October of that year, Cornwallis surrendered at Yorktown. The British sued for peace (and readily agreed to American demands to set the Mississippi River as the western boundary). The formal treaty was signed in 1783.

Almost immediately the economy went aground. Currency issued by the Congress during the war could not be backed up, nor could the government pay its other debts. England, treating America as a foreign nation, denied access to the trade of the West Indies. Tariff wars broke out between the states. New York, for example, taxed cabbages from New Jersey. A mysterious blight hit the nation and caused thousands of farm foreclosures. A deep depression was in effect by 1785.

Early that year, commissioners from Virginia and Maryland met at Mount Vernon to work out a uniform commercial code. The conference made clear the need for a national code and Virginia organized a convention in Annapolis in 1786. Five states attended and they proposed to the Congress that a convention be held to revise the Constitution. Congress agreed and on May 5, 1787, the Constitutional Convention began in Philadelphia under the august chairmanship of General George Washington. Their avowed purpose was to "revise" the Articles. Their true intention was to scrap them and substitute a new Constitution which would strengthen the powers of the central government. Virginia was already at work on the blueprint.

The thirteen states, each having a single vote, sent fifty-five delegates to the convention. Although many were heroes of the revolution, they were for the most part conservative toward change in the social order. They were wealthy, protective of property, and suspicious of the rabble. They were not too interested in demo-

[4] *The Articles of Confederation* by Merrill Jensen (Madison: University of Wisconsin Press, 1966), pages 186–87.

cratic reforms but instead were anxious to have a stronger government to guarantee order and property rights. They wanted protection of the propertied class from popular insurrection, having been impressed by the 1786 rebellion of Massachusetts farmers led by Captain Daniel Shay.[5]

The delegates, however, were not unaware of the libertarian basis of the revolution, the rabble's desire for equality and improvement, nor were they completely cynical about such desires. Desirous of protecting property, they were equally determined to have safeguards for individual rights, and they strove for a balance between the two. Finding that balance would be the linchpin of the convention.

The convention got off to a slow start as delegates arrived by twos and threes to present their credentials. Finally there was a quorum of seven states. Rules were drawn up by the Williamsburg attorney George Wythe and, on May 29, 1787, the main business began.

Edmund Randolph, six feet tall, thirty-three years old, governor of Virginia and noticeably handsome, rose and introduced the Virginia Plan.

He observed, first, that the delegates were gathered to revise the Articles, but that he would offer instead a new national government, with a President, a national judiciary, and a national legislature of two branches. The first house, the Representatives, would be elected by the people. The second branch, the Senate, would be elected by the first branch.

Precisely who designed the Virginia Plan is not known. James Madison's biographers claim he drafted it. Randolph said it "had originated from Virginia." This was undoubtedly the case because it followed very closely the Virginia constitution which had been in operation since 1776.

Randolph was on his feet three or four hours answering questions. When he sat down, Charles Pinckney, a twenty-nine-year-

---

[5] The farmers felt they were carrying too heavy a share of the tax load, which they were, and that they were being victimized by the merchants and lawyers. They marched on the state supreme court at Springfield and were eventually dispersed by a four-thousand-man army.

old Charleston, S.C., lawyer and veteran of the Continental Army, stood up and said he, too, had reduced his ideas of government to a new and simple system, but they were very similar to those presented by Randolph. He then read his paper to the convention. It was not discussed and no record of the details have survived.

The debates began. Details of the Virginia Plan would be hotly argued, but there were only two challenges to the basic structure. The foremost of these, a true alternative, was the New Jersey Plan, submitted by William Paterson.

It was in direct contrast to the Virginia Plan. Where Virginia offered a new governmental structure, New Jersey wanted to revise and strengthen the existing Articles, pointing out that that was the purpose of the convention, "to revise." New Jersey offered a one-house legislature with delegates selected by the states and each state having a single vote. The central authority, however, would be strengthened by granting it an increased number of specific powers over the states.

A challenge to both the Virginia and New Jersey plans was then mounted by Alexander Hamilton, the thirty-year-old delegate from New York and former aide to George Washington.

Hamilton, whose pro-mercantile, pro-industrial views would eventually set the permanent course of American economic policy, was ironically the most foreign member of the convention—foreign-born (in the West Indies) and foreign in his outlook. He liked aristocracy and admired the British Constitution above all governments on earth. (Jefferson later accused him of being "bewitched and perverted by the British example.")

After listening to Virginia and New Jersey, Hamilton offered his alternative—a government modeled on Great Britain's King, its House of Lords and its House of Commons.

He wanted a chief executive chosen for life by a privileged class and with powers of absolute veto. He wanted a lower House to be elected by the people for a term of three years. He wanted an upper House chosen by an Electoral College for life. State governors would be appointed by the national government.

Hamilton was suspicious of democracy, fearful that a national government based on the popular vote would soon become a government ruled by Virginia. "What in process of time will Virginia be? She contains now half a million of inhabitants—in twenty-five years she will double the number . . . The national government cannot long exist when opposed by a weighty rival."[6]

Hamilton's plan did not even gain the favor of the remainder of the New York delegation, which instead supported New Jersey's proposal. The New Jersey Plan, too, was soon disposed of and the Virginia Plan became the basis of discussion for the remainder of the convention.

For three months the convention strove to find the balance between protection of property and protection of rights. George Mason of Virginia wanted an executive and legislature based only on popular vote. His view was backed to an extent by James Madison, who insisted that at least one house of the legislature should be directly elected by the people. It was, he said, "a clear principle of free government."

John Dickinson, the Pennsylvania delegate who had written the Articles of Confederation and who was now a Delaware delegate, proposed a Senate elected by the state legislatures.[7]

Another Northerner, Roger Sherman of Connecticut, seconded him and Madison endorsed the proposition. The Senate's usefulness, said Madison, lay in its proceeding with more coolness, more system and wisdom than the popular branch. Madison said the Senate should have the twofold purpose of protecting the people against their rulers, and to protect property against democratic passions.

This was it. The tool the delegates had sought to balance private property and private rights. The idea of a Senate as a cooling chamber caught hold. Other delegates offered other refinements. The Senate would not only be elected by state legislatures but its

[6] *Miracle at Philadelphia* by Catherine Drinker Bowen (Boston: Little, Brown and Co., 1966), page 113.

[7] Dickinson is not well remembered but he was among the largest talents of his era. He had a remarkable career, wandering at will between Maryland, where he was born, Pennsylvania, and Delaware. He was, at various times, a member of the Delaware legislature, the Pennsylvania legislature, delegate to the Stamp Act Congress and the First Continental Congress, president of Delaware 1781–82, president of Pennsylvania 1782–85, writer of the Articles, presiding officer at the Annapolis Convention, founder of Dickinson College, and an author of considerable political clout, e.g. of *Letters of Fabius on the Federal Constitution*.

members would have longer terms than the House. An age restriction was put in. Senators must be at least thirty years old, House members only twenty-five.[8]

There remained only one final obstacle to adoption of the Virginia Plan. This was the question of state representation in the Congress. One vote for one state? Or votes in proportion to each state's population? The solution, the Connecticut Compromise, came from Roger Sherman. The states would have equal votes in the Senate, votes proportionate to population in the House.

With the adoption of the Dickinson and Sherman modifications, the basic work of the convention was complete. The new Constitution was acceptable. There remained, however, many details which were argued over, most of which were not acted upon, some of which were compromised. Foremost among these was the question of slaves.

There was never any expectation that slavery would be abolished. The argument was, again, whether slaves were property or part of the general population.

This time the South found it convenient to switch its position. Slaves indeed were property, but they also were part of the population and should be credited when apportioning votes in the Congress.

Northerners, such as Gouverneur Morris of Pennsylvania, though Pennsylvania still had slaves, took gleeful opportunity to lash out at the South properly for its hypocrisy, and for its clinging to slavery. "A nefarious institution, the curse of heaven on the states where it prevailed." He compared the misery and poverty of Virginia and Maryland with the "rich and noble cultivation" of the Northern states.

Charles Pinckney was the only delegate to attempt a moral defense of slavery, saying, "In all ages, one half of mankind have been slaves. If the Southern states were let alone . . . they would probably stop importation." He added brusquely, however, that South Carolina would not agree to any government which prohibited the slave trade.

---

[8] Election of senators by the state legislatures continued until 1913 when adoption of the Seventeenth Amendment provided for direct popular election.

After the rhetoric was done, the compromising began. The South agreed to stop importing of slaves by the year 1808. In return, one slave would count as 60 per cent of a white person for purposes of apportioning the Congress. In effect, this gave each white resident of the South 1.6 votes in the Congress to each Northern vote.

Unjust and unfair as the slavery compromise was (it gave the white Southerner a larger vote, and it implicitly legitimatized slavery), it was practical. Alexander Hamilton later said that without it the Constitution would never have been ratified.

The convention adopted the Constitution, sent copies to the states for ratification, and adjourned.

Slavery had been recognized in the organic structure of the document. This point would be made much of by Southern lawyers and law professors in the years preceding the Civil War. But slavery at least had the dignity of discussion. Other groups fared less well. More than half the nation's adult population was not considered for representation by vote. These included women, slaves, indentured servants, and, in most states, propertyless males. The rights and status of women and indentured servants was not even debated at the convention. Nor was a Bill of Rights discussed. There were no guarantees in the Constitution for freedom of religion, speech, press, or peaceful assembly; no right to "speedy, public" trial, due process, or protection from unreasonable searches and seizures, or from cruel and unusual punishments.

It was not that the delegates opposed a Bill of Rights. Eight of the participating states had one. It seems that the delegates felt the rights were implicit in the Constitution.

It was unnecessary, said Alexander Hamilton, to specify "that things shall not be done which there is no power to do." A Bill of Rights, he said, would be a rhetoric which "would sound better in a treatise of ethics than in a constitution of government."

When copies of the Constitution were printed in the newspapers there was a great uproar over the lack of a Bill of Rights. The people wanted a protective law. Delegates attempted to defend the omission, mostly invoking the Hamilton argument of a bill being unnecessary. In South Carolina, Charles Pinckney raised a more novel explanation. A Bill of Rights, he told the boys at the legislature, "generally begin with declaring that all men are by nature born free. Now, we should make that declaration with a very bad grace, when a large part of our property consists in men who are actually born slaves."[9]

The absence of a Bill of Rights became the major obstacle to ratification. Thomas Jefferson, who was then in Paris as minister to France, was sent a copy by George Washington, and a second copy by Madison. He replied, "I like the organization of the government into legislative, judiciary, and executive . . . I will now add what I do not like. First, the omission of a bill of rights . . ."

Ratification by nine states was needed for the Constitution to become law. By May 1788, eight months after adjournment of the convention, eight states had ratified. Massachusetts and Pennsylvania had ratified, but the other two large states, New York and Virginia, had not. New York's convention to ratify seemed hopelessly deadlocked and attention was on Virginia where a debate raged over the Bill of Rights.

The leader of opposition to the Constitution was Patrick Henry. Arrayed against him were Washington, Madison, Edmund Randolph, and George Wythe. Henry was making a stiff fight of it, holding forth in country speeches on the probability of the President enslaving America and the horrid consequences which would result.

At the state convention, as voting time neared, Henry prepared a Declaration of Rights which he insisted must go into the Constitution. These comprised twenty articles of rights. On June 24, 1788, George Wythe moved for a vote on ratification and, to forestall Henry, attached a Declaration of Rights very similar to Henry's. The vote came, and Henry lost technically, as the Constitution was ratified 89–79. But his Declaration of Rights was attached and the opposition forces agreed to present it to the Congress.

Word was sent by quick rider to the national capital at New

[9] Bowen, page 247.

York. The ninth state had ratified, the Constitution was law.[10]
Two years later, in 1789, the Virginians made good their promise
to Patrick Henry. James Madison stood in the House of Representatives and introduced the ten amendments to the Constitution
known as the Bill of Rights. They were Henry's amendments,
though phrased in clearer, briefer language.

The eighteenth-century South took its lead in things cultural
and social from the romantic myth of Virginia, Shakespeare's
magic wood of dale and forest, mead and rushing brook where
"we met . . . to dance our ringlets to the whistling wind."

The nation took its political institutions from a more real Virginia, the ever so practical agrarian democracy of farmers who invented constitutions and bills of rights.

Why Virginia? From what wells did its intellectual energies
spring?

Colonial America as a whole owed its character to England,
that arena of eccentrics and heretics, of adventurers and meddle-
some inventors. Virginia was even more so. It was initially populated by Elizabethans full of the spirit of adventure and zest for
life, freer in style than the Pilgrims and Puritans. The colony was
reinforced for more than a century by the same stock of people
and became very close to a society of Cavaliers. (The planters of
Virginia, Maryland, and the Carolinas proved the point in
1642–52 during the English Civil War when they sided well-nigh
unanimously with the Stuart kings and the Episcopal Church
while the New Englanders came down squarely on the side of
Cromwell and the Puritans.)[11]

On this base, the Virginians built a manorial system of serfs and
slaves and villeins ruled by a landed aristocracy which was so
scornful of modern economics that the colony did not deal in
coins or currency for much of its history but used tobacco leaves as
a medium of exchange. This was the Virginia which held the
South in an enchantment.

---

[10] Actually, New Hampshire had ratified four days earlier and was the
ninth state to do so. But the information traveled slowly and at the time it
was believed that all depended upon Virginia.
[11] Virginia's colonial government formally surrendered to the Parliament in
1652.

Virginia's role as an inventor of uniquely effective political systems is less easily theorized. Part of it was character. Jefferson had observed that Southerners were "zealous" to protect their own liberties but, in contrast to the North, "careless" toward the liberties of others. Perhaps it was a recognition of this carelessness in their own makeup that caused the Virginians to set up safeguards for liberties.

It could partially explain their constitutional activities. Certainly Virginians were aware of the selfish nature of men. But it cannot be the only factor, for otherwise we might expect that Virginian's libertarian reforms would exist very early in its history.

This turns out not to be the case. For the first 150 years Virginia invented nothing more radical than the tobacco trade and the tobacco currency. It isn't until 1765 that it organized the Stamp Act Congress, followed by thirty-five magnificent years of historic creativity. The burst of genius, however, tails off around 1800 and after about 1810, Virginia's contributions *as a society* cease. (Although individuals such as Jefferson, Madison, Monroe, Randolph, and Marshall continue to have large national influence.)

We must look further, particularly for something that existed uniquely in Virginia during the 1765–1800 period. And the most obvious phenomenon is the Williamsburg intellectual community. Washington, Henry, Wythe, the Randolphs, the Lees, Jefferson, Madison, Marshall, Monroe—to mention only the most illuminary—all coming together in some grand cosmic accident. Meeting and stimulating one another in a village which had only three diversions: talk, scholarship, and politics. These diversions centered about the village's three main enterprises, the university, the capitol, and the taverns.

The men of Williamsburg came together in a time of enormous excitement, the breaking off of the American colonies from the world's largest power. In cutting itself loose, Virginia was forced to devise some sort of government and the talent was on hand to make it an exceptional one.

But there must be something else to cause Virginia's creativity because Boston had a brilliant community, though less intimate in its associations due to the much larger population and the wider

range of diversions. Nevertheless, Massachusetts' political contributions, however impressive on their own, were inferior to Virginia's.

There was a second factor present in Virginia during the
1765–1800 period, something that Massachusetts lacked. This
was an exploding frontier of new land and opportunities. To fill
the frontier, Virginia needed a population and the most practical
source was Europe. To attract Europeans, Virginia chose to offer
both economic opportunity and political liberties.

This motive was in fact suggested by Patrick Henry in one of
his speeches to the Virginia legislature urging the recruitment of
emigrants by offering them liberties.

"We have, sir," Henry told the legislators, "an extensive country without population. What can be a more obvious policy than
that this country ought to be peopled? . . . Encourage emigration,
encourage the husbandmen, the mechanics, the merchants of the
old world to come and settle in this land of promise. Make it the
home of the skillful, the industrious, the fortunate and happy, as
well as the asylum of the distressed. Fill up the measure of your
population as speedily as you can by the means which Heaven
hath placed in your power—and I venture to prophesy there are
those now living who will see this favored land amongst the most
powerful on earth . . .

"Do you ask how to get them? Open your doors, sir, and they
will come in . . . They are already standing on tiptoe upon their
native shores, and looking to your coasts with a wishful and long-
ing eye . . . They see a land in which Liberty hath taken up her
abode—that Liberty whom they had considered as a fabled god-
dess, existing only in the fancies of poets, they see her here a real
divinity."[12]

Thus we arrive at a theoretical formula for Virginia's creativity:
(1) There was opportunity, in the fact of American independence
and the need to create some sort of replacement government. (2)
There was economic motive, in the profit to be gained from enticing, with liberties, a population into the frontier. (3) There was a

[12] *Sketches of the Life and Character of Patrick Henry* by William Wirt
(1817). Wirt was a lawyer and author and as U.S. attorney for Virginia
prosecuted Aaron Burr for treason in 1807.

catalyst, the freakish concurrence of genius at Williamsburg. This, of course, was an accident.

Finally, (4) there was a second accident, the Frankfort advice.

John Adams' contention that the impromptu and unplanned Frankfort meeting was *entirely* responsible for Virginia's lead is impossible to accept. Virginia wrote her own constitution, her Bill of Rights, and the Virginia Plan without help from John Adams and his crowd. But the sponsorship of the Massachusetts delegation, agreed upon at the meeting, certainly helped Virginia sell her thinking to the rest of the nation. The result was the American government.

The cause of Virginia's creativity remains theoretical, probably based on accident. An astrologer could make as good a case that it had to do with the ascendancy of Jupiter in conjunction with Venus having an appendicitis operation. How to explain accidents? America itself is a series of accidents. It was discovered accidentally by a seaman looking for something else and most of its early exploration was done in the hope of getting through it or around it.[13] By accident America was discovered, by accident it got its liberty.

The pre-eminent role of the South, which in this period was overwhelmingly Virginian, was likewise accident. There was no intrinsic quality in the Virginia society to make its people more brilliant at politics than were the Puritan Yankees or the frontiersmen of the West. Virginia was in the right place at the right time and got a lucky roll of the dice.

Upon ratification of the Constitution, Virginia would no longer hold the national lead. Northern interests, led by Adams and Hamilton, moved surely and skillfully into control. Détente with the South was no longer important politically to Pennsylvania, New York, or New England. George Washington would become increasingly charmed by the spell of Hamilton. And the laws and policies of the nation would increasingly favor the North.

---

[13] Samuel Eliot Morison has postulated in *The Oxford History of the American People* that if European discovery had been delayed for a century or so, it is possible the Aztec or Iroquis would have established a native state capable of maintaining their independence, as Japan kept her independence from China.

In defense, the South created the Democratic party. And if the genius of Virginia can be attributed to accident, the political skills of the Southerners henceforth would be a deliberate matter of learning and evolving parliamentary techniques.

Chapter 5
THE DEMOCRATS

The first U. S. Congress convened in New York City's Federal Hall in April 1789.[1] Formerly the New York City Hall, the building had been remodeled by Pierre Charles L'Enfant with money raised by public donation. The House chamber was in the center

[1] In 1790 Virginia and Maryland donated land along the Potomac and Congress established the District of Columbia. George Washington had surveyed the land and he proposed that the capital be called "Federal City." The various capitals of the United States have been:

Meetings of the Continental Congress

Philadelphia	September 5, 1774 to December 12, 1776
Baltimore	December 20, 1776 to February 27, 1777
Philadelphia	March 4, 1777 to September 18, 1777
Lancaster, Pa.	September 27, 1777
York, Pa.	September 30, 1777 to June 27, 1778
Philadelphia	July 2, 1778 to June 21, 1783
Princeton, N.J.	June 26, 1783 to November 4, 1783
Annapolis, Md.	November 26, 1783 to June 3, 1784
Trenton, N.J.	November 1, 1784 to December 24, 1784
New York City	January 11, 1785 to March 2, 1789

Meetings of the U. S. Congress

New York City	March 4, 1789 to August 12, 1790
Philadelphia	December 6, 1790 to May 14, 1800
Washington, D.C.	November 17, 1800 to present

of the building on the first floor, a large octagonal room with a public staircase on the left, and a private one on the right.

Both stairs led to the Senate chamber on the second floor. The Senate itself was closed to the public. (The Senate remained closed to outsiders until 1795 when newspaper editors were permitted in. In 1802 the general public was allowed to attend sessions.)

This Congress, and the presidency, was largely inhabited by "federalists," with a small "f." During the debate throughout the various states on ratification, the term had come into use to denote proponents of the Constitution. Persons in opposition were "anti-federalists." Neither group could be considered a political party. They were not organized on any common political ground other than their position on the Constitution, and they did not cooperate to help one another achieve political office. More importantly, they did not consider themselves to be political parties. The drafters and signers of the Constitution had almost unanimously agreed that permanent political parties were evil and that the "spirit of faction" should be put down because it encouraged competitive instincts often adverse to the public interest. As a consequence, the Constitution made no recognition of, or provision for, political parties.

The lineup of federalists and anti-federalists is significant, however, because their social views soon would become embodied in the nation's first two political parties.

The federalists may be broadly characterized as the more wealthy, more conservative people seeking a strong central government and weaker state governments. (Although some federalists such as George Mason of Virginia and Patrick Henry, who after opposing the Constitution became a federalist, were ardent supporters of states' rights.) The federalists tended to be, and to represent, the vested interests, the plantation aristocrats, the Northern shipowners, bankers, and manufacturers.

Federalists favored encouragement of industries, attention to the needs of the great merchants and landowners, and establishment of strict law-and-order society. In foreign affairs they were pro-British. They favored a strong central government to regulate and protect the currency and commerce at home and abroad.

The antifederalists were, on the whole, less aristocratic, more liberal, antimonarchical, small farmers, businessmen, and artisans who wanted less government control. They did not want the social and economic system frozen into a status quo but instead wanted the freedom to improve their own condition. In foreign affairs they tended to be anti-British and pro-French.

Neither group could be considered a political party. Indeed, in the First Congress, traditional authorities do not list the members by federalist or antifederalist labels. Instead, the Senate had seventeen "pro-Administration" members and nine "opposition." The House had thirty-eight pro-Administration and twenty-six opposition.

Three and a half years later, by the second session of the Second Congress, the members of Congress are listed as "Federalist" with a capital "F," and "Democratic-Republican" (members of the Democratic party). What had happened in the meantime was the formation of political parties around the differing philosophies and interests of Thomas Jefferson and Alexander Hamilton. These parties were Jefferson's Democrats and Hamilton's "Federalists." The Federalists represented a loose interpretation of the Constitution; Northern states and Northern interests; and big business, big government, big banking, and big industry. The Democrats were essentially Southern farmers, small businessmen, and artisans demanding a strict interpretation of the Constitution, states' rights, and a small central government.

The evolution of the parties came about accidentally out of George Washington's decision to put the best men in his cabinet, and, apparently, to give it a sectional balance. The President, the Secretary of State (Jefferson), and the Attorney General (Edmund Randolph) all were Southerners. The Vice President (Adams), the Secretary of the Treasury (Hamilton), the Secretary of War (Henry Knox), and the Postmaster General (Samuel Osgood) were Northerners. Score: South 3; North 4. (But one of the South's three, Washington, was more equal than the others.)

Washington had hoped that this balance would erase, or at least disguise, the sectional differences in the country. Such was not the case. Jefferson and Hamilton came into immediate conflict on virtually every issue. They got along like a knee in the groin. They did not like each other's looks, or manners, or speech. They particularly did not like each other's view of the new nation, and their views were mutually exclusive. There could not be a Jeffersonian *and* a Hamiltonian America. There could only be a Jeffersonian *or* a Hamiltonian America.

Hamilton saw the nation as a great industrial power and designed his Treasury programs accordingly. Jefferson envisioned an agrarian democracy such as he had known and seen working well in Virginia. Each man represented his section, North versus South.

Hamilton's perception, less charming, was by far the more accurate. America evolved the industrial economy he predicted. Indeed, in most all of their areas of conflict, at that time and in subsequent history, Hamilton would win.

Their classic clash came over the Bank of the United States, invented by Hamilton in imitation of the Bank of England. The bank was nationwide, with headquarters in Philadelphia and branches in eight other cities. The government subscribed one fifth of the capital of $10 million but this investment was loaned by the bank right back to the government without interest. The bank was to be a fiscal agent for all government income and disbursements and would handle general commercial business, including making loans in return for interest.

The government thus set itself up in command of the oasis' largest well. Water, the raw supply of money, would be doled out in the form of loans to those favored by the government. Persons or business in disfavor would not get water. Hamilton, indeed, saw this as the major advantage of his bank. Out of self-interest, he said, the powerful business houses would be forced to support the policies of the national government.

The bank was clearly designed to favor mercantile over agricultural interests and Jefferson attacked it immediately as unconstitutional. There was no authority anywhere in the Constitution to charter a national bank.

Hamilton replied with his famous doctrine of "implied" powers. The Constitution, he said, gave Congress authority to pass any laws "necessary and proper" to carry out designated powers. One of the designated powers was to levy taxes and coin money. This implied, said Hamilton, the power to create a national bank to safeguard and disburse the money.

A weak structure of logic, but it carried the day and the bank was established in 1791. It was well managed and almost from the beginning paid good dividends. Its conservative, pro-bigness policies, however, tended to restrain private banks and antagonized the more exuberant business and farming people in the South and in the West.[2]

A Federalist political party began to form in support of the bank and other Hamilton financial measures. By November 1792 the opposition, mostly in the South and West, had coalesced into the "Democratic-Republican" party.

The creator of the party, and in its early stages its most conspicuous member, was James Madison, congressman from Virginia. He had begun the Democratic party, with cabinet member Jefferson's discreet cooperation, on a small scale in Virginia and its earliest adherents were, in fact, called "Madisonians." It grew very quickly in that same year of 1792 and became the rallying flag for a majority of small farmers in the West and South, and a growing proletariat in the eastern cities. In 1794 it would win a temporary, two-year majority in the House of Representatives. In 1800, it would win a majority in both houses and the presidency of the United States.

Jefferson's dispute with Hamilton accelerated during 1793 and the outcome would see Jefferson quit the Cabinet and emerge as the Democratic party's national leader.

The disagreement arose out of the French Revolution. During the American Revolution, a Treaty of Alliance had been signed with France. After the beheading of Louis XVI in 1793, France declared war on Great Britain. Pro-French Jeffersonians clamored to honor the alliance with France—and go to French aid. (The position rested on a happy marriage of revenge and opportunism. There was large anti-British sentiment among the lower classes of

[2] The bank lasted until 1811, when a Democrat-dominated Congress defeated its rechartering. A second bank was chartered in 1816 and lasted until 1836.

the United States, and captains and merchants in Southern ports speculated hungrily on the ample supply of British loot to be had by privateering in the nearby West Indies.)

The pro-British Hamiltonians, on the other hand, professed themselves in horror of the excesses of the French revolution and worked to help the British.

George Washington sided with Hamilton in the matter and Secretary of State Jefferson, convinced that Washington had come under the complete influence of Hamilton, on matters domestic *and* foreign, quit.

Jefferson would later write that he saw the nation turning to monarchist principles; that the North was rising at the expense of the South; that mercantile and industrial interests were being favored by the government against agrarian interests; and that the Federalist party was the tool and creation of these prejudicial interests.

After winning a House majority in 1794, the new Democrats put up a presidential candidate against the Federalists.

Jefferson did not want to take the lead in the party and urged Madison to be its candidate for President. Madison deferred, however, and Jefferson went ahead.

In the Federalist party, Washington had declined to run because of his belief that no President should exceed two terms. Hamilton was, in philosophical terms, the logical candidate, being the chief strategist and having the most creative mind in the party. But it was felt that he could never be elected. He was rather thoroughly disliked because of his domineering manner, his arrogance, and his openly expressed dislike for those outside his narrow circle of the "rich, the wise, and the good."

Another difficulty for Hamilton was the Jay Treaty, signed to ease difficulties with Britain in 1794 and with which Hamilton was thoroughly identified.

The relations between Britain and the United States had by then reached a point near war. Britain had repeatedly and arrogantly violated treaty terms signed at the end of the Revolution. Most Americans, spurred by the rhetoric of the Democrats, wanted to pin England's ears back.

To avert war, northern Federalist senators prevailed on Washington to send a mission to London and adjust differences. The senators wanted Hamilton to head the mission but due to fevered opposition from Jefferson, Washington sent the Chief Justice, John Jay.

Jay concluded the treaty in five months and upon his return the Federalists tried to steamroller it through the Senate for ratification.

Public opposition was hot, particularly in the South and on the frontier where the treaty was viewed as a groveling before England. One Southern senator who favored the treaty was Humphrey Marshall of Kentucky. He was burned in effigy, denounced at public meetings, and scalded in the papers. Former friends avoided him. At Frankfort he was stoned. He was finally seized by a mob which threatened to drown him in a Kentucky river.

Arriving on the bank of the river, the senator called a halt and with inimitable humor, coolness, and courage said in substance, "My good friends, all this is irregular. In the ordinance of immersion as practiced in the good old Baptist church, it is the rule to require the candidate to relate his experience before his baptism is performed. Now, in accordance with established rules and precedents, I desire to give my experience before you proceed to my immersion."

The appeal tickled the humor of the mob and Senator Marshall was placed on a convenient stump and ordered to relate his experiences. He proceeded first in a way to amuse them, then warmed to his work and with all the pent-up indignation of a man at the end of a long series of outrages and injustices, let loose. He blistered his listeners with the well-timed fury of his scathing tongue until one by one they sneaked away ashamed and left him master of the field.[3]

The ruckus over the Jay Treaty provided the final crystallization of the two-party system.

In 1794, there were no nominating conventions and, except for the press libel and the stump speaking, very little of the modern

[3] *U. S. Senate, 1787–1801,* dissertation by Roy Swanstrom, Senate Document 64.

political entertainments. Instead, the party leaders in smoke-filled rooms in the eastern cities chose John Adams, two times Vice President, to be Washington's heir. Thomas Pinckney of South Carolina was named the Federalist candidate for Vice President. As always, an effort was made for sectional balance.

Under the system then existing, the candidate receiving the highest vote in the Electoral College was President. The candidate with the second highest vote was Vice President.[4]

Hamilton was outraged at the selection of Adams and hit on a vindictive scheme of sabotage. He worked with Federalist electors in the South to omit Adams from their ballot and to vote for Pinckney and Jefferson. He thought that the withholding of Adams from the Southern ballot would result in Thomas Pinckney being elected President, and to hell with John Adams. The addition of Jefferson, he hoped, would encourage votes for Pinckney.

Jefferson, and very few of his supporters, expected to win, although they did make the customary gesture to sectional balance by signing on the superb New York politician Aaron Burr as their vice presidential nominee.

The situation then was this: Hamilton and his people were working for Pinckney to be President; the loyal Federalists were working for Adams; and the Democrats had hopelessly entered Jefferson and Burr.

Jefferson looked at the situation and in a letter to Madison wrote: "I have no expectation that the Eastern states will suffer themselves to be so much outwitted, as to be made the tools for bringing in Pinckney instead of Adams. I presume they will throw their second vote away." He thought this would increase the electoral vote for his party and that it might throw the presidency into a deadlock to be resolved by the House of Representatives.

[4] Then as now, the state's vote in the Electoral College was equal to the number of its senators and representatives in the Congress. The electors are directed by the Constitution to vote in their respective states. The vote is transmitted to the Congress for counting. In the earliest days, electors were chosen by state legislators. Very quickly, however, each state changed its system and electors were chosen by popular election, often being pledged to vote for a specific presidential candidate. The system whereby the candidate with the second highest electoral vote for president became Vice President was changed in 1804 to the present system, whereby Vice President is on a separate ballot.

In that event, Jefferson would put the interests of the country first: "This is a difficulty from which the constitution has provided no issue. It is both my duty and inclination, therefore, to relieve the embarrassment, should it happen; and in that case, I pray you and authorize you fully, to solicit on my behalf that Mr. Adams may be preferred. He has always been my senior, from the commencement of my public life."[5]

The election was not a tie, but it was almost as close. The New England states, as Jefferson had predicted, thwarted Hamilton's scheme by dropping Pinckney from the ballot. With Adams' name dropped in the South and Pinckney in the North, Jefferson emerged with sixty-eight electoral votes, a very strong second to John Adams' seventy-one votes. The result surprised virtually everyone. That it came as a direct consequence of Federalist Hamilton's scheme to defeat Federalist Adams is ironic. The Democratic party owed its first national office, the vice presidency, to its arch rival, Hamilton.

The true reading on the parties' relative national power came in the Congress, where the Federalists increased their majority in the Senate and regained control of the House.

The parties had now emerged into their true personalities. The Jeffersonian Democrats were pre-eminently the "popular party," appealing to the poorer classes, North and South, even though a large proportion of the poor could not then vote. They were the party of reform, of innovation, favoring protection of the individual from big government and big business.

The Federalists were the party of the rich, the wellborn, the established interests. They favored status quo, and regarded democracy with the suspicion that it would lead to either dictatorship, or the opposite pole, anarchy.

The Jeffersonians stood square on states' rights and strict interpretation of the Constitution. The Hamiltonians believed implied powers of the Constitution allowed the federal government to override the rights of the states.

The Jeffersonians insisted that the national government be operated on a rigid economy and be kept out of debt. The Hamil-

[5] *Memorial Edition, Writings of Thomas Jefferson*, edited by P. L. Ford (New York, 1892), vol. vii, page 91.

tonians believed in a large national debt to foster the growth of business and to give business a direct stake in the continued health of government.

The Hamiltonians favored taxes on the masses. One of their taxes, for instance, was on whiskey, being directly applied to the small Jeffersonian farmer who could not profitably ship bulk grain to the eastern markets, but could do nicely if the grain were converted to liquid form. Another favorite tax was the tariff, again being directed at the masses in the form of higher consumer prices. The Hamiltonians would have regarded today's capital gains tax as outrageous and confiscatory.

The Jeffersonians hotly opposed the whiskey tax, the tariff, and similar mass taxation. They wanted a small government and preferred those governments small enough to be brought regularly to account, such as the governments of the states and localities. These political concepts can be summed up to be: on the Federalist side, pro-big government, pro-big business, anti-states' rights; on the Democrat side, pro-small government, pro-small business, pro-states' rights.

In the succession of major political parties since 1796, the Federalist *philosophical* view has been represented by the Federalists (1792–1816), the National Republicans of Henry Clay and John Quincy Adams (1825–34), the Whigs of Daniel Webster and Henry Harrison (1834–54), and the modern Republican party organized in 1854.

The Jeffersonian Democrat view has been represented by the Democratic party more or less consistently from 1796 until the election of Franklin Roosevelt in 1933. While the Roosevelt New Deal did not prejudice itself in favor of big business, it was certainly big government and anti-states' rights. In reaction, since 1933 the Republicans have taken on more and more of the position against big government and in favor of states' rights.

In reviewing the succession of American political parties, a significant characteristic emerges: The Democratic party has been a constant historical factor. It was created in 1792 as a Southern reaction to Northern control of the national government. It succeeded so well that every major political party since then has been created as a reaction to the Democrats (the National Republicans and Whig parties, both created to unseat Andrew Jackson, and the modern Republican party).

The main strength of the Democratic party after 1796 was the Southern wing. The picture altered in 1933 when the New Deal began to sail in a direction opposite to Southern political tradition. Since then, of course, Southerners have defected in larger and larger numbers.

In 1948 several Southern delegations to the Democratic National Convention expressed their opposition to the civil rights plank and walked out to form the States' Rights party with Strom Thurmond of South Carolina as candidate for President. Thurmond got thirty-nine electoral votes, all in the South, and the party expired shortly afterward. Nevertheless, Southern states delivered electoral votes to the Republican candidates from 1952 onward and—more significantly in terms of party loyalty—began in the 1960s to elect Republicans to the House and Senate.

By 1972 it was a commonplace that there was no longer a "solid South" for the Democratic party. Its hold on the South was broken in the 1960s. A "solid South" did exist, however, in terms of political philosophy. The Southern white majority of the 1970s was still adhering to the tradition laid down by the Jeffersonians of the eighteenth century, the tradition of small government, pro-states' rights attitudes, and strict interpretation of the Constitution.

The pattern that emerges from two hundred years of American history is that the Jeffersonian tradition had and has a stronger hold on Southerners than the tug of party loyalty. The Democratic party in its original form was invented to implement those traditions. When it failed to do so, beginning about 1933, the South began looking for a new partner.

The Southern political tradition, viewed in this light of two hundred years of constancy, becomes a very real influence in the shaping of American political history. It is older, and more enduring, and more constant in its aims, than any American political party.

Chapter 6
NORTH VERSUS SOUTH, 1790s

Party politics was born in America in the 1790s and was essentially a contest between North and South. The first victory went to the North as the Jay Treaty of 1794 was rammed through by the Federalists with bribes, patronage, and extortion in a manner which would set the political ethic for the next decade. The two parties bowed their backs and shoved out their fists for some really gutter-level set-tos. No holds barred, ear-biting and knives allowed.

A second vicious partisan battle occurred in 1797 over the rascally carcass of William Blount, Democratic senator from Tennessee and the first man impeached by the U. S. Congress. The third clash came in 1798, an alarming and vicious event when the Northern Federalists, led by John Adams, attempted to suspend the Bill of Rights.

We begin with Blount's obscurely known story. It carries a certain symbolism, for if Jefferson's life encompassed the noble and lofty aspects of the Southern character, then William Blount illustrates the common clay, the ambitious frontiersmen and land-grabbers who put together the western wing of the Deep South.

Territorial expansion and land acquisition is another powerful feature of American history which, as political policy, received its impetus from Southerners. (As will be discussed later on, virtually every acre added to the United States after 1776 was acquired during the administrations of Southern Presidents.)

The Blount impeachment had its origins in the opening of what was then called "the West" and which is now the states of Kentucky, Tennessee, Alabama, and Mississippi. It was an Eden, a citadel of nature with abundant water, forests lush with game and fertile soil bounded on the north by the Ohio, on the east by the Appalachians, on the west by the Mississippi River, and on the south by the Gulf.

Explorers from Virginia had probed for a pass through the Appalachians early in the seventeenth century. These Virginians had penetrated across the mountains by 1671 and returned with stories of fabled lands. The passage, however, was lost and for two thirds of a century no white man was known to have crossed. As Virginia, Maryland, and the Carolinas began to fill, ever so slightly, with people the older inhabitants became uncomfortable. In their eyes the country was becoming too thickly populated, the operation of the law too onerous, the forests too meager in game.

In 1749 a lunatic, wandering as was his wont during his paroxysms, crossed the dividing ridge beyond the great valley of Virginia, and upon his return asserted that he had been upon streams whose waters flowed to the West. No great public notice seems to have been taken of his discovery. Yet, an early historian tells us that a reconnoitering party crossed the mountains in the same direction in 1751 and fell upon the waters of "what is now Green Brier river, a tributary of the Kenehawa, and found two solitary white men. "These first white inhabitants of Kentucky were not Southerners but New Englanders, "living on the banks of the river, though some hundred yards distant from each other."[1]

The Virginians who crossed in 1751 established a settlement on the Green Brier which lasted until 1763, when it was abandoned because of Indians. The next attempt came four years later when

[1] *Journal of Latrobe* by Benjamin Henry Latrobe (New York: D. Appleton & Co., 1905), page 76.

a North Carolina farmer named Finlay, returned to his family
after a long absence "with accounts of the marvellous beauty and
riches of the country beyond the mountains."[2]

Finlay returned to Kentucky that same year with a party which
included a Pennsylvania frontiersman who had drifted South by
the name of Daniel Boone.[3]

This land across the mountains was a paradise the likes of
which had not been seen in the new world or the old. North of the
Ohio was a forest home for numerous Indian tribes. But south of
the river was a wide tract of country unclaimed even by Indians,
stretching across some 240,000 square miles, five times the size of
England, larger than the nation of France.

Watered by many streams, it was the Indians' legendary "happy
hunting ground" in which there were vast herds of elk and deer
disturbed only occasionally by a hunting party. Here, for the first
time, white families saw the buffalo, buffalo which roamed in
herds of thousands; buffalo which, within sixty years, would no
longer exist east of the Mississippi. Here were forests, unencum-
bered by brushwood, stretching like a vast park from horizon to
horizon. Poplars and sycamores grew a hundred feet high. Abundant springs and streams, vast meadows and numerous salt licks.
Pheasant, grouse, and passenger pigeons, delectable to eat, which
made the sky dark with their flight, putting the sun into eclipse.

News of all this spread among the frontier settlements of Virginia and the Carolinas. Soon, more numerous parties traversed
the ridges seeking out new gaps. The first permanent Kentucky
settlement was established by Daniel Boone at Harrodsburg in
1778 and thereafter a steady stream of immigration poured in

[2] Ibid., page 77.
[3] Boone soon had a quarrel with Finlay and subsequently led his own parties across the mountains. Kentucky politics have been marvelously frac-
tious ever since. The Kentuckians split on the Jay Treaty. Prior to statehood in 1790, they seriously considered becoming an independent nation
and making a treaty with Spain. It was the birthplace of both Abraham
Lincoln and Jefferson Davis and split down the middle on the Civil War issues, its men fighting on both sides. It manufactures 40 per cent of the
whiskey made in the United States, is world-famous for its thoroughbred
horses, and traditionally ranks second to Mississippi in number of illiterates. Its people have a saying that "if Jesus Christ were running for sheriff,
he'd get opposition in Kentucky."

from the east, settling present-day Kentucky and Tennessee and filtering south into Mississippi and Alabama.

These frontiersmen were an amazement to the world. Nothing like their migration fever had been seen in history. Unlike the German barbarians, the Mongols or Vikings, these were neither raiders nor soldiers. They were settlers, unarmed and helpless victims dying by the thousands to establish their families. They were farmers and carpenters, mechanics and small businessmen driven to free land by the need for space and opportunity. Finlay and Boone first crossed the Appalachians in 1767. By 1843 the migration had swept across two thousand miles of continent, broached the Rockies and cleared the first farms in Oregon.

The settlers had crossed into Kentucky and drifted south at the last moment before the outbreak of the Revolution. For seven terrible years they withstood the slashing raids of the British and the Indians. They held on, and they inspired awe.

The Spanish governor of the Louisiana territory stretching from St. Louis to the Gulf feared them: "This prestigious and restless population, continually forcing the Indian nations backward and upon us, is attempting to get possession of all the continent . . . Their method of spreading themselves and their policy are so much to be feared by Spain as are their arms . . . A carbine and a little maize in a sack are enough for an American to wander about in the forests alone for a whole month."[4]

A visiting French official, Pierre Clément de Laussat, saw humor in the phenomenon: "Wherever the Anglo-Americans go, the earth becomes fertile and progress is rapid . . . They are the first to immigrate, clear the land, people it, and then push on again and again without any end or trade but to open the road for new colonists . . . When twenty of these colonists collect together in one place, two printers arrive, one a Federalist, the other an anti-Federalist; then the doctors; then the lawyers; then the adventurers. They drink toasts; they elect a speaker. They lay out a city. They beget children at pleasure. Finally they advertise vast territories for sale. They inveigle and fleece as many buyers as possible. They inflate the figures of population in order that they may

[4] *Ark of Empire* by Dale Van Every (New York: Mentor, 1963), page 39.

appear to have 60,000 inhabitants as soon as possible, for that gives them the right to become an independent state and must be represented in Congress . . . and behold, one more star in the flag of the United States."[5]

This land east of the Mississippi, though populated and claimed by the Americans, also was claimed by Spain, France, and England. Furthermore, while the land between the Ohio and the Cumberland was devoid of Indians, the equally pleasing land south of the Cumberland was inhabited by the politically sophisticated and militarily competent Creek nation. And they did not intend to share it.[6]

Into this caldron of ambition—the ferment of white settlers and Creeks; of French, Spanish, and English intriguers—stepped William Blount, scion of an aristocratic North Carolina tobacco farmer.

William Blount was born in 1749 in North Carolina, a race of people already bearing a reputation for dangerousness. ("Familiar with the horse and rifle and unaccustomed to restraint," said General Light-Horse Harry Lee, "they are a race of wild and ardent temper, less capable of labor and less willing to endure it than most."[7]) The Blount family was English gentry and arrived in America in 1664 with their family crest.

William's father, Jacob, was a versatile moneymaker, raising tobacco, cotton, cattle, and hogs on his farm. He had a mill for grain, occasionally traded in slaves and horses and lent money to neighbors at profitable interest.

The boy William was tall and strong, standing above six feet. He had orange, curly hair and surviving portraits show a pug-nosed and combative Irish face, despite the English heritage. He and his brothers were allowed to run wild in regards to horses, servant girls, and booze, provided they did their work. But the

---

[5] *Creole City* by E. L. Tinker (New York: Longmans, Green & Co., 1953).
[6] The Creeks successfully held their own against the schemes, bribes, and aggressions of Spain, England, France, and the United States for three hundred years—from Ponce de Leon's encounter with them in Florida in 1513 until they were finally defeated by Andrew Jackson's army in 1814.
[7] *Memoirs of the War in the Southern Department of the United States* by Light-Horse Harry Lee (New York: Arno Press, 1969), page 215.

work was hard, their father a demanding foreman, and by the end of a normal week they had little energy for sinning.

By the time he neared his majority, William had taken on the bulk of the family fiscal affairs, the lending of money and the transaction of real estate. Through these activities he became knowledgeable in local politics.

With the advent of the Revolution, he took a relatively safe and comfortable post as paymaster to a North Carolina contingent of the Continental Army. In 1782, with the war still going on, he was elected to the Continental Congress and almost immediately set in motion schemes to enrich himself.

First among these was Blount's buying up of western land given as bonuses to war veterans. The land, located in Tennessee, sold cheaply because of the disputed international claims. Next, Blount worked in both the Congress and the North Carolina legislature to have U.S. sovereignty extended to the territory. U.S. annexation would legitimize Blount's land titles. During the course of this, he obtained North Carolina legislation establishing the town of Nashville (Tennessee), where his agents sold lots.

He was doing not badly for himself as a freshman congressman and he shored up his position by deferring to his colleagues, earning their gratitude by serving on numerous tedious minor committees, and in general working conscientiously and keeping a low profile. One can look hard and long for his path on the national scene and not find a footprint.

In 1786 he bid to be elected president of the Continental Congress. Just at that time, however, his half brother, Reading Blount, got caught up in one of his land schemes and was indicted for fraud in North Carolina. A man can't choose his relatives, said Blount, or words to that effect. A cautious Congress elected Arthur St. Clair of Pennsylvania.

In 1787, with the advent of the Constitutional Convention, North Carolina appointed Blount as one of its two delegates. This was largely a matter of economy. North Carolina, nearly bankrupt, wanted to save expenses and Blount, already at the capital in New York, had only to travel to Philadelphia. He thus became one of the signers of the Constitution and a Founding Father.

His work at the convention was, as was his work in the

Congress and as he sought to make his work everywhere, without trace. One of his comments does survive, in the form of a letter to a business partner. Calmly ignoring the convention's pledge of secrecy on its doings, he described the Virginia plan in detail and gave his opinion of it: It was useless. "We shall, not many years hence, be separate and distinct governments, perfectly independent of each other."[8]

He concentrated on social and business contacts. When the convention was done, he found himself impressed by the class and wealth of those supporting the Constitution. He threw in with them and went home to politic for the federalists, having decided, he said in a private letter, "there is a continent for sale."[9] North Carolina, however, did not like the new Constitution and did not immediately ratify. It waited two years, until November 1789, seven months after the convening of the new government. Blount got the signal of disapproval somewhat earlier, being voted out of Congress in the election of 1788.

It was his stand on the Constitution that beat him and Blount served notice on the Washington administration that he hoped he hadn't sacrificed in vain. He wanted to be named governor of the Southwest Territory, the region of his vast landholdings.

The post was not to be had without stiff competition. Patrick Henry, who also held extensive western lands, put up his business partner George Mason, writer of the Virginia Constitution, for governor. And Anthony Wayne, the Pennsylvania war hero, wanted the post for similar reasons.

Somehow, and the means are unclear (but it appears that Blount offered to further the business of Henry, Mason, and Wayne as profitably as his own), Blount obtained the appointment.

In September 1790, Blount went to Mount Vernon to receive his commission. He was awed. It was "the most agreeable place I ever saw, though the General's dignity was too daunting . . . too awful for I verily belief he is as awful as a God," but "great and amiable—indeed admirable . . . The style and manner of his liv-

[8] *William Blount* by W. H. Masterson (Baton Rouge: Louisiana State University Press, 1954), page 126.
[9] Ibid., page 136.

ing surpasses that I have before seen particularly in dignity and I suppose I saw him living on his own funds, not those of the United States. In fact Major (Andrew) Jackson so informed me." Jackson, born in North Carolina too, was a protégé and friend of Blount's.

Blount transferred to Tennessee in 1791, establishing his capital at White's Ford on the Tennessee River. Here, he entered the last ten years of his life, years of daring schemes and his only moments of heroism and stature.

He named the twenty-four-year-old Andrew Jackson as attorney general. The territory they governed encompassed, roughly, present Tennessee, Mississippi, and Alabama. The inhabitants, who had but lately borne a reputation for drunkenness, brawling, and the biting off of ears, were in a state of transition into family settlements with inns, churches, and schools. Nevertheless, each week saw Creek raids and brought accounts of violence and pillage. The typical "house" was a half-forted cabin, called a "station." The largest town, Nashville, had but two frame houses.

In 1792, Indians, bribed by the Spanish governor of Louisiana, hit Nashville with a particularly fierce raid. An epic fight ensued with whites maintaining hot and accurate musket fire and Creek Indians shooting arrows and bullets and hurling burning brands on the little fort outside the town. The Indians were eventually beaten back and Blount followed them with militia in a campaign throughout the region. This cost money and when public funds dried up, Blount paid the bills out of his own pocket.

When Congress and the Federalist administration learned of the militia campaign, they ordered Blount to desist. The militia movement, they feared, would arouse Spain. Furthermore, they informed Blount, the Indian attacks were instigated by unlawful white encroachments. Curb the white settlers and disband the militia, he was told. The Administration disbelieved Blount's reply that the Indian raids were in fact instigated by Spain. It was one of those rare times in his life when Blount was telling the truth.

The militia activity was halted and the territory settled into a siege existence. For the next two years the Indians struck with fire, theft, and murder in all parts of the territory and the settlers were driven to live in miserable crowds within the walls of the various stations. The government in Philadelphia continued to snipe at Blount and refused to believe his statements on the true affairs in the territory. His never-strong link to the Federalists snapped.

Meanwhile, in the old Blount spirit, he did not neglect his money-making and continued to buy up land, accompanied by descriptions sent to the Carolina newspapers reporting the peace, salubriousness, and fertility of the territory. He also lobbied tirelessly for statehood. Then came Tennessee's pivotal year.

In 1796, having put together a greatly exaggerated census of seventy-seven thousand people, Blount led Tennessee to apply for statehood. Jefferson, Madison, and the fledgling Democratic party put their weight behind the move and statehood was obtained by a Southern bloc vote in which only a few Northerners joined. In return, Blount campaigned for the candidacies of Jefferson and Burr, "Tennessee's very warmest friends," he said, and was himself elected as a Democrat to the U. S. Senate. His election was challenged by the Federalists, but he obtained his seat in the fall.

In October of 1796, Britain and Spain went to war. The Southern frontiersmen, who had hoped to seize the Mississippi and Florida territories from weak Spain, now feared they would be moved forever beyond their grasp. Their fear would impel Blount to treason.

In March 1797, Senator Blount watched "with little joy," he wrote, the inauguration of John Adams. About the same time, on April 21, 1797, he wrote a letter to a business agent of his, James Carey, who was U.S. interpreter to the Cherokees, enlisting Carey's help in a military move. In the explaining of it, Blount spelled out the treason.

Blount said he had entered direct negotiations with the British Government to mount an attack on Pensacola and New Orleans. Blount would send an army of Tennessee volunteers and Indian allies to attack by land while the British fleet struck by sea. As a reward, New Orleans would be named a free port, the Mississippi would be guaranteed to Americans, and portions of Florida would be divided among the participants.

Carey proved an insecure recipient of such a confidence. Shortly after receiving the letter, he got drunk and told the story to a minor member of the Federalist administration. When the Federalist challenged the statement, Carey gave him the letter to prove it.

The Federalist, a factor named James Byers, dropped all other business and rode to Philadelphia to give the document to Secretary of State Timothy Pickering, a long-time enemy of Blount's and a highly partisan politician. Pickering was ecstatic, but he was an astute politician and before leaping into the water he reread the letter several times and pondered the risks. There was only one. The letter seemed to suggest that Blount had been in direct contact with the British minister. If this were true, then it would compromise the Jay Treaty, and to compromise the treaty would compromise the party. Pickering went to see the minister, and, using utmost tact, had his suspicion verified. The minister had been in contact with Blount, on the supposition—said the minister—that Blount was an agent of the government.

Pickering decided not to publish the contents but to use it in other ways. First, however, he informed President Adams.

Adams reacted electrically. The conversation between him and Pickering is not recorded, but it seems he was so anxious to strike a blow against the Democrats that he ignored all other considerations and prepared the letter for delivery to Congress.

On July 3, while the Senate debated consular salaries and taxes on parchment, Blount, bored with proceedings, strolled out of the chamber. On the steps he met Samuel Malcom, the President's secretary. Recognizing the bearer of a presidential message, Blount asked him what it was. Malcom replied it was confidential, and went into the Senate. Blount, content, continued his walk.

He returned a few minutes later to find the Senate in an uproar. Every head turned at his entrance. It was like a nightmare. There was a motion to reread something or other and, to his utter horror, Blount heard the damning letter read to the clerk. Adams' accompanying message spelled out the conspiracy in completely treasonable terms. Ignoring the American *quid pro quo,* the President said it was a scheme to transfer Louisiana and Spanish Florida to British control.

Thomas Jefferson, as Vice President the presiding officer of the Senate, asked Blount if the letter was his. Pale and shaking, Blount said he could not identify it without reference to his papers and asked for a delay. This was granted and he quickly left the chamber.

The same day, Secretary of State Pickering made an imaginative move designed to simultaneously put Blount in prison, destroy the Democratic party, and exonerate the British minister. He announced that it was a Spanish plot, assisted by Jefferson, to blackmail the administration. The Federalist press played it to the hilt and, incredibly, the First Lady, Mrs. John Adams, lamented—in print—the absence of a guillotine in Philadelphia for Senator Blount and Vice President Jefferson.

Blount did not return to the Senate the next day. On the third day, July 5, he sent a letter which said he did "not recollect" writing such a letter, and that he had never written anything intended to injure the United States or the Senate and that if given time he could justify or refute "whatever may be deemed offensive."

Having sent the letter, Blount attempted to board a boat out of town but was intercepted. As escape seemed impossible, he returned to his lodgings to prepare his legal fight. To friends in Tennessee, however, he wrote an admission of the letter saying, "it makes a damnable fuss here. I hope the the people . . . will see nothing but good in it, for so I intended, especially for Tennessee."

He returned to the Senate on July 7, having built himself into a righteous rage. The Senate had seized his clothes, his trunks, and his private papers. A message of impeachment arrived from the House and demanded that the Senate "sequester" Blount and insure his appearance for trial. The Senate invited all House members to attend the Senate and hear the impeachment action. Blount waited in his seat. It was worse than Indians.

Here, however, the nation's first impeachment ran into a legal mistake. Instead of taking time for trial, the Senate expelled Blount forthwith, by a vote of 25–1. (Henry Tazewell of Virginia cast the only negative vote.) Blount was ordered to appear for trial three days later.

Blount was asked for, and gave, assurance that he would appear for trial. He then promptly returned to his hotel, packed his bags and waited for midnight. He lit out for Tennessee.

He chose back roads, avoiding towns to stop at hamlets. He was seized once, by a troop of horse near Lexington, Virginia, but released after they verified he had been expelled. Pickering, who got the news, chafed in disgust as Blount eluded further capture and entered Tennessee. There he was joyously received and all the scandal was laid to vicious Federalist politics being played by Adams and Pickering. The Democratic party, led by Andrew Jackson, announced that Blount would be put up for immediate re-election to that same Senate which had expelled him.

The Senate Democrats were not too unhappy about Blount's escape. The Federalist majority, however, wanted his skin. They sent the Senate messenger, acting as Sergeant of Arms, to Tennessee to arrest Blount. The messenger arrived, somewhat cautiously, but soon found himself handsomely entertained as Blount's house guest and feted with utmost ceremony at parties. He was informed firmly, however, that his host could not conveniently accompany him to Philadelphia.

For the remainder of 1797, Blount's case became a fevered issue between Democrats and Federalists. If public opinion can be measured by the press of the era, the two sides lined up on strictly sectional lines. The Northern newspapers viewed Blount's action as treason, pure and simple. They saw no mitigating circumstances.

The Southern press, while it found it hard to get around a technical treason (though some newspapers managed to do even that), argued that Blount in fact was a patriot. He was protecting lands already inhabited by Americans, mostly Southern Americans it was pointedly noted.

Vice President Jefferson took the lead for the Democrats, lashing away at a "Federalist conspiracy" to use impeachment to persecute a member of the opposition. He wrote Madison that he saw in the impeachment proceedings a formidable weapon of the dominant party to get rid of a man dangerous to their program.

The Democrat press warned that if the House could impeach a senator on such a "vague charge," then the Senate would be completely at the mercy of the House. This argument of Senate self-interest would eventually prove decisive.

Meanwhile, in Tennessee, Blount chose not to run for re-election, having no desire to expose himself to Philadelphia jurisdiction. In his place the Tennessee legislature elected Andrew Jackson and thus launched that political career.

The impeachment trial was finally held on December 17, 1798—a year and a half after the initial charges. Blount was not present but his counsel offered a clever argument.

On the one hand, he said Blount was not subject to impeachment because he was already expelled from the Senate. On the other hand, Blount's alleged treason had occurred in the jurisdiction of Tennessee and he could only be tried there. (A Tennessee jury would have acquitted Blount in approximately thirty seconds.) The Senate dismissed charges for lack of jurisdiction. The vote was 14–11, with all thirteen Democrats and one Federalist voting for dismissal. Seven Federalists abstained. Vice President Jefferson banged the gavel and ordered Blount freed from charges.

The minority Democratic party had won the battle hands down against a Federalist majority in both houses and a passionately partisan Federalist President. It had won, primarily, because it had convinced Federalist senators that the integrity of the Senate itself was the issue, not the treason of William Blount. It had built up the fear that House impeachment could jeopardize the rights of all senators.

The ferocity between Federalist and Democrat from 1794 to 1816 is matched by only one other period in American history— the radical Republicans versus Democrats from 1854 to 1876. Political gutting since compares to them like a petty pickpocket to Attila the Hun.

The two truly vicious periods had common characteristics: both were sectional, North versus South; and both were essentially based on interpretations of the Constitution, the North in general favoring a loose and implied interpretation, the South a strict interpretation.

The Federalist party passions appear to have been ignited by the Jay Treaty of 1794. The hot politics prior to then had been contests between the two leaders, Hamilton and Jefferson. It was the Jay Treaty which put the organizational identity of both parties on the line. Fuel was added by a series of smaller sectional quarrels, such as over the whiskey tax. With Blount, the Federalists burst into flaming paranoia.

It was in 1798, at the height of the Blount scandal, that the Federalists exploded into full volcanic excess and passed four laws aimed expressly at destroying the Democrats and putting the leadership into prison.

Collectively, these were called the "Alien and Sedition Acts." The acts would directly cause the South to invent the doctrine of Nullification and indirectly cause the North to invent the doctrine of Secession.

The four acts were passed in June and July of 1798. The first raised the residency requirement for citizenship from five years to fourteen years, thus disenfranchising thousands of immigrants who had enrolled in the Democratic party.

The second authorized deportation of aliens—anyone who hadn't lived in the country fourteen years—who were *suspected* of treasonous activities. The third authorized the banishment in wartime of subjects of enemy powers. The fourth, the most outrageous, prohibited spoken or written criticism against (1) the government, (2) the Congress, or (3) the President. It nullified the guarantees of freedom of speech and freedom of press. Ten people were eventually convicted under the acts, all of them Democrats, all of them journalists, and all went to prison.

Four months after the acts passed, the Kentucky legislature declared them unconstitutional and not binding on citizens of Kentucky. In December, Virginia made a similar declaration. These were the famous "Virginia and Kentucky Resolves."

The first, the Kentucky resolution, was secretly written by

Thomas Jefferson and it bore the fire of the Declaration of Independence. It warned the government that such unconstitutional acts, "unless arrested on the threshhold, may tend to drive these States into revolution and blood."

The Virginia resolves were written by James Madison and were cooler and more logically laid out. Jefferson had stated that the states had the right to nullify federal laws which the state decided were unconstitutional. Madison carried it further with the procession of a mathematical demonstration. He said that in the case of the federal government exercising a power not given in the Constitution, the states "have the right, and are in duty bound, to *interpose*" their authority between the individual and the federal government and to maintain "the rights and liberties" of the individual.

Together the resolves laid down the basis of nullification.

A debate was set off which carried into the election of 1800.

The writers of the Constitution had not foreseen the issue. There was no provision to resolve disputes between the states and the federal government. And this fatal gap, the "states' rights" dispute, would be a wound in the American side into the next two centuries.

Should there be a state-federal conflict, how would it be settled? By state courts? Federal courts? Secession from the Union?

In *The Federalist,* Hamilton had suggested the Supreme Court as arbiter, although even there he was inferring a power that the Constitution did not specify.

Jefferson and Madison viewed the Constitution as a contract and, as in other contracts, when there was no common judge each party had an equal right to judge the terms for itself. In the case of an onerous federal action, such as the Sedition law, each state in their view had the right to judge it unconstitutional and declare it void.

Hamilton preferred the federal courts. Jefferson opted for the states. Jefferson also addressed himself to the third alternative: secession. He rejected it, though he recognized the temptation of its charms.

"It is true," he wrote, "that we are completely under the saddle of Massachusetts and Connecticut [i.e., the Federalist administration and congressional leadership], and that they ride us very hard, cruelly insulting our feelings, as well as exhausting our strength and subsistence." And it irritated him that the Federalists could so skillfully use sectional politics to dominate the country. "Their natural friends, the three other eastern States, join them from a sort of family pride, and they have the art to divide certain other parts of the Union, so as to make use of them to govern the whole."

Nevertheless, he felt, secession was suicide. "In every free and deliberating society, there must, from the nature of man, be opposite parties, and violent dissensions and discords . . . (but) . . . if on a temporary superiority of the one party, the other is to resort to a scission of the Union, no federal government can ever exist. If to rid ourselves of the present rule of Massachusetts and Connecticut, we break the Union, will the evil stop there?"

It would not, said Jefferson; it would break into anarchy.

"Suppose the New England states alone cut off, will our nature be changed? Are we not men still the south of that, and with all the passions of men? Immediately we shall see a Pennsylvania and a Virginia party arise . . . What a game, too, will the one party have in their hands, by eternally threatening the other that unless they do so and so, they will join their northern neighbors . . .

"Seeing, therefore, that an association of men who will not quarrel with one another is a thing which never yet existed . . . seeing that we must have somebody to quarrel with, I had rather keep our New England associates for that purpose."

If one adhered faithfully to the doctrine of secession, Jefferson concluded, then even the institution of the family would be destroyed, for there would always be quarrels between individuals.

The debates on the Constitution and the Alien and Sedition acts swept the country, involving the famous and the unknown. A typical debate occurred in front of a tavern in Virginia in 1799. Two to three thousand people were on hand to hear Patrick Henry, grown conservative in his dotage, defend the Administration.

Using an argument that would become traditional among future

Southern moderates, Henry did not defend the correctness of the new laws but instead concentrated on the hopeless consequences of defying them. "Defy the President and the Congress," said Henry, "and George Washington will roll over the dissenting states at the head of a federal army, and who will go against him?"

For perhaps two minutes there was silence. No individuals among the thousands present dared answer Henry. Finally, a tall, slender young man stepped forward and took the speaker's stage. He bowed his compliments to Henry, to the crowd, and asked any federal officers present to pay close attention. "For I herewith damn John Adams as a tyrant. I damn his Congress as the tool of tyranny and I stand here in defiance of the Sedition act and dare arrest." He spent the next two hours lashing away at the acts in full challenge of the penalties and when he quit the day and none dared arrest him he had driven old Henry into defeat.

His name was John Randolph. It was his first known public speech and it began his successful campaign for election to Congress as a Jeffersonian Democrat.

The final political phenomenon to arise out of the North-South competition of the 1790s was the doctrine of Secession. It represented the death rattle of the Federalist party.

The pivotal year was 1800 when the Democratic leaders Jefferson and Burr succeeded in putting together a coalition of the have-nots of the country—the agriculturists of the South and the proletarians of Northern cities. They won control of the nation. They took the Senate with eighteen seats to fourteen Federalist, and the House with sixty-nine seats to thirty-six Federalist.

They took the presidency by an equally comfortable margin, although the quirks of the Electoral College arrangement caused Jefferson and his vice presidential candidate Burr to receive an equal number of electoral votes for President.[10]

[10] The election was thrown into the House of Representatives. And the House which had jurisdiction to decide the vote was not the incoming Democratic House but the outgoing, still-in-office Federalist majority House. The Federalists, thus, were in the queer position of deciding which Democrat they wanted for President. Burr, the best practical politician in America who in putting together the New York City vote was the first to

The Federalist party survived another sixteen years, although it never again won control of the House, Senate, or presidency.

It did not not take defeat well. Barely three years after the Democratic rout, Northern Federalists began arguing for the secession of the New England states from the Union. It would be their sullen tom-tom call, a summons to defect, until they passed from the national scene in 1816.

There was nothing understated about their secessionist position. It was widespread, and if it could not be done peaceably, they said, it should be done violently.

Listen to one of the many secessionists, Josiah Quincy III, scion of the New England Quincys, future mayor of Boston and future president of Harvard University. In 1811 he was a thirty-eight-year-old congressman standing opposed to the admission of Louisiana as a state.

"It is my deliberate opinion," he said, "that if this bill passes, the bonds of this union are virtually dissolved, that the States which compose it are free from their moral obligations, and that as it will be the right of all, so it will be the duty of some to prepare, definitely, for a separation; amicably if they can; violently if they must."

One man who listened carefully that year was a freshman congressman from South Carolina. He was John C. Calhoun, who had been taught the secessionist doctrine in the law schools of New England, who had listened to it in the Congress, and who would one day carry it back down South and make it the basis for the Civil War.

---

use the Tammany Society for political purposes, did not withdraw. He sensed a prize near his grasp and intrigued actively to gain the presidency.

Thirty-five ballots were taken over seven days. Jefferson refused Federalist offers of a deal for the presidency in return for certain rewards. On the thirty-sixth ballot, Hamilton threw his weight to Jefferson, hating and fearing Burr even more than he did the Virginian. Jefferson was elected. (What weight this denial of the presidency had in Burr's subsequent killing of Hamilton is open to conjecture.)

The law on the Electoral College was changed in 1804. The only other election thrown into the House was in 1824 when Andrew Jackson had a plurality in electoral votes and in popular vote, but not a majority. The House, with each state having a single vote, chose the second-place candidate, John Quincy Adams.

Meanwhile, it is an unfair stroke that history has identified the South with secession when in fact the earliest and clearest arguments against it were proposed by Jefferson and Madison. The creators of secession doctrine, and the teachers of it from 1800 to 1817, were New England Federalists.

Chapter 7
TWO STYLES, ARISTOCRAT AND DEMAGOGUE

Jefferson was the first President inaugurated in Washington, D.C., a city which he had helped to design. Once installed, he did away with the trappings of White House ceremony which under the Federalists had begun to resemble a royal court. He installed a republican simplicity in the new capital.

Jefferson believed that the federal government should concern itself mostly with foreign affairs and leave local matters to the states and smaller governments. He made budget cuts in all branches of government, replaced Federalist appointees with Democrats, and sought to curb the growing power of the judiciary.

In domestic affairs he believed in minimal government. In foreign affairs, he was somewhat to the contrary, being the first of the expansionist Presidents. He made the Louisiana Purchase, which added virtually all lands bordering the Mississippi River to the United States. And he initiated the Lewis and Clark expedition which opened a trail to the Pacific for American settlers.

The Madison presidency (1809–17) continued the Jefferson style and Jefferson policies.

Madison was succeeded by another Virginian, James Monroe. Monroe would be the last of the Virginia Gentlemen Presidents. The next Southern President, Andrew Jackson, would be the first

President who gained popularity and then office by arousing "the emotions, passions and prejudices of the people."

Andrew Jackson, by dictionary definition of a word which has since taken on uglier meaning, was the first demagogue.

Prior to Jackson, the Southern politician was almost always a member of the elite, such as Jefferson, Madison, or even Blount. These aristocrats usually were elected by vowing to increase opportunity for the working classes. They represented the working classes, but were not one of them. After Jackson, the working classes would increasingly hold office for themselves. They eliminated the middle man between themselves and power.

James Monroe was born in Moreland County, Virginia, and served in the Revolutionary War, where he rose to the rank of captain. He studied law under Jefferson when Jefferson was governor.

Monroe was a founding member of the Democratic party and served in the administrations of both Jefferson and Madison while they were presidents.

In 1816, with both Jefferson and Madison having served the by now traditional two terms, Monroe was designated as heir apparent.[1] He rolled over the Federalist candidate, Rufus King of New York, piling up 83 per cent of the electoral vote. It was the fifth consecutive national election in which the Democrats carried the White House and both houses of Congress. The Federalists evaporated as a national party.

For the next eight years, America had a one-party system. Even John Quincy Adams abandoned his father's party and became a Democrat. In 1820, Monroe became the second and last President to run for office unopposed by a rival candidate. (Washington was the first.)

When Monroe was due to leave office four years later, the Democratic party disintegrated into sectional fights. Various states put

[1] Washington had retired after two terms because he was fatigued by office and wanted to return home. It was Jefferson, not Washington, who left on grounds a third term might set a precedent for dictatorship. The tradition of a third term was of course not violated until Franklin Roosevelt's candidacy in 1940.

up their candidates for office in the election of 1824 and the two leading candidates were John Quincy Adams (an ex-Federalist) of Massachusetts and Andrew Jackson of Tennessee.

Unlike Monroe or Adams, Jackson was not a member of the elite. He was instead a man of the new South, the frontier, backwoods South, a man whose fame was not built upon accomplishment in government or statesmanship, despite two brief terms in the U. S. Senate. His fame and popularity were built on his military successes. He had a string of victorious campaigns against the Indians which had earned him the admiration of the frontier. And in the Battle of New Orleans in 1815 he had gained the most one-sided victory ever struck against a British army, before or since. This had won him the glory of the nation. He added to his heroic reputation three years later by making an unauthorized raid into Spanish Florida, capturing Pensacola and hanging two British subjects as punishment for stirring up the Seminoles against Americans.

(Jackson thus in one stroke stirred up war threats from both Spain and England, neither of whom, however, relished any further military encounter with Andrew Jackson.)

Jackson operated with the high-handed confidence that was for so long the American style, a belief that Americans could do just about anything they set their mind to.

In political theory, Jackson was a throwback to Jefferson. The legitimate line of the Democratic party, running from Madison to Monroe to the aspiring John Quincy Adams, had become too fat and comfortable in office, too accommodating to eastern interests. Jackson advocated a return to the interests of "the people," to the farmer, the artisan, the mechanic, and the small businessman. His creed was undiluted Jeffersonian doctrine. "The federal Constitution," he would say in his first inaugural address, "must be obeyed, states' rights preserved, our national debts must be paid, direct taxes and loans avoided, and the Federal Union preserved."

He differed from Jefferson in one fundamental aspect: he had a strong prejudice against anything smacking of class privilege. This attitude would color the entire Jackson presidency and would have a substantial influence on future American politics.

In the election of 1824, the Democratic party split into two wings. The Adams wing took the name "National Republicans" and shifted their column of march toward the old Federalist goals. States' rights would be de-emphasized, the central government strengthened, and the Hamiltonian economic theories reinstalled as national policy. They favored manufacturing interests, big government, and a loose construction of the Constitution.

The Jackson wing declared themselves the true heirs of Jefferson, which they were, and the election was on.

The splintering Democratic party had no official candidate, but by various means, mostly by state legislative nominations, five men emerged as nominees. These were Adams, Jackson, Clay, William Crawford of Georgia, and John C. Calhoun of South Carolina. Calhoun soon withdrew to run for the vice presidency on Jackson's ticket, and when the dust settled, Jackson surfaced with 42 per cent of the popular vote and ninety-nine electoral votes. Adams had 32 per cent of the popular vote and eighty-four electoral votes. Calhoun got the vice presidency in a walk but neither of the presidential front-runners had a majority. The election went to the House of Representatives.

It was expected that the House would simply certify Jackson as the nation's preference. But on the first ballot, with each state having a single vote, the Clay supporters lined up behind Adams and he was named President. This was not necessarily unjust or illogical since Adams and Clay were philosophical partners. But Jackson claimed a sell-out and shortly afterward, when Adams named Clay his Secretary of State, he was convinced a deal had been made.

The Jacksonites put up a roar which lasted the next four years. They dropped the name "Democratic-Republican" for plain "Democrats" and got long mileage out of the Adams-Clay "bargain." They painted themselves as honest new reformers and their rivals as corrupt old office-holders.

They swept in easily in 1828 on the slogan "Let the People Rule" and at the inaugural Jackson intemperately invited the people to the White House. The people grabbed up food and punch, stood on chairs and tables, broke china, tore up draperies. Jackson himself prudently escaped through a window.

His eight years as President changed the office. In 1832, for the first time, presidential nominees were chosen by national convention. The spoils system was installed with members of the opposition being discharged from federal jobs wholesale and being replaced by party loyalists. Both of these innovations greatly increased the President's hold on his party. Where his predecessors ruled by gentlemanly persuasion, Jackson ruled by carrot-and-stick.

He was, furthermore, bold, enterprising, skillful at politics and decisive in action. Where previous Presidents had used the veto only to declare a law unconstitutional, Jackson used the veto on matters of routine policy. And where Congress attempted to block his wishes, he was quick to go over their heads directly to the people, the individual congressional constituencies, and rouse up public passions. He was the first of the modern Presidents and the first of the important Southern demagogues.

In their political philosophy, Monroe and Jackson were alike. Both were traditional Jeffersonian Democrats. Where they differed was in class prejudice. And this difference affected their electioneering style and consequently their conduct of the presidency. Monroe, a member of the gentleman class and a veteran of the Revolutionary War, had seen the masses stirred up and knew its dangers to property. *The people, they are a Great Beast,* was a lesson of the early United States.

It was not that work itself was scorned. The idle rich did not exist as a class. Americans worked for what they owned, be they Southern planter or Northern merchant. But the men who wrote the Constitution considered property to be the criterion of citizenship. If one didn't work, one lacked character and property and responsibility. If one did work, one acquired property and deserved citizenship.

They believed that intelligent, responsible men did not casually stir up the masses and endanger property. They believed that a very substantial function of government was to protect property. And to protect property from the passions of the masses they installed a system whereby citizens, even property-holders, did not directly elect senators, Presidents, or even presidential electors. Such offices were elected by state legislatures.

Jackson changed all this. With his dislike for the elite and privileged classes, he inspired the states (all but two) to let the people directly elect presidential electors. His constituency thus became the people themselves and not the gentlemen of the various state legislatures. He did not extend the vote to propertyless classes. But he did cause, through frequent public appearance, the President to become more closely aligned with the people. This gave him the opportunity to go directly to the people and rouse up support against Congress or any other institution which got in his way. He was a demagogue, a quite helpful one for the people to have around, as it so happened.

The Virginia model of the gentleman planter, the gentleman President, had greatly impressed the old South. The Jackson model had an equal effect on the frontiersmen of the new South, of Tennessee, Georgia, Alabama, Louisiana, and Mississippi. And when the Southerners spilled into Texas, Missouri, and what became Oklahoma, the tradition of demagoguery went with them. Meanwhile, the people north of the Missouri, the Ohio, and the Potomac never did care much for the excesses of demagoguery and instead have basically carried on in the style of the Adamses.[2]

Jackson furthermore introduced the poor Southern white to the possibilities of gaining office by demagoguery. It would be used with increasing frequency through the succeeding years. Politics would become a minor profession in the South, a means by which a poor man, armed only with some good stories and a merciless character, could advance his prospects. Sometimes, as would be the case of Huey Long and Tom Watson, the demagogues steered close to the truth and the issues. But more often, as with Bilbo and Gene Talmadge, they engaged in the rhetoric of "Soak the Rich-Carpetbagger-Vested Interests-Eastern Banks" and "Nigger, Nigger, Nigger." A candidate didn't have to be too specific. Just point in the general direction of north and name an oppressor.

The tradition of Virginia politics and *noblesse oblige* was not immediately routed from the field. For much of the nineteenth century and the early twentieth century it represented the best in Southern politics and still lingers today. The tradition has even

[2] Boston, New York, and other cities with large immigrant populations have flirted with demagoguery during brief periods.

maintained one area of strength in national politics—being an ethic and ideal in the U. S. Senate.

Monroe and Jackson represent a turning point in Southern political style. Both, too, were important Presidents. But neither would have the impact on the course of Southern politics as would the theories of Senator John C. Calhoun. It can also be argued that the Calhoun theories would have greater effect on the future of domestic American politics than either the Monroe or Jackson presidencies.

These theories were worked out while Calhoun was a member of that unique institution, the U. S. Senate.

Book Two
THE MEANS OF POWER

Chapter 8
"THE MOST REMARKABLE INVENTION OF MODERN POLITICS"

The bastion of Southern political strength in the nineteenth and twentieth centuries would be the U. S. Senate. In the Senate, the states had more equal powers than in the other departments of government. And in the Senate, an organized minority could postpone or alter or sometimes defeat the will of the majority. But it took several decades before it was fully perceived what peculiar powers the Senate held for a skilled minority.

In the beginning, the House was considered the more important branch of the Congress. The important early debates on the Constitution, states' rights, nullification, and secession took place in the House. The House, with its open session and its democratically elected membership, was the forum most sought by politicians ambitious for themselves or their ideals. What was the good to speak in the Senate, a closed closet? In the secret sessions of the Senate neither citizen nor editor could repeat one's words. What public advantage could be gained from identification with a small band of snobbish millionaires, not submitting themselves to direct election by the people but appointed by legislatures to protect the privileged classes? The House by its nature attracted the more candid, direct, and public politicians, men like Madison, the young Randolph, the young John Calhoun.

The Senate, with its hidden but very real powers over the executive, the house, and the judiciary, attracted more subtle men—Aaron Burr, the elder Randolph, the elder Calhoun—behind-the-scenes men who desired not a public forum so much as power for its own sake.

The potential for Senate power and its relative insulation from public accountability were recognized early. During the ratification of the Constitution, the Senate was widely attacked as a club of sable-clad aristocrats ever ready to line their pockets. The Senate was feared because of its small membership, because of its long, six-year terms, and because—unlike the House—the Senate powers extended into all three branches of government; it was a house of the legislature, it confirmed appointment of the judiciary, and it shared powers in foreign affairs with the executive.

The greatest fear of the Senate was attached to its making of treaties. Ten senators, a bare two thirds of a quorum, could in secret session desert the dearest interests of the people, making treaties to sell territory and commercial rights of the United States. Foreign gold, it was feared, could buy off the Senate. Such fears were especially felt in the South where it was expected that Northeast interests would permanently yield navigation rights of the Mississippi to Spain. (The North would do so in its own self-interest to maintain dominance in American shipping, it was felt.)

The Senate was criticized for being inefficient, incapable of helping to run the nation because it was too insulated from public accountability, too preoccupied with its own interests and prerogatives. Such criticism would continue into modern times.

The Senator Lyndon Johnson once called it a "great beached whale." It was alive, it thrashed about flipping its tail here and there and once in a while striking a blow for freedom. But it was incapable of governing the affairs of the nation. The Senate, said another observer, is "unfitted to handle the reins of a one-hoss shay, much less the reins of government."[2]

The Senate is too slow, too insulated, too antidemocratic. Those are the criticisms that have echoed and re-echoed over the two

---

[1] Fourteen senators constituted a quorum in the twenty-six-member Senate of 1789.

[2] Joseph Alsop column, *Washington Post,* June 7, 1974.

centuries. And not only is the Senate aloof from the public mood, but it is ruled by an internal *establishment* of elite senators who are even further removed from public accountability. Joseph Clark, a respected senator from Pennsylvania, voiced his frustrations against this establishment in 1963.

"The Senate establishment," he said, ". . . is almost the antithesis of democracy. It is not selected by any democratic process. It appears to be quite unresponsive to the caucuses of the two parties, be they Republican or Democrat. It is what might be called a self-perpetuating oligarchy with mild, but only mild, overtones of plutocracy."

It came to be viewed in the twentieth century as a creaking relic of the past, outmoded. President Richard Nixon, once its presiding officer, believed it obsolete and declared "that a superior executive branch is now required" to deal with problems of the 1970s.[3]

Yet it should be remembered that these criticisms of slowness, aloofness, and insulation were designed into the Senate. It was conceived as the cooling agent against impulsive passions of majority rule. At its best, it has always acted in the powerful eighteenth-century tradition of independent men willing to put their personal convictions against the forces of Hell, if need be.

At its best, said Daniel Webster, "This is a Senate of equals, of men of individual honor and personal character, and of absolute independence. We know no monsters, we acknowledge no dictators."

Webster's remark, a matter of self-congratulation, is a recurrent Senate characteristic. The historian Henry Brooks Adams, son of Congessman Charles Adams, grandson of President John Adams, had made a note of it:

"Although the Senate is much given to admiring in its members a superiority less obvious or quite invisible to outsiders, one Senator seldom proclaims his own inferiority to another, and still more seldom likes to be told of it."

This practice of reciprocal self-congratulation is a very human characteristic. Very human, and this is proper. The Senate is the

[3] Richard Nixon speech, June 9, 1974.

most human institution in our national government. It is a country legislature picked up and removed from the 1800s and given a place in our times.

Many of the mahogany desks used by the senators today are the original desks made in 1819, when, following the burning of the Capitol by the British, forty-eight desks were furnished by a New York cabinetmaker at a cost of thirty-four dollars each. Desks used today are desks used by Henry Clay, Daniel Webster, John Randolph, John Calhoun, and Jefferson Davis. (A small block of wood inlaid on the left side of the desk used by Davis marks the spot where a Union soldier reportedly thrust his bayonet.) On the marble ledges flanking the rostrum are two tiny snuffboxes of black lacquer, adorned with Japanese figures. They are kept filled with snuff, though never used.

Another custom is blotting sand. Each of the hundred desks has a small crystal bottle with a silver cap, much like a salt shaker, which holds a fine, dark-gray sand.

The Senate is in touch with history and the least visitor to the gallery is in touch with the Senate. It is of a size which can be absorbed by the mind. The House is too large for such absorption; it is like getting intimate with Grand Central Station. The House spectator is bewildered by the comings and goings of 435 members, their staffs, and the pages.

The Supreme Court, with its nine men, is too hushed and dignified and deliberately awesome. Commoners approach it as did Egyptian peasants making obeisance before the temples of Karnak.

As for the executive branch, well, it is easier to penetrate to the sacred Kaaba of Islam than to see even a minor official of the White House. It is in the Senate, and only the Senate, where one can be reassured that the government is actually run by the living.

It is a place so human that it is, in a sense, alien to the rest of modern government. It is intimate. But for all that it is powerful, for it uniquely reaches into all branches of the government.

In legislation, it is directly equal to the House.

In the executive, it has the power to say yes or no to choices for the Cabinet, for ambassadorships, and other appointees. And while the President usually initiates foreign treaties, only the Senate can make them law.

In the judiciary, it has the power to approve or deny, as it sees fit, the appointments of all federal judges up to and including the Supreme Court.

The Senate is an advisory council to Presidents, a protector of the states, a guardian of the privileged, and an easily accessible agency of redress and aid for small businessmen, small farmers, minorities, and beleaguered individuals whatever their classification. Be one a President or a common laborer, a foreign potentate or a Havasupai Indian farmer, a senatorial ear will listen, although, certainly, satisfaction is not guaranteed. But the listening will happen. There is uniquely in the Senate a tradition of *noblesse oblige*.

Among the American institutions, the Senate is the most eccentic and aristocratic in its character and the most deliberate in its pace, the most versatile in its powers and the most human in its conduct. This was the institution that the South, very gradually, came to find most comfortable for its style. The Senate, like the South, was very conscious of history and when it moved forward it did so with an eye on the past.

There are lots of tempering influences in the Senate which make it possible for minority-interest senators to defend themselves.

First, the voting power of each senator and of the states is equal.

Second, there is the seniority principle. The senator from the smallest state in the Union may become chairman of the most powerful committee in the nation. A Senate chairman is always in a position to block temporarily legislation and appropriations of interest to other factions in the nation. He is in a powerful bargaining position to defend or assist his own constituency.

Third, there is the filibuster. The Senate rules and custom of unlimited debate allows even a single senator to tie up national business. The threat of filibuster is also a powerful bargaining tool.

The above three factors, collectively, make the U. S. Senate unique among world parliaments. The English Prime Minister Gladstone viewed the Senate with such admiration that he called it "the most remarkable invention of modern politics."

It is primarily a Southern invention, being based on the identical blueprints submitted to the Constitutional Convention in 1787 by Edmund Randolph of Virginia and Charles Pinckney of South Carolina, drafts which were submitted simultaneously and without knowledge of the other's existence.

Prior to the 1830s, the men of the South had exercised their political strength in a variety of national arenas—the Continental Congress, the Confederate Congress, the House, the Senate, and the presidency. They had created radically new governments and written new chapters in the Rights of Man. The agrarian, Jeffersonian South was as strong as any other facet of the country, political, sectional, or economic. Beginning about 1830 the states north of the Potomac and the Ohio began rapidly to outdistance the South in terms of population, industrialization, and political weight. Each passing year made the South relatively smaller. Furthermore, the nonslave states west of the Mississippi seemed to add on at the rate of one a year. And in the 1830s, the nation's second and final Abolition movement began, a civil rights spearhead thrust by the industrial North into the bowels of the manorial South.

It was in the Senate, beginning about 1831, that the South would take up a no-retreat position on white supremacy, states' rights, and strict interpretation of the Constitution. The South's line of Senate generals would extend from Calhoun and Jefferson Davis to Oscar Underwood, Walter George, Richard Russell, John Stennis, and Sam Ervin. The first was John Calhoun.

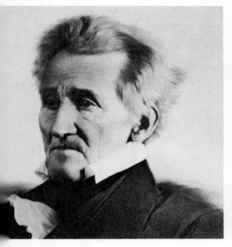

drew Jackson: The "people's choice" cheated out of the White House in first national election. *(Library of ıgress)*

John Calhoun of South Carolina: The "American Marx" learned his secession theories at Yale. *(Library of Congress)*

Jefferson Davis chained in prison at Fort Monroe: "All we ask is to be left alone." *(Library of Congress)*

Hiram Revels of Mississippi: The man who succeeded Jefferson Davis in the Senate was revulsed by Republican party excesses. *(Library of Congress)*

Joseph Rainey: The first black congressman showed no ill will toward Southern whites. *(Library of Congress)*

Senator Blanche Bruce of Mississippi: He helped eliminate Northern reprisals against the South. *(Library of Congress)*

Woodrow Wilson: The most intellectual President since Jefferson. His inauguration had a definite Southern flavor. *(Library of Congress)*

Presidential candidate Franklin Roosevelt meets with running mate
John Nance Garner at Hyde Park, 1932: Beginning with the Roose-
velt-Garner election, Texas would hold national power for thirty-
five years. *(National Archives)*

Speaker Sam Rayburn, left, and W
Atherton, Commander of the Ame
Legion, examine petitions for a G
of Rights: Rayburn passed the Ma
Plan, "the most unsordid act in his
(National Archives)

Chapter 9
THE FORGOTTEN MAN

Jefferson's successor as the navigator of Southern politics was not a man whom the future would remember and respect such as Madison, Monroe, or Jackson. The heir instead was John Calhoun, a man who thirty years prior to the Civil War caused his home state of South Carolina to take up arms against the Union.

No political party looks back to Calhoun as its founder or its philosopher. No group of public men today proclaims allegiance to his memory or can recite his doctrines. Few people outside of the South have heard of him. And in the past, while all major political parties, including the post-World War II Dixiecrats, Republicans, and Democrats, have named Jefferson as their founder, none has dared admit a descent from Calhoun. There are Jeffersonians, Hamiltonians, Wilsonians, Jacksonians, and New Dealers by the ton, but you will not find a Calhounian in America, save possibly for some unaccounted-for lunatic wandering in a swamp.

Yet, Calhoun's doctrines were the most powerful of his era and they are still in heavy use today. Furthermore, while he lived, he was among the most respected and feared men in America, and in the South the most popular.

He was born near Abbeville, South Carolina, in 1782. His father died when he was thirteen years old and the boy's early education was largely informal and out-of-doors. He was, never-theless, well tutored. He easily passed the exams to enter Yale. After graduation he attended law school at Litchfield, Connect-icut, and then went home to South Carolina to practice law and attend to the family business.

His first foray into national politics came in 1811 when he won election to the House of Representatives. He was then a nation-alist, not a sectionalist, and as a campaigner and freshman con-gressman whipped up enthusiasm for a war against England. John Quincy Adams would later declare him to be "above all sectional and factious prejudices, more than any other statesman of the Union with whom I have ever acted."

In the House and in the Senate, he was an impressive figure, bearing a stern visage which had strong resemblance to Mi-chelangelo's Moses. It was a face which seemed not to have gone through the experiences of youth. The posture was bolt upright in the chair. The lips were pressed tight in censure. The eyes were deep and appeared to give out a burning light from beneath heavy eyebrows. And dominating all was a broad, massive forehead, usually lined with a disapproving frown.

Calhoun's background was less joyful than that of the average son of a Southern planter. Throughout his life he would know only two environments: the capital of Washington with its merci-less political competitions, and the estates of South Carolina where—because of the death of his father—Calhoun was early on forced to deal with the realities of management, labor, and nature.

The family was newly arrived at wealth, the father having begun as a poor dirt farmer. The first slave, named Adam, was acquired in Calhoun's boyhood and Adam's son was John Calhoun's inti-mate partner at work in the fields and at play in the yards. This relationship, however, had no tempering effect on Calhoun's strictness toward his own slaves or on his view of the correctness of the slavery institution. (While in Washington, a house servant ran away and Calhoun was strangely resentful. He wrote his brother-in-law to catch the slave immediately and have him "se-verely whipped." When the slave was caught, he repeated his in-struction: "I wish you to have him lodged in jail for one week, to be fed on bread and water, and to employ someone for me to give him thirty lashes, well laid on, at the end of the time.")

In social pleasures, Calhoun was stoic. He did not seek out friends, or welcome those who sought him out. Solitary sports such as hunting and fishing did not interest him. He took little interest in what he ate and none in what he drank. He liked only to work.

In his Scotch Presbyterian background, in his joyless surveillance of the natural pleasures, in his stoic emotions and stern discipline he hewed far more closely to the Roundhead tradition of New England than to the Cavaliers of the South. It is not paradoxical then that he sought out his education at Yale and at Litchfield.

It was there that he learned his secessionist doctrine. His law teachers at Litchfield had been the intellectual backbone of the Federalist movement to secede from union with the unholy Jefferson, the "Virginia Delilah," and make a nation of their own and a government after their own hearts.

Calhoun took his seat in the House in 1811, at a time when South Carolina was replacing Virginia in political leadership of the South, and of the Congress. The Carolinians, in particular William Lowndes, Langdon Cheves, and Calhoun, were not so fortunate in wealth and education as the Virginia dynasty but they were quite as able. All were young, all were Democrats, and all were from the same up-country section of their state. Their skills were so obvious that when they entered the Congress the Democrat majority gave them chairmanships of the major committees: Naval, Appropriations, and Foreign Relations. Calhoun was chairman of the latter.

The decline of Virginia and the rise of Carolina was a product of a shift in population and opportunity in the South. Under the Virginia dynasty, population had poured into Tennessee and the other Mississippi lands. The back country of the nation had fallen to the South. Economic leadership of the expanding region had shifted from the gentlemen of Virginia to the aggressive frontier-oriented small capitalists of the Carolinas. William Blount had been one of the first. There had also been a shift in the economic market which worked against Virginia.

This shift was in the typical pattern of North-South economic relations: Northern initiative and action followed by a Southern reaction. Eli Whitney of Massachusetts and Yale had in 1793 invented the cotton gin, a machine which separated cotton from its seed and significantly reduced labor costs. The North built cotton mills and the South planted cotton fields.

The cotton gin put South Carolina in the lead of Southern economics. In 1810, South Carolina's exports totaled $10.6 million while those of Virginia had fallen to $4.5 million. Tobacco, the great Virginia staple, had given way to cotton.

With this economic clout, it was not unnatural that South Carolina forged to the front in politics.

The men of the old Virginia South were almost everywhere supporters of the Democrats. But the party leadership by 1810 had become visibly Federalist in its views. Young Democrats, such as the Carolinians, were particularly outraged about the foreign policy toward Great Britain. Resentment against British impressment of American seamen was very high. In addition, there was a smaller imperialist faction in the party, called "the War Hawks," who wanted to seize Canada and Florida.

Calhoun was one of the leaders of the War Hawks and, along with Henry Clay of Kentucky, one of the men most responsible for forcing the Madison administration into the War of 1812.

The resultant victory saw the emergence of numerous political careers, most especially those of Andrew Jackson, Clay, and Calhoun. Clay split off quickly to the pro-Hamiltonian wing of the party but the Jeffersonians—Jackson and Calhoun—remained partners through the election of 1824 and that of 1828 when Jackson won the presidency and Calhoun his second consecutive term as Vice President. They fell out that same year.

The surface cause was an increased tariff on foreign goods which favored the manufacturers of the East and penalized the consumers of the South. The tariff was expressly designed to (1) protect Northern industry from foreign competition and (2) raise up revenues to pay off debts incurred in the War of 1812.

The tariffs had long been a sectional issue. Prior to Calhoun, the most forceful opponent had been John Randolph of Virginia.

And it seems to have been the issue of tariffs, not slavery, that converted Calhoun from the nationalist Congressman of 1811 to the pro-South, anti-North Vice President of the 1820s onward.

Calhoun from his entry to the House had been a protégé of John Randolph's. He attended all of Randolph's speeches against the various tariffs in which Randolph took the position that the Southern consumer had a right to buy goods in a free and competitive market. Like Randolph, Calhoun viewed each penny paid in tariffs as a direct subsidy to Northern interests. From this both men had leaped to the logical conclusion that the political forces of the North were aggressively attempting to dominate the South. To make it an agricultural colony.

Randolph believed that all the storm-tossed issues which were to torment the South were the product of the North's economic imperialism. The antislavery movement, like the tariffs, was a Northern attempt to break down the economy of the South and subject it to Northern domination. Randolph, who for most of his life opposed slavery, would not allow emancipation to be imposed from without. Where Randolph led, Calhoun followed.

Slavery, and its corollary, white supremacy, would eventually become *the* sectional issue. But in the beginning the issue of tariffs was equally important.

In 1820, South Carolina had led a petition of Southern states to declare the tariffs "unconstitutional, oppressive, and unjust." The other signers were Georgia, Virginia, North Carolina, Alabama, and Mississippi.[1]

As the tariffs, and the debates, continued to increase during the 1820s, the South fell back more and more to its main line of parliamentary defense: states' rights.

In 1832 the tariff again was raised and Calhoun, now the undisputed leader of the Southern bloc, announced that Northern states so completely dominated national politics that the South was being reduced to poverty. Calhoun set about to reassert Southern political power.

His first weapon was nullification. Using precedents laid down

[1] Calhoun did not always oppose tariffs. A tariff was passed in 1816 to pay war debts and Calhoun, because of his role in starting the war, had little choice but to endorse it.

by Jefferson and Madison on the primacy of states' rights over federal rights, Vice President Calhoun sent a letter to the governor of South Carolina (James Hamilton) laying out the specific means to nullify the new tariff charges.

Jefferson and Madison had justified the general principle of nullification. Calhoun now gave specific instructions on how to do it. The process, and the reasoning, went like this:

1. The state would select delegates and convene a sovereign convention to declare the offending law unconstitutional.

2. All citizens of the state would thereby be legally obliged to regard the law as unconstitutional.

3. If a federal court tried a defendant for violation of the unconstitutional law, the jurors—being state citizens—would be obliged to acquit the defendant.[2]

"Beaten before the courts," said the August 28, 1832, letter to Governor Hamilton, "the General Government would be compelled to abandon its unconstitutional pretensions, or resort to force; a resort, the difficulty (I was about to say, the impossibility) of which would very soon fully manifest itself . . ."

The letter took pains to observe that nullification was a different and separate doctrine from secession. Like Jefferson and Madison, Calhoun viewed nullification as working within the constitutional system. Secession was a withdrawal from the system. But unlike his Southern predecessors, Calhoun did not reject secession. To the contrary, he found it a very useful threat of last resort.

"Without the power of secession, an association or union formed for the common good of all the members might prove ruinous to some, by the abuse of power on the part of the others." This advocacy of the threat of secession was a consequence of Calhoun's Northern Federalist education. It was a significant and disastrous departure from Southern political thought.

To overcome objections to piecemeal secession—state by state dropping off whenever it was offended—Calhoun laid down rules. Secession was permissible only when more than one fourth of the states agreed to it. Such a secession, by a bloc of states, would

[2] Until the 1870s, federal courts had no express power or jurisdiction to rule on the constitutionality of federal law.

guarantee that a very serious issue was involved, an issue which applied to more than one state.

The fraction of one fourth was arrived at by some ingenious arithmetic. Calhoun based it on the Constitution's requirement that three fourths of the states were necessary for ratification. The corollary, said Calhoun, was that if at any time more than one fourth of the states desired to secede, then the constitutional contract was voided.

Calhoun did not advocate Civil War. He offered a safety valve to negotiate differences among the majority and minority state blocs.

Should the secession issue arise, he wrote in this same letter to Governor Hamilton, then there should be convened a convention of all the states to settle and remedy differences.

All of these matters—nullification, secession, and the proposal for a convention of the states—arose out of the Constitution's failure to specify the means to resolve differences between the states and the federal government.

Following Calhoun's letter to Governor Hamilton, South Carolina called a convention and declared the federal tariff law null and void. The nullification would become effective in February 1833.

In the fall, the state legislature elected Calhoun to the U. S. Senate. He resigned his vice presidency so that he might more effectively present South Carolina's arguments in the national chamber. In the meantime, South Carolina armed her militia and prepared for war with Jackson's Federal Army.

The other states refused, despite Calhoun's arguments, to follow South Carolina's lead, although the Virginia legislature—in its old tradition of leadership—came forward and offered to mediate between the Jackson administration, the Congress, and South Carolina.

Jackson was livid with rage, but the old soldier was unsure if he had the force to put down militarily the Carolinians. As he was in the process of assessing his army's capabilities, the Congress backed down. It passed a law of Solomon wisdom which allowed Jackson and the federal government to save face and at the same

time gave South Carolina a reduction of tariff. (The law provided
for a steady reduction of tariffs during the next ten years until they
reached a point of insignificance.)

Tocqueville, present in America at the time, wrote: "Thus
Congress completely abandoned the principle of the tariff . . .
The Government of the Union, in order to conceal its defeat, had
recourse to an expedient which is very much in vogue with feeble
governments. It yielded the point *de facto* while it remained
inflexible on the principles." After the matter was settled, Congress then passed a law investing Jackson with extraordinary
powers to overcome by force a resistance which was no longer
present.

South Carolina was not gracious in its victory. It promptly convened a new session and declared Jackson's extraordinary powers
to likewise be null and void. For the time being, that was the end
of the matter.

Following his victory, Calhoun became increasingly submerged
in a cold personal ambition for the presidency and a monomania
for the interests of his state and the South.

Austere and monumental as an iceberg, he spoke in the Senate
with a voice frigid and harsh. It had a rapid-fire, staccato quality
and was precise in laying out his unbeatable arguments. He was
generally regarded as the supreme intelligence of his day, although
a review of his speeches and writings suggests that this had as
much to do with his abrupt and superior speaking style as it did
with any intrinsic brilliance in his logic. Indeed, upon inspection,
his written logic is not so clear as that of Jefferson, Madison, or
Alexander Hamilton.

Where he excelled was in political analysis. Nourished on Aris-
totle, Machiavelli, and Burke, he possessed an uncanny ability to
cut through to the substance of a problem. He had a facility for
analysis equaled in his time only by Tocqueville. He understood
his era to be, as he wrote, "approaching change in the political
and social condition of the country." It revolved, he said, around
wealth.

"The great question of the future . . . will be that of the distribution of wealth—a question least explored, and the most impor-

tant of any in the whole range of political economy." In America and abroad, said Calhoun, society was being shaped by a class struggle. His theories on class struggle and distribution of wealth were enunciated while Karl Marx was a boy.

The emerging American industrial state depressed Calhoun. He feared the few would be enriched at the expense of the many. The tendency "of Capital to destroy and absorb the property of society and produce a collision between itself and its operatives would lead to anarchy . . ."

"The capitalist," he wrote, "owns the instruments of labor and he seeks to draw out of labor all of the profits, leaving the laborer to shift for himself in age and disease. This can only engender antagonism; the result will be hostility and conflict, ending in Civil War, and the North may fall into a state of social dissolution."

This arch defender of slavery was among the earliest thinkers to enunciate government's duty to protect the individual against the predatory tendencies of capitalism.

Majority government was tyrannical. "The government of the absolute majority," he wrote, "instead of the government of the people, is but the government of the strongest interests; and when not effectively checked is the most tyrannical and oppressive that can be devised." Money, he said, could capture a majority and "unless unchecked could despoil the land and the people."

By 1837 Calhoun had developed a concept known as the "Concurrent Majority," which meant that each state would have "a concurrent voice in the making of laws—or a veto on the execution." The doctrine of minority veto did not originate with Calhoun. It had been used irregularly for three centuries in Europe.[3] Calhoun's twist was to make the states and their congressional delegations the instrument of the veto.

As it would be developed by Calhoun and his followers, the theory of Concurrent Majority became a parliamentary doctrine whereby the states, usually working through the senators, could obstruct the will of the majority by nullification, by filibuster, by procedural footstepping and by locking up in committees. "The

---

[3] The most extreme example of minority veto was the Polish Government of the seventeenth and eighteenth centuries which allowed the veto of any single deputy to dissolve the Parliament and annul its previous decisions.

various interests in the [nation] would thus be protected," said
Calhoun, "because government could not act without the consent
of all."

One cannot fault Calhoun's analysis of the power of economic
forces in society and the government. Nor can one fault the effectiveness of his Concurrent Majority doctrine. Where he goes off
the track, tragically, is that he used these to defend slavery, the
most primitive form of exploitation and tyranny.

Why? Did he believe slavery was a counterforce to the chaos
and tyranny of capitalism? Or was he simply a racist who engaged
in intellectual rationalizations?

The answer appears to be neither. Instead, Calhoun's conduct
seems based on a sense of racial loyalty to the Southern white
tribe. From whatever direction the tribe was threatened, Calhoun
attacked back.

His first strong sectional activities, beginning about 1820, were
not based on slavery but on the question of tariffs. Slavery doesn't
become his primary issue until 1833, but for the remaining seventeen years of his life it will be his only issue.

The 1833 event that so affected Calhoun and the South was the
Abolitionist movement as presented by William Lloyd Garrison,
twenty-eight-year-old black Massachusetts journalist, printer,
founder of the *Liberator* newspaper, and a man who accepted
prison in Maryland rather than pay fines for free speech against
slavery and who had been nearly lynched in Boston for pro-
nouncing the same views.

On December 6, 1833, at the convention of the American Anti-
Slavery Society in Philadelphia, William Lloyd Garrison invoked
the words of Thomas Jefferson.

Said Garrison: *"All Men are created equal; they are endowed
by their Creator with certain inalienable rights* . . . We have met
together for an achievement of an enterprise without which that of
our fathers is incomplete . . . [to declare] that all those laws
which are now in force, admitting the right of slavery, are therefore, before God, utterly null and void . . . and to secure to the
colored population of the United States all the rights and privileges which belong to them as Americans—come what may to our
persons, our interests, or our reputations."

Calhoun reacted to the Abolition movement with a tribal reflex. Slavery was not an abstraction to be judged on the issues of justice, morality, or even economic advantage. No, the Abolition movement was an ultimate Northern weapon aimed at Calhoun's community, his race, and his class. He reacted with his own threat.

"The relation between the two races in the Southern section constitutes a vital portion of her social organization," he told the Senate. "The Southern section regards the relation as one which cannot be destroyed without subjecting the two races to the greatest calamity, and the section to poverty, desolation and wretchedness; and accordingly they feel bound, by every consideration of interest and safety, to defend it."

Calhoun took the lead in defending slavery. He saw in it a means to bind the South together politically and make it once again equal to the North in Congress, in power if not in absolute numbers. The South gathered round him as Calhoun passed from a coldly intellectual analyst to a fanatic demagogue on slavery and the South. The predecessor to Marx died in 1850, the greatest reactionary of his time.

The factor which turned Calhoun and the South toward the path of fatal decline was not so much the desire to defend slavery but fear—fear of the Northern threat from without and the black from within. Calhoun said so much in one of his last speeches to the U. S. Senate, in the year of his death, 1850:

"The North has acquired a decided ascendancy over every department of this Government, and through it a control over all the powers of the system. A single section governed by the will of the numerical majority, has now, in fact, the control of the Government and the entire powers of the system. What was once a constitutional federal republic, is now converted, in reality, into one as absolute as that of the Autocrat of Russia, and as despotic in its tendency as any absolute government that ever existed.

"As then the North has the absolute control over the Government, it is manifest that on all questions between it and the South, where there is a diversity of interest, the interest of the latter will be sacrificed to the former, however oppressive the effects may be."

Calhoun said the South had no recourse to put up with this domination, save in matters which would end in "destruction to the South." The foremost of those matters, he said, was "the relation between the races."

The twin Southern white fears—of being overwhelmed by the North from without and by the blacks from within—have shaped much of American history. The Southern reaction to those fears accounts for much of the Southern political inventions. Threatened, the South has responded creatively. The origin of the outside threat from the North has been tracked in earlier chapters. The origin of the internal threat deserves a further brief examination.

Fear of race war was as endemic to the white South as mother's milk. Slave rebellions had long been a feature of early American history, North and South. But in the South, with its more intense experience with slavery, the threat was felt longer and deeper. It was a peculiar anxiety, being seldom acknowledged. The condition was similar to that of living with atomic missiles in the twentieth century. Each person lived beside the beast from the bottomless pit. The beast was dormant, but its very presence shaped events.

Slave rebellions went back to the beginning of the colonies.

In 1663, black slaves and white indentured servants had revolted in Virginia . . . In New York City in 1712 the "conspirators tying themselves to secrecy by sucking ye blood of each others hands" . . . Again in New York City in the 1730s and thirteen blacks were hung in a row . . . In Charleston in 1720, in Virginia and Louisiana and again in Charleston in 1730 . . .

The preamble to a South Carolina statute of 1740, in defining the duties of slave patrols, stated that many "horrible and barbarous massacres" had been committed or plotted by the slaves who were "generally prone to such practices."

The rebellions in the seventeenth, eighteenth, and nineteenth centuries were so numerous that nobody has ever and probably will never be able to count them all. We know of at least three rebellions in South Carolina alone in 1775.

The Abolitionist movement of 1833 was not the first attempt by an outside power to use slave agitation against the South.

In Virginia in 1775—the battles of Lexington and Concord having been fought—the royal governor, Lord Dunmore, attempted to raise a loyalist army of black slaves by promising them emancipation. Within a few weeks nearly three hundred runaways had joined him. They were enrolled as the Ethiopian Regiment, given arms and fitted into uniforms bearing the words "Liberty to Slaves."

The whole South was horrified. Patrick Henry declared Dunmore's action "fatal to the publick safety." Rebel propagandists churned out white supremacy pamphlets. The British Government, they said, was behind this "hellish plot." Dunmore was holding nightly meetings with the blacks "for the glorious purpose of enticing them to cut their masters' throats while they are asleep." The report spread throughout the South that British secret agents were arming slaves and Indians. It was rumored that the King had promised each Negro who murdered his master the plantation and all the property.

For the Southern colonies, the action of Lord Dunmore was one of the mobilizing factors of the war. Patrols went through towns every night to enforce curfews. Troublemakers among slaves were rounded up and jailed or hung. And Virginians finally engaged Dunmore, some three hundred Loyalists, and the Ethiopian Regiment in a battle at Great Bridge and defeated them. Dunmore retreated to the sea and his black troops were hit by a smallpox epidemic.

As slave populations grew, slave revolts became larger and more frequent. At least a thousand slaves were implicated in a plot in 1800 centered around Henrico County, Virginia. (Betrayal of the plot, combined with a severe storm which postponed a projected march upon Richmond, enabled whites to put it down.) Eleven years later, another massive revolt involving a thousand slaves was put down just west of New Orleans. The slaves, armed with cane knives and stolen muskets, were marching to sack New Orleans. (Intercepted just outside the city, they were delayed long enough by white sharpshooters to enable the militia to mobilize.) Rebellions and plots continued to accelerate between 1820 and

1860. All were put down with severe measures. In Louisiana, the heads of sixteen slaves were stuck upon poles along the Mississippi River as a grim warning to other rebels. White men caught in such conspiracies were cut down without mercy. In an 1835 revolt in central Mississippi, of the thirteen conspirators hung in the town square eight were white.

The problem and threat of slavery was so apparent that Americans several times tried to curtail its growth. By 1750 most of the American colonial legislatures, including the Southern colonies, had banned the further import of Africans. But the British Government, preferring "the immediate advantage of a few African corsairs, to the lasting interests of the American states, and to the rights of human nature," suspended the bans in the interests of their own traders. The *rights of human nature,* the lofty high road motive, was a Massachusetts concept. Virginia planters took the low road. They said flat out they wanted the ban because Virginia would cease to be a "white man's country" if the blacks were not kept out.[4]

The fear of black population growth was so intense that prohibition of slave-trading—as opposed to slave-owning—became one of the first acts of the newly independent states. Delaware banned it in 1776, Virginia in 1778, Maryland in 1783, South Carolina in 1787, North Carolina in 1794, and Georgia in 1798.[5] Through these trading bans, the states hoped to gradually reduce black population through natural attrition and eventually phase out slavery. (A ban on owning was felt to be impractical because it raised enormous problems of compensation.) The national government didn't prohibit the trade until 1808. Thereafter the major source of slaves was the offspring of domestic population. (The proportion of blacks to whites immediately began to decrease.)

Every state had a slave code and, with the exception of Louisiana, they were much alike. The slave was not to be "at large" without a pass, which he must show to any white who asked. He was prohibited from hiring out his own time, finding his own employment, or living by himself—again with the exception of Loui-

---

[4] *Massachusetts Spy,* November 10, 1774.
[5] South Carolina reopened the trade for a five-year period commencing in 1803 and imported thirty-nine thousand additional African laborers.

siana. Slaves had curfews. Slaves could not make contracts or bear witness. Except in Louisiana.

Louisiana's exceptional policies in regard to slave laws were a result of class identification. As stated earlier, it was the class not the race of slaves which was feared in the South.

In Louisiana, there was as much difference between a free black and a slave as there was between a white and a slave. "Free persons of color" had full business and contracting rights. They could acquire by inheritance and transmit property at will. They were tried by the same law and the same court as the white.

There were two reasons for this relative liberality. The first, in chronological terms, was that free blacks were among the first settlers of New Orleans in 1718. They intermingled with whites and they owned property. To handle property transactions, the colonial government found it convenient to bestow contractural rights equally among blacks and whites. From this basis, the blacks acquired the legal parity which existed in Louisiana until the Civil War.

The second factor accounting for the liberality was that French Creole Louisiana practiced a systematic miscegenation, which had the effect of raising slaves out of the ignorant, impoverished class. Official marriage between the races was forbidden (as was marriage between free blacks and slaves). But common law marriages between creole gentlemen and quadroon women were a basic part of the culture. These liaisons were formal and highly protected by custom. The quadroon wife was guaranteed a house for the remainder of her life, the name of her husband for their children, and the support and education of the quadroon children.

However, Louisiana had time and again proved itself quite as merciless as any other Southern state in crushing slave revolts. Gradual working out of the black-white problem was acceptable; immediate freedom for slaves was not.

Ironically, until the time of the Abolition movement, the black slaves of the South had been peaceably arranging their own freedom through economic development. For the first third of the century, everywhere in the South, blacks had an economic grip on the skilled trades. It was blacks, not whites, who knew how to bake bread, build wheels, repair engines, construct houses and buildings. In the South prior to 1840, practically all mechanics, carpenters, blacksmiths, tinsmiths, masons, bricklayers, bakers, and other craftsmen were black. Some who were slaves were buying their freedom. Others who were slaves were sending their freed sons to high schools and colleges. Had this all continued, it is probable that full democratization of the South would have occurred by around 1900.

This favorable development was stopped by two events. One was the Abolition movement, which tended to polarize the races. A second factor, of which scant notice has ever been paid, was more important. It was the wave of Irish and German immigration into the South which began about 1840. These immigrants organized unions and went on strike if black labor was hired. And this was so effective that within ten years the black advantage was gone. And it was not only the best jobs the blacks lost. Charles Lyell, touring the South in 1849, wrote:

"Ten years ago all the draymen in New Orleans—a numerous class—and all the cabmen were colored. Now they are nearly all white. The servants at the great hotels such as the St. Louis and the St. Charles, were formerly of the African race. Now they are of the European race."

By the end of the Civil War, the immigrant whites, throughout the South, dominated all but the most menial job markets. The blacks were forced out of the economic mainstream and had no recourse but to do farm labor or servant work. They would not recover from it for a hundred years.

The *economic* turning point for the Southern black may be figured approximately at 1840, when he was displaced by European immigrants. It coincided with the Abolition literature flowing down from the North. The more advanced of the Southern blacks, robbed of working within the Southern system, took advantage of the Northern movement, began to assist its agents and disperse its pamphlets. Pressure built. And as the pressure built, so did the polarization between the races, and the polarization between North and South.

By the time of Calhoun's death in 1850, the pro-slavers had control of the national Democratic party. In the Southern states themselves, the threat from the North, exploited by demagogues, built such acute anxiety that a rigid doctrinaire conformity set in. Nothing like it had been seen before in the South. For the next century no dissent was allowed on the question of white supremacy. That this should occur in the states which invented the American guarantees of liberty and individualism was tragic.

Southerners who would not conform departed from the South and from the Democratic party. Typical of these was Frank Blair, a native Southerner who moved to Missouri, was elected to the Congress, and in 1856 joined the newborn Republican party.

On behalf of the nonslaveholding people of the South, he arose in the House to scold his former neighbors.

"I make no complaint . . . of having been read out of the Democratic party. I should as soon think of complaining of being read out of a chain gang."

Slavery was now the one issue of the Democratic party. In 1860, at the national convention, the pro-slavers demanded that the party adopt a platform to put slavery in the new western territories. The Western Democrats refused. The party split. The Southerners walked out and Lincoln was elected. That election and its aftermath would set off a full century of bitter contest, North versus South, black versus white. It would be the central problem for Abraham Lincoln and Lyndon Johnson, for Jefferson Davis and John Stennis, for William Lloyd Garrison and Hiram Revels and Martin Luther King.

Chapter 10
THE BLACK BREAKOUT

And now we arrive at the Civil War. In the South it was called the
War Between the States, the War for Secession, and the War for
Southern Independence. In the North it was the War of the Rebellion (the official government designation). The name "Civil War,"
which came to be accepted on both sides, is somewhat misleading
for it was less a struggle between religious or political factions of
the same nation than a sectional combat between two cultures.
Historians still do not agree on its basic cause, but it had its roots
in complex economic, social, and cultural elements.

For the South, the changes brought on by the war are represented in the careers of two statesmen, one white and the other
black. The white was Jefferson Davis who resigned from the U. S.
Senate in 1861 to become President of the Confederacy, was imprisoned and indicted for high treason. The black was Hiram
Rhoades Revels, who began the war as a pastor and schoolteacher, went on to become the first black in the U. S. Senate, and
spent his last years as president of a Southern university. Davis
was the prewar senator and Revels the postwar senator from the
sovereign state of Mississippi.

Mississippi began as a prosperous state and, like Virginia, was
an agrarian democracy without large cities. Unlike Virginia, it

lacked the direct influence of an English aristocracy and never developed a tradition rich in the humanities.

The state grew up around the Natchez Trace, a wilderness highway which ran from south of the river port of Natchez into Nashville, Tennessee, and which played an important role in the development of four states (Mississippi, Alabama, Louisiana, and Tennessee).

The Trace was an unusual-looking highway, being for much of its length a tunneled road. The path, with time, had been worn deep into the earth—twenty-five feet in some places—and was overshadowed by ancient trees. It had been first carved out by buffalo looking for salt licks and then used by Indians to link the Natchez, Choctaw, Chickasaw, and possibly Cherokee tribes. It came into general use by Europeans about 1763 after the Mississippi was opened to Americans. By 1795 it was among the most heavily trafficked highways in the nation.

The Trace owed its importance to the Mississippi River. All the country west of the Alleghenies floated its goods down the tributaries of the Mississippi to New Orleans for sale or export. The boatmen, instead of trying to row back upstream against the currents of the Mississippi, the Missouri, and the Ohio, sold their barges and flatboats for scrap wood and returned home via the Trace.

Many wandered away from the Trace into the virgin lands of Mississippi, Tennessee, and Alabama and later returned with their families. Small farms and large plantations grew up. Slaves were brought in from the Trace. Through the Trace came blacks and whites, gentlemen and riffraff, highwaymen and future Senators.

An early user of it was the boy Jefferson Davis, coming down from Kentucky with his parents.

The boy was raised like a Virginian. He received a classical education at Transylvania College in Kentucky and was afterward given an appointment to West Point, from which he graduated in 1828. He was twenty years old.

For the next seven years he served in various army posts and took part, in 1832, in the Black Hawk War, a shameful expedition against the Sac Indians in Wisconsin. He married the daughter of the war hero Zachary Taylor, but his bride died three months later. He thereupon left the Army and for the next ten years lived in solitude as a Mississippi planter and gentleman. In 1845 he came out of seclusion and was elected to the House of Representatives, but a few months later—with the advent of the Mexican War—he resigned to command a Mississippi regiment. Under Zachary Taylor he distinguished himself, most notably in the capture of Monterey and, shortly after, at the Battle of Buena Vista where Taylor defeated Santa Anna's fifteen-thousand-man army. A year later, 1847, Davis, with the honors of Buena Vista "thick upon him," was appointed to the U. S. Senate.

It was a distinguished Senate. Calhoun was the most eminent, fighting for the South in the last ditch. Webster was there too, and Benton of Missouri and Lewis Cass of Michigan.

Davis was placed on the military affairs committee of which the Democrat Cass was chairman. Cass was soon to be named party nominee for the 1848 presidential election and appointed Davis to work out for him the committee policies, which was to say the military policies of the nation. General Winfield Scott was driving deep into Mexico and Davis came forward with a simple blueprint: The United States would annex all of Mexico, from California to Guatemala.

This could easily have been done, from a military point of view, for the Mexican Army was being decimated by Scott. But John Calhoun, the presiding Senate power, was concerned about Mexico's nonslave status if annexed and doubted the U.S. ability to hold 1.9 million square miles of foreign territory. He proposed that Mexico proper (a thickly populated 761,000 square miles) remain independent. For its share, the United States obtained California, New Mexico, and clear title to Texas (a total of a thinly populated 1.2 million square miles).

Calhoun's course, though the one adopted, was not popular and Davis became a national campaigner for the Whig party in 1848 on the issue of annexing all of Mexico. Davis' father-in-law, Zachary Taylor, was the Whig candidate and won the election. (He died a year after taking office, however, and sixty-four years would pass before another Southerner, Woodrow Wilson, was elected President.)

Jefferson Davis retired from the Senate in 1851 to run for governor of Mississippi but was narrowly defeated. In 1853 the Democrat Franklin Pierce welcomed Davis back into the party and appointed him Secretary of War. From that position, Davis created imaginative policies aimed at expanding American power. Among these were:

—The building of a Southern Pacific railway from Memphis to California.

—Acquisition of the isthmus of Panama and construction of a U.S.-owned railroad across it.

—The purchase of Cuba.

—The opening of trade to Japan and China.

—Cultivation of closer commercial relations with South America.

All of these programs, with the exception of course of buying Cuba, were eventually effected. In this expansion, Davis continued what had become a Southern pattern. Southern presidents and cabinet members had from the time the Virginians crossed the Alleghenies taken the lead in expanding the boundaries of the United States. Jefferson had added the Louisiana Purchase, Madison Florida, Monroe portions of the Dakotas, and James Polk—James Polk of Tennessee had added more square miles of territory than any President in history.[1] (The only major territorial acquisitions made by non-Southern leaders were the Hawaiian Islands under William McKinley in 1898 and Alaska acquired through the policy of Secretary of State William Seward, a Lincoln appointee from New York who was carried over into the administration of Andrew Johnson.)

With the death of Calhoun, Davis had become one of the leaders of the South, sharing that role with Howell Cobb, R. M. T. Hunter, and Henry A. Wise, all but one heads of the chief committees of the U. S. Senate.

[1] Polk was the most startlingly effective President in the nation's history. When he ran in 1844 he announced four major goals: reduction of the tariff, re-establishment of an independent treasury, settlement of the Oregon boundary dispute with Great Britain, and acquisition of California. When he retired four years later, choosing not to run again, he had accomplished them all. The territory he added included all of Texas, New Mexico, Arizona, California, Utah, Nevada, Idaho, Washington, Oregon, and portions of Montana, Wyoming, Colorado, Kansas, and Oklahoma.

Davis was the ablest and the wisest of this group and was accepted and recognized throughout Washington as Calhoun's successor.

Unlike Calhoun, Davis did not believe in frontal warfare. Secession and nullification were not his style. He preferred guerrilla warfare and felt the South could hold on to its interests through control of the Democratic party and the committees of Congress. He felt he himself could steer the course of the nation through his knowledge of the powers affecting the Senate. The Senate was the protector and the representative of the propertied interests and he felt it was the great property holders who would not allow the nation to be broken up on the issue of slavery.

In the election of 1856, the Democrats found it increasingly difficult to reconcile their Northern and Southern wings. The Whigs had disintegrated entirely and, for the first time since the demise of the Federalists, the North put together a truly sectional party: the Republicans.

After a bitter convention fight, the Democrats got together behind a Northerner acceptable to the South. He was James Buchanan of Pennsylvania. Part of Buchanan's favor in Southern eyes was based on his land hunger. He had been an expansionist Congressman and, as Polk's Secretary of State, Buchanan had overseen the acquisition of the Oregon country and the vast territory in the Southwest taken from Mexico. He had supported the annexation of Cuba and proposed, as President, to acquire Cuba. This latter goal was a pet Southern project and led to charges that Buchanan was pro-slavery.

The Republicans nominated John Frémont of California. The campaign was run on the issue of extension of slavery to the territories. The Republicans opposed it strongly. The Democrats said each territory should decide for itself. Buchanan, carrying a solid South, won with 45.6 per cent of the popular vote. Frémont, however, ran a strong second with 33.3 per cent, pulling all his electoral votes from free states and thereby confirming the sectional nature of the newborn Republican party.

In the election, Jefferson Davis returned to the Senate where he continued to oppose secession and instead worked for a compromise between North and South. Buchanan likewise wanted a compromise, but one which leaned to the Southern view. In his inaugural address, Buchanan stressed the need to preserve "the sacred balance of the Union," giving equal congressional representation to slaveholding and free states. He declared that only the courts should decide the question of slavery in those territories not yet admitted as states. This view was, of course, the Southern position, and Buchanan uttered it with confidence as he had already learned privately how the pending Dred Scott case would be decided by the Supreme Court. (Dred Scott was a slave who had accompanied his master to the Wisconsin Territory where slavery had been prohibited by Congressional legislation known as the Missouri Compromise. After returning to a slave state, Scott sued for his freedom on grounds his residence in a free territory had ended his bondage. The justices ruled in 1857 that the Missouri Compromise, passed in 1820–21, was unconstitutional. They said the Congress had no power to prohibit slavery in the territories.)

The Dred Scott decision, and Buchanan's acceptance of it, was roundly denounced in the North where antislavery, anti-South passions began to reach the proportions of a fever.

The South, meanwhile, withdrew into a hard shell, forming a stolid, sullen resistance to change. The South was afraid.

The fear was an ancient one: the inundation of one people by another. It was not racism per se that made whites so anxious. It was not so much the race of blacks but the class of black slaves that the whites regarded as dangerous and were so determined to keep suppressed. For example, even at this late date skilled blacks —mechanics and the like—were tolerated and, indeed, respected for their skills. They were not considered a threat to the social order and were allowed to participate in the advantages of the general society provided they adhered to rules laid down by the whites. These rules for free, educated blacks amounted to an unwritten code whereby the blacks could participate rather freely in the economic system but would keep to themselves in the social and educational areas. It was the ancestor of the separate-but-equal doctrine invoked by the South after the Civil War and so greatly abused by the South.

An example of this white attitude toward upper-class blacks

was printed July 16, 1859, in the New Orleans *Daily Picayune,* less than two years prior to the Civil War.

The newspaper was responding to an offer of emigration made by Haiti to Southern free blacks. The *Picayune* responded:

"The appeals of the Haytian government to the free blacks, inviting their immigration, have been principally directed to the free colored of New Orleans. It is evident that Hayti expects to find the class of people she needs to achieve the salutary reaction which is to save her from barbarism and to put her once more on the road to life.

"Our free colored population forms a distinct class from those elsewhere in the United States. Far from being antipathetic to the whites, they have followed in their footsteps and progressed with them, with a commendable spirit of emulation in the various branches of industry most adapted to their sphere.

"Some of our best mechanics are to be found among the free colored men. They form the great majority of our regular settled masons, bricklayers, builders, carpenters, tailors, shoemakers, etc., whose sudden emigration from the community would certainly be attended with some degree of annoyance; while we count them in no small number among excellent musicians, jewelers, gold smiths, tradesmen and merchants.

"As a general rule, the free colored people of Louisiana, and especially of New Orleans—the 'creole colored people' as they style themselves—are a sober, industrious and moral class, far advanced in education and civilization.

"From that class came the battalion of colored men who fought for the country under General Jackson in 1815 and whose remnants, veterans whom age has withered, are taken by the hand on the anniversary of the glorious eighth of January by their white brethren-in-arms, and proudly march with them under the same flag."

So, two years prior to the Civil War, the largest newspaper in the South stated that the class of free blacks was among the primary elements of the society. They were appreciated, they were needed, and their presence was much desired. Educated black people, a class which was not perceived as a threat, were acceptable.

Free blacks resided in proportionately large or larger numbers in four other Southern states: Virginia, North and South Carolina, and Tennessee. On the whole, the free blacks of those states were less educated, less skillful, and less integrated into the white society than those of Louisiana. They were closer to the class of slaves and accordingly the legislation of Virginia, the Carolinas, and Tennessee gave substantially fewer liberties to free blacks than existed in Louisiana. But there is a body of evidence in the newspapers of Richmond, Charleston, and Nashville which implies that the laws were irregularly enforced. Influential whites, connected with the free blacks by ties of commerce and sometimes by ties of blood, often intervened between them and the law. In addition, they provided for their private education, their religious instruction, and their economic opportunities.

The free blacks enjoyed standing even in Alabama, which along with Mississippi had the most restrictive laws and which in the 1860 census listed only 2,690 free blacks.

The English traveler Sir Charles Lyell, touring the South in 1846, was amazed at the number of "men of color" who had made fortunes in trade. "One of them," he wrote, "by standing security for a white man had lately lost no less than 17,000 dollars; yet he was still prospering and kept a store."[2]

The storekeeper resided near Tuscaloosa, then the state capital and seat of the University of Alabama. Lyell noted that wealthy free blacks had ample resources, and ambition, to send their sons to the university but were prevented by state law, which prohibited formal education for blacks. In some instances, the sons were sent to Northern colleges. And even in Alabama, churches got around the law to an extent by establishing "Sabbath schools," which provided some exposure to reading and writing. Presbyterians had such a school in Tuscaloosa. In Alabama, too, Lyell encountered blacks who owned slaves and was told of a blacksmith named Ellis who "had taught himself Greek and Latin and is now acquiring Hebrew."

Throughout the states with a large free black population, there are repeated contemporary mentions which suggest they did not

[2] *A Second Visit to the United States* (New York: Harper & Bros., 1849), page 71.

assume the cringing posture of debasement which has characterized them in fiction. While the whites were superior to them in
the pecking order, they in turn were superior to the class of slaves
and objected just as strenuously as whites to association or inter-
mingling with them.

The slaves, because of economic, social, and legislative oppression, had been kept so deprived of education that they seemed to
be almost creatures from another planet. Consequently, slavery
and antislavery was a class struggle, a social survival issue upon
which the dominant classes of the South would not budge.

Matters came to a head in the election of 1860. The Democratic
party, meeting at Charleston, failed to agree on a candidate after
fifty-seven ballots. Eight Southern states walked out during the
debates over slavery. By midsummer, the nation had four national
parties in the field:

The Democratic party, the remnants of the original organization
who were striving for a national ticket and put up Stephen
Douglas.

The National Democratic party, a new party formed by the
Southern walkouts who nominated John Breckinridge of Kentucky.

The Constitutional Union, a party composed mainly of former
Whigs and strongest in the border states. They put up John Bell of
Tennessee.

The Republican party, the most revolutionary major party in the
nation's history. It was dominated by a radical wing which was
animated in part by an ideological hatred of the Southern aristocrats—they called them the slavocracy—and imbued with an
ideal of a racially egalitarian society with elevation of the black to
a full political equality and the dismantlement of Southern political power. They nominated Abraham Lincoln.

Lincoln of course won in the November election and would
take office in March 1861. Though he received only 40 per cent of
the popular vote he piled up more electoral votes than the other
three parties combined. The Southerners' Breckinridge ran second, showing that the South was solid, regardless of party banner.
The Democratic nominee, Douglas, ran fourth.

Lincoln's election was a signal. A month later, South Carolina seceded from the Union.

The action, though extreme, was not considered as arbitrary or as illegal then as it is now. Indeed, though the incumbent President Buchanan in a legislative message had denied the right of secession, when it arrived he did little. He said that except for defending U.S. property in South Carolina and collecting customs he lacked any authority to act. Many state and municipal governments considered secession legal. Even New York City took a vote on whether it should secede.[3]

Within the next six months, nine more slave states seceded.[4] Virginia remained loyal but threatened to secede if the Buchanan administration used force against her Southern sister states. Buchanan would not.

When the Congress convened in late January, the senators from the Southern states rose to announce the will of their legislatures. All eyes were upon Jefferson Davis, who had become the most respected man in the Senate, the leader of the South, and who had thus far taken no role in the secession movement.

He rose and addressed the Senate:

"Mississippi, by a solemn ordinance of her people, in convention assembled, has declared her separation from the United States . . . It is known to Senators who have served with me here that I have for many years advocated, as an essential attribute of state sovereignty, the right of a state to secede from the Union."

He turned and left the chamber. A group of radical Republicans jumped up and made an attempt to have the name of Davis and all other seceding senators stricken from the Senate roll. This the Senate refused to do. Instead, ten days after the inauguration of Lincoln, it passed a resolution simply stating that the seats of

[3] The journalist Mary Louise Booth of New York kept a contemporary journal which was published in 1867 as *A History of New York City*. She wrote that the general reaction to South Carolina's secession was to avoid interference "with the existing institutions of the South, which many deplored, but which most regarded as a painful necessity beyond the reach of outside interference . . ." In January 1861, Mayor Fernando Wood sent a message to the city council suggesting that New York City secede from the union. It was voted down.

[4] In chronological order, they were: Mississippi, Florida, Alabama, Georgia, Louisiana, Texas, Arkansas, North Carolina, and Tennessee.

Davis and the others had "become vacant . . . the Secretary be directed to omit their names respectively from the roll."

(Shortly afterward, the Senate gave another example of its dignity and strength. An effort was made to expel the Kentucky Senator Lazarus Powell for his statements, outside the Senate, that the North was "invading the South." The Senate Judiciary Committee held that, "He is entitled to his own opinions and no man is to be expelled from this body because he disagrees with others in opinion.")

Davis and his people had taken the position that secession was their rightful remedy. The North angrily declared it to be an illegal rebellion, and this was ironic for, less than fifty years earlier, the attitudes had been completely reversed. It was the Northern states which had argued the legality of secession and the Southerners who had opposed it.

The Southerners had been driven to their position by the ideological pressures, the ethical pressures, the moral pressures of the antislavery movement. They had been driven half-crazy by their need to protect their cultural identity, whatever the iniquities. They wanted survival. And in the main they did not want war, they wanted divorce. They wanted to be rid of the pressures. They wanted out of their marriage with the North.

On February 4, 1861, in Montgomery, Alabama, the seceding states organized a provisional government and drafted a Constitution for the Confederate States of America. It strongly resembled the U. S. Constitution written by Southerners of the preceding century and repeated much of its language. Stronger and more explicit guarantees of states' rights were added, however, and slavery was "recognized and protected," though a brake was put on its growth by the addition of a clause prohibiting the importation of slaves from any foreign countries or non-Confederate territories. Another significantly Southern clause was the prohibition of any protective tariffs.

Jefferson Davis was elected President and in his inaugural speech at Montgomery stated a position similar to the Declaration of Independence:

"Our present political position . . . illustrates the American ideal that governments rest on the consent of the governed, and that it is the right of the people to alter or abolish them at will whenever they become destructive of the ends for which they were established."

A month later, in his address to the first Confederate Congress at Montgomery, he pierced right to the core of the Southern mood:

"All we ask is to be let alone."

Davis continued to work for a settlement between the Union and the Confederacy. In the meantime, he had ordered occupation of Union military posts in the South. Due to the actions of three subordinate officers, the Union fort at Fort Sumter, South Carolina, was fired upon by the Confederates and war began.[5]

Both sides fell to with a blood lust. The South was defending itself from what it felt was an unjust aggression. The North was led by the radical Republicans, who were determined to reduce the South to ashes and on the ruins build a new world, supervised by themselves, a region in which neither the federal government, nor the Republican party, nor the black man's place in the light would ever be challenged.

The fierceness of both sides is embodied in a letter written in August 1863 to President Lincoln from General William Tecumseh Sherman of Ohio.

The smaller farmers, mechanics, merchants, laborers, "probably three-quarters of the population of the South," he wrote, "in all things follow blindly the lead of the planters . . . The Southern politicians understand this class, use them as the French do their masses . . . consult their prejudices, while they make their orders and enforce them . . ."

The Southern ruling class, said Sherman, must be rooted out. "These men must all be killed or employed by us before we can

---

[5] Davis had authorized General P. G. T. Beauregard to fire on the fort if it refused to surrender. The message was delivered to the fort by three of Beauregard's subordinates: Roger Pryor, Louis Wigfall, and S. S. Lee. The Union commander, Major Robert Anderson, replied he would surrender in two days. The subordinates, knowing that Jefferson Davis was trying to reconcile matters with the North, but wanting war themselves, did not relay the Union reply to General Beauregard. The latter, thinking surrender had been refused, ordered the attack.

hope for peace . . . particularly fearsome [are] the young bloods
of the South, men who never did work and never will. War suits
them, and the rascals are brave, fine riders, bold to rashness . . .
They care not a sou for niggers, land, or anything. They hate
Yankees *per se,* and don't bother their brains about the past, present, or future. As long as they have good horses, plenty of forage
and an open country, they are happy.

"This is a larger class than most men suppose, and they are all
the most dangerous set of men that this war has turned loose upon
the world . . .

"No other choice is left us but degradation. The South must be
ruled by us, or she will rule us. We must conquer them or ourselves be conquered. They ask, and will have, nothing else, and
talk of compromise is bosh; for we know they would even scorn
the offer . . . I would not coax them, or even meet them halfway, but make them so sick of war that generations would pass
away before they would again appeal to it."[6]

More than 186,000 black men served in the Union armies during the war, 93,000 of them being recruited from Confederate
states. They fought in segregated units and were mostly led by
white officers assisted by black noncoms. They fought with a special determination to prove themselves. A running account of one
of their biggest battles was put together by black historian George
Washington Williams, who interviewed survivors for his *History
of the Negro Race in America from 1619 to 1880.*

The battle was at Port Hudson, Mississippi, and there was,
wrote Williams, "a question of grave doubt among white troops as
to the fighting qualities of negro soldiers. There were various
doubts expressed by the officers on both sides of the line. The
Confederates greeted the news that niggers were to meet them in
battle with derision, and treated the whole matter as a huge joke.
The Federal soldiers were filled with amazement and fear as to the
issue . . ."

Six times the black brigade, its white officers shot dead, as-
saulted the Confederate redoubt and were beaten back. On the

[6] *Abraham Lincoln: The War Years* by Carl Sandburg (New York: Harcourt, Brace & Co., 1939), vol. ii, pages 390–91.

seventh charge, they entered the trenches and wiped out a company of Confederates.

They were eventually beaten back but, writes Williams, "they convinced the white soldiers on both sides that they were both willing and able to fight the battles of the Union. And if any person doubts the abilities of the negro as a soldier, let him talk with General Banks [the Union commander], as we have, and hear his golden eloquence on the black brigade at Port Hudson."

By the conclusion of the four-year war, 258,000 Confederate soldiers had died in battle, from wounds or disease. The Union Army had 304,000 dead.

Obviously, the toll was great on both sides, but for the South it staggers the imagination. Seldom in modern history has a people suffered more proportionately. Of the white Southern males between the age of fifteen and fifty, 75 per cent served in the Confederate armies. Nearly one third of them were killed in the war. Nearly another third were wounded in battle or suffered debilitation in Northern prisons. A single staggering statistic tells the story: A year after the war, one fifth of the revenues of Mississippi were allotted for artificial arms and legs for her veterans.

An additional loss, after the war, was the migration of unknown thousands of Confederate veterans and their families to the new lands of the West and Southwest (and in smaller numbers to Brazil and Mexico) to escape Northern domination and poverty.

The South was whipped. Johnny Reb, often barefoot, undergunned, and existing on half the daily ration of his Union brother, had put up a terrible fight for four years. The South's generals, such as Robert E. Lee and Stonewall Jackson, had become legends in the North, repeatedly defeating Union armies two and three times their size. Lee in two short years sent six massively superior Union armies reeling back to Washington ("The Great Skedaddle," Lee's troops called it). He even piled successive defeat after defeat upon the great Grant until the final months of the war, when there was nothing left with which to fight.

The Union, with its great weight of industry and population, with its own military abilities developed to deadly efficiency by Grant, prevailed. Total war was waged. Southern cities were burned by the hundreds. Millions of acres of crops were scorched.

Southern industry, meager enough in the beginning, ceased to exist. The South was thrown back into the pre-industrial age. No nation has been, before or since, so thoroughly sacked by the force of American arms as was the South. No nation has suffered such a severe postwar occupation and looting by American arms and American politicians.

Following Lee's surrender to Grant, the last cabinet meeting of the Confederacy was held (April 1865) at Charlotte, North Carolina. Jefferson Davis dismissed the government and fled.

A few weeks later, President Andrew Johnson, using flagrantly false evidence, charged Davis with aiding in the assassination of Abraham Lincoln and put a $100,000 reward on Davis' head. He was captured in late May 1865 in Georgia and hauled off in chains to Fort Monroe, Virginia.

For the first five days of his captivity, Davis was kept in chains. For the next five months he was forced to keep a light burning in his cell day and night and every fifteen minutes of the clock he was inspected. He was not given normal prison conditions until October 1865, and he would remain in prison long after every other Southern leader had been released.

Davis did not comment or complain publicly on his treatment. He did not ask for mercy, nor did he seek the pardon available to recanted rebels. He stood fast, and around him a new Southern pride began to build.

He was freed in 1867 after the New York publisher Horace Greeley posted bail. Greeley received much criticism for his act but replied that the South, and Davis, were honorable enemies, honorably defeated, and should be honorably treated.

Davis never relinquished his belief in the right of secession. In March 1884, addressing the weeping, cheering members of the Mississippi legislature, virtually all veterans of the war, the old leader cited the hundreds of thousands of compatriots who, by refusing to apply for federal pardons and thereby forfeiting their property rights, had upheld the legality of secession. "Repentance," said Davis, "must precede the right of pardon and I have not repented. Remembering as I must all which has been lost, disappointed hopes and crushed aspirations, yet I deliberately say, if it were to do all over again, I would again do just as I did in 1861."

For nearly a half hour the chamber rang with rebel yells.

In this same speech, touchingly, Davis said the "happiest time of my life was when I held the office of United States senator from Mississippi—one which I preferred to all others." He died in New Orleans eight years later at the age of eighty-one.

The South had been laid flat by the war. Stepping into the gap came the newly created federal bureaucracy, the Freedmen's Bureau. It was the one bright spot of the Northern occupation. Designed to aid and protect the newly freed blacks, it also aided destitute whites. It provided massive relief for a conquered enemy, a world phenomenon in its time which would become a standing feature of U.S. policy in most future wars.

In its two years of operation, the Bureau issued twenty-one million rations, three fourths to blacks, one fourth to whites. Of its work, a white reporter in Atlanta wrote: "I cannot help but remark that it must be a matter of gratitude as well as surprise for our people to see a government, which was lately fighting us with fire and sword and shell, now generously feeding our poor and distressed . . . There is much in this that takes away the bitter sting and sorrow of the past . . . Even crippled Confederate soldiers have their sacks filled and are fed."[7]

Although the Bureau later became inefficient, oppressive, and corrupt, its finest contribution was to Negro education, building schools and founding or assisting colleges and universities.

The black historian George Washington Williams, writing in 1883, took a look at the Freedmen's Bureau work and the aftermath. He felt his people were ignoring the skilled trades at their own peril.

"The work of education for the Negro at the South had to begin at the bottom. There were no schools at all for this people; and hence the work began with the alphabet . . . All the way from six to sixty the pupils ranged in age . . . Some ministers of the Gospel after a half century of preaching entered school to learn how

[7] *The Angry Scar* by Hodding Carter (Garden City, N.Y.: Doubleday & Company, 1959), page 58.

to spell out the names of the twelve Apostles. Old women who
had lived out their threescore years and ten prayed that they might
live to spell out the Lord's prayer . . .

"[But] the majority of the colored students in the Southern
schools qualify themselves to teach and preach, while the remainder go to law and medicine. Few educated colored men ever return to agricultural life . . . Such silly ideas should be abandoned
—they must be abandoned. There is great demand for educated
farmers and laborers . . .

"The need of the hour is a varied employment for the Negro
race on this continent. There is more need of educated mechanics,
civil engineers, surveyors, printers, artificers, inventors, architects,
builders, merchants, and bankers than there is demand for lawyers, physicians, or clergymen . . .

"It matters not how many million dollars are given toward the
education of the Negro; so long as he is deprived of the privilege
of learning and plying the trades and mechanic arts his education
will injure rather than help him. We would rather see a Negro boy
build an engine than take the highest prize in Yale or Harvard."

Williams' hope for a strong black re-entry into the skilled labor
market would not be realized for many generations.

A major block was the resurrection of Southern politics, a politics that took a vicious demagogic turn on the question of race.
The South, so able at national politics, seems never to have been
so capable at handling its domestic affairs.

The South remained determined to keep the class of poor
blacks suppressed. The stiffest opposition came on black voting
rights, which Southerners—and many leading abolitionists including Harriet Beecher Stowe—viewed as giving power to a propertyless class. (Most states still restricted voting to property
holders.) The second strong objection was to the flight of black
labor from Southern agriculture.

Immediately following the peace, the legislatures of the Southern states set about to reharness the black to the white plow. Not
a single Southern state gave the vote to former slaves—although
Andrew Johnson had recommended, without insisting, that educated and property-holding Negroes be enfranchised. Furthermore, with the exception of Arkansas and Tennessee, which had

proportionately the fewest blacks, the South enacted laws—known as the Black Codes—to restrict blacks.

The severest of these, but not untypical, was in Mississippi, where blacks could not testify in court. Nor could they own property except in towns and cities. Blacks under age eighteen whose parents did not support them could be bound out by probate courts as apprentices, with their former owners having first choice. Blacks could not make "dangerous" speeches, sell liquor, or move from job to job without special license or contract.

The radical Republicans, determined to liberate the blacks, overturned the codes in 1866 and followed this up with the Reconstruction Act, which established new state constitutions and sent in federal troops to enforce Republican rule.

And now came the years of the locust for the South: Republican rule, implemented by Northerners, blacks, and turncoat white Southerners and backed by Yankee bayonets. At the national level, laws were passed empowering the President to use his armed forces against civilians to enforce law specifically in the South. Polling places were often guarded by armed soldiers. A law of 1871 gave the President authority to suspend habeas corpus, again specifically and exclusively in the South. Southerners, viewing the laws as unconstitutional and supported only by bayonets, called them "force bills."

In lower levels of government, public and private property was looted by legislatures and lesser bodies. The blacks went on an emotional binge and not a single Southern state was without its true tales of horror: of white men murdered, of white women raped, of white homes burned and pillaged. These were, however, individual actions, for there was no mass revenge by the blacks against whites. What the blacks did do by tens of thousands was to abandon the plantations and farms where they had been slaves and allow themselves to be supported by the Freedmen's Bureau.

Meanwhile, blacks were taking public office for the first time. What has come down through history is an image of circus legislatures, bribed and corrupt and openly passing bills to enrich themselves and their Republican allies.

The classic account of radical reconstruction was written by James Shepherd Pike, a Northerner and former editor of the New

York *Tribune,* in his book *The Prostrate State: South Carolina Under Negro Government.* Pike's account begins with a condemnation, a view of a black legislature as something out of the Congo jungles. It ends with a perception of it as a place of dignity and humanity.

"In the place of this old aristocratic society stands the rude form of the most ignorant democracy that mankind ever saw, invested with the functions of government. It is the dregs of the population habilitated in the robes of their intelligent predecessors, and asserting over them the rule of ignorance and corruption, through the inexorable machinery of a majority of numbers. It is barbarism overwhelming civilization by physical force. It is the slave rioting in the halls of his master, and putting their master under his feet. And, though it is done without malice and without vengeance, it is nevertheless none the less completely and absolutely done.

"Let us approach nearer and take a closer view. We will enter the House of Representatives. Here sit one hundred and twenty-four members. Of these, twenty-three are white men, representing the remains of the old civilization. These are good-looking, substantial citizens. They are men of weight and standing in the communities they represent. They all are from the hill country. There they sit, grim and silent. They feel themselves to be but loose stones, thrown in to partially obstruct a current they are powerless to resist. They say little and do little as the days go by. They simply watch the rising tide . . . They accept their position with a stoicism that promises no reward here or hereafter. They are the types of a conquered race . . ."

Of the remainder, "ninety-four are colored, and seven are their white allies . . . the body is almost a Black Parliament, and it is the only one on the face of the earth which is the representative of a white constituency.

". . . The Speaker is black, the Clerk is black, the door-keepers are black, and the chaplain is coal-black. At some of the desks sit colored men whose types it would be hard to find outside of Congo; whose costumes, visages, attitudes and expression, only befit the forecastle of a buccaneer."

But even here is seen an instinctive Southern political skill and

Pike observes that "the old stagers admit that the colored brethren have a wonderful aptness at legislative proceedings. They are 'quick as lightning' at detecting points of order, and they certainly make incessant and extraordinary use of their knowledge . . .

". . . Seven years ago these men were raising corn and cotton under the whip of the overseer. Today they are raising points of order and questions of privilege. They find they can raise one as well as the other. They prefer the latter. It is easier, and better paid. It means escape and defense from the old oppressors. It means liberty. It means the destruction of prison walls only too real to them. It is the sunshine of their lives. It is their day of jubilee. It is their long-promised vision of the Lord God Almighty."

Despite this picture, blacks never truly ruled a Southern state. No black man was ever elected governor, though Mississippi, Louisiana, and South Carolina did elect Negro lieutenant governors. And Louisiana's, P. B. S. Pinchback, served very briefly as acting governor. Blacks in other high offices were rare but there were significant exceptions. Mississippi sent two blacks to the U. S. Senate. Louisiana elected Pinchback to the Senate, but it was contested and he never took his seat. Between 1868 and 1870, seven Southern states sent twenty-six blacks to the U. S. House of Representatives, still not much representation for 3.5 million Southern blacks.

At the lower levels, the majority of Negro office-holders were either so incompetent or so corrupt that they angered even the old-line radicals, North and South. But what the white South was to resent the most were the Negro constables and sheriffs, the superintendents of education and justices of the peace, and other lesser county and local officials. They compounded, in the aggregate, all the faults of the blacks in higher office.

All of this was expected, by the North and South, for there had been no preparation for black citizenship. The marvel is not that the blacks produced so many inferior politicians but that they produced so many able ones.

Among these was Jonathan Jasper Wright, born in Pennsylvania of free parents, self-educated, who came to South Carolina in 1865 to organize Negro schools. A justice of the South Carolina Supreme Court, he signed the legal order in 1876 that, at cost to Republican rule, returned legality to the state's election process. This cost him his position with the party. He resigned the following year and died only eight years later at forty-five, an impoverished and forgotten man.

There was Joseph Hayne Rainey, the first Negro to be a member of the U. S. House of Representatives, taking his seat in 1869. He was the son of a South Carolina barber who had bought his family's freedom. A prominent radical Republican, he nevertheless showed no ill will toward Southern whites. He was a champion of civil rights legislation and felt so strongly that his people should have access to public places that he once refused to leave the dining room of a white hotel in Virginia and was forcibly ejected. It is revealing of his love for the Southern homeplace that after he lost his health and fortune in Washington, he returned in 1886 to his birthplace of Georgetown, South Carolina, to live out the last year of his life.

And finally there were the two U.S. senators from Mississippi, both of whom were exceptional. The first of these, the first black elected to the U. S. Senate, was Hiram Rhoades Revels. Revels, born in North Carolina, had organized a pair of negro regiments in the Civil War and after the surrender had settled in Natchez. A moderate Republican, he was elected by the radical-dominated Mississippi legislature to take Jefferson Davis' seat in the U. S. Senate in 1870. He served there but one year, resigning to become president of Mississippi's newly founded Alcorn College. So disgusted did he become with the excesses of radical Republicanism that in 1875 he joined the Democrats to defeat the carpetbag government and—most remarkable—in an open letter to President U. S. Grant declared that the good men of Mississippi, regardless of party or race, had combined to defeat the graft-ridden Republican organization. Liked by blacks and whites alike, he remained active in Mississippi public affairs until his death in 1901 at the age of seventy-nine.

Mississippi's second senator, and the first Negro to serve a full term in the U. S. Senate, was Blanche K. Bruce, a Virginia-born, Missouri-raised freeman. He came to Mississippi in 1868 as a planter. He was elected to the Senate in 1875 and served until 1881. As a Senator he energetically opposed Southern white election frauds, but likewise tried to remove the radical Republican excesses imposed upon the South. He was an outspoken defender of the rights of minority groups, including blacks, Southern whites, and those of the Chinese and the American Indian. He also worked to improve navigation on the Mississippi in the hope of increasing interstate and foreign commerce. Like Revels, Bruce helped eliminate Republican reprisals against whites who had opposed emancipation. Following his Senate term, Bruce held several important federal appointment posts in Washington until his death in 1898.

At the close of the century, only one black remained in Congress—George White of North Carolina. By 1902 there were not only no blacks in Congress, but none in any state legislature, North or South. It would not be until 1929 that another black would be elected to the U. S. House of Representatives. He was Oscar DePriest of Illinois. And it would not be until 1967 that another black would take his seat in the U. S. Senate, Edward Brooke of Massachusetts. It is an enlightening lesson in hypocrisy that, despite Abolition, the Civil War, Emancipation, and radical Republicanism, DePriest and Brooke were the first blacks ever elected to Congress from a Northern state.

So, it was in the South, not the North, that blacks first made their break-throughs in the skilled trades. It was in the South, not the North, that blacks first gained elective office. Backed by Yankee bayonets, it is true, but the bayonets were withdrawn in 1876 when the U.S. troops were recalled. Southern blacks continued to be elected to Congress regularly through 1899. All this was fitting, for the South was the home of the American black.

To assume his rightful place he nevertheless had to fight all the way. White resistance began firming up in 1875 with passage of the first "Jim Crow"[8] laws, which set up a color line in public transportation, in hotels, restaurants, barbershops, schools, hospitals, even jail cells. (The segregation laws, proposed and backed by fanatical, lower-class white organizations, were stiffly opposed by middle-class and upper-class Southerners of the period. This observation is made repeatedly by writers contemporary to the

[8] Jim Crow was a clownish black character in a nineteenth-century minstrel show.

event and even a casual perusal of the era's newspapers' editorials and letter columns supports the impression. This pattern was repeated in the 1950s and 1960s when lower-class white organizations such as the Klan and the White Citizens' Councils imposed their will on the general Southern community. In each instance, the Southern political leadership knuckled under to the prejudices and fears of the lower-class whites.)

Jim Crow laws remained in effect for three quarters of a century, through grandfather, father, and child. Then, in 1955, Mrs. Rosa Parks, a Montgomery, Alabama, seamstress, refused to move her tired body to the back of a bus. She was arrested and jailed. And after that, Jim Crow was dead. He was put in his grave by a black minister, newly arrived from Atlanta, named Martin Luther King, Jr. From the pulpit he convinced forty-two thousand Montgomery Negroes to quit riding Jim Crow buses. They could walk. And a boycott began, lasting 380 days and ending in victory when the U. S. Supreme Court ruled that the bus discrimination, the Jim Crow law, was illegal.

> Free at last, free at last,
> Thank God Almighty, we're free at last.

In the 1960s, the American black, after 350 years on the continent, would finally achieve his full civil rights. His great opponent for most of those years was the Southern white, who employed all the arts of war, economics, and politics. Of these Southern white weapons, one of the most enduring is the seniority-committee system.

It is a system whereby Congressional committees are chaired by the most senior member of the majority party. It is a system used to suppress the blacks and other minorities. But—true to the Southern love for contradiction—it is an institution which has great strength to protect liberties.

Chapter 11
SENIORITY

I know not how better to describe our form of government in a single phrase than by calling it a government by the chairmen of the standing committees of Congress.

Woodrow Wilson

Toward the end of John Calhoun's career the seniority system evolved in the Congress. It was a simple invention. The majority party in each house selected as committee chairman the party member who had continually served longest on that particular committee. Simple, but unique. No other parliamentary body in the world has the system. And no other institution of the Congress has been attacked with such relentless persistence.

As early as 1859, a Northern Democrat damned the system for giving "senators from slave-holding states the chairmanship of every single committee that controls the public business of this government. There is not one exception."

The system was invented to give Congress independence against strong presidents. Originally, it was the custom for Presidents, acting through the party machinery, to select committee chairmen. This was how freshmen such as Randolph and Calhoun received chairmanships of the Ways and Means or Military Affairs com-

mittees. It gave the President a control over the legislative branch
not envisioned by the Constitution.

Presidential control of the Congress is almost always popular
with the public and with politicians. Presidential control provides
the means for quick action, fast change. It is a more efficient
means of instituting programs and legislation, whether the goal be
the acquisition of the Louisiana territory, the kickoff of the New
Deal, guarantees of civil rights, or firing up a race to the moon.

But presidential control subverts the balance of powers principle of American government and in the long run causes a very
dangerous erosion of individual rights. The seniority system was
created to reassert the balance of powers in government.

But the seniority system has not conveyed any image of itself as
a guarantor of liberty. Instead it has endured silently the attacks
made upon it as an oppressor of liberties.

These attacks stem from two basic causes. First, and foremost,
the seniority system acts as a brake on change and, since virtually
all American social and political movements advocate some sort
of change, seniority, as entrenched power, becomes a natural tar-
get. Second, although the system is a guarantor of liberties for all
against a tyrannical President, users of the system traditionally use
it to defend a minority against the will of the majority. The most
noticeable example of the latter case in the past century has been
the Southerners using the system to sustain white supremacy.

Most of the criticism against the system has centered around the
Southerners' domination of it. But the system also has been criticized for putting a binding jacket on young talent. It has been
damned for being undemocratic. It is a system whereby, in 1975,
an elderly, conservative collection of self-employed small-town
lawyers and farmers, mostly from the South and entirely white,
share with the President and the Supreme Court the running of a
national population which is largely liberal, city-dwelling, and salaried, a population which is 51 per cent female, 87 per cent white,
and 79 per cent younger than forty-four years of age.

And the system has been damned for being out of touch with
the times. In 1975 the chairman of Senate Appropriations was
John McClellan, who was first elected to Congress in 1934. James
Eastland, chairman of Senate Judiciary, came to the Senate from

Doddsville, Mississippi, in 1941. John Sparkman, Foreign Relations chairman, left Huntsville, Alabama, in 1936 to join the Congress. Wright Patman, former House Banking chairman, was elected in 1928, the same year Herbert Hoover was sent to the White House. And the next four most senior House members—George Mahon, W. R. Poage, Wilbur Mills, and F. Edward Hebert—all were elected before Pearl Harbor.[1]

The system has been battered and flogged by forces inside and outside the Congress. It has sometimes been overwhelmed by strong presidents, majority leaders, House speakers, and revolt in the Congressional ranks.

Yet it survives, and this is remarkable. It has no official standing. It is not recognized by the Constitution nor in lesser law. It has no precedent in any other national parliament. It is not even embodied by formal rule in either chamber. Why does it survive? What is its secret?

Its secret simply is seniority. The Kentuckian Alben Barkley, congressman, senator, and Vice President of the United States, once said that as a young senator he never saw the wisdom of the system. "The longer I stay here," he added, "the wiser it seems."

The seniority system exists because the committee system exists. But unlike seniority, parliamentary committees are neither new nor unique. Virtually every private and public organization, a Congress, a parent-teachers organization, or General Motors, appoints internal committees to handle specific business.

However, one aspect of the American congressional committee system is unusual. This is the use of committees as a counterweight to block executive power, or for that matter to block the public will. The concept of a "power" committee was revealed by James Madison in 1794.

All the early U.S. governments—colonial legislatures, Stamp Act Congress, Continental Congress—had committees. The U. S.

---

[1] In a House revolt against the seniority system in December 1974, Poage, Mills, and Hebert were deposed, respectively, from the chairmanships of the Agriculture, Ways and Means, and Armed Services committees. Mahon, after agreeing to surrender virtually all of his powers, was allowed to survive as a figurehead chairman of House Appropriations.

Congress appointed committees at its first session in 1789. Those committees were not "standing committees," held over from Congress to Congress as is the case today, but were instead temporary committees named to handle specific bills.

The first committees were dominated by representatives and senators loyal to the Administration and were used as tools to further administration policies. The only committee in either house which handled a general category of bills was House Ways and Means which oversaw appropriations. It was the one committee which, though its membership changed each election year, was in operation from Congress to Congress.

In 1794, when the fledgling Democratic party achieved for two years a majority in the House, James Madison perceived that he could use Ways and Means to oppose the federalist administration.

Until that moment, the nation's fiscal affairs had been handled by Alexander Hamilton, Secretary of the Treasury. Appearing before the House, Hamilton would make recommendations on the "ways and means" for the nation to raise revenues.

When the Jeffersonian Democrats won their House majority, Madison raised the question of whether "the ways and means should be referred to the Secretary of Treasury as heretofore, or to a Committee." He then pushed through, by a slim majority, establishment of a Ways and Means Committee which could itself determine fiscal systems. The Federalists were bitter. David Cobb of Massachusetts, complained: "The favorite object which our Southern friends have long been wishing to obtain—that of excluding the Secretary of the Treasury from reporting systems of finance—they effected on Wednesday last."

Through Democratic pressure, the Ways and Means became the first de facto standing committee of Congress—it would not formally become a standing committee until 1802—and has appeared in every Congress since 1795.

The Federalists, when they returned to power in the Fifth and Sixth congresses, displayed a remarkable reluctance to use the Committee as a power tool.

The Democrats had no such reluctance when they returned to power in the Seventh Congress (1801). Named as chairman of

Ways and Means was John Randolph of Virginia. The long succession of Southern chairmen had begun.[2]

For the next 185 years, though the fortunes of the South and the Democratic party waxed and waned, Southerners would hold the chair of Ways and Means 46 per cent of the time. Between 1900 and 1975, when the seniority system was in full operation, Southerners held the chair fifty years. Other major House committees have followed the same pattern. They were originally formed as a block against executive power, and for much of their history they were dominated by Southerners.

Senate committees evolved more slowly. In the beginning they were appointed not so much to handle specific legislation but to organize rules of the Senate and to handle communications with the House. Having a smaller number of members, it was not so necessary for the Senate to divide up its work.

The Senate's first standing committee didn't appear until 1806 and it was a minor one composed of three members charged with ensuring that all bills which left the Senate were properly signed. It was called "Committee on Engrossed Bills, etc." By 1816 the appointment of temporary committees for specific bills had become quite common (there were ninety such in the 1816 Senate), but only three standing committees had been added, all of them minor.[3] In late 1816, eleven standing committees were appointed and the practice has existed since then. At various periods until 1833, chairmanships were appointed by ballot of the entire Senate, or by selection of the Senate president pro tem, or by selection of the vice president. From 1833 onward, committee chairmen were appointed by the majority party.

Seniority was introduced in 1845, the year John Calhoun returned to the Senate. Aware of the growing tide against the South,

[2] The chairman of the first of the "standing" Ways and Means Committee in 1794 was also a Southerner, William Smith of South Carolina. But Smith was a weak chairman, very much in the shadow of committee member James Madison. Strong chairmen such as Randolph and his successors came afterward.
[3] They were: Joint Committee on Enrolled Bills; Joint Committee on the Library; and Committee to Audit and Control the Contingent Expenses of the Senate.

Calhoun suggested to his Senate colleagues that a seniority system would reduce tension between the political parties.

By having committee members automatically held over from Congress to Congress, and by letting them accrue seniority to become chairman, it would eliminate the horse-trading between parties that characterized the system of selecting committee members at each Congress.

Furthermore, it would strengthen the Senate against control of its machinery by the executive. Presidents with strong grip on party machinery, such as Andrew Jackson, would no longer be able to dictate who would be placed on a committee. Nor would a strong President be able to hold out a committee appointment or chairmanship as a bribe in return for a vote. Though other means of owning a senator would remain available to a President, committee appointments would be no longer at his disposal. This was a great blow to the presidency, for committee appointments were a President's strongest weapon against an individual senator.

Seniority was formally introduced in December of 1845 when Ambrose Sevier, senator from Arkansas, proposed that the majority party chair the standing committees, that members of the committee be carried over from Congress to Congress, and that rank on each committee be determined by length of service on that committee. The most senior member of the majority party would automatically be chairman. It is the same system that exists in the Senate today, unchanged. As Southerners already held most committee chairmanships and would be the first beneficiaries of the system, adoption was not difficult to obtain.

Democratic support of the system hardened during the sectional polarization of the 1850s and control of the system seesawed between North and South, Republicans and Democrats, until about 1875, when it settled down to the present arrangement whereby parties consult on committee appointments and committees are the primary units of Congress.

Concurrent with the evolution of House and Senate committees was the creation of the "conference committee." This is one of the least known, least reported, least supervised, but most powerful institutions in American government.

The conference committee is neither complex nor unique. It exists, formally or informally, in every legislature that has more than one house. Its function is to resolve differences between the houses on a specific piece of legislation. It is not a standing committee and is dissolved once the agreed-upon legislation is finally passed by both houses.

In the U. S. Congress, conference committees have existed since 1789. House members are chosen by the speaker, Senate members by the vice president or the president pro tem of the Senate. The committees' power rests on two bases: (1) the lack of supervision —the committees almost always meet in secret—and (2) the traditional practice of both houses to adopt the compromises reached by the conference committees. These exceptional powers have aroused criticism.

Senator William Fulbright of Arkansas once sarcastically suggested that the Congress save time and money by turning over all its business to the conference committees. "It is clearly evident," Fulbright told the Senate, "that to save the world and the people of this country from disaster, all that is needed is to reconvene, preferably in secret, only those incomparable sages, the conferees of the Appropriations [Conference] Committee. From their deliberations the same results would be achieved and without the expense and trouble to everyone that is involved in going through the archaic ritual of pretended legislation.

"It is quite clear that regardless of what the common Members of this body may wish, the conferees make the decisions."

Southerners, because of their lengthy control of committee chairs, have long held a disproportionate power in conference committees. This stems from the tradition of allowing the chairman having charge of a particular bill designate which members the House Speaker or Senate president will appoint to the conference committee.

Southern control of the congressional committees is an extension of Calhoun's doctrine of the Concurrent Majority. Through such control, the South has maintained a veto position on national policies. The degree to which Southern Democrats have managed to maintain the doctrine through the years was demonstrated in the makeup of the 1974 Senate.

In that year, the eleven Confederate states were represented by fourteen Democrats who had been elected by 13 per cent of the people who voted in the national elections.

The Southerners chaired nine of the Senate's seventeen standing committees and all of the most powerful committees (Finance, Appropriations, Armed Services, Foreign Relations, and Judiciary). They were elected by, again, only 13 per cent of the vote-casting citizens and constituted only 14 per cent of the Senate membership itself.

Nevertheless, through seniority and other devices, as James MacGregor Burns observed in *The Deadlock of Democracy,* the Southern Democrats "make up for their lack of numbers in the quality of their political craftsmanship, their grasp of the relation of policy goals and political means, and of course their control of Congressional machinery."

The seniority system has always been weaker in the House and, although the general public and even most House members believe it is an ancient House tradition, it in fact was firmly entrenched in the House only during the period 1945–74.

From the Second Congress (1791) until the sixty-second Congress (1911), House committee chairmen were appointed by the Speaker. It was a custom some of that time for seniority to be only one of the factors involved in selection.

In 1911 a House revolt aganst Speaker Joe Cannon stripped him, and his successors, of the power of committee appointment. The power went to the House as a whole. As a practical matter, it evolved that the majority party in the House chose the chairmen, often on the basis of seniority but with frequent exceptions.

From 1911 to 1945, about three of every four House chairs were filled by the most senior member. From 1945 until December 1974, seniority was the only basis of selection.[4]

The seniority system was invented in the Senate and there it has remained for nearly a century and a half in inviolate condition.

---

[4] In December 1974 a coalition of House liberals and incoming freshmen intimidated a weak Democratic party leadership and overthrew the system. Chairmen from then on have been chosen by a coalition-controlled party caucus which has voted by secret ballot.

For the public, the seniority and standing committee systems provide very real benefits. The members and their staffs gather information, hold hearings, bring other branches to public account, prepare bills for appropriations, regulation, and laws of the land. Holding office year after year, engaged in specialties such as banking or agriculture, they provide continuity in government.

But the picture of the chairman that has emerged over the years is that of an aging tyrant, ruling with an iron hand, entombing legislation he dislikes, dispensing favors whimsically. He runs the committee like the Pharaoh ran Egypt. He indulges disagreement with all the toleration of Ivan the Terrible.

This is very rarely the case. The system, while it does select the chairman, also restricts his powers and duties and lays down the rights of other members. These rules can be, and often are, spelled out to stop the chairman from ruling as an autocrat. Instead, he is transformed into a presiding officer who must give and take with his fellow members.

In addition, there is the give-and-take of the entire Congress. Not a day passes but that the chairman of, say, Senate Agriculture has an interest in bills before a dozen committees of the Senate and House, or in action by the executive branch. Should Senate Agriculture prove unreasonably obdurate on a matter, then House Appropriations might reply in kind. It was in the U. S. Congress that the phrase was invented, "To get along, go along."[5]

The image of the autocratic chairman has survived because it is politically useful to all the Congress. When individual members or the Congress as a whole does not wish to take the heat for the passage of a particular piece of legislation—such as a civil rights bill—discreet word is sent to the chairman that there is no objection to having it killed in committee. The chairman takes the blame, and does not mind at all, because, though it often makes him the object of national vilification, it increases his image of power with the folks at home.

The seniority system is a truly congressional phenomenon. Representative Morris Udall of Arizona once asked the Library of

[5] Sam Rayburn's advice to freshman Congressman Lyndon Johnson.

Congress to determine its use elsewhere. The answer was nowhere
—not in any of the fifty state legislatures, not in any municipal or
county governments, nor in the British, French, Swedish, German,
Russian, Australian, or any other foreign government, nor in the
Fiji Islands. But in the U. S. Congess it determines not only committee assignments but also the allotment of parking space, office
space, and other emoluments.

One of these, discovered only about 1971, was "hideaway"
offices. These were secret rooms, some seventy-five in number,
tucked away in the U. S. Capitol for senior senators and, in a few
instances, senior House members. They varied widely in quality,
some luxurious and others windowless and like closets.

One of the most impressive then belonged to Allen Ellender of
Louisiana, the most senior senator. His huge room featured a
built-in stove, a freezer stocked with seafood, and was the only
hideaway to boast two chandeliers.

The custom of hideaways dates back to 1935, when the
Supreme Court moved from the Capitol to its present site. The vacated offices were quickly occupied by the senators and congressmen.

Sam Rayburn's was the scene of so much political activity that
it became known as "the board of education," and it was there—
while swapping bourbon and stories with Rayburn—that Harry
Truman learned that Franklin Roosevelt had died and that he was
President.

Another of the early hideaways belonged not to a member of
Congress but to a bootlegger named Cassidy who used it as a drop
for his whiskey.

Lyndon Johnson's spread was the most sumptuous of all and,
by the time he became Vice President, consisted of seven rooms
on two floors. It was known as "Johnson Ranch East."

The spaces are assigned by the Senate Rules Committee and the
House Administration Committee.

The seniority and committee systems have undergone some
changes since World War II. In 1946, Senator Bob La Follette,
working with House and Senate liberals, caused the number of
House committees to be reduced from eighty-four to thirty-one

and the Senate committees from thirty-three to fifteen (though a few more have been added since in each house).

Southerners, through skillful shifting, nevertheless managed to control the key committees. Of the twelve Senate committee chairmen in the seventy-ninth Congress (1946) who returned to the Eightieth Congress (1947) only four were Southerners. They were, however, first-ranking on three of the most important committees: Appropriations, Finance, and Foreign Relations, and soon would assume control of Armed Forces.

Typical of the shuffling was the movement of Lister Hill of Alabama and Richard Russell of Georgia. Hill gave up chairmanship of Expenditures in Executive Departments to become number four on Armed Services. Russell gave up chairmanship of Immigration to become number two on Armed Services.

Within a few years, Southerners again dominated the standing committees.

In 1953, Lyndon Johnson—the new Democratic majority leader—responded to a growing restlessness among less privileged senators by implementing a system whereby each senator would be given at least one important committee post, instead of having to wait in line for years as had been the case.

Major posts were handed to such freshmen as Mansfield of Montana, Symington of Missouri, and Jackson of Washington. Southerners, nevertheless, managed to hold on to the power committees while giving up control of lesser committees, like Public Works or Labor and Public Welfare, to their liberal colleagues.

Thus, through their own skillful shifting, the Southerners kept the strongest possible congressional positions for themselves while at the same time keeping the chances of revolt to a minimum.

As the decade of the 1970s began, the South still held its position, chairing ten of the seventeen Senate committees and fourteen of the twenty-one House committees.

But there was handwriting on the wall. The South had become increasingly disenchanted with the Democratic party and as the solid South fell apart, so did its power. By 1975 the total number of Southern Democratic senators was fifteen. In the House, between 1955 and 1975, the number of Southern Democrats had shrunk from one hundred to eighty-one. Two of Mississippi's five congressmen were Republican. Half of Virginia's ten congressmen were Republican. Southerners held only one power committee in the House—Appropriations—and the chairman, George Mahon of Texas, was a figurehead.

In the Senate, its traditional stronghold, the South held on grimly. In 1975 it retained six of seventeen committee chairmanships and held all of the most powerful committees—Judiciary, Foreign Relations, Finance, Armed Services, Appropriations, and Agriculture. But because of the attrition of age, because of the swing to the Republican party where the South had no seniority, it is likely that by 1980 there will be only one Southern chairman in the Senate and none in the House.

In other words, it is probable that for the first time since Reconstruction, for only the second time since the beginning of the nation, Southern power will be broken on the national level. Or will it?

The South has shown a strong historical pattern of resilience. It snapped back from the stagnation of the Articles of Confederation by inventing a new Constitution. It rebounded against a Federalist-dominated government by creating the Democratic party. And when the Democratic party splintered into anti-South factions, the Southerners implemented the doctrine of the Concurrent Majority and invented the filibuster and the seniority committee system.

The Civil War struck the South low. It took nearly fifty years before the region could reassert its power on the national level. That reassertion came in 1912 with the re-election of Woodrow Wilson and would see the Southerners enter a sixty-year era during which they held positions of power unequaled since the days of John Calhoun.

Chapter 12
NEW FREEDOM

It may fairly be said that the eighteenth century marked the intellectual and physical birth of America, the nineteenth century was its era of territorial growth, and the twentieth saw the new nation advance into the world arena and occupy the center position. Southerners played a key role, in many instances the central role, in all these American experiences.

The Southerners also gave impetus to a fourth episode of the American pageant, the vast increase in the size of the federal government. This increase in size, caused mostly by expanding demands for "government regulation" of areas of the economy, was directly contrary to Jeffersonian philosophy. Yet, as a matter of economic and political necessity, Southern political leaders were instrumental in laying down the precedents of government regulation in farms, banks, and industry.

The turn away from Jefferson began with the election of Woodrow Wilson in 1912.

The Republican party had held the White House for forty-four of the preceding fifty-two years.[1] In 1912, former President Theodore Roosevelt challenged incumbent President William

---

[1] Democrat Grover Cleveland of New York was elected in 1884 and 1892.

Howard Taft for the Republican nomination. Roosevelt was undoubtedly the choice of rank-and-file Republicans but Taft held the party machinery and carried the nomination. Roosevelt, feeling strong as a "Bull Moose," bolted and created the Progressive party—thus confirming an ancient axiom that the party in power isn't defeated but splits into factions and defeats itself.[2] House Speaker Joe Cannon, surveying his party's wreckage, said it now became a simple question of which corpse would receive the most flowers.

The Democrats, after a long and exciting convention, nominated Dr. Woodrow Wilson, native of Virginia and newly elected (1910) reform governor of New Jersey.

In Wilson, the Democrats had their most intellectual nominee since Thomas Jefferson. Wilson was a professor of history and political science and his writings included *Congressional Government* and *Constitutional Government,* two of the most profound analyses of American politics ever written. In 1902, Wilson had been chosen president of Princeton University, where he did much to improve its academic standards and to democratize its social system. He resigned the university position in 1910.

Wilson campaigned for what he called the New Freedom, freedom for the ordinary man from exploitation by big business and high finance, something the ordinary man had seen a lot of during a half century of government ruled by robber barons who specialized in looting national lands for the railroads, busting unions, controlling prices, enshrining the seventy-hour work week as a holy object, and engineering recessions to keep wages down and Wall Street profits up. The New Freedom was, of course, a reutterance of the goals of Jefferson and Jackson.

The fractured Republican wings between them collected 50.5 per cent of the national vote. Wilson, with only 41.8 per cent, carried a majority popular vote in only one state otuside the South —in Arizona.[3] He nevertheless piled up 81 per cent of the electoral college ballots.

[2] The commonplace theory is that to achieve an enduring majority a party must embrace so many differing interests and prejudices that it falls apart of its own weight.

[3] The Socialist party's Eugene Debs had 6 per cent of the vote. Eugene Chafin, Prohibition party nominee, had 1.4 per cent.

Wilson thus went into the White House as a minority President who had been elected on a sectional vote, a Southern vote.

The inauguration had a definite Southern flavor. Wilson was sworn in by Chief Justice Edward Douglass White, a former Confederate soldier and senator from Louisiana.[4] Southerners had crowded into the capital by the tens of thousands and the air resounded with repeated rebel yells. An estimated three hundred thousand persons marched in the inaugural parade and whenever a Southern figure rode by or a band played "Dixie" the very sidewalks seemed to shake with sound.

Wilson had lived in the North since taking his law degree at the University of Virginia. But his upbringing had been in Virginia, Georgia, and the Carolinas and he once said that "the only place in the country, the only place in the world where nothing has to be explained to me is the South."

Five of Wilson's ten cabinet members were Southerners—the attorney general, the postmaster general, the secretaries of the Navy, of Agriculture, and the Treasury. The Secretary of State, William Jennings Bryan of Illinois, was a long-time Southern favorite.

On Capitol Hill, the South held an even stronger position. In the House, two fifths of the Democratic majority were Southerners and the South took over eleven of the thirteen major committee chairs. In the Senate, which under the impetus of the New Freedom would soon (1913) convert to popular election of senators, more than half of the Democratic majority were Southerners. The South chaired twelve of the fourteen major committees.

The Southerners had for some time dominated the Democratic party but the emergence of the Democrats as the majority party, and the appointment of Southerners to committee chairmanships, all happened in the election of 1912.

What had occurred was that the South, with its agrarian mystique and its abundance of small businessmen and farmers, had never abandoned its well-placed mistrust of big business, high tariffs, trusts, railroads, and Wall Street. And the nation, after half a century of exploitation by the robber barons and corrupted governments, in 1912 joined with the South in disgust.

[4] White was of Cajun-French descent. The family name was originally LeBlanc.

So the South had regained its national influence. But at a price. In the process of battling the vested interests it had become apparent that the most effective tool was government regulation. Regulation of railroads, regulation of trusts, regulation of warehouses, regulation of the money and credit system. This meant a swing to big government, a turn away from the tradition of small government, states' rights and Jeffersonian principles. It had been accepted by the working classes throughout the nation, including the South. But it had been accepted with the greatest reluctance in the South. It was a marriage of convenience, one which the white South, the Jeffersonian South, would never be comfortable with.

This discomfort was particularly felt by the Southern political leadership. Nevertheless, carried along by party loyalty and the temper of the times, conservatives like Senator John Bankhead of Alabama followed Wilson's march.

The reforms came tumbling out of the Congress on an assembly-line basis. First was a drastic reduction in tariffs, led through the Congress by Congressman Oscar Underwood of Alabama. Next came the first "income tax," led through the House by Underwood, Cordell Hull of Tennessee, and John Nance Garner of Texas. In the Senate, James Vardaman of Mississippi attached an amendment which put a higher tax on very large incomes. Opponents screamed that it was class legislation and a Southern raid on Eastern wealth. It passed.[5]

Other reforms followed in the fields of banking, currency, and credit. When those bills were signed by Wilson two days before Christmas, Alabama's Congressman Thomas Heflin rose on the floor in elation. "Mr. Speaker," he said, "let the calamity howlers howl. Let the croakers croak, and the chronic kickers kick. Labor is employed, wages good, the earth has yielded abundantly, the Democratic party is in control, God reigns, and all is well with the Republic."

In the 1914 Congress, the Wilsonians passed the Clayton Anti-Trust Act and created the Federal Trade Commission while—in a

[5] The first U.S. income tax was passed in 1864 but was abandoned in 1872. A second income tax passed in 1894 but was declared unconstitutional. The tax of 1913 was the first to be held legal by the courts.

bow to the Southern farmers and Northern workers—partially exempting farm and labor organizations from antitrust laws. In succeeding Congresses, there was created the county agent program to give farmers access to new agricultural techniques and knowledge. And Georgia's Senator Hoke Smith passed a bill giving federal aid to secondary schools. Also passed with active participation by Southern leadership were laws expanding the federal highway construction program, regulation of child labor, and an eight-hour work day.

Then came World War I.

Other than the Civil War, no event more changed the social profile of the South than did the first World War. Among the changes would be a great increase in prosperity, but this wasn't foreseen. The South thought it had already entered the Garden of Eden. In Thomas Heflin's words, wages were good, the earth abundant, and all was well.

At the outbreak of war, the South was enjoying an unusual conjunction of rising agricultural production and rising farm prices. Cotton in 1914 came in with a high price and the largest crop in history. Then, when the Europeans went to war, it fell to rock bottom, banks foreclosed, businesses closed, the economy faltered. Things looked gloomy and the Southerners, usually not so opposed to war, was cursing this one like an assembly of Quakers.

There had always been some nonmilitarist sentiment in the South. John Randolph had once pointedly reminded President Madison that the Constitution empowers the government "to make war for the *defense* of the nation, Sir. Nowhere is there a power for *offensive* war."[6] But such lectures had of course been put aside as genial eccentricities by the riding, shooting class of young Southerners that General Sherman found so awesome.

Now in 1915, however, with many Southerners having had firsthand experience of the ravages of the Civil War, the opposition to involvement in European affairs was widespread and inflexible.

[6] Randolph's reference was to Article I, section 8 of the Constitution which gives Congress the power to "provide for the common defense" of the United States.

Wilson wanted the nation to arm, to prepare. But there was a deep suspicion in the South that "preparedness" was no more than a scheme to enrich the steel companies, the munitions makers, and the financial interests. The Southern mood was deepened by a mistrust of large armies. It was "the lesson of history," said Martin Dies of Texas, "that the spirit of liberty, equality, and free government can not live in the military atmosphere." Populists like Tom Watson of Georgia and demagogic Populists like Jim Vardaman of Mississippi were very vocal about the class aspects of war, that the lower classes bled blood while the upper classes made money.

The opponents of the war were, however, quite careful to avoid a break with Wilson, as the President continued to have an enormously popular following. And by the end of 1916, much of the war opposition had evaporated because of the success of his submarine policy, rising farm prices, and a successful presidential campaign.

When war finally came in April 1917, public opinion in the South was for it and the war declaration was opposed by only five Southern congressmen (four from Alabama, one from South Carolina) and one senator (Vardaman).

Once the declaration came, there was overwhelming Southern support of war services, bond drives, recruitments, and a thousand other ventures.

In the Congress, the Southern leadership abandoned almost completely their states' rights principles and handed sweeping emergency powers to the federal government and the President. Some Southerners, their brains swollen shut with patriotism, advocated suspension of the Constitution. "I challenge any lawyer here," said Alabama Congressman William Bankhead, to produce a court ruling that states "the Constitution . . . in time of war can stand in the way of any measures necessary for the saving of the life and very sovereignty of the government itself when in desperate peril."

It was ignored that suspension of the Constitution would strip away the foundation of authority of the Congress, the military, and the presidency. Apart from the force of arms, they'd have no more legality or justification than any other mob that might want to get itself together and give out orders.

The most significant effect of the war on the South was a dramatic change in prosperity and awareness for a previously static society.

Nearly a million Southern men, black and white, left their local environments and joined the military where, though military units themselves were segregated, they mixed in camps and towns with men of different locales, different languages, races, religions, and national origin. They saw the peoples of England and France, of Italy, Africa, and Greece, of Russia and Japan.

In addition, the people of the South who did not go off to war were also introduced to different customs and peoples. Because of climate, space, and clout in Congress, the majority of the Army training camps were located in the South. The greatest naval complex in the United States was developed in the area of Norfolk, Virginia, a town whose population of seventy thousand leaped, nearly overnight, to three times that number. Other large installations were activated at New Orleans, Pensacola, the Florida Keys, Parris Island in South Carolina, and Charleston. Shipyards opened on the Mississippi Gulf Coast, in New Orleans, and very quickly a complex of yards existed from Texas to Virginia.

The South entered an economic boom unknown in its history. Industry expanded, farm prices rose, and workers had money in their pockets and could take their pick of jobs. It was in this period that Southern textile industry was set off on a climb that, in the 1920s, would carry it past New England. Coal mining boomed. Harlan County, Kentucky, had been an Appalachian retreat of log cabins, few roads, scratched-out farms, and a culture closer in its language, its folklore, and its living style to Elizabethan England than to twentieth-century America. In 1911 it had 169 mines. By 1915 it had 1,496 mines, and by 1923 the mines numbered 9,260.[7]

The wealth spread throughout the class structure. Those at the

[7] The economic summaries and figures are from *The Emergence of the New South, 1913–1945* by George Tindall (Baton Rouge: Louisiana State University Press, 1967), pages 4–60.

top, as usual, got the most but the coal miners were earning as much as forty dollars a day and black tenant farmers were settling debts, buying goods and land, and had cash money in their hand. Indeed, this last aspect was so unnerving that newspaper editorialists began wondering if the boom were a healthy thing after all.

The worries came sharply into focus in the congressional elections of 1918. During the war, the Congress had put price ceilings on commodities purchased by the government. Cotton had been noticeably exempted (after vigorous lobbying by Southern congressmen and the Farmers Union). In 1917, legislation was passed to put price controls on food, fuel, fertilizers, and agricultural implements (the Lever Food Control Act). Again, cotton was exempted.

Wheat farmers in the Midwest, whose own product was price-controlled, howled at the discrimination. The Republican party took up the charge of cotton profiteering and added embellishments that made it appear that the entire federal government was biased in favor of the South. The war, said the Republicans, was being financed by Northern taxes to build Southern industry.

The administration remained strangely unresponsive to the charges and the 1918 election became a corrosive sectional contest. Despite the winning of the war and general prosperity, the Democrats lost twenty-six seats in the House, six seats in the Senate. The Republicans held a majority now in both houses and installed their own committee chairmen.

This sectional election had an unexpected result a few months later. It constitutes one of the most provocative "what ifs" of history.

In January 1919, Wilson headed the American delegation to the Paris peace conference where the Allied nations were to decide the fate of Europe, and for that matter most of the industrial and colonial worlds.

Wilson was received with ovations throughout Europe, even by defeated Germany. He came armed with a fourteen-point program designed to create a new world society.[8] It would be governed by

[8] The general points were: (1) no secret diplomacy or treaties among nations; (2) freedom of the seas in peace and war; (3) removal of economic

the "self-determination of peoples"; would be free from secret diplomacy and wars; and would have an association of nations to maintain international justice.

This golden age appeared to have every chance of success. Germany had already expressed agreement with the fourteen points and the convening Allied nations represented the industrial and military might of the world. Even Bolshevik Russia, though not invited, had expressed a strong desire to be included in the settlement. But such was not to be the case. England had made too many secret agreements granting territories to minor allies. Japan wanted a huge chunk of the Pacific and Far East. And Clemenceau of France, Wilson's most obdurate opponent, wanted revenge on Germany and a return to the old order.

What came out of the conference was the Treaty of Versailles, punitive to the defeated Central Powers, and the League of Nations.

Wilson accepted the treaty as the best obtainable and went home to drum up popular support and obtain the two-thirds vote needed for ratification in the Republican Senate.

In the ensuing debates and votes, the foundation of Wilson's support, not unexpectedly, was the Southern Democrats. But their strength was insufficient and the treaty was defeated. A few days later, John Sharp Williams told the Mississippi legislature, "Men sometimes disparage idealists . . . But the idealists point the way and cheer men's souls." And Carter Glass of Virginia later lamented the lost opportunity for "the nations of the earth to enter into a Covenant which contained the very essence of the Sermon on the Mount . . ."

Woodrow Wilson's hopes for a "new freedom" for the underprivileged of America, and for the underprivileged elsewhere in the world, applied only peripherally to the nation's blacks. It was

---

barriers, including tariffs, as much as possible; (4) reduction of armaments to needs for domestic safety; and (5) adjustment of colonial claims based on negotiated compromise between inhabitants and colonists. The remaining nine points were specific in nature and dealt mostly with territorial adjustments in Europe but included the provision for a "general association of nations."

Wilson who brought blacks into the Democratic party, courting their votes in the 1912 campaign and promising "absolute fair dealing . . . in advancing the interests of their race." But he did not, and would not, present any concrete civil rights programs. His attitude was essentially Southern-paternal. He wished them well, provided they stayed to themselves. He wished for advancement of the race along "sound and sensible lines."

In fact, despite Wilson's lukewarm rhetoric and encouragement of black votes, the growing Jim Crow segregation in federal government expanded under his administration. Jim Crow was becoming the rule not only in the South but in the nation and Wilson went along with the times.

Concurrent with the rise of Jim Crow was the great migration of blacks from the South to Northern cities. This was a direct result of World War I when industries of the North invited black labor and had money and housing and jobs for them. Black aspirations rose and when black soldiers returned from the war the aspirations rose further. In Europe the blacks had not been regarded as inferior but as exotically different and—to hear the stories— desirably different to European women.

Tales spread in the North and South about black soldiers who had been "Frenchwoman-ruined," and reports of black rape and lusts rose to a height unknown since Reconstruction. Race riots and lynchings became weekly occurrences in Michigan and Texas, in Chicago and Little Rock.

Adding fuel to the conflagration was the rise of a secret society which had political ambitions, the Ku Klux Klan.

The first Klan, headed by Confederate General Nathan Forrest, and largely composed of ex-officers, was formed after the Civil War as a guerrilla unit to combat excesses of the radical Republicans and to maintain white supremacy. It withered away after about 1870.

The second Klan had no connection with the original save for one thing, the organizer had seen a story about Forrest's organization in a movie.

The movie was *The Birth of a Nation,* released in 1915.[9] A few months after it appeared in Atlanta, William Simmons, a self-styled Methodist preacher and a man bankrupt in character, assembled a meeting of white-robed figures atop Stone Mountain, Georgia. A cross was burned and the second Klan was begun.

It was a distinct breed from the original, being fanatically antiblack and to only slightly lesser degree anti-Catholic, anti-Semitic, and antiforeign.

From top to bottom it was heavily populated with thugs, swindlers, cowards, and low-life in general. In its appeal, its crude ambitions, and its constituency it closely resembled the National Socialist party which would rise later in Germany. Like the Nazis it seemed to provide an outlet for the militant patriotism aroused by the War and like the Nazis it heavily stressed purity of race.

It built membership during the war under the slogan of "Americanism" and for a short time beginning about 1922 became the dominant political power in many small towns in the states of Texas, Oklahoma, Indiana, Oregon, and Maine, and in big cities like Indianapolis, Little Rock, Dallas, Fort Worth, Houston, Atlanta, and Birmingham. Throughout the nation, unknown thousands of local politicians owed office directly to the Klan and thousands more were so intimidated that they would say or do nothing about it.

In 1922 the Klan, through fund-raising, propaganda, and general electioneering, elected Clifford Walker governor of Georgia, sent Earle Mayfield to the Senate from Texas, and captured the Oklahoma legislature. It contributed to the victories of other prominent politicians, including the election of Alabama's Hugo Black (1927) to the Senate.[10]

The Klan rise did not go unopposed. Its most outspoken enemy was Oscar Underwood of Alabama, who lost his Senate seat to Black because of it. But the most effective opposition came from major Southern newspapers which kept up a steady barrage

[9] The film ran continuously in Southern states until 1930. Wilson reportedly said that any man "who sees it is a Southern partisan for life."
[10] Black later turned against the Klan. He was appointed to the Supreme Court by Franklin Roosevelt.

against the Klan, stirred up the public conscience, and gave courage to politicians who around 1926 began piling up a steady succession of victories in elections against the Klan. The Klan went into rapid decline and disappeared shortly afterward.[11]

There are three reasons why the Klan failed while its European counterpart, the Nazi party, succeeded. First was the American tradition of a free press. When German newspapers spoke against the Nazis, party thugs broke the presses. When Klansmen attacked American journalists, it only increased opposition. Second was the tradition of free speech. American politicians could not be silenced by beatings or murders, such as in Germany. The public wouldn't stand for it. Oh, they'd stand for one or two, but not several in a row. (It should be noted that it is indeed tradition, not rights, that is the operative factor here. The right of free speech and press existed in postwar Germany but the tradition was absent. Therefore, when the right was abrogated, no one thought too much about it.)

The third factor was the absence of a skilled leadership. The Nazis, and Mussolini's Fascists, had politically skillful, decisive men at the top. The Klan was as bankrupt in these areas as it was morally.

In the sixteen-year period between 1912 and 1928, the nation, and most of all the South, went through a rapid series of staggering change—the emergence of the Democratic party and the new freedom, prosperity, then the economic boom of the war and the mixing up of peoples and cultures, the black migration and the phenomenon of the Klan. In addition, there were other powerful forces stirring up the old social order—automobiles and highways and airplanes, the radio, and the movies. More change was of course to come.

In 1928 a series of agricultural disasters hit Southern farms. In late 1929 came the Great Depression, followed in 1930 by the

[11] A third Klan arose in the South in the late 1950s in reaction to school integration and other civil rights advances. It never achieved significant political power, although it did for short periods control some Southern towns, such as Bogalusa, Louisiana, and some counties, such as Neshoba in Mississippi.

worst drought "in the climatological history of the country," according to the Weather Bureau.

The three successive blows completely unsettled the economic and credit system of the South. In desperation, Southern congressmen put aside their Jeffersonian principles and joined other parts of the nation in asking for federal relief. In early 1932, Wright Patman, congressman from Texas, proposed that veterans' bonuses, averaging one thousand dollars per man and due in 1945, be paid immediately. An army of fifteen thousand unemployed veterans marched to Washington to lobby for the Patman bill but were driven out by General Douglas MacArthur, acting under orders from President Hoover.

The bonus bill was defeated and Patman responded by attempting to impeach Andrew Mellon, Hoover's Secretary of the Treasury, who had openly ridiculed the bonus bill.

Patman, pink-cheeked, curly-haired, and thirty-five years old, had come to Congress in 1928 out of northeastern Texas, Hard-Shell Baptist country where the people frowned on music, dancing, public drinking, and cards. (What they favored was church-going, rabbit for Sunday dinner, and Levi Garrett snuff.)

Patman was a good country-style rabble-rouser and the bonus bill was his first big issue in Congress.[12]

He took the floor and accused Mellon of "high crimes and misdemeanors." For two days he argued, and produced a few supporting documents, that Mellon had used his office to enrich himself. Mellon put up a stiff defense and the matter was temporarily tabled. Within a month, Mellon resigned and the impeachment charges were dropped.

In this same year, another Texas congressman, Maury Maverick, then a young tax collector, set out on a hobo trip through Texas, Oklahoma, and Louisiana. He and his companions, he later wrote, "slept in jungles, got lousy, and, what was worse, got preached and lectured at by fourflushing racketeers."[13] He estimated that two thousand people a day, broke and jobless, passed

---

[12] Patman was the most senior member of the Ninety-fourth Congress (1975), having served forty-seven consecutive years.
[13] *A Maverick American* by Maury Maverick (New York: Covici Friede, 1937), pages 150–76.

through such cities as Dallas and New Orleans. Most were farmers and farm workers, but many were insurance men, car salesmen, lawyers, mechanics, and a fourth of all the people were women and children. Maverick said he saw filth and degradation and promiscuity and crime to sicken the mind for life.

Out of this misery came the campaign of Franklin Roosevelt.

Chapter 13
NEW DEAL

Franklin Roosevelt, like Woodrow Wilson, was the hand-selected presidential choice of Eastern machine Democrats. It was not so much that they liked him but that they thought he could win. The previous Democratic candidate, Al Smith of New York, the first Roman Catholic nominated by a major party, had lost heavily in the Protestant South. It was felt that Roosevelt could bring the South back in the fold. Roosevelt was to do better than that. Like Wilson, he was to make the South the very foundation of his political base.

Southern support for Roosevelt was organized by Cordell Hull of Tennessee, long-time congressman (served all but two years from 1907 to 1931) and recently elected U.S. senator. Hull, in meetings with Southern leaders, stressed Roosevelt's patrician background, his part-time residency in Georgia, his commitment to do something about the Depression, and most of all his potential for carrying the Democrats into control of the Congress and the White House. With control of the Congress, the South would regain its committee chairmanships.

By the time the Democratic convention rolled around in 1932, Roosevelt had carried primaries in Georgia, Alabama, and Florida and had the support of every Southern state delegation except three, all of which were supporting "favorite sons."[1]

The favorite sons were House Speaker John Nance Garner of Texas, Harry Byrd of Virginia, and Governor "Alfalfa Bill" Murray of Oklahoma.

The only one of these who had the least chance to become a serious candidate was Garner, who had won the California primary. But he wasn't that interested and his campaign manager, Congressman Sam Rayburn, felt that Roosevelt was the only man who could win the national election for the Democrats. A deal was worked out, Garner released his delegates to Roosevelt and was named the party's vice presidential nominee.

During the convention, the Democratic party was steered further to the left than Roosevelt had intended. The stimulus came from two Southerners: young Claude Pepper of Florida, later senator and congressman; and the boss of Louisiana, acting governor and incumbent Senator Huey Long. Long's push was by far the more effective of the two and Roosevelt's campaign manager, James Farley, later said that in 1932 Roosevelt was "persuaded" to move to the left, and in the mid-thirties moved left again out of fear Long would run against him.

The New Deal took office in March 1933. It was not so heavily dominated by Southern cabinet members as Wilson's government, but Cordell Hull was Secretary of State, the Virginian Claude Swanson was Secretary of the Navy, and South Carolina's Dan Roper was Secretary of Commerce. In addition, South Carolina's Senator James Byrnes became one of Roosevelt's most influential advisers.

On Capitol Hill, the Southerners were back in power. During the Twenties, they had been about the only Democrats in Congress, suffering along under Republican chairmen and Republican Presidents, but piling up seniority. Now, in the House, due to seniority, they chaired twelve of seventeen major committees.

---

[1] This is a strategy whereby a state's convention delegates are pledged to vote for the "favorite son," usually the state's governor. There is rarely any expectation that the "favorite son" can win. Instead, his state's votes for presidential candidate are regarded as negotiable and will be traded off to the nominee who offers the most in return, such as a cabinet appointment of particular interest to the state's political machine.

In the Senate they chaired nine of fourteen major committees. This situation would prevail until the committees were reorganized in 1946.

Southerners also held the party leadership in Congress, which is not dependent upon seniority. Joseph Robinson of Arkansas was majority leader in the Senate, to be succeeded when he died in 1937 by Alben Barkley of Kentucky. In the House, the speaker was Henry Rainey of Illinois (1933), but he was succeeded by Joseph Byrns of Tennessee (1935), William Bankhead of Alabama (1936), and Sam Rayburn of Texas (1940).

It would be these Southern-dominated Congresses which, ironically in view of their political tradition, would rubber-stamp Roosevelt's design for a bureaucratic state.

The proposed laws, each of which required an administering bureaucracy, came to Congress fast and quick. There was an omnibus farm bill, a Tobacco Control Act, a Bankhead Act for cotton, a quota system for sugar, all oriented to the agricultural South. The Southerners found it impossible to oppose them and, indeed, proposed most of them. There followed, in quick deluge, all the relief, job, and regulatory programs of the New Deal. In putting these through, Roosevelt worked closely with a Southern team. The most important of them were:

—Congressman Sam Rayburn of Texas, chairman of the Committee on Interstate and Foreign Commerce, who guided through the Securities Act, the Securities Exchange Act, the Public Utility Holding Company, and that marvelous boon to rural America, the Rural Electrification Act (REA).

—Congressman William Bankhead of Alabama, the quarterback of the House team and one of Congress' most skilled parliamentarians. His brother John was a U.S. senator and also a key figure in the New Deal legislation.

—Joe Robinson of Arkansas, Roosevelt's majority leader in the Senate and somewhat the Lyndon Johnson of his day. In 1935 he pushed through the Emergency Banking Act in seven hours. He was regarded as a "slave driver who kept the Senate under his whip."

—Pat Harrison, senator from Mississippi, a highly effective, though lazy, tactician in the art of compromise, who, as chairman of Senate Finance, guided through laws on social security, revenue acts, and reciprocal foreign trade agreements.

—James Byrnes of South Carolina, a former senator who was Roosevelt's liaison with the Congress. Raymond Moley, a Brain Truster, later said, "I seriously doubt that any other man on Capitol Hill could have carried through" the New Deal legislation as effectively as Byrnes.

Meanwhile, Roosevelt's main Democratic opposition also came from Southerners, three senators: Carter Glass of Virginia, Joe Bailey of North Carolina, and Harry Byrd of Virginia. They viewed the economic regulation and the growth of federal government with horror.

A fourth Senate critic took an opposite view. He didn't think Roosevelt or the Congress was doing enough. He was Huey Long. It was Long that Roosevelt watched the most. Without Long's help in the 1932 convention, Roosevelt would not have been nominated, or so thought James Farley and some others. But this alliance had evaporated, partly because of Long's dissatisfaction with New Deal economics and, to an equal degree, due to Roosevelt's alarm over Long's vote-gathering success. Among other awesome displays, Long had recently guided, through direct intervention, Hattie Caraway of Arkansas into the U. S. Senate, the first woman ever elected. And Long had a talent for the added little touches, like keeping his hat on when he and Roosevelt sat down for a talk.

The Roosevelt presidency, viewed originally as a victory for the South, actually marked the end of the South's 150-year love affair with the Democratic party. Virtually from the day of Roosevelt's election in 1932, the Southerners' power in the party began to dwindle. Their power in the Congress, due to committee appointments, seniority, and something called "The Club," would remain. But it had no solid organizational foundation. It depended too heavily on individual skills and ingenuity. From the election of 1932 onward, Southern political power was engaged in retreat and its successes were the successes of rear-guard actions.

The cause of the falling out had come in 1932 when the party reached out to embrace Northern liberals and blacks everywhere.

These Northern Democrats, who would come to dominate party nominations, party policies, and party seats in the Congress, had differing goals than the Democrats from the South.

Prior to the Roosevelt campaign—with the exception of Wilson—blacks had traditionally voted Republican. But in Roosevelt they saw their true interest—relief for the poor—and they shifted to the Democrats in amazing numbers. The black vote became increasingly important to the Democratic machines in great Northern cities. And the states with the largest electoral votes—New York, California, Texas, Michigan, Ohio, Illinois—all had large black populations who tended to vote in a bloc that could swing close elections.

As the New Deal became more and more Big Government, as it became more and more pro-civil rights, particularly as it became more and more pro-civil rights, Southerners defected and would defect in growing numbers of thousands for the next three decades. And each defection, each election of a Southern Republican, each Southern vote for a Republican presidential nominee, made the South less important to the Democratic party. The gap widened by mutual agreement.

The first visible indication of the rift came not in the election of 1932 but in the election of 1936.

Huey Long, Roosevelt's greatest fear, had been assassinated in the fall of 1935. The Republican opposition looked harmless. The President, possibly having geared up for a fight with Long and now having energy to burn, announced his intention to intervene in Democratic primaries and help his friends and hurt his enemies.

His first stop was Kentucky, where he helped Alben Barkley, who needed no help. He then went to Georgia and took on Senator Walter George, who gleefully joined battle and dealt Roosevelt a resounding defeat. Roosevelt went on to South Carolina, where he got drubbed by senatorial candidate Olin Johnston. He went to Maryland and got flattened again. Friendly Southerners then prevailed on Roosevelt to stay out of any more of their primaries and the President went back to Washington to attend to his own campaign (in which he carried every state but Maine and Vermont). His myth of total political invincibility, however, had been shattered.

In February 1937, Roosevelt took on the Southerners again. He had lost patience with the Supreme Court, which had overturned his National Recovery Act legislation, and called a special meeting of the Cabinet to announce a remedy. Majority leader Robinson, Speaker Bankhead, and three other congressional leaders were present.

They listened stunned as Roosevelt spelled out his plan. He wanted a law giving him, essentially, the power to appoint a new justice for each justice past the age of seventy who had not resigned. Since there were six justices in this category, the effect was to give Roosevelt six new Supreme Court appointments—enough to shape the court to his desires.

Congress clearly had the power to pass such a law. (There is no provision in the Constitution setting out the number of justices.) The Supreme Court itself raised no great fuss outside the walls of its own private dining room. Indeed, Chief Justice Charles Evans Hughes was overheard to remark, "If they want me to preside over a convention, I can do it."

The Congress was not so placid. The Southerners who had been fighting Roosevelt, such as Carter Glass of Virginia, and the Southerners the President had recently enraged in the 1936 primary elections, such as Walter George, raced each other to be the first to denounce the bill.

"I shall oppose it with all the strength which remains to me," said Glass, and added artfully, "But I don't imagine for a minute that it'll do any good. Why, if the President asked Congress to commit suicide tomorrow, they'd do it."

The Republicans stood aside to let the Democrats fight it out. The Southerners were not alone in their opposition. Montana Senator Burton Wheeler, a progressive Democrat, announced, "I tell you, it isn't going to pass, and what's more, I'm going to fight it with everything I've got."

Millard Tydings of Maryland organized a steering committee to beat the bill. Wheeler was chairman and the other key members were Joe Bailey of North Carolina, Harry Byrd of Virginia, Walter George, Carter Glass, and Tom Connally of Texas.

Using the radio—Roosevelt's tool, to great extent—the Democrats stressed the Constitutional issue. Compromise the judiciary, said Bailey, "and it would be violated again and again; and our people would be reduced to the very conditions under which our forefathers suffered." The latter clause was a reference to the so-called "Force Bills" following the Civil War whereby the federal government had used military force in the South to implement its will.

Carter Glass, in another radio speech, said the plan would result in enforced integration and "practically committed the administration . . . to a new Force Bill for the South."

Roosevelt countered with a dishonorable, but slick, bribe. He summoned Senate majority leader Joe Robinson to the White House and promised that if the bill passed, Robinson would be named to the court. Robinson was very popular in the Senate and the Southern bloc of twenty-six senators seemed to be split 50–50 on the issue. Unexpectedly, Robinson (opponents claimed he was probably overtaxed by his work to get on the Supreme Court) dropped dead of a heart attack. Roosevelt was beaten.

To save face for Roosevelt, Vice President John Nance Garner stepped in with a compromise and arranged for approval of certain reforms in court procedures, but no new judges.

In the process of the Supreme Court issue, conservative Republicans and Dixie Democrats had joined together on a few procedural votes. This would come to be called the "conservative coalition" and it would hamstring Democratic Presidents for the next generation. The conservative coalition was an entity with which both the Republican and the Democratic parties would have to deal in the future. In terms of passing or defeating legislation, it would be the main weapon of Southern Democrats for the next thirty years.

With creation of the conservative coalition, the South and the major parties completed a full circle waltz.

Wilson, with Southern backing, had steered the Democrats toward big government but the party had retained its tradition of representing workers, small businessmen, small farmers, states' rights, and a status quo on race. Under Roosevelt, while still identified with the struggling and disadvantaged, the party had gone full sail into big government, massive federal regulation, deficit spending and anti-states' rights. Jefferson's party had become, in a word, Hamiltonian. It had, furthermore, cautiously begun to identify itself with the movement to improve opportunities for blacks.

The Republicans, descendants of the Federalists, remained identified with big business, but in all other respects had become Jeffersonian—pro states' rights, balanced budget, small central government, and implicitly favoring the racial status quo. The Republican party, created to destroy the South and to destroy the Democrats, found itself in alliance with Southern Democrats.

The most consistent performer in the three-party waltz was the South. Throughout, it had adhered somewhat faithfully to the Jefferson principles, advocating, in essence, very little federal activity except to keep the post office running and to tax the rich to benefit the poor, instead of the reverse. The South had, of course, adhered even more religiously to the idol of white supremacy. It followed that idol wherever it was carried and whoever carried it. No backsliding Israelite ever trailed the golden god Baal with more determination.

There were, however, prophets. The South prior to the Civil War had realized the race problem was a class problem, knowledge which was buried in the Jim Crow era. Huey Long resurrected the information. He cared not a damn about black or white. He was keen on the class struggle and improved the black condition without ever mentioning civil rights or states' rights. He stood at the crossroads, signaling his discovery of a new path. We can only ponder what the results would have been had history followed his road.

Chapter 14
HUEY LONG

"Before Huey Long we had nothing. After Huey Long we had something. That was the difference."

Louisiana farmer, 1935

He had a ridiculous button nose, a wad of curly hair, a crumpled suit, and resembled a circus clown. He tended to eat with his mouth open. He got drunk in public, cussed openly on the radio, and his best friends in the East were Mafia bosses. His only close friends in the U. S. Senate were George Norris and Bill Borah, both liberal Northern Republicans. He ruled Louisiana with a near-totalitarian fist. His schemes ranged from the hiring of a professional football squad to play under fake names at Louisiana State University, to a Share-the-Wealth program which would have revolutionized the social and economic system of the nation.

The football team won and the Share-the-Wealth program might have worked. Huey Long was neither crazy nor moronic. He was a brilliant political phenomenon and no Southern politician since Andrew Jackson has so captured the national imagination.

This was fitting, for Huey Long came out of the same populist-frontier soil as Andrew Jackson and had the same give-'em-hell, knock-'em-down style.

The most sensational demonstration of his energy and technique came in 1931–35 when Long was both U.S. senator and acting governor of Louisiana. He would, on whim, rush back to Baton Rouge to dominate committee hearings and storm into the chamber of either house of the state legislature while in session to shout orders to his floor leaders. Laws were jammed through at a rate never seen in an American legislature. On one occasion, forty-two bills were passed in twenty-two minutes. During seven special sessions, he put through 463 bills including 19 amendments to the state constitution.

"The interesting thing," said Long's biographer T. Harry Williams, "is that he was a surprisingly introspective politician. His techniques were condemned as dictatorial [but] he wondered about his role and conduct in the democratic process." He was a dictator who wondered about the morality of his conduct and— typical of the species—decided there was no other way to accomplish his goals.

Long, in a public address, once said, "They say they don't like my methods. Well, I don't like them either . . . I'd much rather get up before a legislature and say, 'Now this is a good law, it's for the benefit of the people, and I'd like for you to vote for it in the interest of the public welfare.'

"Only I know that laws ain't made that way. You've got to fight fire with fire." On another occasion he summarized his operational philosophy: "The means justify the end. I would do it some other way if there was time or if it wasn't necessary to do it this way."

Long was elected governor of Louisiana in 1928. He was assassinated in the state capitol in 1935. In those seven years he brought the state from a semifeudal condition into the twentieth century. Forty years after his death, his legacy was everywhere in the state, in the form of bridges, public buildings, airports, and superhighways. And it was also present in the form of political heirs. His son was a U.S. senator, and his campaign manager, Allen Ellender, who died in 1972, served thirty-five years in the Senate. Another Long was a congressman. The immediate ex-governor, the Secretary of State, federal judges, and justices of the state supreme court were all direct products of the Long machine, holding power forty years after his death, along with a raft of lesser Long office holders.

In his Louisiana domain, Long launched some of the most advanced public works of the time—a network of roads, the largest charity hospital in the nation, free textbooks, and an expanded black-vote registration. He established a generous welfare system and medical system, launched a free-lunch program in the schools and a school-bus transportation system that was in advance of anything in the nation. Louisiana had a medicare and medicaid program thirty years ahead of the nation.

He was among the first to build a superhighway, constructing during the Depression a four-lane, ninety-mile highway between New Orleans and Baton Rouge. He didn't say he did it to create jobs. He said he wanted to cut down his own travel time between the cities.

All poor people, black and white, shared in the work and the benefits. He did not go out and stump for civil rights. There is no evidence anywhere that he cared one way or the other about racial matters. But he did believe in class opportunity. "In Louisiana a Negro's just the same as anybody else; he ought to have a chance to work and to make a living, and to get an education," he said.

Once he explained to a Negro leader how he had managed to get better medical care for colored people: "Why, down in Louisiana . . . the whites have decided niggahs have got to have public health care. Got to give 'em clinics and good hospitals. Got to keep 'em healthy. That's fair and it's good sense. I said to them: 'You wouldn't want a colored woman watching over your children if she had pyorrhea, would you?' They see the point."[1]

When the Ku Klux Klan leader Hiram Evans threatened to come to Louisiana and campaign against Huey's racial position,

[1] *Romance and Realism in Southern Politics* by T. Harry Williams (Baton Rouge: Louisiana State University Press, 1966), page 81. Professor Williams also reports an anecdote where Huey's brother Earl Long put a reverse twist on prejudice. Earl, in his 1960 congressional campaign, would tell black audiences that he would take care of school integration for them. "Now don't worry. I'm not going to let them make you send your kids to schools with white kids, where they'll lord it over 'em. You're going to have your own schools."

Long gave a statement to the press: "Quote me as saying that that Imperial bastard will never set foot in Louisiana, and that when I call him a sonofabitch I am not using profanity, but am referring to the circumstances of his birth."

Southern politicians as a class are notoriously realistic. The Southerner is not as transient as other Americans and has deeper roots in his community. Politics is his profession and usually he has decided upon it early and studied it from the county courthouse to the state legislature to the governor's office and to the Congress, if he gets there. He knows his constituency and he knows his legislative colleagues, for he has studied them all his life. He rises or he falls in direct relation to his ability to predict what will work with his voters and what will work with other politicians.

Huey Long was the most coldly realistic of them all. He rose far and he had his eye on the White House, a national constituency, and he was not about to be bogged down by prejudice. Asked once if he saw any similarity between himself and Hitler, Long was outraged—not about Hitler's racism, but about Hitler's stupidity.

"Don't liken me to that sonofabitch," he roared. "Anybody that lets his public policies be mixed up with religious prejudices is a plain Goddamned fool."

Louisiana of the 1920s had less than 330 miles of paved road— 300 miles of it a two-lane road tying together Shreveport, Baton Rouge, and New Orleans, leaving 30 miles to service the other 48,000 square miles of the state. The state had only three major bridges and a public educational system that was about on a par with Albania's. There was one small and archaic public hospital. In general, the public services were about the same as when the territory had been settled in 1718. Maybe worse. More than half of the streets of New Orleans were unpaved and the downtown French Quarter had no sewerage. (Outhouses were used and the contents cleaned out periodically by what amounted to a caste of "untouchables"—men who hauled the sewage in wagons to the Mississippi River and dumped it.)

After seven years of Huey Long, financed by state-issued bonds,

Louisiana had 3,800 miles of paved roads, more than forty major bridges, and a grandly expanded educational system with such details as the free lunch and the free textbooks (innovations which boosted enrollment 20 per cent). Long repealed the poll tax and inaugurated free night schools for more than a hundred thousand illiterate blacks and whites. He actively recruited black voter registration and, in sum, in a few years had taken Louisiana from a backward tropical colony into what was then America's most innovative and progressive state.

Throughout its history, the South has been keenly conscious of class structure and class struggle. Jefferson's Democratic party was founded as a defensive reaction to the power of New England's mercantile class. And until the 1840s, the South's most obvious problem—the status of Southern blacks—was viewed by native Southerners such as Jefferson, Madison, and Randolph, and by visitors like Tocqueville as a matter of class prejudice rather than racial prejudice. John Calhoun, called by later historians the "American Marx," firmly believed that the North-South struggle, waged on the ostensible issue of states' rights and slavery, was in fact a class war.

The polarization of the racial issue in the 1840s, however, blinded the South to the class basis of its predicament for a century and more afterward. But there were interludes of perception and among these was the phenomenon of Huey Long. Both the man and the phenomenon were born in Winn Parish, the Populist stronghold of Louisiana.

The Populist movement began in the 1870s when farm prices dropped so low that farmers of the West and South found that, because of deflation, the money they had to repay on debts was worth more than the money they had borrowed. But they were growing poorer, bankers and capitalists of the East were growing richer. And while they burned their crops because costs of fuel and transportation were too high to make marketing profitable, owners of mines and railroads had become millionaires.

By 1891 the class consciousness of the farmers climaxed in creation of the Populist party. At a party convention in Omaha the following year, the Populists adopted a platform calling for abolition of national banks, government ownership of railroads, a graduated income tax, plenty of paper money, civil service reform, an eight-hour work day, direct election of senators, and free coinage of silver.[2]

The goal of the Populist party was to replace the Democrats as the nation's second major party by forming an alliance of the farmers of the West and the South with the industrial workers of the East. This of course was the major coalition of the original Democratic party.

The Populist party was formed in the Midwest but by any standards the South was the center of Populist strength. The Southerners were more radical than their Western allies, led by William Jennings Bryan. (Bryan thought that the unlimited coinage of [Western-mined] silver would remedy the economic ills of farmers and industrial workers by putting a greater amount of money into circulation.)

The Southerners, led by the nation's most able Populist, Tom Watson of Georgia, were the principal architects of the Populist platforms which proposed an income tax, public election of senators, government ownership of railroads, plenty of paper money, postal banks, Civil Service reform, and an eight-hour workday. Many of these planks were later put into law by Southern Democratic leaders during the Wilson administration.

Watson was the acknowledged Southern leader. Born in 1856, he served one term in Congress (1891–92), where he worked for free delivery of rural mail. He was the Populist nominee for Vice President in 1896 and for President in 1904. And he served in the U. S. Senate from his election in 1920 until his death in 1922.[3]

[2] "Free silver" became a slogan of the Populists and, later, of William Jennings Bryan of the Democratic party. Like all slogans, it meant many things to many people, being primarily a rallying cry of the "outs" and the underprivileged against the "ins" and the privileged. Specifically it was a narrow sectional issue involving Westerners who wanted the government to begin buying western silver for use in coins.

[3] Watson was replaced in the Senate by Rebecca Latimer Felton, an eighty-seven-year-old Populist and leader of the women's rights movement. Mrs. Felton, appointed as a gesture to Watson's Populism and a political power in her own right, was the first woman senator.

Watson's invective, covering half a century of politics, was uncompromising. Bankers, railroaders, merchants, and corporation executives were given regular floggings. Watson kept alive the Southern class consciousness during the worst years of racial polarity. Over and over he stressed that the poor white man and the poor black man were equally victims of economic exploitation. They could save themselves, he preached, only by working together. "You are made to hate each other," he told them, "because upon that hatred is rested the keystone of the arch of financial despotism which enslaves you both. You are deceived and blinded that you may not see how this race antagonism perpetuates a money system which beggars you both."

To implement the principles of Watson and other Populists, the party put in platforms enunciating the right of blacks to vote and hold office. Blacks, though usually only in token numbers, were present at important party functions. When, at a national convention, it was proposed to put a black into high party office, the Southern delegates roared their approval and a Georgian rose to say: "I wish to say that we can stand that down in Georgia."

In the presidential election of 1892, the Populists, with James Weaver of Iowa as their nominee, put together 1,029,960 popular votes. In the congressional election two years later, they pulled 1,471,000 votes. That election marked the high-water mark of the Populist party ceased to be a national force, though a few leaders adopted by the Democratic party in 1896 and soon thereafter the Populist party ceased to be a national force, though a few leaders such as Watson survived.

The Populist party had been absorbed by the Democrats but "populism" was not dead in the South, only dormant. It resurrected itself briefly during the Wilson era in a modified form known as "Progressivism." Class consciousness and the awareness of exploitation were still present but the rhetoric had become moderate enough to embrace professional classes and city dwellers. The extreme language of revolution was put aside and Progressive leaders were more likely to be lawyers, editors, and businessmen rather than farmers. They talked of controlling big corporations, enlarging public education, and federal aid for agriculture, things which Progressives such as Senator Hoke Smith of Georgia helped put through during the Wilson administration.

Populism rose up again in its radical form with the launching of the career of Huey Long.

Huey Long's birthplace of Winn Parish had a history of Populist sassiness. Among the leaders was his father, Huey Pierce Long, Sr., who in a 1935 interview, at age eighty-three, was still thumping for revolution.

"There wants to be a revolution, I tell you. I seen this domination of capital, seen it for seventy years. What do these rich folks care for the poor man? They care nothing—not for his pain, nor his sickness, nor his death . . . Why the (rich) women don't even comb their own hair . . . They tried to pass a law saying that only them as owned land could vote. And when the war came, the man that owned ten slaves didn't have to fight . . . Maybe you're surprised to hear talk like that. Well, it was just such talk that my boy was raised under, and that I was raised under."

Winn Parish is located in northern Louisiana and it has a reputation for cantankerousness that dates back to before the Civil War, being known, scornfully, as "the free State of Winn." When Lincoln was elected, Winn instructed its delegate to the state convention to vote against secession. Why fight to save another man's slaves? When Louisiana joined the Confederacy, many of Winn's youths fled to join the Union Army while wiser ones took to the woods rather than risk death with either side.

During the 1870s, Winn formed its own People's party and kept its distance from the Democratic machinery. When the Populist party was born, Winn sent three Populists to the state legislature. And Winn went Socialist in 1908 when, after a visit by Socialist presidential nominee Eugene Debs, Winn's parish government declared itself to be "Socialist."

The American Longs began in Maryland sometime prior to the Revolutionary War and were fairly well off, an ancestor, James Long, being an Episcopal minister and a physician with a degree from Baltimore College. They had drifted for a short time into Ohio where Huey's grandfather, John Long, was born and then down into Mississippi where John Long married Huey's grand-mother, a Wingate. John Long established a farm in Winn Parish in 1859, and arrived as a typical Southern farmer, neither poor, nor a slaveowner, nor a gentleman planter.

From the beginning they were substantial members of the community. One of John Long's sons became president of the bank and another, Huey's father, expanded the original farm until it was one of the largest of the region. There Huey was born in 1893.

For his entire political career, Huey Long would identify himself with the poor and spread tales of his red-necked family scratching a bare existence out of the Winn Parish soil. In fact, the family was well-off and influential and, though radical in its politics, middle class in its comforts and in its emphasis on education. Huey and his brothers all received either a high school or college education.

Huey's first involvement in a public controversy came at the beginning of World War I. Huey and his friend, State Senator S. J. Harper, opposed American participation.

Harper was a wealthy Winn parishioner and Huey a young lawyer. Together they worked up a pamphlet asserting that the war in Europe was being fought by the poor for the benefit of the rich, a view which then was neither as acceptable nor reasonable as it might seem today. Harper, who signed the pamphlet, said that 2 per cent of the American people owned 70 per cent of the wealth and that if a war was to be fought, why it should be a war of the poor against the rich.

Harper was indicted for the pamphlet by a federal grand jury on a farfetched charge of violating the Espionage Act. Huey defended him, saying that the indictment "was nothing less than an attempt to coerce a reputable official of this state, whose views are not in accord with the war profiteers."

Huey sailed into the case with a plan to turn the government's policeman-like suspicions to his own advantage. He explained his tactic in his autobiography *Every Man a King:*

"I felt the case rested on the selection of the jury. We found out that the prospective jurors and ourselves were being closely shielded, either by agents of the government or by somebody else. I ventured upon the expedient to take advantage of such surveillance. I would take off Juror A, whom we did not desire to serve on the jury. Always where I could be seen, I would buy him a drink. I would buy him something to eat. I would talk with him in close, confidential tones, even to the point of whispering in his ear about everything under the sun except the Harper case. I did that with several of them, all prospective jurors whom we wanted excused."

When the trial got under way, each of the would-be jurors was asked if Huey had talked with them about the case. Each, quite truthfully, said no. The prosecution, convinced they were lying, excused them until the list of potentially hostile jurors was exhausted. Huey won the case.

In 1923, on his thirtieth birthday, Huey announced for governor. He revealed his "Share Our Wealth" program and stressed the class struggle, the poor were being exploited by the rich. With shirt half-open, wet with sweat, he campaigned from atop tree stumps and farm wagons at nearly every town and country crossroads in the state. On the eve of election, he felt he had won the farm vote to his cause and he predicted that if the next day were sunny he would win. The dirt roads would be dry and the farmers could get to town for their vote. It rained, the state turned into a bog, and Long lost.

He ran again in 1928. Where he had been a wild man before, he was now a one-man revolution. He had, in the intervening years, developed a windmill, arm-flailing style. He would squinch up his eyes, tear off his coat, and burlesque the dignified style of his opponents. He laid them out with invective and elaborated on the details of their ancestry and their morals. The laws of slander did not bother him and he would accuse former governors, judges, legislators, and newspaper editors of cracking safes, of whoring with women, of selling their souls to the oil companies.

The state in fact had been owned lock, stock, and barrel by the vested interests, the oil companies, the banks, and the lumber industry. Their financial contributions, their bribes, and their political machines controlled state and local government. The common people were regarded simply as a source of controlled votes and a pool of unskilled cheap labor. They were malnourished, diseased, and illiterate. They could not read newspapers and they were kept without roads or schools or other forms of communication with the outside world. They depended upon the landlord, the company store, and the political boss for their survival and were as firmly locked into their condition as the most primitive inhabitant of the Amazon jungle. Prior to 1928, Louisiana and its people were little more than a subtropical colony, a source of raw products for outside interests.

Long, going from crossroads to crossroads, changed this. He denounced the masters as "thieves, bugs and lice . . . plundering high-binders." He lashed the state administration as being worse than carpetbaggers. In Cajun country, at a river landing beside the Evangeline Oak, the source of Longfellow's poem, he dwelt eloquently on unfulfilled promises:

"Where are the schools that you have waited for your children to have, that have never come? Where are the roads and the highways that you spent your money to build, that are no nearer now than ever before? Where are the institutions to care for the sick and disabled? Evangeline wept bitter tears in her disappointment. But they lasted through only one lifetime. Your tears in this country, around this oak, have lasted for generations. Give me the chance to dry the tears of those who still weep here."

Everywhere, Long's greatest joy, and his greatest huzzahs from the crowd, revolved around his pledge to shove a new tax of five cents a barrel down the throat of Standard Oil. That tax would pay for the schools and the hospitals.

In the election of 1928, the day held sunny and Long won. His inauguration in Baton Rouge reminded one of Jackson's as President a hundred years earlier. The people, at his invitation, came to see *their* governor. They came from farms and towns from across the state. They came on foot, by mule wagon, on horseback, by model-T Ford and by bus. Some poled their pirogues through swamps that reached almost to the capitol steps.

The women were in their calico Sunday best. The men were gallused, tobacco-chewing, and felt-hatted. Some of the visiting farmers were timid and awed by the city, but others swaggered triumphantly on the streets.[4] The revolution was on.

Once in office, Long swept out the old bureaucracy and installed his own men. Though faced with a balky legislature, he began making good on his promises of paved roads, free hospitals, free schoolbooks, and the five-cent tax on every barrel of refined oil and gasoline. The newspapers and businessmen howled that he would drive industry out of Louisiana and Standard Oil began suggesting to friendly legislators the possibility of impeachment. The House impeached him on a charge that Long had intimidated a newspaper publisher by threatening to expose the fact that the publisher's brother was in an insane asylum. Other formal charges followed but Long beat the impeachment and seized control of the legislature.

In 1930, Long decided to run against incumbent U. S. Senator Joseph Ransdell. He would run while still governor and he faced the problem that if he won he would be both governor and senator. (Ransdell's Senate term expired in March 1931; Huey's gubernatorial term didn't expire until fourteen months after that time.) The normal course would have been for Long to resign in favor of the lieutenant governor. He had no intention of doing that, however, because Lieutenant Governor Paul Cyr was a member of the anti-Long machine.

Putting that problem to one side, Long sailed into Ransdell as a creature of the vested interests. He claimed Ransdell had entered into some unspecified corrupt arrangement with Sam Zemurray, a millionaire fruit importer, and had U. S. Marines sent to Central America to protect Zemurray's investments. Huey also liked to point out the results of Ransdell's long years in office:

1. *We lost the United States Mint.*

2. *We lost the Federal Reserve Bank.*

3. *The United States Navy Yards in New Orleans were closed down.*

---

[4] Nearly half a century later, Louisiana continued to have the most colorful gubernatorial inaugurations in the South and in the nation. Every new governor since Long has staged an open-house celebration with barbecues, music, dancing, and gospel singing—hoe-downs seldom attended by fewer than a hundred thousand people and often more.

4. *The United States Army abandoned the military post at Jackson Barracks.*

5. *We lost a station on the Transcontinental Air Mail Route.*

WE HAVE NOT YET LOST THE POST OFFICE.

Two million of the above and other posters were distributed during the campaign. And Huey carried on with his stump-speaking:

"If you believe that Louisiana is to be ruled by the people, that the poor man is as good as the rich man, that the people have a right to pass on issues themselves; if you believe that this is a state where every man is king but no man wears a crown, then I want you to vote for Huey Long for the United States Senate."

There was a huge turnout in the senatorial election and Huey Long buried Ransdell.

While waiting to take his Senate seat, Long styled himself "Governor and United States Senator-elect." He vowed that his ambitious lieutenant governor, Cyr, would "not serve as governor one minute."

Cyr impulsively took the oath of governor before a notary public and declared that Huey had legally vacated the office when he was elected senator. There was one hitch. Cyr had to present his oath-of-office papers to the secretary of state, Alice Lee Grosjean, a close friend of Huey's. Long placed National Guard troops around her office and Cyr was unable to present his papers.

Long then announced that insofar as Cyr had taken the oath as governor, he had vacated his office of lieutenant governor. Long appointed his own lieutenant governor, the president pro tem of the state Senate, and went off to Washington. The state was still in Long's control. He would serve, in fact, from 1931 until his death in 1935 as both governor and senator.

Huey Long's impudence made him a national figure long before he reached the Senate. He was once photographed with former President Calvin Coolidge and he suggested to photographers that they use the caption, "The ex-President of the United States and the future one." He asked Coolidge if the Herbert Hoovers were good housekeepers. Coolidge was taken aback, and Huey explained, "When I was elected in Baton Rouge, I had to tear down the mansion. It started a hell of a row. I don't want to have to tear down the White House."

From the day he set foot in the U. S. Senate he began shattering tradition. He ignored the regulation against smoking and used the clerk's desk as a resting place for his cigar while he took the oath.

Then the senior Louisiana senator, Edwin Broussard, approached Long and said, "Huey, there is a rule here that a senator from one state should escort a new senator from that state when he takes the floor."

Long replied, "Edwin, when I reached here this morning, I read in the newspapers . . . that you had not decided whether you would or would not introduce me."

"I won't introduce you," said Broussard, tight-lipped with anger, "unless you ask me to."

"Don't hold your breath until I do," Long replied and strolled into the chamber alone.

It was also customary for freshmen senators to wait many months, even years, before making an important speech. Long made his within three months. As they were presented in the first speech and refined in later speeches, Long's arguments went along these lines:

"There is no rule so sure as that one that the same mill that grinds out fortunes above a certain size at the top, grinds out paupers at the bottom. The same machine makes them both; and how are they made? There is so much in the world, just so much land, so many houses, so much to eat and so much to wear. There is enough—yea, there is more—than the entire human race can consume, if all are reasonable.

"All the people in America cannot eat up the food that is produced in America; all the people in America cannot wear out the clothes that can be made in America; nor can all of the people in America occupy the houses that stand in this country." There is enough for everyone, said Long, if the wealth of the super-rich were re-distributed.

"If," Long told the Senate in his maiden speech on April 4, 1932, "we could distribute this surplus wealth, while leaving these rich people all the luxuries they can possibly use, what a different world this would be."

His program envisioned limiting individual fortunes to $5 million. Everyone would be guaranteed a homestead allowance of $6,000 and an annual income of at least $2,000. No one would be permitted to earn above $1 million per year, and surplus millions would be taken by taxes. The government would provide old-age pensions, free education for children through college, a radio, an automobile, and perhaps a refrigerator for each family. The government would purchase farm surpluses and store them until needed by the people. Hours of labor would go up and down to balance consumption against production and, finally, the veterans would receive their bonuses immediately.

Huey ran into instant hostility from the bulk of the Senate. It did not disturb him. He replied, "Rockefeller and Morgan would sleep much safer tonight if they had $100 million under their pillow instead of a billion or two." Then he'd stroll across the chamber and massage the backs of Norris and Borah with the reassuring explanation that they were his ideals. He'd return to his seat and explain he was not a Communist. "I would not take a single luxury away," he would smile, neither "fish ponds for fishing, estates for following the hounds."

His most frequent challenger was the Democratic minority leader Joseph Robinson. Why, said the indignant Robinson, the Louisiana senator's ideas were little less than confiscation of wealth, and Long would advance on him, saying that Robinson was in bed with Herbert Hoover, saying that he wanted Robinson for Vice President—on the Republican ticket.

For Robinson, Huey sprang a new tactic on the Senate, one he had perfected back in Louisiana. Out came a notebook, a list of corporations which were law clients of Robinson. "When a man comes into the Senate," Long shouted, "without enough clients to make a corporal's guard, and winds up representing every big corporate interest, if that don't mean something, what does?"

Huey got tougher each day. Other senators who opposed him had skeletons taken out of their closets and swung high up in the air for all to see. Long mimicked the speech and walk of those he didn't like, goading his victims while the gallery howled with glee. One day Long sent out and bought two big Bibles for the guidance of his Senate colleagues. He said they needed them. One

Bible was insufficient for the work. He so enraged Carter Glass in a mocking speech that the dignified Glass charged to thrash him. Friends intervened.

Meanwhile Long was still running Louisiana and rushed back periodically to push bills through the legislature at a furious pace. He used a marvelously undemocratic system to unclog the legislative calendar. The system was invented by a Cajun legislator during a private meeting in Baton Rouge. The situation was that anti-Long members of the legislature had introduced a flood of private interest bills in the hope to so clog the machinery that Long's bills would fail to pass.

What to do? Long asked at a meeting of floor leaders.

The Cajun replied with a question of his own:

"What would happen if we passed all those bills, enemy and friend alike?"

Long thought a long while, then chuckled. "Well, it wouldn't take long would it? We got the votes to just read the title and pass them without debate."

Some excited discussion followed and Long announced, "Tomorrow morning as fast as a number is read on a bill, allow as little talk as possible and let the Speaker recognize our floor leader and let him move the final passage and a previous question. You can clear the calendar in a day that way. I will veto every bill after it is passed that I don't want."

Long handled the private sector with equal dispatch. When he inaugurated his program of free textbooks for the schools, it developed that the state had to borrow $500,000 to pay for the books. Long went to the banks in New Orleans to make the loans.

"They hesitated," he later recalled, "and informed me that their attorneys doubted the legality of loans to the [state] Board of Liquidation."

"We must be guided by our lawyers' advice," the bankers told Long.

"Then I will be guided by your attorneys' advice, too," said Long. "Did you know that the state owes you $935,000 on previous Board of Liquidation loans?"

The bankers replied yes, and that the amount had been ordered paid in the last session of the legislature.

"But it isn't paid yet," Long rejoined, "and what's more it ain't going to be paid. Your attorneys ruled those loans illegal, and if it's illegal to make them it's illegal to pay them. You must follow your lawyers' advice, right?"

Long said he'd keep the $935,000, pay for the schoolbooks, and have $435,000 to spare. He thereupon walked out of the meeting and went to a restaurant "and told the waiter to bring me a thin sandwich. One of the bankers came into the dining room," Long recalled.

"Governor," he said hurriedly, "let's stop this talk where it is. We voted to make you the loan—right now."

Long turned and shouted to the waiter, "Take back that sandwich and fry me a steak!"

In other instances, Long worked to protect the banks. During the Depression (and Long said repeatedly that "Louisiana would not have a Depression were it not part of the United States") many banks closed, having insufficient funds to pay their depositors. In Louisiana, such closings were rare. Long forbade it. He ordered banks to bail each other out or face a crackdown by state examiners.

In one instance among many, Long heard a New Orleans bank was facing a run. He appeared as the doors opened in the morning and informed the long lines of depositors that the state had money deposited and that if they insisted on withdrawing their assets, he'd do the same with the state money. The state had priority and its claims were more than the amount of the bank's cash on hand. The run stopped.

In another example, a leading Mississippi bank prepared to close without paying depositors. Nervous Mississippi depositors, needing money to meet payrolls and other immediate debts, proposed to siphon their long-term deposits from New Orleans banks. The falling domino effect could lead to a bank crash for the entire Mississippi Valley.

A delegation of New Orleans bankers called on Long to propose a Louisiana moratorium so that deposits could not be withdrawn. Long was appalled and shouted to a bodyguard, "Joe, keep these bastards here till I come back. Shoot any of them that try to leave." He went out and phoned the Chase Manhattan in New York. A heavy loan staved off bank runs in both states.

All these stories were told, around the state and around the nation. Long became a folk hero. He was the common man who said "ain't" and wore rumpled clothes and who used good sense to straighten out bankers and other muddleheads. The idea began to build that Long might do equally well if he ran the country.

Long's personal touches, his language and dress, his impudence in the Senate, his sassiness toward Coolidge and Hoover, were quite genuine, not premeditated to build an image. He had an enthusiasm for life and a talent for doing the interesting thing. And the least thing could become interesting.

Once, while driving to Alexandria, Louisiana, he passed a woman and two small children trudging along the road. Long ordered his driver to stop the car. "Going my way?" he asked the woman.

"Yes," she said, "we are headed for Missouri."

Without identifying himself, Long invited the family into his car. He learned they were without money, tired and hungry and trying to hitchhike to Missouri where relatives lived.

Long drove the family to the train depot and personally purchased Pullman tickets to their destination. He gave the woman some cash and left.

"Who was that man?" the woman asked the ticket agent.

"Why, ma'am," he replied, "that is Huey P. Long himself."

By the spring of 1932, with a presidential election due in the fall, Long had enrolled six million Americans as dues-paying members of his "Share Our Wealth" program. He was a political force and when leading Democrats asked him his preferences for President he spoke kindly of John Nance Garner but said the man he most favored was the dark-horse governor from New York, Franklin Roosevelt.

Long got his affairs in order back home by installing a puppet governor, O. K. Allen, a friend of his from Winn Parish. He attended a New Orleans dinner and announced:

"I'm leaving state politics for good. I've done all I can for Louisiana; now I want to help the rest of the country. The liberal element is running all over the world and they'll soon be in power in America. When they are, we'll put an end to multimillionaires and bring back prosperity." He left, but he had no intention of "leaving state politics." Instead, he drove back to Baton Rouge and marched into his new thirty-four-story capitol skyscraper. (Long wanted the state capitol to be the tallest structure in Louisiana, which it was until the 1960s.)

He sat down in Governor Allen's chair and began giving Allen orders. (Allen was accustomed to being bossed. One day during a recent legislative session, Long had called out roughly, "Oscar, go get me those goddamn bills we was talking about. Embarrassed, Allen pretended not to hear. Long howled, "Goddamn you, Oscar, I can break you easy as I made you! Now hop to those goddamn bills!" Allen hopped.)

As Long went on the campaign trail for Roosevelt, *Time* magazine gave a box score on Long's accomplishments:

"During his four-year rule in Louisiana energetic Huey Long has reduced property assessments 20 per cent. He has distributed 600,000 free school books. At his free night schools 175,000 illiterates over 21 learned to read and write. Senator Long is responsible for 2,500 miles of new paved roads, 6,000 miles of new gravel roads. Thanks to him, twelve new bridges are about to span Louisiana rivers."

Long reveled in such statistics. "There may be smarter men than me but they ain't in Louisiana," he liked to brag.

Roosevelt, of course, got the Democratic nomination and won his election and shortly afterward James Farley, the campaign manager, publicly stated that Huey Long was one of six men most important in winning the White House for Roosevelt. Huey returned to the Senate, expecting to have a large voice in the New Deal. Instead, differences between Long and Roosevelt arose almost immediately. They came down to one thing: Roosevelt didn't go quite far enough to suit Long.

Roosevelt took office in March 1933, and the first thing he asked for from Congress was a banking bill which gave him dictatorial powers over banks, authorized the impounding of all gold, and provided for a new issue of paper money.

The bill was the first business of Congress and it passed through the House two hours after being introduced. In the Senate, where it would pass five and a half hours later, it was delayed by Huey Long.

Long took the floor while Eleanor Roosevelt sat in the visitor's gallery with yarn and needles, knitting, knitting, knitting. The benefits of the bill extended only to Federal Reserve member banks. State banks were omitted from coverage and Long offered an amendment to sweep every bank in the land under the shelter of the Federal Reserve.

Carter Glass of Virginia rose in anger.

Glass: The Senator has such ignorance of the whole problem that he wants the President to cover fourteen thousand state banks into the Federal Reserve without knowing a thing in the world about them.

Long: What will the little banks do in the little county seats?

Glass: Little banks! Little corner grocerymen who get together ten thousand dollars and then invite the deposits of their community and then at the very first gust of disaster topple over and ruin their depositors! What we need in this country are real banks and real bankers.

Glass won the vote, the bill passed 73–7, but Long won the votes and hearts of innumerable little corner grocerymen.

In this year of 1933, Long began to use the filibuster and within three years was the acknowledged world champion filibusterer of the United States Senate, the title good for life and no challengers need apply. In one record-breaking instance, Long held the floor for fifteen and a half consecutive hours of talk.

The filibuster and Long were natural partners. The filibuster was invented to protect minority interests and Long often was a minority of one against the rest of the Senate. He could talk and block all other legislation and Senate business for as long as he could hold the floor. In other words, for as long as he held the floor, one man could block the legislation of the Republic and its 140 million people. Business could not resume until the Senate majority leader negotiated with him or wore him out.

The filibuster does not exist in the House of Representatives, nor in the houses of any other national parliament. It exists only in the United States Senate, and it is a truly great, an inspiring invention. Huey Long was a master of it.

The Senate has abided by the filibuster despite enormous aggravations, and Long was probably the most exasperating of all filibusterers. During one filibuster, Long noticed he was playing to an almost empty house.

"Mr. President," he told the chair, "I desire to ask that every senator be made to stay here and listen to me, unless he has himself excused."

"In the opinion of the present occupant of the chair," said Vice President John Garner, "that would be unusual cruelty under the Bill of Rights." But he gave Long what he asked for.

Although Senate rule and custom requires that filibusters have some relevancy to the bill in question, Long made no pretense of relevancy, nor did he have restraint in the vitriol he heaped upon opponents. His enemies were "chinch bugs," "scoundrels," "garbage politicians," and as "worthless as tits on a boar."

Like John Randolph's filibusters a century before, Long's discourses rambled over all the knowledge of man. He quoted from Frederick the Great, Victor Hugo, and Joseph Touro (an obscure nineteenth-century Louisiana philanthropist). He would dictate recipes for the Congressional Record. "First let me tell senators what potlikker is. Potlikker is the residue that remains from the commingling, heating, and evaporation"—and here he got mixed up—"anyway, it is in the bottom of the pot!" It should be prepared, he said, by first boiling turnip greens, and then Long held up a wastebasket and showed how to put the greens in. He also told how to make a Sazerac cocktail[5] and oysters Rockefeller.

Long mused aloud: "I wonder if we could not print these recipes as a [separate] Senate document and send them out—it would do an immense amount of good" for the country.

---

[5] Long's driver and bodyguard, Jim Brocato, was thoroughly instructed in making the Sazerac so that Long could have it wherever they traveled. It consists of one ounce Bourbon, one teaspoon sugar, one teaspoon Pernod, two drops Angostura bitters, two drops Peychaud bitters, and a twist of lemon. The ingredients are stirred, then strained into a chilled glass.

One of Long's most skillful and successful filibusters came on the last day of the second session of the congress, June 18, 1934. Long wanted a law which would block foreclosures on bankrupt farmers and instead allow overdue mortgages to be paid off in installments. The bill, not much liked by the Administration or the Republicans, had been approved by the House and was in conference committee, where minor differences between the House and Senate versions were being worked out. On this last day, however, the conference committee had "lost" the House bill and Long was suspicious.

He took the floor and said it would have to be "found" and acted upon. "There is something miraculous about this. There is a malignant influence pursuing the House every time it deals with the farm bankruptcy bill. They are all set, ready to go, and lo and behold, they have lost the papers again." He said he would filibuster until they were found.

Administrative leaders recognized that all the emergency bills awaiting passage would be jammed up and perhaps lost entirely by a Long filibuster. There was a flurry of inquiries to the House. Then, Majority Leader Robinson, hating Long, announced: "I have just been informed that the papers to which the senator refers are on their way to the Senate now."

"Glory be!" said Long, but he would not give up the floor until the bill arrived. "It will not hurt Congress to wait awhile and listen to me. Do not be in a hurry. Many people have gotten into their buggies and have driven forty miles to hear me, back home." The bill showed up shortly thereafter and was passed.

Such tactics, because they were successful, did not endear Long to the Senate power structure. During another filibuster, Long was interrupted by an angry Kenneth McKellar, senator from Tennessee. McKellar, apropos of nothing except frustration at seeing a Long filibuster, said Long had no influence in the Senate. He could not "get the Lord's Prayer endorsed in this body if he undertook to do so . . ."

This brought laughs, including a laugh from Long, and Tom Connally of Texas, annoyed at the outburst, reminded the chair, "The occupants of the galleries are not in order."

Alben Barkley of Kentucky interrupted: "I appeal to the Chair not to be too harsh with the occupants of the galleries. When people go to the circus they ought to be allowed to laugh at the monkey."

Long gave a wickedly smiling riposte: "Mr. President, I resent that statement about my friend from Tennessee."

In between filibusters, Long attended to his business in Louisiana and became a frequent visitor to New York. There, in 1933, he became friends with several Cosa Nostra leaders and most particularly with Frank Costello, Lucky Luciano's chief aide. In the New Yorker Hotel the two made a deal whereby Costello received an illegal—and secret—franchise to control casino and slot machine gambling in Louisiana. In return, Long was to receive approximately 10 per cent of the gross revenues. (The New York racketeers set up shop in Louisiana shortly before Long's death and paid the agreed-upon "tax" to Long's political heirs.) The arrangement is peculiar because Long never in his career showed much interest in money for his personal use. He probably intended that the Cosa Nostra graft would be used in his political campaigns. This fit with Long's doctrine: "The ends justify the means." Graft, in the millions, honeycombed the Long machine, but none of it stuck to Huey. He wasn't interested. He died with a modest estate of $115,000.[6]

[6] According to *Huey Long,* the Pulitzer Prize-winning biography written by T. Harry Williams, Huey kept huge amounts of cash in a secret "deduct box." When Huey was in Louisiana, the box was kept in a safe in his suite at the Roosevelt Hotel in New Orleans. While in Washington, it stayed in a safe at the Mayflower Hotel and was later moved to the Riggs National Bank. It was supposed to contain more than $1 million and affidavits of evidence damaging to President Roosevelt and other political enemies of Long. The box disappeared immediately after Long's death and its contents have never been made public. Long's connections with the Mafia and Cosa Nostra are equally mysterious. At Huey's 1928 gubernatorial inauguration, the only celebrity guest was Mayor Big Bill Thompson of Chicago, a partner of racketeers Johnny Torrio and Al Capone. Thompson and Long were the major speakers at the ceremony and watching from the wings was another gangland figure, Bob Maestri, a New Orleans professional gambler who was Huey's chief financial contributor and adviser and later mayor of New Orleans. Professor Williams in *Huey Long* states that Long had no organized crime connections and that Mayor Thompson was present only because he and Huey both "were interested in flood control." With due re-

Meanwhile, in 1932 Long gave a startling demonstration of just how effective he could be in the public arena.

It was the year of course in which Huey had contributed so greatly to Roosevelt's victory. In the same year, Huey invaded Arkansas on a seven-day blitzkrieg to elect the first woman to a full term in the U. S. Senate. (Mrs. Felton, who succeeded Tom Watson of Georgia and was the first woman senator, was an appointee.)

Long's candidate was Hattie Caraway, wife of Senator Thaddeus Caraway, a colorful but not particularly talented senator who had died abruptly in November 1931 with more than a year of his term to serve.

The Democratic party leaders of Arkansas had arranged an unopposed, *pro forma* election to install the widow Mrs. Caraway for a brief interim term in her husband's seat. When Huey Long was sworn into the Senate in January 1932, he had been assigned the desk next to her. She stood up and shook hands and, as she said later, "treated him like a human being in the general to-do about him." They became friends. Long was further impressed

---

spect to Professor Williams, Mayor Thompson had about as much interest in flood control as does a lobster in the orbit of the planets. Huey Long's arrangement with Frank Costello was first revealed in New York City grand jury testimony given in August and September 1939, four years after Huey's death. Costello and other associates of New York Cosa Nostra families reluctantly spelled out the details of the gambling franchises given by Long in return for a percentage of the take. Additional corroboration came from the fact that Costello's organization, using slot machines shipped down from New York, began operation in New Orleans and elsewhere in Louisiana two months prior to Huey's death, and continued to operate and expand until the Kefauver investigations of 1951. Professor Williams and Huey's son U. S. Senator Russell Long disbelieve the Costello testimony and point out that it came four years after Huey's death when he could not refute it. Nevertheless, there is substantial documentation of close relationships between members of the Long machine and the Cosa Nostra following his death. For instance, Huey's bodyguard, James Brocato, was chief collector of the New Orleans slot machines operation. A final curiosity is that Senator Russell Long in 1946 purchased his Baton Rouge house from Frank Coppola, a Costello lieutenant sent down from New York to supervise the Louisiana operation. In an interview with the author, Senator Russell Long said the sale was a coincidence, that he never met Frank Coppola and learned of his notoriety only when Coppola was deported to Sicily months after the real estate transaction.

when she was one of the few senators to vote for his bill limiting income to $1 million per year.

Back in Arkansas, an election had been scheduled for August 1932 to fill the upcoming six-year term. Several powerful Arkansas politicians had already entered the lists and it was expected Mrs. Caraway would gracefully retire to her home and leave the work to the men. Privately, she had made up her mind. She would run. When she mentioned this to Huey Long, who had become her political adviser, he counseled against it. "You haven't a chance to win." She agreed that she had no prospects but said she would go down fighting.

Twenty-four hours later, Huey came into her Senate office. "Mrs. Caraway," he said, "I'm going to come into your campaign." She objected, saying she feared he would use it as an excuse to jump on Majority Leader Robinson, the senior senator from Arkansas. Huey promised he would not. The partnership was formed.

Before dawn on August 1, 1932, a caravan left Shreveport and headed for the Arkansas line. In the lead was a huge black car in which sat Huey and a bodyguard of Louisiana State Police. He was followed by seven trucks. Two of them were constructed as mobile offices with loudspeakers attached and a platform on the roof so that Huey could use them as a stage. Huey would be with one truck while the other set up at the next stop on the itinerary. That way he could cover five and six towns every day. The other trucks carried campaign propaganda, batteries, electrical tools, electricians and carpenters, and other conveniences for setting up political rallies.

Huey's first stop was Magnolia, Arkansas. He hit it at nine o'clock in the morning and the dusty town square was jammed with people, the town being swelled to double, triple, and, by some estimates, quadruple size by farmers and their families from the surrounding area.

His speech was typical of all the speeches he gave in Arkansas:

"We're all here to take the feet of six bullies off the neck of one little defenseless widow woman . . . We have more food in this country . . . than we can eat up in two years if we never plowed another furrow or fattened another shote—and yet people are hungry and starving. We have more cotton and wool and leather than we could wear out in two years if we never raised another boll of cotton, sheared another sheep, or tanned another hide— and yet people are ragged and naked. We have more houses . . . and yet people are homeless . . .

"You people wonder why your belly's flat up against your backbone?" Because wealth had become concentrated. Five hundred and forty men on Wall street made more millions in their private income than did all the farmers of the country put together. They controlled the Congress like an owner controlled his restaurant. "They've got a set of Republican waiters on one side and a set of Democratic waiters on the other side, but no matter which set of waiters brings you the dish, the legislative grub is all prepared in the same Wall Street kitchen."

He recounted how his "Share the Wealth" legislation had been defeated in the Congress. Sure, he had proposed to limit income to one million dollars. "One measly, lousy, silvery million dollars . . . Why, it was awful! That meant that if one of those birds stepped under an electric fan in the summertime to cool off, he wouldn't be getting but about four dollars a minute while he was doing it. That meant that if he went to bathe and shave, he wouldn't get but about five hundred dollars richer by the time he got his clothes back on."

In his campaign against the rich, Long asked the audiences, who had supported Huey Long? Very few senators, but one was Hattie Caraway.

She was a brave woman who had defied Wall Street and now the big politicians had "their feet on her neck." Huey swore they would take them off before he left Arkansas.

Mrs. Caraway spoke briefly at this and subsequent meetings, improving rapidly as she gained experience. Huey said she was learning at the hands of the master. Arkansas politicians and newspapermen, drawn from across the country, were amazed at the efficiency of the campaign, the military-like precision by which the Long forces moved from town to town, set up, and moved on. Huey's own car drove over the gravel roads at seventy to eighty miles an hour and he blew out six sets of tires during the campaign. Candidates for lesser offices began to follow the caravan, seeking the crowds to hand out their own pamphlets. At Little Rock, Huey and Mrs. Caraway drew thirty thousand people or more. Newspapers tagged it the largest meeting of any kind ever held in the state.

Everywhere he demonstrated the personal touch that made him unique. At almost every stop, somewhere during the talking, an infant would cry. Huey would stop and, with outstretched finger, direct one of his men to go into the crowd with a glass of water. If the infant continued to cry, Huey would reach into his pocket and send out an all-day sucker. While this was going on, he would lecture the audience:

"Ninety-nine times out of a hundred, when a baby cries, it's only thirsty and if you give it a drink of water it goes right back to sleep. That's a good thing to know when you're not so fixed that you can hire nurses to take care of your children like the rich people do."

Arkansas had not seen a campaign like Huey Long's and one observer compared it to "a circus hitched to a tornado." It lasted seven days, no longer, and on election eve Huey was back in New Orleans. The returns came in and it was a Caraway landslide. She piled up more votes than all six of her opponents combined, no runoff was necessary, and Hattie Caraway became the first woman elected to a full Senate term.

Immediately upon his return home, Huey launched another Senate campaign, the September Louisiana election for the seat of incumbent Edwin S. Broussard, the man who had refused to formally introduce Huey Long to the Senate.

"Broussard's been one of Wall Street's own," Huey roared. "Watch us clean that bird's plow for him."

Huey's hand-selected candidate was John Overton, a Long protégé and state legislator. To run the Overton campaign, Huey named Allen Ellender, later a U.S. senator himself. Overton had very little to do with his own campaign. Asked once if he had been consulted about the selection of Ellender and a co-manager, Harvey Peltier, Overton replied, "I was consulted this way, I was

advised that they had been selected." Overton won handily over
the incumbent Broussard and Long had installed his second senator. Then he went on to the campaign to elect Roosevelt.

In his campaigning, Long steered clear of the racial question.
His biographer, Professor Williams, who interviewed hundreds of
people who knew Long personally, concluded that he had no personal sense of race prejudice and, indeed, seems to have genuinely
liked blacks. In contemporary newspaper accounts of his
speeches, there is little trace—not even in hostile newspapers—of
racial rhetoric. Blacks from the beginning were included in his
welfare, medical, and education programs. Asked how blacks
would be treated under the "Share the Wealth" program, Long
replied:

"Treat them just the same as anybody else. Give them an opportunity to make a living . . . In Louisiana a Negro's just the
same as anybody else; he ought to have a chance to work and to
make a living, and to get an education."

Long's politics was based on one principle: to hold power, you
had to produce something. You must make promises and you
must keep enough of those promises to maintain your hold. He
was perhaps the best campaigner America ever saw, and he
backed his gift for oratory and a sense of the people with a brilliant mind. Two Supreme Court justices declared him one of the
outstanding attorneys to appear before them.

Long himself was certainly convinced of his intellectual abilities. Once, in the middle of a discussion on his attributes, Huey
yawned: "Just say I'm *sui generis,* and let it go at that."

With the election of Roosevelt, Long felt he would have much
to say about national policy.

Very quickly, Roosevelt's distaste for Long and for Long's welfare proposals became evident. Long threatened he'd get him in
the 1936 election, that he'd break him.

He began in his public speeches to compare Roosevelt with
Herbert Hoover.

Hoover was a hoot owl. Roosevelt was a scrootch owl. "A hoot
owl bangs into the roost and knocks the hen clean off, and catches
her while she's falling. But a scrootch owl slips into the roost and

scrootches up to the hen and talks softly to her. And the hen just falls in love with him, and the first thing you know, *there ain't no hen.*"

Roosevelt and his patronage chief, James Farley, responded by denying Louisiana federal patronage. Huey countered by denouncing the New Deal as "a Bad Deal for the poor people." Roosevelt escalated by cutting off all federal relief funds to Louisiana, an excessively vindictive act, and simultaneously launched tax investigations of Huey and his friends. Long, however, had the resources of an oil-rich state, and the welfare benefits did not diminish.

The Roosevelt cabinet held several meetings, according to Farley, to consider ways of dealing with Long. They came up with a plan to have a presidential staff member, Hugh Johnson, attack Long on national radio talks, coast to coast. Johnson did, linking Huey with a pro-fascist Catholic priest, Father Coughlin. In those broadcasts, Johnson used a Negro accent to imitate Huey.

Long responded with his own coast-to-coast broadcast and pulled an even larger audience. Newspapers reported it as the "largest radio audience in the history of America" and the audience heard Long lay it on Roosevelt:

"While millions have starved and gone naked; while babies have cried and died for milk; while people have begged for meat and bread, Mister Roosevelt's administration sails merrily along, plowing under and destroying the things to eat and wear, with tear-dimmed eyes and hungry souls made to chant for this *New Deal,* so that even their starvation dole is not taken away, and meanwhile the food and clothes craved by their bodies and souls goes for destruction and ruin.

"Is this government? It looks more like Saint Vitus Dance."

And Long was making plans for the 1936 presidential election. He didn't then figure to run himself but instead to back a liberal candidate, such as Senator Borah. He told friends, "Nineteen forty will be my real year."

Meanwhile, Roosevelt heard some disturbing information. According to James Farley, in his book *Behind the Ballots,* the Democratic National Committee had conducted a secret poll on Huey

Long. It showed his vote-drawing power to be clearly national, not regional, even if Long used a third party.

"It indicated," wrote Farley, "that running on a third party ticket, Long would be able to poll between three million and four million votes.[7] His probable support *was not* confined to Louisiana and nearby states. On the contrary, he had about as much following in the North as in the South, and he had as strong an appeal in the industrial centers as he did in the rural areas . . . It was easy to conceive a situation whereby Long, by polling more than three million votes, might have the balance of power in the 1936 election.

"For instance, the poll indicated that he would command upward of 100,000 votes in New York State, a pivotal state in any national election; and a vote of that size could easily mean the difference between victory and defeat for the Democratic or Republican candidate. Take that number of votes away from either major candidate, and it would come mostly from our side, and the result might spell disaster."

Huey Long represents one of the most provocative conjectures of American history. Not again in this century has America had such a radical politician with such a large national following.

Long's criticisms of Roosevelt and the New Deal have proved justified and, in the past decade, it has become a commonplace that the New Deal didn't solve the Depression. It only relieved some of its worst aspects. Prosperity returned because of World War II.

America's problem, said Long, was distribution of wealth. The nation's resources were sufficient, he believed, to let all people— black and white—share in that wealth. It was a view which forty years after his death was still radical, but which still made considerable sense.

His program was attacked in his lifetime and afterward as fiscally impossible. But his 1928 program to reform Louisiana had been attacked with equal vigor and Long had proven the critics wrong. His personal brilliance and his record of performance sug-

7 This represented about 8 per cent of the votes cast in the 1936 election.

gest that, at the least, it was possible he might have succeeded nationally.

His apparent strategy to gain the White House in 1940 was sound. He intended to dilute Roosevelt's power in 1936. One means was to defeat Roosevelt outright by using a third party to siphon off Democratic votes and throw the election to the Republicans. Another, and more likely plan, was to use a third party threat as a weapon to force a Roosevelt-Long coalition and implement at least portions of "Share the Wealth." Roosevelt time and again in his career proved himself capable of making deals with the devil, and if Long were the devil, so be it.

By whichever route, in 1940, Long would be the logical contender for the presidency, either as the Democratic nominee or at the head of a "Share the Wealth" party. Roosevelt then had no ambition for an unprecedented third term and tradition was so against it that Wendell Willkie almost beat Roosevelt on that single issue.[8]

An assassin's bullet canceled all such possibilities. On the night of September 8, 1935, Huey Long was in the Baton Rouge Capitol and walking down the hallway to attend the legislature. A young Baton Rouge doctor, Carl Austin Weiss, stepped into the corridor, thrust a gun into Huey's side and fired. Bodyguards responded with their own gunfire and the hallway was filled with bullets. Long fell wounded. Weiss was dead with sixty-one bullets in his body, two in the head. Long died two days later.

There were immediate rumors of a conspiracy, rumors which persisted for decades. It was a plot by a cabal of wealthy Louisianians, it was a plot by friends of Roosevelt, a plot by Long's own people frightened of a tax investigation, a plot by the Mafia. No evidence, however, was ever found to show that the assassin Weiss was a member of any plot. A single bullet by a single assassin remains the only persuading theory. Long was dead and "Share the Wealth," as an organization, vanished shortly afterward.

Long's idea of class struggle had greater persistency. His belief that the poor, black and white, had a common interest in reform

[8] Roosevelt beat Willkie by less than five million votes out of 49.7 million votes cast.

of the economic structure would later be echoed by Martin Luther King, Jr. And, most interestingly, Long-style populism would show signs of reappearing in the South and in border states in the 1970s.

Unlike Thomas Jefferson, James Madison, or John Calhoun, Huey Long was neither an inventor of a complete political philosophy nor an innovator of governmental structure. His contribution to the American experience is not found in any piece of legislation bearing his name, nor in any institution of the Congress or the elective process.

He is remembered in part for his style. But unlike the aristocratic style of John Randolph, the Long style did not enter the Southern tradition. The demagogic, stump-speaking oratory that Long is identified with was not his creation; it existed long before him. What he did contribute in the matter of style was the model of high-handed dictator of a state, and the sarcastic, mocking, scornful loner of the Senate. Neither of those models has been used by successors.

Huey Long's contribution was a single idea, an idea which, though yet unused, is available to the American process: the idea of equally sharing the wealth.

Huey Long was in the Andrew Jackson mold, but with an important difference. He was of the twentieth century. He addressed himself not only to the injustice of excessive wealth and privilege, as had Jackson, but also to the spectrum of racial, sexual, and class inequality.

Long's solution to all was the radical and immediate redistribution of wealth.

Forty years after his death, the major American political parties remained hostile to his proposals. But Huey Long had left a legacy which could not be erased from the public knowledge. He had mapped out an alternative solution to the nation's problems, a solution which, though radical, could nevertheless be accomplished through the Constitutional system.

His life truncated by assassination, Huey Long never acquired the power to test his idea. His less radical contemporaries, the

New Deal Southerners, meanwhile continued to play a large role in shaping national events.

Virtually all of them were introduced into the power circles of Congress through a Southern "protégé" system. This informal system is one of the important methods by which Southerners acquired, and continue to acquire, congressional power.

Chapter 15
PROTÉGÉS

As the story goes, President Roosevelt and Senator Tom Connally of Texas were having breakfast at the White House. Roosevelt asked Connally why his efforts to derail Huey Long had not worked. Connally, the archetypal senator with long white hair and string tie, took a bite of biscuit, a slow sip of coffee, and replied:

"Mr. President, we have a saying in Texas: 'If you want a postgraduate course in politics, go to Louisiana.' "

This was a considerable compliment from a man who was a master of politics in a state which was not a stranger itself to the subtle arts of government.

Part of the reason for Long's success in politics—and also a basis for Texas' success in Congress—was the protégé tradition. It was, and is, an informal practice whereby promising young Southern lawmakers are taken under the wing of older, wiser professionals and steered into positions of power. It amounts to an adoption system similar to that used by wealthy families of imperial Rome. Power is kept in safe and capable hands from generation to generation. The inheritance is not subject to the unpredictable accidents of genetics, but is passed to a selected and qualified adopted heir.

In Texas, for instance, John Nance Garner, speaker of the

House, was patron to young Sam Rayburn. Rayburn in turn was the patron of Lyndon Johnson. And Johnson, while in the Congress, played the role to a platoon of incoming Southern congressmen and senators. In Mississippi, a direct line of heirs and successors runs from James Vardaman in 1902 to Theodore Bilbo to James Eastland in 1975. In Georgia, the Talmadges have been patrons and protégés for more than half a century. The Byrds of Virginia have used the tradition even longer.

The tradition does not restrict itself to state delegations but embraces all incoming Southerners, black and white, man and woman, provided they are Democrats and provided they are willing to accept the protégé status.

A case history example of the system is the career of Barbara Jordan, born in Houston, Texas, in 1936, the first black to be elected to the Texas state Senate since Reconstruction, the first black woman to be elected to the Congress from the South ever.

She was elected to the House in 1972 and within three years was being talked about and written about as Speaker Jordan, Senator Jordan, Supreme Court Justice Jordan, Vice President Jordan.

She achieved such quick eminence because of a sharp intelligence, hard work, strong character, and a solid political sense. She won elections because, in the Huey Long mold, she could produce something for her constituents. Unlike Long, she won power positions, in the Texas legislature and the Congress, by a willingness to participate in the protégé system.

Barbara Jordan has few of the personality attributes of a successful politician. Overweight and careless in her dress, she is far from glamorous. She is not a person who shakes hands, smiles, and presses the flesh in the Lyndon Johnson style. And she has a manner of dealing with slow-witted people, be they constituents or colleagues, that approaches the arrogant. She does not suffer fools gladly and a reporter once wrote that she was "about as cozy as a piledriver."

Once, when a Texas congressman gave the state delegation a seemingly endless lecture on fertilizer, she cut him off with: "Well, I'm glad you're finally talking about something you're into."

Barbara Jordan was the daughter of a Houston warehouse clerk who on Sundays functioned as a Baptist preacher. He drove her hard in school and, drawing from his talents as minister of the Gospel, taught her how to move men with words. At all-black Texas Southern University, her debating team beat Harvard.

She took her law degree at Boston University in 1959 and promptly returned to Texas to take up a political career, serving as an assistant to a county judge. In 1966, following the Supreme Court's one-man, one-vote ruling which threw more congressional seats open to city voters, she won election to the state Senate in a district that was only 38 per cent black.

In her first days at the state Senate, she was spurned and insulted by a number of her colleagues. But the young lieutenant governor, Ben Barnes, a protégé of Lyndon Johnson, recognized her abilities. He could use her as an access to the black community. She could use him as an access to the power structure. They became allies.

Within four years, Barbara Jordan was president pro-tem of the state Senate and had risen to the highest level of state politics. Her legislative accomplishments included sponsorship of a minimum wage bill, a workmen's compensation bill, and the defeat of a bill intended to disfranchise blacks and Mexican-Americans by tightening voter registration.

(After beating the registration bill, Jordan told reporters, in good Lyndon Johnson style: "I checked my little black book and I called on ten senators who owed me.")

Her skills brought her very quickly to the attention of President Johnson, who was constantly on the search for talent, and he appointed her to a White House commission on income maintenance.

In 1971, Jordan decided to run for Congress against a powerful black state legislator. Lyndon Johnson was the guest of honor at the initial cocktail party. Houston moneymen kicked in and Jordan won in an 81 per cent landslide.

Following the election, and before her inauguration, she surprised friends in Houston by saying she hoped to be appointed to the House Judiciary Committee. This was considered odd because Judiciary, which passes on the appointment of federal judges and attorneys, is considered a plum only when your party holds the White House. There were no Supreme Court appointments coming up and Nixon had left very few vacancies in the lower courts. What lay behind her unexpected move was that Lyndon Johnson had advised her to go to Judiciary, to build up seniority for the long line of Democratic Presidents he expected to succeed Nixon.

In this advice, Johnson showed his customary acumen, and a bit of political knowledge not generally perceived. It is that a President, by appointing federal judges attuned to his biases and philosophy, can put a longer-lasting stamp on the future than he can through reform of a bureaucracy or with ordinary legislation. Legislation has a short-term effect, subject to revision from Congress to Congress. A federal judge holds his office for his lifetime and cannot be removed except by impeachment. By this logic, the most sustaining effect of the Nixon administration would not be his foreign policy achievements, nor the legal precedents established in his Watergate defense, but the hundreds of Nixon conservatives appointed to the federal judiciary.

Representative Jordan went to Washington. There, at a meeting of the congressional Black Caucus (a political organization composed of all the black representatives), she was told to forget Judiciary. She would seek, it was decreed, appointment to the Armed Services Committee.

The man who held the power of that appointment was Wilbur Mills of Arkansas, chairman of Ways and Means, whose members then decided on party choices for other committees.

Dutifully, Jordan contacted Lyndon Johnson in Texas and asked his intercession with Mills. He persuaded her to ignore the Black Caucus and go to Judiciary where, because it was less sought after, she'd have a quicker rise to power. She agreed and the appointment was made. It proved wise. Within three years, sophomore Congressman Jordan was midway up the Judiciary seniority ladder (thirteenth). Had she gone to Armed Services, she would have been in 1975 still at the bottom rung (twenty-fourth).

Throughout her rise, her philosophy and her legislation were reminiscent of the Populists. Back in 1962, when she was a county judge's assistant, she had filled out a Houston *Post* questionnaire in which she stated: "Politics has no meaning except as a means of getting things done, making our democratic system work better for every family, giving every child a chance to succeed, and eliminating injustices. That states my political philosophy."

In the Congress she sponsored legislation to increase Social Security benefits and, in a Huey Long stroke, a law requiring oil companies to report their reserves and their production.

In the meantime, she slowly and steadily built her effectiveness in the House. A fellow Texas representative attributed it to her ability to work with the power structure. "Barbara indicates quickly a willingness to follow and be loyal to a leader. She avoids positions where leadership could imagine she is in any way a threat to them."

She herself said, "I didn't get here by being black or a woman. I got here by working hard . . . I am neither a black politician nor a woman politician. Just a politician, a *professional* politician."

She came into national prominence in 1974 during the televised Nixon impeachment debates, making an eloquent opening remark on the Constitution: "When that document was completed on the seventeenth of September in 1787, I was not included in that *We the People* . . ." But she supported the Constitution, believed in its supremacy in law, and expected Presidents to support that supremacy.

She supported all five impeachment resolutions against Nixon, including two the committee refused to adopt, and would likely have been named a manager of the House's case had a trial been held in the Senate.

Several months later, Barbara Jordan, pupil and protégée of Lyndon Johnson's, was at the podium of a meeting of national Democrats in Kansas City. The man beside her was Robert Byrd, born in North Carolina, senator from West Virginia, Democratic whip of the Senate, a former Ku Klux Klansman who had called Martin Luther King "a self-seeking rabble-rouser." But he was also a rising power in national government.

The ex-Klansman and the Houston black woman stood side by side before the thousands of cheering Democrats. And Barbara

Jordan introduced Byrd, admiring "the depth of his intellect and capacity for human understanding and compassion . . . his ability to lead."

Afterward, as they left the platform together, Byrd, obviously moved by the introduction, told her: "You'll never be sorry that you introduced me . . . If there's anything I can do for you, don't hesitate to let me know."

Barbara Jordan smiled and said, "I won't."

The protégé tradition which so helped the career of Barbara Jordan is not an invention of politics but a product of the general Southern culture.

In September 1974, Judge Hoke Smith II, grandson of Georgia Senator Hoke Smith,[1] put his feet on the desk at his Atlanta law office and explained the South in which he was raised. "There is a Southern tradition to learn parliamentary procedures. I served eight years in the Georgia legislature and before I took my seat the first day I knew the rules backward and forward. I *had* to know the rules, or I'd get my teeth kicked in . . ."

Judge Smith spent much of his childhood and adolescence living in Washington while his grandfather was senator. From that advantaged point, and his own career in state government, he gained several generations of experience in Southern politics.

He went on. "Politics in the South has two cardinal sins: The first is ingratitude. If someone helps you, you are expected—you are *obligated*—to help back. The second is breaking your word. If you give your word, no matter under what circumstances or to whom, keep it! If word gets around that you didn't, you're in trouble. The person who breaks those rules gets no further support. That's the way it is in the home town, the way it is in the State House, and the way it is in the Congress. We're raised that way . . .

[1] Senator Hoke Smith of Georgia was a progressive, self-taught lawyer and career politician. He was Cleveland's Secretary of the Interior (1893–96), resigned to support Bryan, and was governor of Georgia, 1907–9. He was elected to the U. S. Senate in 1911 and served until his defeat by Populist Tom Watson in 1921. Smith was founder of the modern Atlanta *Journal*, buying the paper in 1887 when it was a small community daily and converting it into a major newspaper.

"Another thing about the Southerners up in Washington is that a high percentage of them are lawyers, trial lawyers. The South being impoverished as it was for so long, the lawyers were the only professional class who had enough time to deal with public office." He paused to reflect on the recently ended Senate Watergate hearings:

"Now being a *trial* lawyer, as opposed to an *office* lawyer, can give you an advantage in certain things—like the Watergate hearings. Herman Talmadge and Sam Ervin did trial work. They know that the smiling courteous examination is going to be more effective with a jury. They know that the members of a jury have sense. So you don't have to point out the obvious. Let the jurors figure it out. At the hearings, they had a jury of the United States and they accomplished what they set out to do."

Judge Smith said that he had been helped by older legislators while he was in state government and that his grandfather had been helped in the U. S. Senate.

"When the freshman Southerner goes up there, he gets help from the delegation of his state and he gets help from the delegations of neighboring states. You don't find that among the non-Southerners.

"This tradition goes all the way to the beginning of the South. When you'd travel somewhere to a town you'd never been, your daddy or somebody you'd know would give you a letter so's you could do business or have a place to stay. It still goes on. You get one of those letters, or today it's a phone call, and when I get it I knock myself out to help. Accordingly, I expect the reverse when I make the call.

"Let me put it another way, how it works today. I travel a lot on law business to New York and Chicago and to Southern towns like New Orleans. I know a lot of people in all those towns. But if I was in New York I wouldn't think of calling a colleague and just telling him I was in town. It wouldn't be expected. But if I was in New Orleans, I'd *have* to call 'cause their feelings would be hurt if they found out I was in town and hadn't called. If I ran into a friend I knew in Chicago and hadn't called, neither he nor I would think a thing about it. But if the same thing happened in New

Orleans both me and my family would be embarrassed for a long time.[2]

"You see, when those fellows go up to the House or to the Senate, they go up with introductions to the other Southerners."

An example of the protégé tradition at work in the U. S. Senate can be seen in the career of Bennett Johnston, a freshman senator from Louisiana.

Johnston's background is typical of the Southern career politician: stable cultural roots, rural environment, educated as a lawyer or schoolteacher, and substantial experience in local government. His family, who trace back to Revolutionary times in South Carolina, had transferred to the Shreveport region in the midnineteenth century and stayed. His grandfather was a lawyer and first superintendent of schools for Bossier Parish. His father was also a lawyer active in politics. And Bennett Johnston, after law school and a term in the Army, spent eight years in the state legislature as floor leader for Governor John McKeithen.[3]

His entry into big-time politics was typical of Southern careers. First, a shot at the governor's office to gain a name and experience.

In 1971, Bennett Johnston, unknown except to aunts, uncles, and other immediate relatives, quietly enrolled in a gouging, clawing, eighteen-man Democratic primary for governor. From the standpoint of dazzling variety, the 1971 Louisiana campaign was hard to beat. Not only were there eighteen Democrats engaged in a free-style wrestling match—half of them well known and the other half, like Johnston, unknown—but there were two Republicans running their own tag match primary, and an American party nominee doing a solo act of right-wing loops. All in all, twenty-

[2] In a discussion of the Judge Smith interview, Roy Reed, roving correspondent for the New York *Times*, said he was well aware of the phenomenon. Reed, born in Arkansas, travels contantly on assignment. He said he had taken to slipping in and out of Southern cities incognito, staying at obscure motels, eating at unknown restaurants so he wouldn't be spotted by friends. They would be insulted if he hadn't called and to do so, with so many so often, would obstruct his work to the point where little of it would ever get done.

[3] McKeithen, governor of Louisiana 1964–72, was himself a protégé and floor leader of Earl Long, Huey's brother.

one candidates running at the same time in a mind-boggling display of colors, occupations, and political intentions.

The twenty-one included blacks, whites, and Indians. They included congressmen, a lieutenant governor, state legislators, farmers, grocers, a doctor, two preachers, salesmen, two journalists, and a Klan Kleagle. And one big-time Nashville singer.[4]

Political philosophy ran from far-left socialism (one of the journalists) to modified populism (a third of the candidates) to rightwing fascism in the form of the Klan Kleagle's ideas on how to restore law and order to Louisiana. Everybody got a hearing around the state and it was the democratic process at its best or at its worst, depending on your attitude toward mixing of the classes.

After ten months of campaigning, Johnston emerged from the melee a strong second to Edwin Edwards, a Cajun congressman who became governor.[5]

The following year, 1972, there came another statewide election. The incumbent was Allen Ellender, Huey Long's political right-hand who had become chairman of the Senate Agriculture Committee and the most senior Democrat in the Senate. He was very strong politically but he was eighty-one years old and some people had their eye on his job.

(Foremost among these was outgoing governor John McKeithen who listened with joy to rumors Ellender had grown weak and senile. Early in 1972, however, Ellender—who spent his thirty-six years of Senate vacations working on his south Louisiana farm—popped in unexpectedly, but with deliberate intentions, at McKeithen's office. The supposedly feeble and doddering

[4] He was sixty-nine-year-old Jimmie Davis, writer of "You Are My Sunshine" and other hits and already two-times governor of Louisiana. When inaugurated for his second term in 1960, Davis, with cowboy hat and heavy silver saddle, rode a huge white horse up the steps of the state capitol and into the House and Senate as part of the celebration hurrah.

[5] Edwards had also been a floor leader for McKeithen. The fate of the nineteen other candidates was varied. One, Republican David Treen, later became a congressman. An incumbent lieutenant governor and an incumbent congressman who were running for governor were both beaten so badly they retired from politics. A Cajun private detective was convicted of public defamation, his oratory being a bit too hot even for a Louisiana election. A Shreveport doctor committed suicide in an event indirectly related to his political activity.

senator talked with rapid energy and shook the governor's hand with such force that it seemed it would break. McKeithen was appalled at such vigor and strength. He chose then and there not to run.)

Johnston, having built a statewide following and having a campaign organization of high morale, challenged Ellender's seat. He was given little chance. When qualifications closed in July 1972, Johnston was Ellender's only contender: the young man versus the old. Suddenly, three weeks later, Ellender died and Johnston had the Democratic nomination, and the U. S. Senate seat, by virtual default.[6] Johnston was formally elected in November 1972.

Johnston had thus, in eight years, progressed smoothly up the professional political ladder. He had served as executive-trainee in the state legislature to the governor, his sponsor. He had acquired experience. And he'd then outstepped and outlucked his rivals to take a prized senior vice presidency, a seat in the Senate. At the state level, the protégé tradition had worked to the advantage of his district, his governor, and himself. In the Senate, it would continue to work, to the advantage of his state, the South, and himself.

Johnston had become a resource of Louisiana and this was made clear a week after his election. Following Senator Ellender's death, Governor Edwards, as mentioned, had appointed his wife to the vacant seat. But upon Johnston's election, Edward's wife resigned and the forty-four-year-old governor appointed his chief political rival, Johnston, to fill out the remaining two months of Ellender's term.

This gave Johnston a two-month seniority advantage, and it gave the state of Louisiana that same advantage. Two months doesn't seem much of an advantage to a state, or to a rival. But Senate power positions are often decided on the basis of a few

[6] The immediately former governor, McKeithen, was outraged at this stroke of fortune and ran in the November general elections as an unsuccessful independent. The immediately incumbent governor, Edwin Edwards, probably would have appointed himself to the Ellender seat had the death occurred later in the term. Coming as it did a bare two months after his own inauguration, he consoled himself by appointing his wife to fill three months of Ellender's unexpired term. She performed quite well, according to Senate colleagues.

days' seniority. The early appointment had jumped Johnston ahead of eleven other freshman senators.[7]

Arriving in the Senate, Johnston was taken in hand by the senior Louisiana senator, Russell Long, son of Huey. Long, who sits at the desk used by John Calhoun, had been elected to the Senate in 1948, one day before his thirtieth birthday.[8] Obligated to no one but the oil companies, who heavily finance the campaigns of Long and other oil state senators, he is quick, smooth, brazen, and witty. Longtime chairman of Senate Finance, he is a master of Senate politics and procedure and seemed in the 1960s to be the heir apparent to the Senate majority leader. But, a perennial wrestler with booze, he disgraced himself with repeated episodes of wandering around the Senate chamber barefoot, drunk, and making inane speeches. By the time Bennett Johnston arrived, Russell Long had taken the pledge and restored his prestige.

Long advised Johnston to apply to the Democratic Steering Committee for appointments to Banking and Interior, each of which Johnston received. Long also helped him to build a staff. Russell Long was grooming Johnston as a protégé.

In those first few months, Johnston was very conscious of being observed and judged by his colleagues, particularly by other Southerners. But he had the background of mutual acquaintances to fall back upon, he had the firsthand experience of back-home Southern politics and legislative procedure, and he had the proper manners. It was like coming from the same fraternity at Yale.

His eagerness to work, his discipline, and his integrity became evident to his fellow senators. Long sponsored him. Others, like Sam Ervin, liked him. And John Stennis of Mississippi joined with Long in becoming Johnston's patron. The older men gave advice and led. The younger man listened and followed.

[7] At almost the same moment in Georgia, a similar situation had been caused by the death of Senator Richard Russell. An unknown state legislator, Sam Nunn, won the election. Governor Jimmy Carter, like Nunn a young, sophisticated country boy, acted in the interest of the state and appointed Nunn the following day, on November 8, 1972. Nunn thus went into the Senate with a six-day advantage over Johnston and it helped Nunn win Russell's old seat on the Senate Armed Services Committee.

[8] Russell Long is the only person in Senate history who was preceded in the chamber by both his father and mother. Rose McConnell Long was appointed to her husband's seat after his assassination and served until his term expired in 1937.

A test of Johnston's Senate clout came within a year.

Johnston had sponsored a special interest bill, a $5 million appropriation to benefit Louisiana oystermen. James Buckley, the well-known, conservative, Republican senator from New York, thought he'd make a point on excessive spending and at the same time crush a freshman Democrat. He challenged the bill in committee, saying—correctly as it so happened—that it was a handout to a few Louisiana oyster farmers. The bill would be killed, said Buckley.

The Senate machinery went into action. Not directly, but discreetly so as not to embarrass Buckley. Russell Long's legislative aide told Jim Buckley's legislative aide that "if Senator Buckley does this, he'll never, ever get anything out of Long's committee again." When the bill came up for passage, Buckley did not have to back down publicly. He just didn't show up.

Within three years, Bennett Johnston, forty-three years old, unknown outside of Washington and his home state and a very junior senator, had become a probationary member of the "Club," the Senate's leadership clique. He had moved up to number four position on Interior, and stood a chance to gain the chairmanship within a few years. He held two chairmanships of subcommittees, and he had won a transfer to Appropriations, one of the three "power" committees in the Senate.[9]

Johnston had these gains primarily because when he had entered the Senate he had not been left adrift. Many new senators are not helped even by the other senator from their state. They often represent rival political parties or political factions and the senior will be damned if he'll help the junior. In Johnston's case, as with virtually all new Southern Democrats, he'd been taken in hand by the protégé tradition.

Senior Southerners had taken him around, had helped him put together a competent staff, had advised and endorsed him on committee choices. They had, further, given him schooling in the Sen-

[9] It is obvious that any Senate committee or subcommittee is powerful, through their various jurisdictions of investigation, appointment, federal laws and federal money. But according to *Congressional Quarterly* and to numerous polls of senators and congressmen, the undisputed most powerful committees are Finance, Appropriations, and Armed Services. Judiciary is often ranked next. Foreign Relations, though not a "power committee" is considered a good committee to gain national exposure.

ate system which requires that its followers work hard, work loyally for the Senate as a body, and work with deference to the prerogatives of senior senators.

"Being a Southerner," Johnston acknowledged somewhat in wonder, "is an advantage in the Senate. The Southerners have a reputation for keeping their word, and this is of great benefit in negotiation with other senators. I think there is something in the family roots of the South, in the value system that places a premium on personal integrity."

Johnston had expected some solidarity among Southerners when he first went to the Senate. He was amazed at how solid the bond was.

"They confer together, the Southern Democrats, every day. It is very informal. They have a large table in the Senate dining room and you will almost always find them there at lunch. Sam Ervin, Russell Long, John Stennis, John Sparkman. Committee chairmen and freshmen alike. If you are a Southern Democrat your invitation is automatic.

"On the floor and in negotiations, they have greater flexibility than anyone else in the Senate. Essentially, this is because they owe their election to neither party. On the impeachment [of Richard Nixon], the Southerners would have been the determining factor. The Republicans could figure on so many votes, the Democrats on so many. But the Southerners, either as a bloc or as individuals, hadn't made up their mind. They were going to judge on the evidence. The Southerners pay some loyalty to the Democratic party, because they owe their seniority to them, but they are not blindly obedient. Instead, they stick with each other."

Another witness to Senate doings, the author William S. White, had written while Bennett Johnston was in law school about the Southern advantage. He did not comment on a protégé tradition, he attributed the advantage to the Club. White wrote that the Southern senator, seemingly by right of birth, automatically joined the Club, the inner establishment which White and some others believe runs the Senate.

Congressman and Mrs. William B. Bank-head: To assist Wilson, he advocated suspension of the Constitution. *(Library of Congress)*

Senator Huey Long, center, of Louisiana, with Public Service Commissioner James O'Connor, left, and Governor O. K. Allen. Forty years after Long's assassination, his ideas remain untested. *(National Archives)*

Senator Tom Watson of Georgia: nation's most able Populist proposed income tax, nationalized railroads, women's rights. *(Library of Congress*

The Georgia Populist Rebecca Latimer Felton: She was the first woman to serve in the U.S. Senate. *(Library of Congress)*

Senator Hattie Caraway of Arkansas: With the help of Huey Long, her victorious election looked "like a circus hitched to a tornado." *(Library of Congress)*

Senate Foreign Relations Committee, 1944. From left, Secretary of State Cordell Hull, Senators Walter George, Tom Connally, Arthur Vandenberg, Warren Austin, Guy Gillette, W. H. White, Jr., and Alben Barkley. Without Connally's leadership, there would not have been a United Nations. *(National Archives)*

Senators Richard Russell of Georgia, left, and A. B. Chandler of Kentucky touring battlefronts in the South Pacific, 1943. Russell knocked a hero off a white horse and expertly defused a potential World War III. *(National Archives)*

President Harry Truman deliverin acceptance speech at the Demo National Convention in Philadelph 1948. Truman once told Sam Ray "We're going to save the world." *photo)*

Chapter 16
THE CLUB

Through the years, from the time of Richard Henry Lee, Charles Pinckney, and John Calhoun to the era of Sam Ervin and John Stennis the heart of the Senate has been an inner leadership clique, the Club.

The Club is that body of people from which other senators take their lead. It sets the pace, the style, the ethic of the Senate.

It is not a formal organization which has regular meetings and officers. It is an informal clique. What its members have most obviously in common is a loyalty to the Senate. A belief that the institution ranks above all others in government and ranks even above their own careers. Beyond that, the Club is hard to define, for it is made up of indefinable men, prima donnas, and powerful egos like Joe Robinson of Arkansas, Roosevelt's majority leader who pushed through the New Deal. It has had men like George Norris, the Nebraska liberal Republican who unseated the tyrannical House speaker Joe Cannon, and risked his career to oppose Woodrow Wilson's war powers in 1917. (Norris was drummed out of the Republican party in 1936 for supporting Roosevelt. Rather than join the Democratic party, Norris became an independent.) And it has had men like Richard Russell of Georgia,

Lyndon Johnson of Texas, and Bob Kerr of Oklahoma, all colorful backroom leaders.

The Senate itself in 1955 indirectly defined the types of men
who form the Club. The occasion was appointment of a committee, headed by Lyndon Johnson, to select "five outstanding persons, but not a living person, who have served as members of the
Senate" whose portraits were to be painted in oval spaces in the
Reception Room.

The men selected were Daniel Webster, John Calhoun, Henry
Clay, the Republican Robert Taft of Ohio, and the senior Bob La
Follette of Wisconsin. These men were considered the "five
greatest senators" up to that time. The list is interesting from several angles. First, it is devoid of party dominance. Only one career
Democrat was chosen (Calhoun) and only one Republican
(Taft). There were two Whigs, Webster and Clay, and the independent La Follette. But the list does have some familiar Senate
types. There is the nationalist (Webster), the sectionalist (Calhoun), and the compromiser (Clay). There is the stiff party
loyalist (Taft) and the senator aloof from party, La Follette. And,
most important to the Senate, each of the five put loyalty to the
Senate above other politics, including their own careers. That is
the core of the Club.

Like all cliques, the Club is tyrannical about whom it will select
and whom it will reject. It is a place where one member will be
forgiven anything or everything, and another be forgiven hardly
anything at all.

A Eugene McCarthy, a Birch Bayh, can conduct themselves
with intelligence and courtesy and decorum and never be accepted
in the core of the Senate because, in part, they regard the Senate
without sufficient awe, as simply another institution of government. On the other hand, a Russell Long can pad around the Senate floor in his stockinged feet, half-crazed with drink, and remain
not only accepted by but a ranking member of the Club. His word
is respected and he knows his way around the Senate, the ins and
outs of procedure and of committees.

In pursuing a definition of the Club, one finds that over the
years it has been dominated, but not controlled, by Southerners.
Being a Southerner, as Bennett Johnston found, helps a great

deal. But Southerners are sometimes ostracized. James Eastland seems to be such a case. He is from Mississippi and chairs the powerful Judiciary committee and is number one in Senate seniority. He must be dealt with by all, but he is not considered a member of the Senate establishment, the Club.

Why? His outspoken and crude racism is a factor. Sam Ervin of North Carolina disliked Eastland virtually on sight, from the time Ervin entered the Senate in 1954. Indeed, a comparison of the two men demonstrates the mysteries of Senate acceptance. Both Southerners. Both hard and diligent workers. Both opposed to the series of civil rights bills in the 1950s, 1960s, and 1970s. But their styles differed and this has a bit (but not a lot) to do with Senate acceptance.

Eastland was openly hateful against blacks and supporters of civil rights for blacks. Ervin was not at all hateful against blacks, though he held an anti-rights position, indeed was the Senate leader of it for ten years. He argued courteously that special legislation for the civil rights of one group, the blacks, robbed the civil liberties of the nation as a whole.

In any case, their styles were different. But, in trying to define Senate acceptance, one would expect that Ervin's more likeable style would be offset by Eastland's greater power. Eastland had seniority and was chairman of one of the four most powerful committees. Ervin never had much seniority and chaired Government Operations, a minor committee. Yet Ervin was a member of the Club, Eastland was not. Ervin had something called "character," which—whatever it is—Eastland seemed to lack in the eyes of the Club.

Character and Club. The two concepts are better understood by giving examples than by giving definitions.

The inner Club, or clique, seems to have been present at the beginning of the Senate. The basis of it was probably the Constitutional Convention. Half of the senators in the First Congress had attended the convention. They knew each other and they conferred. They set the style, the pace, and the ethics of the first Senate.

Since then, the Club has been the most ephemeral of the Senate processes. Transitory. It appears and disappears at irregular intervals over the years like an unpredictable comet. In the first twelve years of the Senate (1789–1801) it was dominated by New England Federalists. It vanished with the Federalist defeats in the election of 1800. For the ensuing hundred years, we hear little about any inner establishment of the Senate. There is a suggestion of something like the Club in the Calhoun era. And there is an antithesis of a Club in the 1880s and 1890s, when the Senate was controlled by an inner ring of corrupt Republican plunderers who'd sell their mothers to a white slave ring if they could get a price.

It reappears around 1913 when the Democrats put Wilson in the White House and won a majority in both houses of Congress. Southerners, who were the Democrats with the most seniority, became chairmen in the Senate. Like the Federalists of 1789, they had a common experience, being Democrats—which had been an endangered species for fifty years—and Southerners. And like the Federalist clique, they had power and a desire to direct the Senate along dignified and proper, even aristocratic, lines with a sense of noble obligation.

Though senators have come and gone, the Club has existed since then.

In the Senate of the 1970s, as in the Senate of 1913, the definition of what is proper is mostly made by Southern Democrats. They deal, however, not entirely from their strength on committees, but because of their knowledge of political realities and their experience in precedents and parliamentary rules.

This Southern role of guidance, while objected to by many inside and outside the Senate, is not without historical justice. It should be recalled that Southerners—Madison, Pinckney, and Randolph—invented the Senate. Indeed, it should also be recalled, the Virginia Plan and the Pinckney Plan were the foundation designs of the national government. So it is not too outrageous that the heirs of the Madison tradition should continue, by example, to set the style of the Senate.

The Southern senator, at his best, is a model for all senators. He views his role as one to "slow down history." He respects—

and in some cases *loves* is not too strong a word—tradition, the Constitution, and the national institutions. One of his primary obligations is to guard them from tampering. He is the custodian of what his Virginia and Carolina ancestors gave to the world two hundred years ago.

In the fast-moving American Republic, those affections are regarded as at least unfashionable, if not downright reactionary. But in the Senate those affections are much admired, by Northerners and Southerners, by Democrats and Republicans.

To hear the Southerner stand and debate his beliefs can be a thrill to the ear, for—to the best of them—the English language is a living friend. The best American talkers are Southerners such as Sam Ervin or Herman Talmadge. They appear to speak *plain*. They palm off the impression that they are themselves as plain as they speak and as plain as everyone else. Of course, they are not plain at all, they are cunning. And when they speak they intend for those who are also cunning to recognize their cunning, too. They communicate at many wonderful and artful levels.

Listen to Sam Ervin of North Carolina describe the Nixon White House:

"To achieve what they considered a worthy purpose—the re-election of the President—they willingly resorted to evil. They had forgotten, if they ever knew, that the Constitution is designed to be a law for rulers and people alike at all times and under all circumstances."

That came at a time when academically gowned constitutional experts and even judges were debating whether President Nixon was above the law. Incredible as it seemed afterward, there was about a ten-month period in the Nixon regime when the courts, the law schools, and the press were actually arguing over whether application of the law extended to the President of the United States.

In the middle of the debate, Ervin said it plain and simple: it applies to everyone at all times.

Another plain, every-day Southern senator is Herman Talmadge of Georgia. He begins softly, with wry self-deprecation. Apologetic, almost humble, he will say that he has only a few words; all too well aware, he seems to say, that it is not for *him* to take up the time of his betters.

It was with such a manner that Talmadge questioned John Ehrlichman, during committee hearings on the limits of law in the Nixon White House. Ehrlichman, number two man in the Nixon White House, was in a position to know, but he had not cracked despite hours of rigorous questioning by other senators.

"Now," asked Talmadge, "if the President could authorize a covert break-in and you say you do not know where that power would be limited, you do not think it could include murder, do you?"

Ehrlichman: "I do not know where the line is, Senator."

It became unmistakably clear that nobody in Nixon's White House was willing to draw the line anywhere.

Talmadge was the best cross-examiner in the Senate hearings on Watergate. He was a joy to behold. Even the unflappable ex-attorney general, the cool Wall Street lawyer John Mitchell, lost his temper in an exchange with the polite but deadly Talmadge. With the whole nation watching, Mitchell exploded and said he considered the re-election of Richard Nixon in 1972 "so important that it outweighed all other considerations!"

"*All* other?" asked Talmadge softly.

Mitchell refused to reply.

The Talmadge style is the style of the Club. Polite, but deadly when aroused.

The 1972 *Ralph Nader Congress Report* defined the Club mostly by who was out.[1]

John and Robert Kennedy were out, too independent. Wayne Morse, too belligerent and wasp-tongued. Eugene McCarthy was too detached. Joseph Tydings of Maryland too aloof. "Those who best qualify have power, Lyndon Johnson and Robert Kerr; dignity, Richard Russell and Paul Douglas; homespun friendliness, Warren Magnuson; or seniority, the Southern patriarchs."

A 1974 poll of Senate staff members indicated that the Club

[1] *Who Runs Congress* by Green, Fallows, and Zwick (New York: Grossman Publishers), page 175.

consisted of about eighteen senators.[2] Seven were Southerners, but contrary to the myth of "Southern Patriarchs," only three—Long, Stennis, and McClellan—had any significant seniority.

It is widely believed that Southerners hold power positions in Congress because they amass great seniority. This has not been true since about 1950 when the Southerners began to forfeit their Democratic party seniority by bolting the party and running on Republican or third party tickets. Since then, and increasingly each year, the South as a region has had no greater seniority statistically than any other political grouping. (Of the twenty most senior senators in 1975, only six were Southerners.)

The secret of Southern power rests not on seniority in Congress but seniority in the power committees. (For example, in 1975 William Barrett of Pennsylvania was the seventeenth most senior member of the House, having been first elected to Congress in 1948. He had amassed great seniority in Congress, but was not a member of any "power" committees. In contrast, Gillis Long of Louisiana, elected in 1972, applied for and was promptly placed on House Rules and was the ninth ranking Democrat on that power committee.)

The power committees of the Senate are Finance, Appropriations, Armed Services, and Judiciary. The power committees of the House are Ways and Means, Appropriations, Armed Services, and Rules.

Since Roosevelt's election in 1932, Southerners almost without interruption have been chairmen of the power committees, until the 1974 "Freshmen's Revolt" overthrew their reign in the House. They continued to hold all the power committees in the Senate, and also held Agriculture, another committee traditionally chaired by a Southerner.

[2] The survey was conducted by the author. Members of the Club cited most often were Stennis of Mississippi, Talmadge of Georgia, Long of Louisiana, Hansen of Wyoming, Jordan of North Carolina, Harry Byrd of Virginia, Magnuson and Jackson of Washington, Allen of Alabama, Robert Byrd of West Virginia, Cannon of Nevada, Hruska of Nebraska, Mansfield, McClellan of Arkansas, Pastore of Rhode Island, Symington of Missouri, Scott of Pennsylvania, and Young of North Dakota. Several other senators were, in effect, probationary members. They included Bentsen of Texas, Johnston of Louisiana, and Nunn of Georgia.

There is but one method to obtain seniority on a choice committee: One must be appointed to it early in his career.

These appointments are formally made, in the case of Democrats, by the Democratic Steering Committee of the Senate. When a Bennett Johnston or a Sam Nunn enters the Senate, he presents his assignment preferences to the Steering Committee. The Steering Committee, composed of the party leadership and six other senators, supposedly allots assignments the way it sees fit. But most senators are not sure how much independent judgment the committee exercises. They suspect that it is guided by the Club.

Through the protégé tradition, incoming Southerners usually gain the sponsorship of a senior Southern senator who is a Club member. This, in turn, leads to choice committee assignments early in the freshman's career, and seniority and chairmanship later.

Despite its importance, the existence and nature of the Club has only recently been public knowledge. The first deliberate investigation of the Club seems to have been in the 1950s by the newspaper columnist William S. White, doing research for his book *Citadel: The Story of the U. S. Senate.*

The Club, White wrote, is composed of men "for whom the institution is a career in itself, a life in itself, and an end in itself." The Club member is a master of Senate rules and precedents, and has an instant, acute sensitivity to the moods of the Senate. "His head swims with its history, its lore . . . To him, precedent has an almost mystical meaning . . . His concern for the preservation of Senate tradition is so great that he distrusts anything out of the ordinary."

A striking thing about the makeup of the Club is how few of its members are publicly known. The reason is that famous senators usually have other ambitions, like the White House. The Club demands complete loyalty and will not accept flirts. The Club usually, for a short time, will not test its power against a man who may become President. A contender, of course, has much power. Such was the status enjoyed in the 1970s by Henry Jackson and Ted Kennedy. But the very act of seeking the presidency is a disqualification for membership in the Club. In all cases, save that of Richard Russell, who for a few weeks reached for the Democratic nomination that went to Adlai Stevenson—a fleeting apostasy which was forgiven—a contender who fails is ousted. Estes Kefauver, Hubert Humphrey, and Barry Goldwater all fell from the Club once they announced for the presidency and were not picked up following their defeats.

Somehow, though no one has ever explained when or where, the Club casts blackballs on potentially eligible senators. John Kennedy, who was elected to two terms as senator, was never at any time a member. It was quite clear to his colleagues that his life was directed at a national constituency. He would not dutifully adhere to the Club rules of self-effacement, routine chores, and cultivation of his elders. (Kennedy did not need the Club as senator; he would need them if elected President. That would be the time to defer to the sensitivities of the Club, not while he was a junior senator.)

The Club is quite conscious of its own identity and the type of people it wants. Joseph Clark, a maverick senator, once described a lunch that Majority Leader Lyndon Johnson gave for Clark's class of freshmen Democrats in 1957:

"As we sat down to our steaks at the long table . . . we found at our places copies of *Citadel: The Story of the U. S. Senate,* autographed 'with all good wishes' not only by its author . . . but by the Majority Leader as well. During the course of the lunch, which was attended by the other recently re-elected [party] leaders, Senator Johnson encouraged us to consider Mr. White's book as a sort of *McGuffey's Reader* from which we could learn much about the 'greatest deliberative body in the world' and how to mold ourselves into its way of life."

Newspaper columnist Clayton Fritchey, took a look at the Club in 1967 and found himself agreeing with William White's view of the Club as the guardian of the Senate.

"Aside from its quiet satisfaction at squelching activist Presidents," wrote Fritchey, "the influence of the Club is mainly focused on important . . . matters affecting the Senate as an institution." The Club member is dedicated to "promoting the Senate's primacy in the American Constitutional system, whether the Constitution calls for it or not."

Fritchey polled senators and the wives of senators, and a cross section of Senate staffers, lobbyists, Capitol journalists, and administration liaisons to come up with a list of the Club in 1967. At the core of the Senate were twenty-five names.[3] The membership was nonsectarian, nonpartisan, and nonideological. There were Democrats and Republicans; there were liberals like Pastore and conservatives like Stennis. Even seniority wasn't an absolute criterion. Robert Byrd of West Virginia, for instance, was already in the Club despite the fact he had been in the Senate only six and a half years.

There was a sectional dominance in the list. Eleven of the twenty-five were from the South.

Fritchey observed that two other senators were provisionally on the list: Stuart Symington of Missouri and John Sparkman of Alabama. The people polled had "reservations on Symington and Sparkman," said Fritchey, "because both once had outside ambitions; one [Symington] was a candidate for the Democratic presidential nomination and the other [Sparkman] was Stevenson's running mate in 1952." These youthful deviations were ultimately forgiven.

One feature on which all of Fritchey's respondents agreed was that Richard Russell of Georgia was the "president" of the Club.

Russell was the quintessential Club man—a Southerner, and chairman of the potent Armed Services Committee. Personally he was courtly and deferring. His word was his contract and his operating policy was accommodation. Live and let live.

He was the most powerful man in the Senate, even though—and it is significant—he had little to show in the way of legislative

[3] They were Clinton Anderson of New Mexico, Alan Bible of Nevada, Byrd of West Virginia, Cannon of Nevada, Dirksen of Illinois, Ellender of Louisiana, Ervin of North Carolina, Carl Hayden of Arizona, Bourke Hickenlooper of Iowa, Lister Hill of Alabama, Spessard Holland and George Smathers of Florida, Hruska of Nebraska, Jackson and Magnuson of Washington, Jordan of North Carolina, Long of Louisiana, Mansfield of Montana, McClellan of Arkansas, Thruston Morton of Kentucky, Mundt of South Dakota, Edmund Muskie of Maine, Pastore of Rhode Island, Russell of Georgia, and Stennis of Mississippi. As can be seen, the list differs in detail, though not in substance, from the author's list compiled in 1974. The changes were due to attrition. Some men had died (Ellender and Russell), others had been defeated in elections (Smathers) or retired. Muskie was dropped apparently as a result of his presidential ambitions.

initiative or positive programs, despite thirty-three years as a senator.

It is significant because the lack of personal legislation did not reduce him in the eyes of his colleagues. Russell seemed to stand for something bigger than personal glory or temporary laws. He stood for the Senate itself.

This was by no means an act of altruism or self-sacrifice. By attaching and identifying himself with the Senate and the Club, Russell for more than twenty years was one of the most influential political men in the nation. No presidential initiative, no legislation, no foreign or domestic policy could be undertaken without considering Richard Russell. He was a big bear standing in the forest path, amiable enough if not aroused. He could be gotten around, sometimes, but one had to go slow and do maneuvers. It was safest to negotiate.

The direct source of Russell's personal importance was the Senate. He realized this and, accordingly, did his best to preserve and advance the Senate's interests as an institution.

In this, too, Russell was the essence of the Club which as a body has managed over the decades not only to preserve the Senate's constitutional powers but to magnify them.

The Club can be quite awesome in exercising its powers. In the 1950s, Hubert Humphrey was a bright, cocky activist member of the Senate, well-liked by the press and with a national following. In those early years, before being embraced by the Senate establishment, he took on a Club member, the elder Harry Byrd of Virginia.

One of Byrd's special projects was the Joint Committee on Reduction of Nonessential Federal Expenditures, which Byrd liked because of the old Virginia belief that the government shouldn't spend much on anything. Humphrey suggested the committee didn't do much and was itself a "nonessential federal expenditure." He said it should be abolished.

The vast majority of the Senate, privately, couldn't have agreed more with Humphrey's assessment of the committee's value. But Byrd was a member of the Club and had certain privileges.

Humphrey later remarked he had not the slightest awareness of what he had walked into, or why. But an anti-Humphrey demonstration raged on the Senate floor for the better part of a whole day. Democrats and Republicans alike stood to give Humphrey his licks. At day's end, a dazed and battered Humphrey retired from the field. He said he then understood it was a mistake to challenge prerogatives granted by the establishment.

Another newcomer who received a lesson was Edmund Muskie, who arrived in the Senate in January 1959, and crashed head-on into the Club. Muskie, like Humphrey, came in as a phenomenon. His election as governor of Maine in 1954—a unique Democratic victory in normally Republican Maine—had made banner headlines in the newspapers. Biographies were done in *Time, Life,* and *Newsweek.* In 1954, 1956, and 1958 he had earned merit points with the party by campaigning for Democratic candidates in seventeen states. He was much in demand, nationally known. He was hot and he arrived in the Senate with an exaggerated view of himself, exaggerated as far as the Senate was concerned.

The crucial issue in the opening 1959 session of the Senate was a change in Rule 22, the rule which determines the number of votes needed to break a filibuster. At the time, Rule 22 required two thirds of the Senate membership to close off debate. But Southerners had used the filibuster repeatedly to block civil rights bills and there was an angry liberal move to change it. They wanted debate cut off by a simple majority vote.

Majority Leader Lyndon Johnson had offered a compromise on Rule 22 which would allow two thirds of the senators "present and voting" to close off debate. The compromise was illusionary. Theoretically thirty-four senators, two thirds of a quorum, could stop a filibuster. But in a cloture motion virtually every senator would be "present and voting," and the vote of sixty-seven senators would be necessary. Nevertheless, it was a face-saver for those who had taken a public stand on filibuster "reform."

It was the custom then for new senators to see the majority leader and submit a list of their choices for committee assignment. Muskie wanted to be on Foreign Relations, Commerce, and Judiciary and arranged a meeting with Johnson in the leader's office.

Johnson was using such assignment requests as a carrot weapon to bind votes for his compromise. "Jesus, it was rough," recalled a veteran of those days, "Lyndon was going around with two lists in his inside pocket. One was for committee assignments and anything else you wanted and the other was for Rule 22. He didn't talk about the first until you'd cleared on the second, and that's all there was to it."

The forty-five-minute meeting began pleasantly. Johnson gave some advice about adjusting to the role of senator from that of governor. "There'll be times, Ed," said Johnson with a smile, "when you won't know how you're going to vote until they start calling the M's."

Muskie, who has a penchant for the flash-tempered one-liner, replied, "Well, Lyndon, we haven't gotten to the M's yet," and he turned and left. "I thought it was a pleasant way to let him know that I hadn't made up my mind yet [on Rule 22]," Muskie said later.

What followed was the humiliation of Ed Muskie. It was as if his swift rise to national prominence had never happened. Johnson gave him punitive committee assignments and did not even deign to speak to him for months. Muskie was frozen out of the process by which legislation was drafted and decisions made in the Senate.

Instead of Foreign Relations, Commerce, and Judiciary, Muskie got Public Works, Banking, and Government Operations. But even these were trick bag assignments. Public Works, for instance, was important enough on the surface (it hands out pork-barrel grants). But it was ruled by the iron grip of Bob Kerr of Oklahoma, who did not accept initiative from newcomers. It was also where the leadership sent young malcontents to be disciplined.

Banking had less power, its jurisdiction having been handed over to independent agencies such as the Federal Reserve. Furthermore, its chairman, A. Willis Robertson of Virginia, was opposed to most legislation it did review and therefore did as little as possible. It was another of what the *Wehrmacht* would have called a discipline battalion.

Government Operations was a minor committee, but even there Muskie was blocked from meaningful activity because its chairman, John McClellan of Arkansas, disliked Muskie personally.

Muskie found all this a "very depressing experience" but

buckled down to the realities of the Senate, working hard and
doing the chores. Finally, at the end of a long, lonely year, Muskie
attempted to get a bill creating a commission on Intergovernmen-
tal Relations. It needed the approval of Carl Hayden of Arizona,
chairman of Appropriations. Hayden was agreeable, provided
Lyndon Johnson didn't object.

A Muskie staffer recalled, "I was on the floor one night when
one of Mr. Johnson's emissaries came up and asked me, 'You
think Muskie would [like] . . . to get that advisory commission
of his going?' I said, 'Christ, yes; anything so he doesn't draw a
blank for the year.' 'Okay' the man said, '. . . the leader worked
it out.' " The commission was funded. Muskie had served his sen-
tence, getting time off for good behavior.[4]

At a glance, it might seem that Muskie was punished for his individualism, his independence of thought. It might be inferred that
the Club demands uniformity and anonymity from its senators.
Such is not the case, however. Richard Russell, Lyndon Johnson,
Tom Connally, Everett Dirksen, Sam Ervin, and the others were
prima donnas all and certainly were not lacking in independence.
What the Club did demand was cooperation, "You have to go
along to get along."

The Senate, and its leadership group the Club, can be viewed as
a mini-society and what shocks it is not individualist or even eccentric behavior but antisocial behavior. The Senate is like any
small town with a stable population, towns such as are found most
often in the South. In such communities, eccentrics abound. There
is black Joe Cooper who gets drunk on Saturday nights and shoots
up his barn; Maybelle Ledbetter who is a secret socialist, or her
sister Frances "who takes dope"; or young Billy Tanner who hurrahs the "jook" joints and challenges the police in hundred-mile-
an-hour chases.

They are not ostracized, because the limits of their eccentricities
are known. And they are known, as were their parents and grand-
parents before them, whose behavior was predictable, not aber-
rant or threatening.

---

[4] The details and quotes from Muskie's difficulties with the leadership come
from *Muskie of Maine* by David Nevin (New York: Random House,
1972), pages 102–10.

In meeting with Muskie, Lyndon Johnson was attempting to perceive the New Englander's social attitude. Muskie's anti-Club response caused Johnson to send him off for a stint in the disciplinary battalions. He was isolated in a position where he could not harm the Club's area of interest, and at the same time he could be observed for possible rehabilitation. Muskie chose to be rehabilitated.

Some men are content with the isolation. To join the community requires too great a price. A Kennedy or a William Fulbright is not willing to submerge his ego, or his national goals. Fulbright, indeed, would seem to have been an ideal candidate for the Club. A former president of the University of Arkansas, creator of the Fulbright scholarships, he is intelligent, courteous, knowledgeable, and a man of high integrity. His racial views were compatible with mainstream Southerners. (In 1956, he had shocked his liberal Northern admirers by signing a "Southern Manifesto" objecting to Supreme Court decisions on segregation.) It was only in foreign affairs that Fulbright ran contrary to Southern tradition. He was opposed to foreign commitments, and during the Vietnam War he differed from the other Southern leaders in his refusal to rally around the flag. He opposed the war and said so with frequency and often with eloquence, whereas other Southerners, such as Richard Russell, who, though opposing the war initially, had cooperated with the White House once the war was engaged.

It was not his foreign policy views, however, that kept Fulbright out of the Club. It was his individualism, for from the time Fulbright entered the Senate in 1944 he was not a team player. In private, he was candid enough to concede that as chairman of Senate Foreign Relations his influence with fellow senators was negligible, though his voice commanded respect in the worldwide intellectual community. He, like Paul Douglas and Wayne Morse, would not submerge his individual goals to the interests of the Senate as a whole. Indeed, in their case, their ethics and ideals were too lofty to accommodate the frequent compromises required by the Club.

To be in or out of the Club reflects more on a senator's ambition and temperament than it does on his ability. Some men of great ability, such as Huey Long and John Kennedy, spurn it from the outset. Others are able but are blackballed because of character flaws—the crude racists such as Theodore Bilbo of Mississippi or the men who flout senatorial courtesy, such as Joe McCarthy of Wisconsin. (Demagoguery per se is acceptable, insofar as it helps win elections at home.)

Most men who have sat in the Senate have not been blackballed from the Club, nor have they spurned it. They are the uninvited, the rank-and-file who pursue their individual ambitions and visions of duty. Usually, they are temperamentally unsuited for team work. They prefer to do their act alone, making alliances when necessary and where possible. Two examples of able men in this category are William Proxmire and Harry Truman.

Proxmire is an extreme loner. He is the only senator who runs four miles from his home to the Capitol each morning. The only one to always stand, not sit, at his desk. The only one who has had hair transplants. He is a Democratic liberal who uses filibusters to defeat Southern bills. He is an outsider who specializes in hopeless causes and sometimes wins them. (In 1964, Proxmire began a lonely and seemingly futile campaign to kill billion-dollar funding for a supersonic transport—SST—much desired by the military-industrialist lobby and their senators. It took seven years, but he killed it in 1971.)

Proxmire is accustomed to swimming upstream. In 1952 he ran for governor of traditionally Republican Wisconsin against Governor Walter Kohler. At a governors' conference earlier that year, Kohler had had a conversation with Governor Driscoll of New Jersey.

"Have you an opponent, Walter?" asked Driscoll.

"Yes," said Kohler. "He's the son of an Illinois Republican. He graduated from Yale and Harvard, worked for J. P. Morgan, and married a Rockefeller, and just moved into Wisconsin three years ago."

"My God," exploded Driscoll, "did you pick him yourself?"[5]

When he was elected to the Senate in 1957, Proxmire was only the second Democrat elected to statewide office in Wisconsin in

[5] "The Outsider in the Senate" by Ralph Huitt, *American Political Science Review,* September 1961.

twenty-five years. His victory rejuvenated the party in the state and created almost as much sensation as Muskie's in Maine.

But unlike Muskie, Proxmire took his seat in the Senate as a freshman willing to cooperate and learn. He went beyond that. In the beginning he praised Lyndon Johnson to a degree which embarrassed Johnson's staff. Scarcely a week passed without some fulsome Proxmire tribute to the leader's skill and wonderful talents. Proxmire cheerfully accepted every chore handed to him. Johnson gave him a good assignment on Appropriations.

Proxmire had one frustration. He wanted to talk. It killed him not to talk, but he knew that freshmen bided their time. He did so, speaking only when invited by senior members to do so. He cautiously scheduled his first major speech on the day before Easter when most members would have been absent, being assured that it was proper. (Only two members heard him through, the presiding officer there by necessity, and Paul Douglas, who canceled an appointment in order to give Proxmire an audience.)

But then, the floodgates were opened. "As if he could not help himself, Proxmire became steadily more active in debate until he was one of the busiest [speakers] on the floor." The warnings came, indirect, in the form of the presiding officer looking pointedly at Proxmire while he recognized another member out of turn. And there were friendly tips, usually in the form that someone heard another senator say . . .

The rejection puzzled and frustrated Proxmire. He believed he had exercised restraint. He fell silent—for a while. Then it appeared he had made a decision. To hell with the establishment. In June, his sixth month in the Senate, he stood and offered six amendments to the Mutual Security Act and insisted on a vote.

"Inasmuch as Proxmire was not a member of the Foreign Relations Committee," his aide Ralph Huitt wrote, "the performance was hardly a demonstration of modesty. Criticism was sharp and immediate, though indirect as always, and it spurred Proxmire to a decision: he would be a senator like Wayne [Morse] and Paul [Douglas]; he would talk when he pleased on whatever he chose and would not worry about his influence in the Senate. He had found his role."

He turned on Johnson, calling him a dictator. He discovered

thrift, which was popular in Wisconsin, and set out to eliminate funds for new post offices in Mississippi, Tennessee, Vermont, and Pennsylvania. He was crushed. Not only in the floor vote, but eight senators—representing the four affected states—were alienated for the indefinite future.

Nevertheless, as the lonely years passed, Proxmire built up expertise—in agriculture, because Wisconsin was a farm state, and in military spending (Wisconsin's thrift). Because of that expertise, he gradually, then with frequency, was chosen by the leadership to handle pertinent legislation. As his role as an outsider became more and more consistent, it became more valuable to the Senate leadership. Protest groups in search of a spokesman could be referred to Proxmire. And, where compromise was needed, the value of a middle position could be demonstrated by playing Proxmire against a conservative outsider like Strom Thurmond, the Republican from South Carolina.

Each year, of course, Proxmire's seniority increased until by 1974 he ranked ninth in Appropriations and second on Banking. The big bankers dreaded the day Proxmire might become chairman. That happened in January 1975 when John Sparkman of Alabama moved over to chair Foreign Relations, replacing William Fulbright, who had been defeated back in Arkansas.[6]

Proxmire had found his place in the Senate community. He had been observed and identified as a loner and took his place with Morse and Douglas among the eccentrics of the community. He had in time become comfortable with the Senate Club, and the Club in time had become comfortable with him.

Unlike Proxmire, Harry Truman—Democratic senator from Missouri from 1934 to 1944—never went to war with the Club. Indeed, he may have been an unwitting member of it, though

[6] Sparkman was number two on Foreign Relations after Fulbright, and simultaneously chairman of Banking. The nation's bankers liked Sparkman, who, though relatively liberal, was a known quantity. Proxmire gave them the shudders. As a consequence, when it appeared Fulbright faced a tough election in Arkansas against Governor Dale Bumpers, the bankers pumped money into the Fulbright campaign, to keep him in the Senate as chairman of Foreign Relations and thereby keep Sparkman on Banking.

Truman felt he had not built enough seniority to be considered a member.

"It takes a long time for a person to reach a position of influence in the Senate," Truman told a biographer. "Eight or ten senators really run the whole thing. And you have to have their confidence to get anything done, and I think it can be said that eventually I did have."

As an example, Truman recalled that in a key appointment his advice had been sought by Arthur Vandenberg, the Republican leader from Michigan who was very much in the Club.

"I said, 'Senator, I think he's all right.' I went around to my seat and Vandenberg got up and said, 'When the junior senator from Missouri makes a statement like that, it's worth agreeing to.' And they did. The Senate approved of [the man] for the job."

". . . It shows you," Truman told biographer Merle Miller, "that if you have a fundamentally honest background with senators, you can get things accomplished . . . Of course there are always those . . . whose word you know isn't worth a goddamn. Like Huey Long . . . He was a liar and he was nothing but a damn demagogue . . ."

Truman laughingly recalled he was the acting presiding officer one day during a Long filibuster. Long had a big stack of books and newspapers, reading everything he could lay hands on to kill the hours.

"I adjourned the Senate when he closed his book," said Truman, "and we walked across the street from the Senate, and he said, 'What did you think of my speech, Harry?'

"I said, 'Hell, Huey, I had to sit there and listen to it.' And he never spoke to me after that. Not that I was missing much."[7]

In his second senatorial election, Truman found the Club was of more help to him than the Democratic party.

He had been an enthusiastic supporter of the New Deal, but early in 1940 he had criticized Roosevelt's going for a third term. Roosevelt struck back at him in the Democratic primary in Missouri, sending money to Truman's opponent. At the same time,

[7] *Plain Speaking* by Merle Miller (New York: Berkley Publishing Corp., 1974), page 161.

Truman was publicly tied to his friend Tom Pendergast, the Kansas City boss who was in jail for tax evasion. The implication, never proved, was that Truman was owned by Pendergast. And piling on the handicaps, Truman, the child of Southern parents, came down hard in favor of civil rights. He told Missourians, they should allow "Negroes [to have] the rights that are theirs . . . It is our duty to see that Negroes in our locality have increased opportunity to exercise their privilege as freemen."

Truman had no funds and about the only discernible financial help he had was from the Senate establishment, which caused contributions to be sent out-of-state. They also dispatched a gifted campaigner, Senator Lew Schwellenbach of Washington, to help.

It was an ugly, low-level campaign for the Democratic nomination. Truman's Roosevelt-backed opponents even caused the foreclosure of the mortgage on his mother's farm. But the grassroots expert won against all odds (as he would in 1948). When he returned to the Senate, he received a standing ovation from both parties.

The Club, with its emphasis on character, had given support to Harry Truman. Indirectly, this proved a great national service. In his second term, the establishment chose Harry Truman to chair a Senate investigation of corruption, inefficiency, and bungling on war contracts. He saved at least $1 billion and greatly aided the war effort, and it led to his nomination for the vice presidency in 1944.

None of this could have been foreseen in the Senate election in Missouri in 1940. But by recruiting and developing men of character, the Club has created the potential for such fortunate accidents. By the very nature of its existence, it puts strength into nationally critical positions.

All this is to the Club's credit, although, unlike the unique seniority system, the phenomenon of the Club is not extraordinary. It is simply a leadership clique which might exist in any type of social organization. Its value lies in its longevity and quality, that it is made up of the same type of men over the years. In its current form, it has renewed itself in its own image continuously since the Congresses of Woodrow Wilson.

That image was built around the best qualities of the Southern senator. It explains the essential Southernness of the Club, although Southerners neither control the Club nor constitute a majority of its members.

There is nothing official about the Club, just as there is nothing official about seniority. Both phenomena were developed casually. But they come together—the Club and seniority—to produce a cadre of solid constitutional protectors.

Book Three
THE USE OF POWER

Chapter 17
THE REPUBLIC

Franklin Roosevelt's New Deal put an end to Democratic solidarity in the South. The Democratic party in courting and serving a majority of national voters could no longer tolerate the racial prejudices of the white South. The South, in turn, began to drift away from the Democrats.

A further alienation of the South from the Democratic party was caused by the geometrical explosion of federal powers, a leap occasioned by the New Deal and World War II. Southerners, like Dr. Frankenstein, had created a monster which had grown out of control.

From the Roosevelt administration onward, the federal government increasingly operated on a principle of benign interference. During the Depression, numerous bureaucracies were created to correct existing wrongs and as a result this form of solution became a habit with the Congress and the Executive. Soon benign interference ranged from vast public welfare programs (direct and indirect assistance for multimillion-dollar corporations and starving individuals alike) to prohibitions against racial and religious biases (many Americans thought and think that bigotry is their constitutional right), to employee-hiring quotas, to mandatory auto seat belts, to matchbook covers that had to be closed before striking. All this interference by government was new. It didn't exist before.[1]

To political conservatives, whether any single interference was desirable or not was beside the point. The important thing was the constitutional rights which they felt should be left undisturbed. They held a Jeffersonian-Southern view of minimal federal government and minimal interference in private lives.

The policy of benign interference was a policy of the Democratic party and it greatly changed American life. It also increased the alienation between the South and the Democratic party and between the South and the rest of the nation.

The South's sole resource to oppose this federal interference was in the Congress, where Southerners ruled the committees and where the more responsible Southerners argued that special legislation to ensure the rights of a few was a danger to the liberties of all. To their shame, they did not offer solutions for the rescue of blacks and women, who were second-class citizens. But they did, with wisdom and foresight, object to the growing federal power.

From 1945 onward, the Southerners were engaged in rearguard political actions to protect their vision of Jeffersonian democracy, fighting skirmishes to postpone and delay the rolling weight of the federal government.

They fought in the House and Senate with steadily diminishing numbers, abandoned by their own party, constantly abused in books, magazines, newspapers, on television, and in the lecture halls of universities. The white Southerner, whose prejudice had made miserable the lives of millions of blacks, became himself the victim of a national prejudice.

In the meantime, Southern landmarks disappeared one by one: the one-party system, the one-crop (cotton) system in agriculture and industry, the Jim Crow laws. These visible features of the Southern terrain were replaced by an equally visible, new land-

[1] Prior to the New Deal, the federal government's direct interference with the individual citizen consisted almost entirely of three sets of laws: the antitrust laws, the Opium Exclusion Act of 1909 which was the first antinarcotics law, and the Volstead Act of 1919 which prohibited the making and selling of intoxicating beverages.

mark: a mammoth federal presence in health, education, and welfare.

The Southerners fought on. And an irony of the entire period
from 1945 to 1975 is how often the Jeffersonian Southerners happened to be in the right place at the right time to rescue the American Republic. And they did rescue it, using the individual resources and strength which were a consequence of their honor,
their abilities, and their political tradition.

For instance, the Texan Tom Connally would be the guiding
mind behind creation of the United Nations. A Virginia-educated
Secretary of State, George Catlett Marshall, would create the
Marshall Plan and rescue Europe from economic blight. And a
whole platoon of Southern senators would step in at the proper
moments to affect history: Richard Russell putting down the danger of a right-wing coup, freshman Senator Sam Ervin destroying
Joe McCarthy, and John Stennis speaking four private words,
"unacceptable to the Senate," which drove President Nixon to resign.

In the 1945–75 era, as in 1776, many of the nation's most creative policies would emanate from Southerners. The Southern political contribution to the nation would be unexcelled except, as had
been the case two hundred years earlier, in the matter of race relations.

With the exception of George Marshall, a creative man who was
a presidential appointee, the historically important Southerners of
the postwar era were produced by a system, trained as protégés,
recruited and installed on committees by the Senate Club, and
moved up the ladder by committee seniority.

This Southern system worked most effectively in the Senate,
where, with its small membership and century-long adherence to
the seniority system, men like Russell, Ervin, and Stennis could be
placed in the right place at the right time, but it was no more acci-
dental than the placement of a bishop by a chess master.

The method by which the Senate produced and placed such
men is seen in the careers of John Stennis and Sam Ervin, both of
whom came into the Club fully developed by the Southern political process; in Herman Talmadge, who was converted from a

racist demagogue into a statesman; and in Jim Eastland, a chairman who moved up despite the Club, whose sins are unchangeable, perhaps unforgivable, but whose talents were nevertheless used constructively by the Southerners and the Senate.

Chapter 18
THE MISSISSIPPIAN

There is a saying in Mississippi that one senator should be a gentleman and the other a sonofabitch, that way the whole state is represented. This refers to a tendency there to balance the election of red-neck demagogues, the Vardamans and the Bilbos, with the election of gentlemen, the Percys and the Stennises.

For some thirty years, beginning in the 1940s, Mississippi's senatorial delegation satisfied a version of the equation. The senior senator was James Oliver Eastland, born in 1904, and elected in 1942. Protégé of Bilbo, coarse and rude in his public manner, demagogue, a man who treated the Bill of Rights and other constitutional liberties as concepts dangerous—which they are—to the rulers of the land—whether the land be Mississippi or the United States and whether the rulers be the elected government, the banks, or Delta cotton growers.

The junior senator, born in 1901 and elected in 1947 (ironically as the successor of Theodore Bilbo) was John Stennis. Like Eastland, he was a powerful Senate committee chairman, like Eastland he held a Southern conservative view toward government. On important matters of character and style, however, they differed. Stennis was the "conscience of the Senate," a benevolent baron known for his cautious use of the levers of power. His reputation for integrity and incorruptibility boosted him to the peak of influence and prestige within the Senate. He became the epitome of the Club, the establishment which rejected Eastland.

"Stennis is in. Eastland is out. What gave one man access to the Club and not the other was the test of character," said a colleague of the two.[1]

One aspect of character was their contrasting attitudes toward dissent. Eastland would crush dissent, when, where, and with whatever tools were practical. Stennis would abide by it as a legal right.

For instance, Stennis' maiden speech in the Senate was against civil rights legislation and he was among the leaders in the Southern filibuster of the 1950s and 1960s. Yet, what many Mississippians did not know was that Stennis had quietly worked to desegregate the University of Mississippi law school in the 1950s, prior to the rights confrontations of the 1960s. Stennis upholds his view of the Constitution in matters large and small. One example was when he defended the right of a twenty-five-year-old minister (Wilkes Macaulay) to preach a civil rights sermon in Stennis' home church at DeKalb, Mississippi.

Stennis had come home to find that church elders had prohibited the pastor's speech. He had, according to Reverend Macaulay, given them a stiff lecture along these lines: "The real issue here is freedom of the pulpit. We can't tell Macaulay what to preach. If we're not going to have this pulpit free, we might as well take it and throw it in the street."

His reputation for fairness achieved legendary proportions. One incident which helped build it occurred in 1967 when Stennis was selected to head a very sensitive investigation of charges that Connecticut Senator Thomas Dodd had diverted campaign contributions to his personal use.

It was a delicate assignment. The Senate, that guardian of individualism, is never anxious to investigate any senator, regardless of charges. This basic reluctance was compounded by the nature of the charges. To widely varying degrees, most senators intermingle some professional, personal and campaign expenses.

[1] Confidential interview, May 1974.

Campaign contributions, and in the case of wealthy senators personal funds, are often used to supplement their federal budget, which by itself is insufficient to meet all the mailings, travel, phone calls on behalf of constituents, and other expenses of a senator's office. Operating funds come from intermingled sources, and are spent on intermingled purposes, it being often difficult to define a trip as personal, political, or senatorial.

Dodd, however, was an extreme case of abusing the practice. Nevertheless, there was much sympathy in the Senate for his predicament. At the same time, the public was outraged at his selling of favors and there was a mood to take his scalp.

Stennis proceeded slowly. He gave Dodd every opportunity to defend himself, but at the end the Stennis committee censured Dodd for conduct "contrary to accepted morals." Stennis emerged with an even larger reputation for fairness and justice. Liberal Republican Mark Hatfield, who had done long battles with Stennis over military spending, said: "Some of us freshmen were sitting around once during the Dodd hearings, and we agreed that if we found ourselves charged with some terrible crime and if we could pick our judge we'd pick John Stennis to judge us."

And it was John Stennis who in the spring of 1974 virtually ensured that Richard Nixon would either resign or be removed from office by impeachment and conviction.

At the time, Nixon's implication in the Watergate burglaries, perjuries, and buy-offs of witnesses was known only to the President and his closest aides (Bob Haldeman, John Ehrlichman, and John Mitchell). But thanks to the staff work of the Sam Ervin committee and the interrogations by Herman Talmadge it was known that the crucial conversations were on tape, and that it was they which should prove the extent of Nixon's guilt or innocence.

The President had refused to surrender the tapes and the Supreme Court was considering whether Congress had the right in law to force him. Before the court's decision was released, the White House publicly hinted that should the ruling be adverse, Nixon might defy the court.

At that point, John Stennis secretly sent word to Richard Nixon that such defiance would be unacceptable to the Senate.

"That sealed the fate of the Nixon presidency," said a White

House aide several months after Nixon's resignation. "Although the rest of us didn't know what was on those tapes, the President did. Stennis' message closed off the last exit. The President knew that if he surrendered the tapes, he would be impeached and removed for what was on them. He knew that if he refused to surrender the tapes, he would be impeached for that. His only alternative was resignation.

"Oh, I guess, if you're playing around with scenarios, the President could have surrounded the Congress and the Court with the 101st Airborne. But really, after Stennis' message, the only practical thing . . . was for the President to resign. He waited as long as he could, hoping for some stroke of fortune to save him. When it didn't come, he resigned."[2]

Stennis' manners are as polished as his ethics. He has been known to interrupt important Senate hearings in order to guide a late-arriving woman spectator to a seat. And a dirt-farmer constituent visiting his Senate office receives as much courtesy as a visiting Secretary of Defense.

He likewise requires his committee members to be well mannered. He frowns upon tardiness and insists they pay attention. His presence is such that he doesn't use a gavel. Merely tapping his water glass with a pencil demands silence.

Mississippi, and for much of its history its senators, has been a state of contradictions and surprises. As mentioned above, for every Eastland or Bilbo, it has produced a Stennis or a Pat Harrison. For every James Vardaman, a William Alexander Percy. It produced in Hiram Rhodes Revels and Blanche Bruce, men who were the only black senators prior to the election of Edward Brooke of Massachusetts in 1966, *and* men who were senators of exceptional quality. Mississippi in 1975 had elected more black officials than all but two states in the United States.[3]

It is a state of surprises and contrasts. It has produced some of

[2] Confidential interview, November 1974.
[3] In 1975, Michigan had 179 elected black officials; New York, 160; Mississippi 152; Alabama, 149; Illinois, 137; Louisiana, 130; and California, largest state in the union, 130. In terms of regional distribution, the South had 45 per cent of all elected black officials, while the Northeast had 22 per cent, the Midwest 26 per cent, and the Far West 7 per cent.

the best writers in the twentieth century, William Faulkner, Shelby Foote, Eudora Welty, Hodding Carter, Walker Percy, Tennessee Williams, and Richard Wright. Yet the median education level is 8.9 years, compared to a national average of 12.2 years. Mississippi ranks near the bottom in all statistics: income, housing, health care, illegitimacy. Indeed, while the rest of the nation tends to view the entire South as one large Mississippi, all Southern states have a saying, "Thank God for Mississippi." Were it not for Mississippi, then Louisiana, Arkansas, Alabama, or some other Southern state would be at the statistical bottom.

Mississippi's national politics falls into two simple historical divisions. Prior to 1850, it was aimed at wresting control of the land and the river from the French, the Spanish, the English, and the Indians. Since 1850, it has been aimed at keeping control in the hands of a dominant class of white agriculturalists.

Mississippi's internal political battles have been waged over who would constitute that dominant class of whites, the aristocratic Delta planters or the red-necks. The struggle between these two, V. O. Key observed in the 1940s, distills down to a politics of oratory "because the state is miserably poor. The gap between rich and poor is wide, but as a whole the state is so poor that a welfare politics can only become a politics of fulmination and little more. Louisiana's neo-Populism could tap the state's resources and take action. Mississippi's neo-Populism under the leadership of Vardaman [and] Bilbo sooner or later ran against the limitations imposed by poverty."[4]

Observing the risk of oversimplification, these two classes can be described. They occupy different territorial bases. The planters, masters of huge plantations cultivated largely by black sharecroppers and tenant farmers, reign over the Mississippi Delta country, the northwest fifth of the state which runs from Memphis to below Vicksburg. About two counties wide, the flat, fertile valley soil is easy to farm and constitutes one of the favored agricultural regions of the world. Living beneath towering levees which hold back the river, its masters have a common experience of life-

[4] *Southern Politics* by V. O. Key, Jr. (New York: Vintage Books, 1949), page 230.

long battles against the river. They have the common bond of men
of property everywhere to promote their self interest.

The "red-neck," "cracker," or "peckerwood," as he has been
derisively called since the nineteenth century, lives in a different
world. His country occupies roughly the eastern and southern two
thirds of the state, surrendering to pine forests along the coast.
These hills are the home of the tenant farmer and the small independent farmer. The soil is not so fertile and the labor is hard. He
looks with envy on the Delta occupied by the planter and the
black.

The first successful challenge of Delta supremacy came in 1902
with the election of Governor James Vardaman, a personally kind
and vain man who was more of a showman than a political
thinker. He dressed, or overdressed, much in the style of a cowboy star in a Wild West show, black hair worn long to his shoulders, decorated boots, and a white Stetson. His modest brush with
education was summed up in a passion to quote Bobbie Burns at
the slightest opportunity.

In oratory, he was a demagogue pure and simple. He advertised his love for the "common people," by which he meant the
poor whites, and he stood for them against the "nigger." Those
were his qualifications for office. He was very popular in Mississippi and they called him The Great White Chief.

As his career went on, he gathered unto himself various
Populist doctrines. He was anticorporation, antirich, and favored
increased education for the rural whites. As for the blacks, "Why
squander money on his education when the only effect is to spoil a
good field hand and make an insolent cook?" he asked.

Delta candidates were pushed into a defense of the black. "The
Negro problem," said one, "is being agitated for sinister motives
of gain by those who have not the interest of their state at heart."
Throughout Vardaman's career, the rallying cry of white supremacy carried the day and other politicians watched and learned.

The epitome of the Delta opposition came from LeRoy Percy.
Though by no means did all Delta planters embody the qualities
of the Percys, that family typified the best of the old Southern aristocracy, being bound by a tradition of honor, of fair dealing and
justice, and obligation to the less fortunate.

The story of the Vardaman-Percy senatorial election campaign was told by Percy's son, William Alexander Percy.[5]

"Father wanted to be a force for good government," wrote Percy, "but he did not want to hold office. He did not want to be senator from Mississippi, but he wanted to keep Vardaman from being. Vardaman stood for all he considered vulgar and dangerous. Most people we knew felt the same way about him."

A vacancy had been created by the death of Senator McLaurin in 1910. The election, for a one-year term, would be decided by the Mississippi legislature, not by popular vote. Vardaman looked certain to win, but the Delta faction decided to field five candidates to block him. They figured they could make enough separate claims on the various legislators to deadlock the ballot, then they'd put forth the strongest of the five as the Delta candidate. Percy had agreed to be one of the five.

The strategy succeeded. For fifty-six ballots, the Delta blocked Vardaman's election. On the next ballot, Percy was put forward as the single Delta candidate and won, by a slim five votes. He was senator. But the politics was not finished.

His son wrote: "While the overt issue in father's race before the legislature had been Vardaman's stand on the Negro question, the undeclared issue had been the unanswerable charge against father that he was a prosperous plantation owner, a corporation lawyer, and unmistakably a gentleman." The Percy-Vardaman issue was a Delta-red-neck contest, a class competition. The black as he had been in the class struggle between the North and the South, was also in Mississippi a pawn.

At that point, an obscure Vardaman lieutenant named Theodore Bilbo entered the scene. About two months after the election, Bilbo, a member of the legislature, went to a grand jury and waved currency he said he had accepted as a bribe to vote for Percy. There were two things queer about his testimony: First, the record showed, he had not voted for Percy, and second, an inspection of the bills showed many had been issued by the bank after Bilbo said he had received them. Nevertheless, the charge

[5] *Lanterns on the Levee* by William Alexander Percy (Baton Rouge: Louisiana State University Press edition, 1973). (William Alexander Percy is the uncle of novelist Walker Percy.)

caught fire. And Bilbo fanned it, lecturing across the state, a self-accused bribe-taker, a ridiculous figure five feet, two inches tall with a paunch, sloping shoulders, and a receding chin. He looked like an ugly elf, but he had an attention-getting voice, a theatrical manner and a gift for the platform that brought men leaping into the aisle shouting "Hallelujah" and "Amen" and "Hit it, Bilbo!"

The legislature censured Bilbo and condemned his bribery charge as a "trumped-up falsehood utterly unworthy of belief." But they failed by one vote to expel him.

Bilbo cared not at all. He crisscrossed the state, "a man without honor hounding a man of honor." The youthful William Percy watched his father's reputation being torn to shreds and pondered on the success of Bilbo:

He was "a pert little monster, glib and shameless, with that sort of cunning common to criminals which passes for intelligence. The people loved him. They loved him not because they were deceived in him, but because they understood him thoroughly; they said of him proudly, 'He's a slick little bastard.' He was one of them and he had risen from obscurity to the fame of glittering infamy—it was as if they themselves had crashed the headlines."

Vardaman's own glamour and fame was eclipsed by that of his rising lieutenant. Percy attended a Bilbo meeting and, with the distaste of the aristocrat for the masses, studied the flock.

"I studied them as they milled about. They were the sort of people that lynch Negroes, that mistake hoodlumism for wit, and cunning for intelligence, that attend revivals and fight and fornicate in the bushes afterwards. They were undiluted Anglo-Saxons. They were the sovereign voter."

In 1911, Percy, barely installed in his office, had to run for re-election. Vardaman ran against him but this time Vardaman won, greatly assisted by Bilbo. The "sonofabitch" vote in the state had gained the Senate. In 1915 they regained the governor's office, with Bilbo winning by a slim margin.

As Mississippi law prevented a governor from succeeding himself, Bilbo and Vardaman and their followers played musical chairs with state offices through the Twenties and early Thirties, usually but not always narrowly beating the Delta opposition. In

1934, Bilbo turned on Vardaman and ran against him for a seat in the Senate.

By this time, Mississippi politics had settled down to class rhetoric, rhetoric born during the 1911 Percy-Vardaman campaign: poor versus rich, rural versus city, hill country against Delta. Vardaman had said politics was a contest "between the man whose toil produces the wealth of the country, and the favored few who reap for profit." Bilbo said the same, and he matched his mentor "nigger" for "nigger" and went much further than Vardaman in personal invective.

Bilbo described one opponent as "a cross between a hyena and a mongrel, begotten in a nigger graveyard at midnight, suckled by a cow and educated by a fool." (The man so described later boarded a train on which Bilbo was a passenger and beat him insensible with a pistol butt.)

Bilbo won his 1934 election by a slim margin, the first of three senatorial elections he was to win.

Bilbo and Vardaman constitute a type in Southern politics. They are entertainers more than politicians, a Southern counterpart of Everyman in the medieval morality plays. It is their very commonness and lack of ability that make them popular. As Percy had noted, they are recognized for what they are: lazy, lying, posturing fools who do what most folks fantasize to do. They twist the nose of their superiors, spout the worst trash-mouth invective against enemies real and imagined, flaunt their power, and generally indulge themselves with the excesses of a sometimes amusing child. Commonness is what made Everyman the most popular of morality play characters, and is the factor which helped Bilbo, Vardaman, and Earl Long, and many lesser politicians win election after election.

Significantly, when Bilbo entered the U. S. Senate, and was no longer playing directly to his Mississippi audience, he behaved respectably, except on campaign trips home. In the Capitol, he sat quietly for four years but was consistently shunned by the Club. His first radical move was not all that radical—or new.

In June 1938, Bilbo offered an amendment to a work-relief bill which he claimed, with his limited mental resources, would solve the unemployment problem. His proposal was to ship twelve million blacks back to Africa—reminiscent of the old Liberian scheme and to similar projects endorsed by such as Daniel Webster, Abraham Lincoln, and U. S. Grant, each of whom had spoken in favor of voluntary colonization.

Bilbo's scheme was likewise voluntary and he displayed a voluminous petition which he claimed bore the names of 2.5 million blacks who chose to remove to Africa.[6]

His measure would have established a "Greater Liberia" by taking 400,000 square miles from Great Britain and France as part payment on their World War I debts. The United States would provide transportation and, when the colonists arrived in Africa, it would pay labor battalions army wages to build the colony.

Except for the racist implications, the idea wasn't all that extraordinary. Many white Americans, made desperate by the Depression, would have chanced a subsidized adventure in the jungle, probably to their regret. But they would have attempted it, and it can be supposed that a large number of blacks likewise would have given it a try, being, as always, harder hit by a depression than the whites and being given, simultaneously, an escape from the whites.

Furthermore, the idea had a certain historical legitimacy. It was in the grand Southern tradition of national expansion, and it resurrected the old scheme of deportation to solve the racial problem. Mind you, it overlooked the wishes of the present inhabitants of the new colony, but wasn't that also traditional?

Bilbo contended that eight million of the twelve million American blacks would migrate to Africa if the move were subsidized. He saw it as the high point of his career and said he was carrying out the work of Jefferson and Lincoln, "the solution to the race problem which they advocated . . . When this task has been accomplished, what a great problem we will have solved for ourselves and for our posterity."

Other senators and the press of the nation turned on the proposal savagely and it deranged him. Bilbo responded by arousing the old Southern disgust at Yankee interference, and for the next

[6] Most of the signatures were gathered from forty-five states by Mrs. Mattie Lena Gordon, a Chicago black who headed a group called the Peace Movement of Ethiopia.

eight years he became even more rabidly sectional and racist. When *Life* magazine called him "the worst man in the Senate" or when Robert Taft of Ohio called him a "disgrace to the Senate," Bilbo gleefully repeated the charges at home as more grist for his propaganda mill. Each attack gave him more strength back home, as Mississippians gathered round their endangered member.

He won re-election to the Senate in 1940 and again in 1946. His racial invective reached a peak of hysteria. He had become, with his ridiculous appearance, his sonorous speaking style, and his demented racism an easy victim of caricature and a caricature which was sometimes used to embarrass the Senate as a whole. After his 1946 election, and before he was sworn in for a new term, two Senate committees filed complaints against Bilbo. The first report said that he had gained office by improper practices. The other said that Bilbo had taken bribes, and had improperly used his high office as United States senator for "his personal gain in his dealings with war contractors."

The elections of 1946 saw the Republicans take a majority in the Senate, and they refused to let Bilbo take his seat when the Congress convened in January 1947. But, as a compromise, the Senate agreed not to take up the issue of permanent seating until Bilbo, at that time sick with cancer, was able to return and defend himself. He died shortly afterward without returning.

The Delta planters seized the Bilbo death as an opportunity to install one of their own in the Senate. He was John Stennis, a career politician who had been a state legislator, district attorney, and circuit judge. His slogan in politics since the beginning of that career had been:

"I will plow a straight furrow right down to the end of my row."

John Stennis came from a family of country doctors, though his father was a farmer and merchant in De Kalb, the seat of Kemper County. In Mississippi, Kemper is known as "bloody Kemper" because a villainous carpetbagger judge and his family were lynched there by the Ku Klux Klan during Reconstruction.

History in Kemper County, as it is throughout the South, is a living thing, always present. The lynching is still remembered, at least in legendary form, and for the older generations "the war" refers to the Civil War.

John Stennis told an interviewer that his mother and father missed a college education because of "the war," meaning the Civil War. "Down there for the last hundred years," said Stennis, "people lacked for money and lacked for worldly things. But they got plenty of things money can't buy—like good neighbors, good friends, the community spirit of sharing with the other fellow."

Stennis took his law degree in 1928 from Thomas Jefferson's school, the University of Virginia. He served a short term in the Mississippi House, then was elected district attorney and in 1937 became a circuit judge. He was in that post in 1947 when Bilbo died, and he won election to the U. S. Senate. The Southern Club which had kept Bilbo away from power throughout his twelve-year Senate career, brought the freshman Stennis immediately into their ranks. He came under the wing of Richard Russell of Georgia, leader of the Southern bloc.

"Russell was the biggest man in government in those days," Stennis recalled, "and we knew each other's people. The Southerners often knew each other before coming in. If not, they had a common background and we helped one another."[7]

Russell, who had been in the Senate since 1933, was the teacher and adviser of most of the promising Southerners who entered the Senate in the 1940s and 1950s. He gave them advice, placed them on advantageous committees, and taught them the ways and manners of the Senate. They in turn passed these teachings on to others.

They were respected by their colleagues. In later years, a freshman senator related how he looked to Stennis for advice from the time he entered.

"I would ask him, for instance, what type of committee I should try to get on, or what I should do when I first get to the Senate. There are certain senators that everyone universally respects. At least all of the older senators respect him. You sense it, you feel it. I will give you a strong example: John Stennis. I just sense that everyone in the Senate respects Senator Stennis. He is not a committee chairman [then], he is from Mississippi, but as far as I am

[7] Interview with author, May 1974.

concerned, he is a fine senator, and he is the type of man I would go to to seek advice. He tries to help you. He takes an interest in the new senator. He invites me to breakfast once a week."[8]

John Stennis is another disproof of the myth that Southern power in the Congress rests on raw seniority. His strength is his character, a strength which saw him adopted under the protégé tradition and brought into the Club. In 1945, Senate Minority Leader Lyndon Johnson passed over many more senior senators to place sophomore Stennis on the committee to investigate Senator Joseph McCarthy of Wisconsin. (Johnson also appointed freshman Sam Ervin, who was so junior that he hardly had his bags unpacked before he was rushed into the hot spot.)

Stennis handled another delicate assignment in 1962 after South Carolinian Strom Thurmond, a Democrat turned States Righter turned Republican, charged that the Kennedy administration was "muzzling the military" in its reports to the Congress. Thurmond claimed that high-level military critics of Defense Secretary Robert McNamara were being prohibited from making their objections known to Congress. Stennis chaired the investigation of Thurmond's charges and earned the gratitude of colleagues for keeping a calm hold on hearings that could have degenerated into a sensational witch hunt against liberal Democrats. And in 1965, Stennis was again tapped, to handle the Dodd investigation.

During all this time he was one of the leaders of the Southern effort to defeat civil rights legislation.

Stennis has several times tried to break out of racial politics, but on each occasion he has been jerked back by the realities of Mississippi elections. "He knows," says a friend, "what Mississippi has done to the Negro over the years is wrong. But at the time he grew up, you couldn't take any other position and be in Mississippi politics." He refuses, however, to make statements against black people and has never run a "nigger-nigger" campaign.

Yet, partly due to heavy pressure from his white constituency and partly due to his attitude on constitutional rights, Stennis makes strong efforts to preserve the social status quo in Mississippi.

[8] *Power in the Senate* by Randall B. Ripley (New York: St. Martin's Press, 1969), page 86.

One example of his tactics in this regard came in 1969 when he forced the White House to relax school desegregation pressure in Mississippi. He had done this quietly, but the story exploded into view when a Jackson, Mississippi, newspaper reported that President Nixon had ordered a retreat on Mississippi desegregation after Stennis "threatened to quit as floor manager" of a Nixon-backed military appropriations bill.

The White House press asked Nixon about it and he denied any such thing had happened. "Senator Stennis did speak to me," the President acknowledged, "about the Mississippi situation. But anybody who knows Senator Stennis and anybody who knows me would know he would be the last person to say, 'Look, if you don't do what I want in Mississippi, I'm not going to do what is best for this country.'

"He did not say that [he wanted a quid pro quo] and under no circumstances, of course, would I have acceded to it."

It was a slippery answer and truthful insofar as Stennis would not have presented a blatant threat. He would instead have politely implied it and Nixon, who spent ten years in the Senate as senator and Vice President, had enough experience to read the implication.

Shortly after the Nixon press conference, three cabinet officers made conciliatory calls upon Stennis.[9] A few days later the pressure for desegregating Mississippi school districts was relaxed. (It was undone later that year, however, when the Supreme Court unanimously scolded the Administration for its retreat and said the time had come to integrate "at once" in Mississippi.)

Since the day he first went to Washington, Stennis has kept a practice of returning home to Mississippi about every other weekend. His office was kept in the state capital of Jackson, but most of his time was spent around De Kalb, a town about as antique in the 1970s as it was when Stennis was born in 1901. It has dusty streets and drugstores and sheet-iron façades above the store fronts. There John Stennis holds court at the cafe of an old hotel and gives the truck drivers and dirt farmers information on what

[9] The Attorney General, John Mitchell, the Secretary of Defense, Melvin Laird, and the Secretary of Health, Education and Welfare, Robert Finch.

he is doing, and what other people *might* be doing in Washington. And it works, for in the small towns of Mississippi where John Stennis holds court, they know and discuss for years afterward what is going on in national policy. What John Stennis says will happen usually does happen, for he does not fool them or high-talk them. In Mississippi, there is not the cultural isolation between the powerful and the nonpowerful as there is, say, in New England between the Kennedys and the factory workers.

Stennis by 1969 was number two Democrat on Richard Russell's Armed Services Committee and much desired the chairmanship. In that year, the chairman of Appropriations, Carl Hayden of Arizona, left the Senate. As mentioned above, Russell was number two on Appropriations and chose to become chairman, leaving Stennis as chairman of Armed Services. This move by Russell gave the South chairmanships of all five of the most powerful committees. (Long held Finance, Eastland had Judiciary, and Fulbright had Foreign Relations.)

Stennis came into the chairmanship at the moment the entire congressional military establishment was being rocked by the fiercest budgetary revolt since before World War II. For Stennis, said an observer, it was like being promoted to commander of the fort just as the Indians came swarming over the walls. It was at the height of the Vietnam war and Stennis believed in military defense, though like his mentor Russell he was not a warhawk.[10]

During Russell's sixteen years as Armed Services chairman, the Senate never quibbled about the Pentagon's annual shopping list of missiles, ships, bombers, and other stunning paraphernalia. In 1969, however, with concern about domestic needs on the rise, and with shocking disclosures of runaway waste, the Senate was skeptical. And at the precise moment when skepticism was reach-

[10] In 1954, Richard Russell protested President Eisenhower's idea to send aid to the French at Dienbienphu. From 1961 onward, Russell opposed the Vietnam war, saying, "I don't buy this so-called Domino Theory. We don't have to have South Vietnam to hold back communism. You can't help anybody who won't help themselves." Russell preferred to stay away from war. However, once Kennedy plunged the United States in, Russell backed him up, now saying, "There is no honorable alternative to victory . . . The only thing to do is punish North Vietnam until they're willing to negotiate." Stennis and most Southern senators held identical views throughout the 1950s and 1960s.

ing its height, President Nixon chose to push through a multibillion-dollar antiballistics missile (ABM) appropriation. The revolt was on.

In the ensuing debate, the test of Stennis was not the outcome of the appropriation proposal but the manner in which he allowed or denied each side opportunity to present its case. Feelings ran high. The extremists on one side wanted to emasculate the military; on the other they wanted to continue the blank check. Stennis' position was to let each side prove its case, prove it or default.

The debate took thirty-seven days. Senator Barry Goldwater of Arizona thought it sacrilege to cast suspicions at the military. It is a "left-wing . . . war on American defense." The dovish majority leader Mike Mansfield read it differently: "The Senate has asserted afresh its constitutional role to understand and appraise our defense strategy."

That was oratory, debate for public consumption on the Senate floor. Back in committee, where the issue would truly be decided, Stennis was asking for evidence from all sides. Edward Kennedy of Massachusetts approached him to explain that he felt compelled to make a tough fight against the ABM. Stennis urged him to go right ahead.

When the hearings ended, $20 billion had been approved for military spending. Only $71 million had been cut, but even the harshest critics conceded that Stennis had made the military prove every inch of their request. "The truth of the matter is," said a friend, "that he detests the pomposity of generals and admirals. He thinks those guys play golf all the time."

The military no longer had a blank check and, in most quarters of the Congress, it was felt that the nation was better off for it. That set the pattern of all subsequent hearings, regardless of the issue, by John Stennis until mid-1973, when he was shot by muggers outside his Washington home.

He returned to full physical power in the spring of 1974, taking again his seat in the Senate, where the military had to prove itself, where critics were heard, and where Stennis, arguing courteously in his rich Mississippi drawl, served notice on Richard Nixon not to defy the law. He continued to serve the Republic in his old-fashioned way, with honor and patriotism, determined to "plow a straight furrow right down to the end of my row."

In the weekends of the spring and summer and fall of 1974, John Stennis returned home, to sit in the hotel lobby at De Kalb. He liked to do that, but also he had to do that. In Mississippi it was expected. There is a firm belief among Southerners that it is a good thing for powerful men to be regularly reminded of their roots and origins, for in Washington they are isolated from that.

In the Senate careers of Theodore Bilbo and John Stennis we saw the Southern system of selection at work. Seniority, committee appointment, the protégé tradition, and the Club all came together to deny power to Bilbo, mediocre and irresponsible, and to give power to Stennis, talented and principled. When a crisis came, Stennis—or men like him—were in the proper place to meet it on behalf of the Senate. The Southern system had worked.

As an experienced and skilled infantry squad will automatically entrench itself on the highest ground in hostile country, the Southern Senate establishment has attempted to occupy all the crucial positions of the Senate.

Of course, they do not always succeed. One man who forced his way into Senate power virtually on his own initiative, by dint of massive seniority, was the other senator from Mississippi, James Eastland. A protégé of Bilbo's, a man who seems as destructively racist as his mentor, and more dangerous, for he is energetic and skillful, Eastland is chairman of Senate Judiciary. He is the living symbol of the "dragon chairman," a species which serves a very real and legitimate function in the Congress.

Chapter 19
THE CHAIRMAN

A chairman's power is partially determined by the discipline and cohesion of his committee. The intellectual Arkansan, William Fulbright, as chairman of Senate Foreign Relations, was rarely consulted by either the White House or the Senate leadership on matters before his committee. It was because Fulbright, though important as a national voice, was unimportant as a chairman. He was too often engaged in inspired quarrels on matters of principle with his committee members and with the White House. Fulbright, for instance, was not consulted by Majority Leader Mansfield in 1965 on postponement of an important treaty with the Soviet Union, whereas it would be suicidal not to consult Richard Russell, Bob Kerr, or John Stennis on a matter of interest to them.

Although congressional chairmen are as varied as the human species, they tend to fall into one of three general categories.

The most effective chairmen are of the Stennis type, men who preside as model parliamentarians, giving all sides a hearing, but who reserve for themselves the role of leader and judge. Bills issued by committees that operate this way go to the Senate floor with a blue-ribbon stamp of approval. The Senate as a whole has confidence that issues have been aired and just decisions rendered.

The least effective are the Fulbrights, who allow their committees to proceed without leadership. Their bills are received on the floor with the suspicion that there is much work still to be done before a vote can be taken.

Falling in between these two poles of effectiveness are the committees ruled by autocratic chairmen. Their bills are received as a *fait accompli*. For better or worse, the chairman's bias has prevailed and it will be damned difficult to reverse him.

Why does the Congress endure dictatorial chairmen? It is not impossible to remove their power or their chairmanships. In January 1963 the House Democrats, goaded by President Kennedy, diluted the power of Howard Smith of Rules who had locked up civil rights legislation in his committee and refused to release it for a vote by the full House membership. The House got around Smith by expanding the size of the committee and appointing as new members liberal Democrats who had enough votes to overrule the chairman. (In 1965, the eighty-three-year-old Smith was defeated for re-election and lost his House seat.) And in 1974 the House removed all of the autocratic chairmen and thus made the House more responsive to the will of the majority party. (It had the effect of making the leaders of the Democratic caucus the tyrants rather than the ousted chairmen. Henceforward in the House it would be the handful of leaders of the Democratic caucus who would dictate the life and death of legislation.)

But the Senate has never removed such chairmen and the House did not do so for a long time. The reason is that the "dragon chairmen" serve a useful role for all the Congress.

Consider James Eastland. By image, he is the archetypal dragon chairman, an old man from a safe rural Southern district who holds power through seniority and rules one of those committees which liberals and moderates alike regularly attack as "bastions of conservatism, obstructive units subject to control by special interests, and dictatorships ruled by misfits."[1]

Eastland has the image of a dictator, but he is not. He might like to be, and the Senate and Eastland allow the false image to prosper and grow unchecked. But the fact that Eastland is not a

[1] "Congressional Reform" in *Congressional Quarterly*, Washington, D.C., April 1964, page 18.

dictator and is not allowed to be a dictator is a secret kept within the Senate family. There is an advantage to keeping the secret.

Misfits. When the *Congressional Quarterly* spoke that word it had Eastland foremost in mind. Regularly for two decades he has been trotted out and tied to the whipping post for a public lashing. And it has all the effect of a light rain on the skin of a sleeping alligator. *Misfit.* It is difficult, well nigh impossible, to find anyone —senator, committee personnel, journalist, or elevator operator— who regularly does business on Capitol Hill who is fond of James Eastland. He is narrow-minded, arbitrary, arrogant, bigoted, and vindictive. He is, in sum, simply unpleasant to be around, unless you drive a pickup truck and burn crosses on Saturday night.

To make it worse, there is not much anyone can do about it. He is too strong, and he is too thoroughly respected for his skills and his power.

A basis of his strength is raw seniority. Eastland is the exception that proves the myth about Southerners, for he has true seniority, having served by 1975 longer in the Senate than any of his colleagues. He has been chairman of Judiciary since 1956 and, following the death of senior Democrat Allen Ellender in 1972, he has been president pro tem of the Senate.

Ironically, a second base of his power is his ability to get along with his committee members. He doesn't embarrass them by making dictatorial decisions. And he gives them what they want for their district, be it a judgeship, a special law, or a courthouse, as long as it doesn't conflict with the direct economic or social interests of white Mississippi.

Even if he wanted to, and he sometimes does, Eastland could not enforce a dictatorial decision on the committee because it is composed of men very powerful in their own right. McClellan of Arkansas is a member, as is Robert Byrd of West Virginia, Hruska of Nebraska, and Scott of Pennsylvania. And neither are the junior members exactly weak-kneed pushovers, men such as Birch Bayh of Indiana, Edward Kennedy of Massachusetts, and John Tunney of California. And there is Strom Thurmond of South Carolina, who is about as easy to dictate to as an enraged grizzly bear.

No, Eastland is not a dictator, he just allows the public and the press to think he is. He is, in fact, a master of backroom politics, winning over his members by persuasion and bargain. His skills at this are such that when Edward Kennedy came into the Senate, among the first men he approached was Eastland. He asked Eastland's advice on Senate politics and he sought, and obtained, appointment to Judiciary.

Eastland moves in shadows and he stays so well in the background that twice, with the resignation of Vice President Spiro Agnew in 1973 and upon the resignation of President Nixon in 1974, he was second in line to the presidency and few Americans were aware of his existence.

Jim Eastland, as he is known back home, lives in white "massa" style on a grand, five-thousand-acre plantation in Sunflower County, Mississippi, a red-neck who made good.

The estate was acquired by his grandfather, a hustling hill-country druggist who made up a washtub medicine in his drugstore which became "Dr. Tichenor's Antiseptic," a fortune-building patent medicine very popular throughout the South. Eastland has added to that fortune by feeding fully at the federal trough. On his plantation, Eastland takes full advantage of federal farm subsidies, which have paid him in excess of $150,000 a year for not growing cotton, soybeans, and what have you. He pays his black farm workers seven dollars a day.

Born in 1904, he came up through county courthouse politics as a protégé of Theodore Bilbo. He won a three-month appointment to the U. S. Senate in 1941 to fill the vacancy caused by the death of Senator Pat Harrison. A year later, Eastland was elected senator and his seniority dates from the time he took his seat on January 3, 1943.

A bald man with a boyish face and loose, ambling gait, he isolates himself from public view, both professionally and socially. He will not meet with the press and will not, if cornered, discuss the Senate or himself. "I just don't do it," he says, disappearing down the hall behind a cloud of cigar smoke. This aloofness would lack interest were it not atypical. Most senators are as eager as a Miss America contestant to meet with the press. It is their means of keeping their names before the people back home and they respond as quickly to appointments with the Capitol Press Corps as they do to meetings with other senators.

The Southerners as a group are somewhat of an exception to this behavior and Eastland even more so. (A running joke on the Washington cocktail circuit for a time was that the two southernmost points of the United States were Key West and Jim Eastland.)

He is also isolated in private life. Between 1941 and 1975, in a town built around parties, his only known social appearances were one embassy party and a small number of White House invitations which he accepted, but only if the gatherings were small.

"The only people who see Jim Eastland are the ones who go by his office for a drink after work," said Nixon's attorney general Richard Kleindienst.

Like Stennis, Eastland goes home to Mississippi almost every weekend, either to his plantation or to Jackson, where he holds court for the state capital crowd. Afterward he likes to drive the countryside "looking for steaks." He often ends up at Doe's Eat Place, a restaurant tucked away in the black section of Greenville which serves thick steaks to the region's power structure.

Once at Doe's in the 1960s, Eastland was presiding over a large party. In Congress at the time, an appropriations bill was pending to fund an all-black hospital at Mound Bayou, Mississippi.

A white Episcopal minister, wearing his collar, approached Eastland to ask support for the funding to help the blacks. He introduced himself, mentioned the hospital, and before he could expound Eastland interrupted:

"Don't you worry about it a bit. We're not goin' to give 'em a cent. Not a cent. Glad to see ya'."

"But . . ." said the minister.

Eastland dismissed him with a wave. "Don't you fret now, that'll never be funded," and returned to his steak. Jim Eastland had assumed, as always, that any white man who approached him had to be a segregationist.

In his governmental views, Eastland contrasts sharply with such Southerners as Stennis or Sam Ervin. A lobbyist commented, "The differences between a man like Sam Ervin and Jim Eastland —well, there are so many. Ervin is a conservative, anti-black who believes in constitutional law—that is, all but the Fourteenth Amendment. Jim Eastland does not even believe in the First Amendment."

Philosophically, if such a word can be applied to Jim Eastland, he is an opportunistic demagogue directly in the mold of Vardaman and Bilbo, although more intelligent and less of a showman.

His opportunism was evident when he first entered the Senate. During his three-month appointment in 1941 he won the name "Cotton Seed Jim" for his opposition to Roosevelt's attempts to put a price ceiling on cotton seed oil, a move that would have cost money to Mississippi growers. And, hypocritically calling Roosevelt the "servant of the rich," he rode the cotton issue to his Senate election.

His racism has been evident throughout. In 1947 he opposed black voter registration on the argument, "the mental level of those people renders them incapable of suffrage."

In the 1950s, Eastland was a leader of the "Southern Manifesto," a document signed by 101 Southern senators and congressmen which denounced the 1954 "Brown vs. Board of Education" Supreme Court school desegregation decision as "destroying the amicable relations between the white and Negro races that have been created through ninety years of patient effort by the good people of both races."

This remarkable document, enough to give an honest man the blind staggers, was actually believed by some of the signers but, we may be certain, not by Jim Eastland. He is too clear-eyed for that. He knew full well that it was only another exercise in rhetoric. His attitude toward blacks, as demonstrated by the seven dollars a day wages he was still paying to his farm labor in the 1960s, was not "patient effort" but "keep 'em in their place—down."[2]

To obtain his ends, Eastland doesn't mind the big lie. The chairman of Judiciary denounced the Supreme Court's Brown decision and told Mississippians to ignore it. He asked: "Who is obligated morally to obey a decision whose authorities rest not upon the law but upon the writings and teachings of pro-Communist

[2] Congressional Record, Eighty-fourth Congress, second session, 1956, volume 102, pages 4415–16.

agitators and people who have a long record of affiliations with anti-American causes and with agitators who are part and parcel of the Communist conspiracy to destroy our country?"

Eastland may have believed that. There is a certain type of Southerner—Eastland, Strom Thurmond, Leander Perez, George Wallace for a while—who believed Communists were behind the civil rights movement. And their belief was passed on to their constituency, essentially red-neck whites, and caused much violence and misery in the 1950s and 1960s.

In his fury at the Supreme Court, Eastland found himself a natural ally of the Wisconsin Republican Joe McCarthy. Their relationship is typified by an exchange during a meeting of the Internal Security Subcommittee in 1956:

Eastland: "Could I ask you a question there?"

McCarthy: "Yes, sir."

Eastland: "There is just one pro-Communist decision after another from this court, is there not?"

McCarthy: "You are so right."

Eastland: "What other explanation could there be except that a majority of that court is being influenced by some secret, but very powerful Communist or pro-Communist influence?"

That is the chairman who presides over the appointment of federal judges and whose committee is the spawning ground of civil rights bills, if any. That many of the bills got through is proof that Jim Eastland is neither all-powerful nor dictatorial. If he could have squashed them, he would have. But there was too much pressure.

That pressure, however, did not manifest itself until the mid-1960s. And here we arrive at the reason for the existence of the "dragon chairman" image. It is useful.

Until the mid-1960s, most of the Judiciary members, and a majority of the Senate itself, did not truly desire civil rights reform—for varying reasons, some of them racist and some of them on grounds that it would violate other constitutional rights. For those and other reasons, the majority did not want it. They found it useful to let Jim Eastland take the heat, to carry the blame. The image of the dragon chairman allowed this, the image of one man holding up his hand and commanding the tide to halt. In fact, Eastland could no more halt the tide, when it came, than could Canute.

It was in 1966 that Chairman Eastland walked into the Judiciary hearings on a new batch of civil rights bills. The room was crowded, and the day got off to a humorous start.

"Feel hot in heah?" asked Eastland as he entered.

"Well, Senator," said a staff member, "the thermostat is set at seventy-two degrees but we can make it colder."

Eastland looked puzzled. "I said: 'Feel hot in heah?' "

The staffer was worried that Eastland might be in one of his bad moods, hangover or something. "Not to me, Senator," he replied carefully, "but I'll lower the thermostat."

"Damn it, son!" Eastland thundered. "Is Sen-a-tor Feel, P-H-I-L, Hot, H-A-R-T, in heah?"

At the time, the House version of the bill was stuck in Rules Committee, headed by Congressman Howard Smith, a man even more irascible and dragonlike than Eastland. Yet, in the House, Representative Richard Bolling of Missouri was eventually able to spring it loose and voted the bill out of Rules to victory on the House floor. The House version of the dragon image had served, in that particular instance, its function and when the majority was ready to move the chairman was simply overruled.

In the Senate it would be another story. Eight votes were needed in Eastland's committee to get the bill onto the floor. But four Republicans refused to show up and the bill died in committee.

Eastland took the heat. It blazed out from the White House, from liberals in the House and Senate, from the press. The four senators who failed to appear and vote him down received no mention at all. Eastland took his cremation silently and earned more respect, more gratitude, more power. He was a chairman.

Eastland's function had been a traditional one of the Senate— he had been the means to slow down history until his colleagues, whether wisely or foolishly, decided the nation was ready for the new legislation.

Chapter 20
THE CONSTITUTIONALIST

One career which demonstrates a cautious and wise use of political power is that of Sam Ervin, former senator from North Carolina.

Similar to John Randolph of Roanoke in his political, if not his class philosophy, Sam Ervin has some of the best qualities of the Southern leader, being heroic, humane, and a brilliant constitutional expert. And yet, like so many of his countrymen, he is a man flawed by the Southern racial arrangement.

Sam Ervin's people were among those who began the Southern social structure. The Ervins arrived in the Carolinas from Ireland in 1732, Scotch-Irish Presbyterians among the flood of English-Scotch-Irish Protestants so badly mistreated by the King of England that they arrived ready for revolt. They were the people who provided the fiercest fighters in the American Revolution, in the Civil War, and, according to numerous generals, they were the best soldiers of two World Wars, and Korea, and Vietnam. They remain today, those pure survivors of the Southern colonies, locked in bastions in the Ozark and Appalachian mountains, still using the vocabulary, poetry, and music of Elizabethan and Georgian England, the most historically violent racial group in America.

That they can consistently produce people of dignity and responsibility and law seems contradictory, a bit of a miracle. But they do, turning them out regularly, and almost every small Southern town has one or two of them practicing law, teaching school, sitting on the bench, or from some other vantage point serving as the moral compass of the community. Most of these men and women are never known outside their county, but once in a while one rises high enough to be seen by the nation. Sam Ervin was seen long before Watergate.

"To a casual visitor peering down from the Senate gallery, he might look like some windbag Senator Claghorn, a walking Washington stereotype. There, behind a desk piled high with lawbooks, is Senator Samuel James Ervin, Jr., eyebrows rippling up and down, fulminating against the latest civil rights bill and regaling the Senate with the latest cracker-barrel humor from the mountains of North Carolina. But if stereotypes are always misleading, they are downright laughable in the case of Sam Ervin. After thirteen years in the Senate, Ervin still regularly enrages first the liberals and then the conservatives. He defies all the easy generalizations of political journalism."[1]

In 1925 the North Carolina legislature considered a bill to forbid teaching Darwinism or "any other evolutionary hypothesis that links man in blood relationship with any lower form of life." Sam Ervin, then a twenty-nine-year-old state legislator, a country lawyer, defeated the bill by arguing: "I don't see but one good feature in this thing, and that is that it will gratify the monkeys to know they are absolved from all responsibility for the conduct of the human race."

In 1974, nearly fifty years later, Sam Ervin retired from the Senate, going home to do some fishing. Never particularly ambitious in politics, he nevertheless had served since 1923 in the North Carolina General Assembly, as circuit judge, as associate justice of the North Carolina Supreme Court, and as Representative in the U. S. Congress. He was elected to the Senate in 1954 and in his twenty years there compiled a seemingly schizophrenic record defending civil liberties and opposing civil rights.

[1] James Batten, *Charlotte Observer*, April 2, 1967.

In the process, he did minuets around the Constitution that left onlookers glassy-eyed.

The man who at one time championed the rights of black basketball players against the "economic enslavement" imposed by giant sports trusts could at another time oppose a minimum wage for maids because "if you pay household workers more, people won't be able to afford them."

Ervin's admirers said he was always consistent, focusing on one principle: his opposition to government interference with individual rights. He was "the last of the Founding Fathers, and the Senate's foremost constitutional expert."

His detractors found him a rationalizer and a sophist. A "Claghorn's Hammurabi" with blind spots on race, labor, and sex discrimination.

The detractors' comments arise almost entirely from Ervin's civil rights position, which is essentially that the black minority does not need and should not have special legislation to bring them into the American mainstream. It is unconstitutional, he would say. (He has proved a staunch defender of other minorities —military men, Indians, the mentally ill, government employes; and through his vigorous and successful opposition to government invasion of citizens' rights and privacy he has benefited the American public at large. He has made no such extra effort for blacks.)

Before hearing his defense, let us consider Sam Ervin at the end of his career, the peak of his career, the Senate Watergate hearings when he became probably the last man born in the nineteenth century to be a hero in the twentieth.

At the beginning of the Watergate hearings, President Nixon said he wouldn't produce witnesses. Instead, he proposed, Ervin could personally question executive staff in private.

Ervin exploded in outrage. The eyebrows went up and down, the jowls jiggled, as Ervin, softly tumbling out his words in gentle Southern tones and idiom, his references skittering from Shakespeare to the Bible, replied at a public session:

"Divine right went out with the American Revolution and doesn't belong to White House aides. What meat do they eat that makes them grow so great? I am not willing to elevate them to a position above the great mass of the American people. I don't think we have any such thing as royalty or nobility that exempts them. I'm not going to let anybody come down at night like Nicodemus and whisper something in my ear that no one else can hear. That is not executive privilege. It is executive poppycock."[2]

Then came a stunning threat, reminiscent in itself of the early fiery days of the eighteenth-century American Congress. Ervin said he might recommend to the Senate that it send the sergeant-at-arms to arrest White House aides, or any other witness who refused to testify before the committee. Nixon backed down and produced the witnesses.

The public hearings began, ran their course, and at their conclusion the committee made available its findings to other committees in the House and Senate, thus paving the road for Nixon's impeachment.

Positive proof was lacking of Nixon's personal direction of the illegal actions, however, and when the report failed to single out the President, Ervin replied that it was possible to draw a picture of a horse in two ways. You could draw the picture of a horse with a very good likeness. Or you could draw the picture and write under it, "This is a horse." Well, said Ervin, "We just drew the picture." In this, too, Ervin was a product of his culture, for John Randolph of Roanoke, while making a sinister implication against President Adams in 1826, had said: "I do not draw my pictures in such a way as to render it necessary to write under them, 'This is a man, this is a horse.' "

Ironically, it was Richard Nixon who gave Ervin his first national prominence.

Ervin came to the Senate in June 1954, appointed by the governor of North Carolina to replace the deceased Senator Clyde Hoey. It was the height of the Joe McCarthy era. Three months earlier, the Republican senator from Wisconsin had been labeled a "persecutor" in a television special by Edward R. Murrow. McCarthy's numerous accusations of "disloyalty" against members of government had created a climate of fear. No powerful men had taken him to task, fearful themselves, and Murrow

[2] *Time* magazine, April 16, 1973.

challenged the Senate: "We are not descended from fearful men
. . . dissent should not be confused with disloyalty . . . it is time
for men to speak out."

Now came Ervin. Washington was in chaos. There was not a
member of the Senate who did not risk being branded an "unwitting agent of the Communist Party" by McCarthy. And even before Ervin went to Washington, his wife, knowing her man,
pleaded with him not to tangle with McCarthy. "He is dangerous," she said.

Richard Nixon as Vice President gave Ervin the oath of office.
A few days later, the new senator was asked by a newsman what
he thought of being under consideration for one of six positions
on a select committee to study the censure of McCarthy. Ervin,
who did not know of such a committee's existence, replied that
someone with more experience should be picked. "I don't think it
would be the duty of a country boy who just came up from North
Carolina."[3]

The Republicans were the majority in both houses, holding the
Senate by 48 to 47 members and the House by 221 to 211
members. Lyndon Johnson, minority leader, had three positions
to fill on the committee and was looking for men with judicial experience. Ervin and John Stennis of Mississippi had been recommended to him. Johnson nominated both, who, as a formality,
were approved by Vice President Nixon.[4]

The hearings began on August 3, 1954, with McCarthy, flanked
by his attorney Edward Bennett Williams, the first witness. During
the lengthy questioning of McCarthy, Ervin was quiet. One of
their few exchanges, however, was typical of the differences between the two senators. It concerned General Ralph Zwicker
(who at an earlier hearing had been told by McCarthy: "Don't be
coy with me, General.").

Speaking as "an old cross-examiner myself," Ervin said, "I
rather admired [your words] in a way. Personally, I would never
have been bold enough to have made that observation on a cross-

[3] *Just a Country Lawyer* by Paul Clancy (Bloomington: Indiana University
Press, 1974), page 157.
[4] Francis Case of South Dakota was the other Democrat. Republican
members were Arthur Watkins of Utah, Edwin Johnson of Colorado, and
Frank Carlson of Kansas.

examination of anybody in the military service, unless perhaps it were a WAVE or a WAC, and then I would have been bold enough to do it only under romantic circumstances, where I was surrounded with soft music, moonlight and roses; and I am satisfied I never would have been bold enough to give that admonition to either a general or to a sergeant. But I merely want to ask the senator whether he considered that a proper method of cross-examining a general—that is, General Zwicker?"

McCarthy replied: "I did, because he had been trying to be coy —coy and evasive. That was my system of cross-examining. You might have used different language, Senator Ervin, when you gave an evasive answer. That is my system of trying to pull teeth. I finally pulled some of them and got some of the information."[5]

At the end of the hearings, the committee issued a mild resolution condemning McCarthy's failure to appear before a subcommittee (which was looking into his financial dealings) and his badgering of General Zwicker. Nothing more than a slap on the wrist.

But McCarthy was annoyed, particularly at Ervin and two Republicans, Arthur Watkins and Edwin Johnson, probably feeling that as conservatives they should have defended him. He lashed out at them in a press interview, saying they were "unwitting handmaidens" of the Communists. A month later McCarthy inserted a speech in the Congressional Record stating that the entire select committee was an agent of the Communist party, which "has now extended its tentacles to that most respected of American bodies, the United States Senate."

And he went on: "In the course of the Senate debate, I shall demonstrate that the committee has done the work of the Communist party, that it not only cooperated in the achievement of Communist goals but that in writing its report it imitated Communist methods—that it distorted, misrepresented, and omitted in its effort to manufacture a plausible rationalization for advising the Senate to accede to the clamor for my scalp."

No member of the committee was bold enough to reply, save one—the very junior senator from North Carolina. And he not only replied but also called for McCarthy's expulsion, arguing

[5] Clancy, page 158.

with a logic that left no escape. McCarthy, said Ervin, either believed or did not believe his own statements. In either case, he was unfit for the Senate.

"If Senator McCarthy did not believe those things when he said them about the Senate committee, then there is pretty solid ground to say that he ought to be expelled from the Senate for moral incapacity. On the contrary, if he put those things in there honestly believing them to be true, then he has evidently suffered gigantic mental delusions and it may be argued with much force that he should be expelled from the Senate for mental difficulty."

Mental difficulty. The term had the ring of an eighteenth-century lawyer. And now, finally, someone had squared off face-to-face with McCarthy in the very arena of his power, the Senate. Surprisingly, there was little help for Ervin. The Republican leadership, joined by McCarthy's fanatical followers, strongly resisted expulsion. It would set a dangerous precedent, they said.[6]

(Everett Dirksen of Illinois asked, "If this [expulsion] can be done to one member of the Senate, who is next on the list?" No seat in the Senate, particularly the seat of a conservative, would be safe, he said.)

Even among the Democrats, except for minority leader Lyndon Johnson, there was little leadership against McCarthy.

When the date of the expulsion debate came, Republican Watkins, chairman of the censure committee, declined to present the committee position and asked Ervin to do it.

So, on November 15, 1954, five months after coming to Washington, Sam Ervin stood before a packed Senate gallery and took on Joe McCarthy. It was, perhaps, Ervin's most masterful presentation, and certainly one of the great ones in Senate history.

"I had a vague impression," he began, "that a great storm was raging in the country around the activities of Senator McCarthy. I came to the Senate, however, with the vague impression that, by and large, Senator McCarthy was doing a good job . . . Now, I think not."

He said that McCarthy's claim that he was being persecuted be-

---

[6] The expulsion of Senator William Blount of Tennessee 157 years earlier was apparently not remembered.

cause he fought Communism "has no more substance than a shadow of a dream."

He ridiculed McCarthy's habit of lifting words out of context to make a case. "The McCarthy technique," said Ervin, "was practiced in North Carolina about seventy-five years ago. At that time, the women had a habit of wearing their hair in topknots. The preacher deplored that habit. As a consequence he preached a rip-snorting sermon one Sunday on the text 'Top Not Come Down.' At the conclusion of his sermon an irate woman, wearing a very pronounced topknot, told the preacher that no such text could be found in the Bible. The preacher thereupon opened the Scriptures to the seventeenth verse of the twenty-fourth chapter of Matthew and pointed to the words: 'Let him which is on the housetop not come down to take anything out of his house.' "

The Senate galleries exploded with laughter and the mood changed abruptly in Ervin's favor.

Now he switched to a more serious chord, his smile vanishing, his voice slower and more solemn as he outlined McCarthy's damage to innocent people. He suggested, again, the presence of mental difficulties and then bore home toward his goal with another story.

"Many years ago, there was a custom in a section of my country, known as the South Mountains, to hold religious meetings at which the oldest members of the congregation were called upon to stand up and publicly testify to their religious experiences. On one occasion they were holding such a meeting in one of the churches; and old Uncle Ephraim Swink, a South mountaineer whose body was all bent and distorted with arthritis, was present. All the older members of the congregation except Uncle Ephraim arose and gave testimony to their religious experiences. Uncle Ephraim kept his seat. Thereupon the moderator said, 'Brother Ephraim, suppose you tell us what has the Lord done for you.'

"Uncle Ephraim arose, with his bent and distorted body, and said, 'Brother, he has might nigh ruint me.'

"Mister President," said Ervin. "That is about what Senator McCarthy has done to the Senate . . .

"The issue before the American people is simply this: Does the Senate of the United States have enough manhood to stand up to

Senator McCarthy? Mister President, the honor of the Senate is in our keeping. I pray that senators will not soil it by permitting Senator McCarthy to go unwhipped of senatorial justice."

As he walked back to his seat, Lyndon Johnson told Ervin: "You showed you don't scare easily." Two and a half weeks later the Senate censured McCarthy by a 67–22 vote and McCarthy ceased to be an influence in national politics. The presiding officer was Richard Nixon.

Ervin's storytelling ability had been put to keen use in the McCarthy debates, as it would for the remainder of his Senate career. The expert use of words was part of his heritage. Many of the stories he picked up while he was a circuit judge traveling the state of North Carolina.

"At night," wrote his biographer Paul Clancy, "when he wasn't poring over the law books, he would hold court among the local lawyers and the other judges. Ervin spent many an evening smoothing the benches and rockers on the porches of hotels and rooming houses, exchanging that most precious and enduring commodity, the courtroom story. On summer evenings the laughter of those men rang robustly as they celebrated the humor, the pathos, and the absurdities of the human condition.

"Ervin collected these stories, not in any systematic way, but he remembered them, told them, and retold them until they were part of him. Many years later, the stubborn, cantankerous, wise mountain folk came to life again in the pages of the Congressional Record . . ."

As mentioned above, the two strongest features of Ervin's character that arose during his Senate career were his strong stand for civil liberties and against civil rights.

Freedom of religion; freedom of speech and the press; freedom to assemble and protest; the right to be left alone by government; the protection of life, liberty, and property; the right to a speedy trial before an impartial jury with the aid of legal counsel; freedom from excessive bail—all these were greatly strengthened by Ervin's actions between 1954 and 1974, and many of them, such as the ones dealing with trial, counsel, and bail, were of special importance, to blacks.

These libertarian stances confounded Ervin's enemies. In 1968, while the Senate was considering the Fair Housing Bill, designed to help blacks, Ervin offered an attachment called the "Indian Bill of Rights," which would extend to reservation Indians the same guarantees held by other Americans. Liberals and civil rights lobbyists, convinced it was a trick to kill the Housing bill, opposed it. Ervin replied with a taunt: "I did not think that anybody supporting a bill to give constitutional rights to black people would be opposed to securing constitutional rights for red people. But I am apparently mistaken." The amendment was finally approved 81–0 and the Cherokees made Ervin an honorary chief.

When legislation was drawn on a broad constitutional basis, blacks benefited from Ervin's often courageous defense of liberties.

For instance, he was the principal sponsor of a bill to provide a legal defender system for the indigent, and of bail reform measures. He stood virtually alone in 1970 against the Nixon administration's law-and-order package which allowed preventive detention, police to enter the homes of suspects without knocking, and life sentences for such "crimes of violence" as purse snatching and tampering with bubble gum machines.

And in 1971 he, along with Senator William Proxmire, defeated Nixon's plan, a sweeping villainy, to convert the long dormant Subversive Activities Control Board (SACB) into an American Gestapo.

Nixon had issued a secret executive order granting the SACB vast new powers to investigate any group which appeared likely to engage in "treason, rebellion, or insurrection, riots or civil disorder, seditious conspiracy, sabotage, trading with the enemy, obstructing of the recruiting and enlistment service of the United States, impeding officers of the United States, or related crimes or offenses."

Nothing like it had been seen since the Alien and Sedition Act of 1798 and even that, because it was done openly, didn't quite match up to what Nixon had in mind. The term "impeding officers of the United States, or related crimes" in particular was so broad and vague that any person or agency, including the Congress and the Supreme Court, could come under its terms.

The secret was casually revealed during testimony by the SACB chairman, John Mahon, before Senate Appropriations. Trying to justify SACB's budget, Mahon had described the agency's new powers, and the existence of the executive order. Roman Hruska, a Republican member of Appropriations, commented: "When Sam hears that he'll hit the ceiling."[7] Ervin did just that.

Meanwhile, William Proxmire had been working to kill SACB, not because he then knew its nature, but because he thought it was a worthless expenditure of money.

Ervin and Proxmire joined forces, striking at SACB through two main arguments: first, that it was a violation of the Bill of Rights; second, that it was a prime example of waste in government.

After a year of speeches, committee appearances, and behind-the-scene politicking, Ervin and Proxmire were still unable to kill off SACB. But they did get the Senate to agree that not a cent could be spent to carry out Nixon's executive order. The following year, 1973, Nixon omitted SACB's appropriation from his budget request and the agency passed out of existence.

The other side of Ervin was that he publicly took the lead in opposing the civil rights acts of 1957, 1960, 1964, and the Voting Rights Act of 1965, which have so greatly changed life in the South and raised up 40 per cent of the Southern population, the blacks, into full political participation for the first time in history. Ervin was the center and the pre-eminent lawyer in fighting those bills.

His defense was that most of the acts on behalf of the blacks penalized the civil liberties of the nation as a whole. "It is not the civil rights of some, but the civil liberties of all on which I take my stand."

His position, from which he did not deviate, was spelled out in a committee minority report which he and Senator Olin Johnston of South Carolina submitted against the 1957 Civil Rights Act.

"[The bill] is based on the strange thesis that the best way to promote civil rights of some Americans is to rob other Americans

[7] *Just a Country Lawyer* by Paul Clancy (Bloomington: Indiana University Press, 1974), page 225.

of civil rights equally as precious and to reduce the supposedly sovereign states to meaningless zeros on the Nation's map.

"The only reason advanced by the proponents of [the bill] for urging enactment is, in essence, an insulting and insupportable indictment of a whole people. They say that Southern officials and Southern people are generally faithless to their oaths as public officers and jurors, and for that reason can be justifiably denied the right to invoke for their protection in courts of justice constitutional and legal safeguards erected in times past by the Founding Fathers and the Congress to protect all Americans from governmental tyranny.

". . . If these provisions can be used today to make legal pariahs and second-class litigants out of Southerners involved in civil rights cases, they can be used with equal facility tomorrow to reduce other Americans involved in countless other cases to the like status."

Ervin thus presents a strong and convincing argument against such special legislation. It epitomizes the Southern white philosophy of government: states rights and constitutional guarantees against government interference in life, liberty, and property.

But the contradiction is, and Ervin was well aware of it, that the South used state, county, and municipal governments to interfere with the life, liberty, and property of blacks. Ervin knew this as a native, as a resident, and as a reader of history. And he, like the South as a whole, failed to offer any positive relief. In this, one must conclude that Sam Ervin, whatever his virtues, allowed the oppression of individuals because they were black. He was protecting the status quo of the Southern white society.

Sam Ervin is personally grieved by such accusations because, as with most small-town Southerners, he has grown up with black people, and though he does not believe in "the mixing of the races," he does believe in courtesy and friendship between the races. And he is aware of the black man's condition.

What he often called his "favorite" courtroom story involved a case he reviewed while on the North Carolina Supreme Court bench. A black man had been convicted of raping a white woman and sentenced to die. Suspicious of the case, Ervin pored over the trial's twelve hundred pages of testimony and decided that the evidence was inconclusive. He ordered the man freed. Shortly afterward, Ervin chanced to meet him and asked if he were relieved to get off Death Row.

"Boss," said the black, "we never get off Death Row. We are on Death Row from the day we be here until the day we die."

Chapter 21
LEADERS I

For the sake of metaphor, we may look at the American Congress as one vast orchestra. As we enter the hall, it is a chaos of sound. Violins are being tuned; brass is experimenting with notes high and low; woodwinds are rustling pages of the music and exchanging gossip; cellos are sawing away on their own private enterprise. Then, quite suddenly, order arrives in the person of the first violinist, the concertmaster. With quiet authority, he strides on stage. There is instant silence. He surveys the orchestra and sees that the musicians are in place. Satisfied, he signals to the wings. The conductor enters, takes his position on the podium. He looks to the first violin. They exchange nods. The conductor raises his baton and brings it down. The symphony begins.

The normal appearance of the American Congress is one of chaos, with five hundred and thirty-five artists rehearsing, gossiping, pursuing their individual exercises. They come together only periodically for moments of performance.

Usually those moments are at the end of each congressional session when all the bills that have been rehearsed and worked over are up for final passage. But the finest moments of performance, the magnificent symphonies, have come at instances of recognized national emergencies.

More often than not, the men who have played the role of first violin or conductor in those emergencies have been the Southerners.

A series of such performances came in the late 1930s. Japanese and Chinese armies were in the field in Asia, and Hitler and Stalin were moving aggressively in Europe. The attention of American politics shifted from domestic problems to foreign affairs. And, once again, as had been the case with Woodrow Wilson twenty years before, the Southern legislators became the foundation for American policy, and the President's main support.

The war and its aftermath would be a period of extraordinary Southern performance. It would see Roosevelt's enemy, Walter George of Georgia, put through the President's prewar armament program. It would see George, in concert with Tom Connally of Texas and Elbert Thomas of Utah, convert the Senate Foreign Relations into an unprecedented "council of state," a collection of powerful senators who implemented wartime policy.

And, as the war wound down, it would see Tom Connally design the United Nations.

In the postwar period, George would emerge again as a force, handling the Asian treaties while his junior colleague from Georgia, Richard Russell, defused an explosive situation which could have led to World War III fought with atomic weapons.

This acceptance of leadership in moments of emergency is characteristically Southern and has been examined and commented upon by numerous writers.[1] Southern leaders have been particularly supportive during wars. This is an apparent contradiction because historical evidence shows fairly conclusively that Southern leaders and the body politic have been opposed to most American wars, including the Civil War, entries into World Wars I and II, and the Vietnam War. Once the war was begun, however, they gathered round.

The theories on why the Southern community has been ready to fight, once fighting seemed inevitable, have ranged from ethnic

[1] See especially, *The Fighting South* by John Temple Graves (New York: 1954), *The Southerners and World Affairs* by Alfred Nero (Baton Rouge: Louisiana State University Press, 1965), and *The Waning of Southern Internationalism* by Paul Seabury (Princeton, N.J.: Princeton University Press, 1957).

roots—a pro-British heritage and a desire to protect the British interests, such as in World Wars I and II; to historical obligation —to the French and a desire to aid them; to economic determinism—a desire to protect cotton markets in particular and the American economy in general.

Carter Glass, not indulging himself in humor, said it was a virtue of Southern character, "superior character and exceptional understanding of the problem." Erskine Caldwell, humorously, said it was Southern ignorance.

None of these explains all the times Southerners have supported American wars. The only instances of pro-British feeling was in World Wars I and II, both of which significantly had the result of reducing British power *vis à vis* the United States. (The South instead has a long record of being anti-British, save for the unsuccessful courting of British support by the Confederacy.)

The British "loyalty" theory can be put to rest, as can any obligations to the French—people who saw Bismarck, the Kaiser, and Hitler all invade their country while America sat still.

Economic determinism has played a more constant role, being a prime factor in the Revolutionary War, the War of 1812, the Mexican-American War, and the Civil War. It does not, however, seem to have played much of a role in gaining Southern support for the world wars, nor the Korean and Vietnamese wars.

Economics also fails to supply a reason for Southern patriotism. Furthermore, far from being militarists, Southern leaders were in the forefront of opposition to all American engagements since the Civil War. It was only after American prestige was committed that Southerners rallied round.

Group integrity. That is the simplest answer for Southern patriotism, and perhaps the only answer. Southerners have a strong community identification, and when that community is menaced they strike out.

As the situation of the 1930s worsened, Southerners more than other Americans favored action against the Nazi, Fascist, and Japanese expansions. "In the years before the Pearl Harbor attack, they repeatedly displayed in the opinion polls a greater conviction . . . that the Army and Navy should be enlarged, that young men should be drafted, that neutrality legislation should be revised or repealed. In October 1941, the Gallup poll found 88 per cent of the Southerners convinced that the defeat of Germany was more important than keeping out of war."[2]

In 1920, Southerners had gone all the way with Wilson on the Fourteen Points and the Versailles Treaty, only to be frustrated by the machinations of Republican Henry Cabot Lodge, chairman of Senate Foreign Relations. (The subsequent U.S. failures to include Germany and Bolshevik Russia in the peace negotiations and to join the League of Nations led directly to a German-Russian alliance that lasted from 1921 to 1941 and climaxed in World War II.)[3]

Southern congressmen showed little interest in foreign affairs thereafter and took up an isolationist stance. Then in 1937 President Roosevelt invoked their Democratic party loyalty to give him a freer hand in foreign policy. In January 1938, Southern Democrats furnished the foundation for a majority which blocked an isolationist law which would have called for a national referendum to legalize any declaration of war.

In September 1939, with the invasion of Poland, Roosevelt asked permission to sell arms to Britain and France. Agreement was made quickly in the House under leadership of Speaker William Bankhead of Alabama. In the Senate, Roosevelt kept discreetly in the background and let Tom Connally of Texas and Jimmy Byrnes of South Carolina push the bill through.

Southern support was solid and effective. Claude Pepper of Florida championed Roosevelt's swapping American destroyers to

[2] *The Emergence of the New South* by Tindall (Baton Rouge: Louisiana State University Press, 1967), page 688.
[3] The two defeated nations viewed Poland, a nation re-created by the Treaty of Versailles, as a direct threat to their security—a view occasioned in part by the French-sanctioned invasion of both Germany and Russia by Polish troops in 1919–20. Germany and Russia in 1921 signed the Treaty of Rapallo for economic and political cooperation, which led to an arrangement whereby the Germans trained new Soviet armed forces. In return, the Soviets allowed the training and development on Russian soil, hidden from Allied eyes, of the German Air Force and panzer units. This pact, which probably would not have occurred if Wilson had prevailed with his Fourteen Points, was periodically renewed and strengthened, fizzling briefly in 1936 but climaxing in the Non-Aggression Pact of 1939 and the simultaneous German-Soviet invasion of Poland.

Great Britain in exchange for Atlantic and Caribbean bases. Carter Glass of Virginia in the spring of 1941 urged "doing everything possible to bring about the downfall of Hitler and his gang."

Throughout the prewar period only one (Reynolds of North Carolina) of the twenty-six Southern senators voted consistently against Roosevelt's proposals. In the House, the new speaker Sam Rayburn of Texas, succeeding after Bankhead's death in 1940, won victory after narrow victory in favor of war preparation. (By parliamentary legerdemain, Rayburn blocked reconsideration of a measure which failed by one vote, 202–203, to halt the military draft just four months prior to the attack on Pearl Harbor.)

Throughout the late 1930s and early 1940s, Southern Democrats topped all other regional and party groupings in their votes for American intervention and preparedness.

In this, they often rose above politics and personalities, for many of them were, or had become, anti-New Deal and anti-Roosevelt. Typical among these was Walter George of Georgia.

George was born in 1878, the older of two children raised in a sun-blistered pine house in Webster County, Georgia, where his father worked the thick clay and brought forth thin crops of cotton, cowpeas, and sweet potatoes. His main reading material was his grandfather's collection of the Congressional Record, and George would later recall, "The style was ponderous, but I learned to like it."

He worked full time while attending high school, taking a year off to teach grade school, and thought he would become a dentist. But then politics came upon him.

It happened at an outdoor lecture where the village had congregated to hear a renowned local judge speak on the virtues of citizenship. The judge failed to show up and George, the best high school orator in those parts, stood in for the missing judge. He made a rousing forty-minute delivery on Robert E. Lee and was cheeringly received by the crowd. From then on, he was hooked.

He followed the traditional path of Southern politics, going to law school—at Mercer in Macon, Georgia—and in 1901 set up practice at the county seat of Vienna, taking an office just off the courthouse square.

He plunged immediately into trials, his first one scheduled only two weeks after he came to town. (George figured that opposing attorneys would expect him, as a newcomer, to ask for delays and would therefore neglect their own homework. When court opened, George was ready, the others were not.)

He became the most celebrated trial lawyer in the region and within six years was elected district attorney of Cordele, the local city. In 1912 he was appointed district judge and broke up a lynch mob on the steps of the Cordele Opera House. (The intended victim was the white killer of a county official.)

He moved steadily upward in state politics, finally becoming associate justice of the Georgia Supreme Court. Then, one day while fishing on the Flint River near Vienna, he got word that Populist Senator Tom Watson had died. George ran and won and on November 22, 1922, took his seat in the U. S. Senate, where he would remain for thirty-four years.

He arrived in Washington favoring Prohibition and opposed to the League of Nations and of U.S. loans to foreign countries, especially to Negro Liberia.

George had to bide his time before receiving any choice committee assignments, but in 1926 he was put on the tax-writing Finance Committee and in 1928 on Foreign Relations. On those two committees he would become a national power.

At the beginning of the New Deal, George favored about 80 per cent of the proposals, suffering the typical Southern dilemma of voting against Jeffersonian principles out of necessity. For instance, on farm legislation he said he was against the principle of expanding government, "but the farmers are desperate and need help." He, like other Southerners, supported the REA, TVA, the Securities Exchange Commission, and the Social Security Act for expedient reasons. At the same time, again typically, he opposed the packing of the Supreme Court.

Franklin Roosevelt, unforgiving of George's leadership against his court-packing fight went to Georgia, in August 1938, and campaigned against him. Popular though he was, the President was too shrewd to be unaware of resentments about outside interference. He carefully presented his credentials to Georgia crowds as the "adopted son" of "my other state," and then proceeded to

Senator Leroy Percy of Mississippi: The Percy-Vardaman election was a class struggle between a gentleman and a redneck. *(Library of Congress)*

ar Theodore Bilbo of Mississippi: at little monster, glib and shame- ." *(Library of Congress)*

John Stennis, the junior senator from Mississippi, functions as "the conscience of the Senate." *(UPI photo)*

James Eastland, senior senator from Mississippi, is viewed as a crude, racist, and dictatorial chairman. He is also a master of subtle politics, and his pupils include such liberals as Edward Kennedy of Massachusetts. *(UPI photo)*

Senator Sam Ervin of North Carolina: Of Ervin, Richard Nixon said, "He works even harder than most of our Southern gentlemen. They are great politicians. They are just more clever than the others. Just more clever." *(UPI photo)*

or Herman Talmadge of Georgia: e Watergate hearings his soft, polite ian manner concealed a deadly -examination technique. *(UPI)*

Martin Luther King, Jr., marchir
of Selma, Alabama: "Like Huey
King had a keen perception of the
struggle."

Lyndon Johnson on the Pedernales, brooding in retirement on the
disdain for the South woven into the fabric of Northern experience.
(Frank Wolfe, LBJ Library)

lay his prestige directly on the line against George in a three-way race.

The three candidates all were "country boys" taking the usual line of country-versus-city, and poor-people-against-corporations. Roosevelt, with smiling hypocrisy, claimed Senator George was a lackey of the "dictatorship of the small minority of individuals and corporations" who opposed the New Deal. Roosevelt said the second candidate, two-time Governor Eugene Talmadge was a "demagogue" and should likewise be denied the nomination. This left Roosevelt's candidate, Lawrence Camp, a U.S. district attorney who, Roosevelt implied, would bring honor to the state and New Deal largesse to the people.

While Roosevelt spoke at Barnesville, Senator George sat behind him on the platform, listening politely. When the President had finished, George arose, walked over, shook Roosevelt's hand and said, with a voice strong enough to carry across to the gathered thousands: "I want you to know, Mister President, that I accept the challenge." Replied Roosevelt with equally forceful volume, "God bless you, Walter. Let's always be friends." Neither meant it.

Four days later, George opened his campaign at Waycross, a steaming railroad town near swamp country. He spoke to two thousand people while sweat poured from his face and a red rose in his lapel wilted from the 105-degree heat. Tears streamed down, his voice choked, and he had to pause before answering Roosevelt's charge that he was a pawn of big business.

He gathered himself up and shouted out: "I was born in south Georgia, the son of a tenant farmer. I have known how it feels to want things that I cannot have. Back there in the days when as a boy I plowed the soil . . ."

He beat Talmadge soundly. Roosevelt's man ran a poor third.

During 1939, George's opposition toward Roosevelt was insistent. Early that year, George, the number two Democrat on Foreign Relations said that if the President would stop meddling and avoid predicting war in Europe there would be no war.

But war came and in 1940 George became chairman of Foreign Relations. Now he moved over to Roosevelt's side and support of

American intervention. He backed aid for England, preparing of the American military, and lend-lease.

In June 1941 the chairman of Senate Finance, Pat Harrison of Mississippi, died and George moved over to that chairmanship, where he felt he "was at the heart of the political process." What this referred to specifically was the Finance jurisdiction to set the size of the national debt. The extent to which the United States could arm itself and its allies for war would be determined by Senate Finance.

Walter George had put aside his differences with Roosevelt, and the reservations he held in mid-1940 about war. He put the arming measures through the Senate skillfully and swiftly. But never irresponsibly. Among other things, he kept a close watch on war profiteering. At the beginning, when there was a boiling controversy about how much profit industry should be allowed, George replied: "I'd think about 8 per cent would be *re-e*asonable. Maybe 6 per cent. Possibly as high as 10 per cent. But 8 per cent is probably the most *re-e*-easonable."

Roosevelt never afterward directly referred to the campaign of 1938. Once, however, at the White House while urging a particular tax bill on the chairman, Roosevelt started to argue how popular it would be: "Walter, if I know anything at all about Georgia politics . . ." At that point, George caught the President's eye and Roosevelt finished with a laugh, ". . . and certainly I don't."

The man to whom George had surrendered the chairmanship of Foreign Relations was Tom Connally of Texas, who may have been the best Foreign Relations chairman ever. His accomplishments were awesome.

Born in 1877 in McLennan County, Texas, Tom Connally's entire career was politics. He entered the state legislature at the age of twenty-four, then became district attorney of Falls County and entered the U. S. House of Representatives in 1917 where he served twelve years. He became senator in 1929 and was chairman of Foreign Relations from 1941 to 1946.

Foreign Relations shared with Armed Services and Finance the brunt of war powers and war work. Prior to 1940, Foreign Relations was mostly isolationist. The outbreak of war in Europe and the leadership of Walter George brought it around to an activist, pro-intervention role.

In late 1940, Senator Elbert Thomas of Utah made a startling suggestion. Thomas was a member of Foreign Relations and also of the Democratic Steering Committee which determined committee assignments. He proposed, with chairman George's backing, that Foreign Relations be made into a sort of "executive council," a council of state.[4] Its members would be senators representing strong committees who would in effect function as ambassadors of the other Senate committees.

"It was thought by some," Senator Thomas later wrote, "that senators of long standing would not give up their seniority on other committees to serve in a lower position of the Foreign Relations Committee, but both Senator Glass [of Virginia] and Senator Byrnes [South Carolina] accepted the proposition. Senator Glass told me later how grateful he was for the opportunity it gave him to serve his country. The minority [Republican] party also accepted the theory and Senator Austin gave up his ascendant position on the Judiciary Committee . . ."[5]

Foreign Relations was enlarged to include both majority and minority leaders and the chairmen of eight major committees. The reorganization took place as Connally became chairman.

As the committee made plans for war, it simultaneously made confident plans for the peace to follow. Connally formed a subcommittee of eight senators to design the peace and out of this subcommittee, meeting regularly during the war, came the blueprint for the postwar world.

Through the work of the Connally subcommittee, the Congress proposed forming a world organization to prevent war. Out of this came the Dumbarton Oaks Conference in 1944 where the United States, Great Britain, and the Soviet Union published plans for an organization to be known as "The United Nations." Then, in April 1945, with war still going on in Europe and Asia, the San

[4] George Washington had assumed that the Senate as a whole, consisting of twenty-six members, would function as such a council. It would meet regularly and secretly with the President and develop nonpartisan national policies.
[5] "The Senate During and Since the War" by Elbert Thomas, *Parliamentary Affairs,* winter 1949.

Francisco Conference convened. Delegates of fifty nations completed a charter for the United Nations and its component organs: the Security Council, the General Assembly, the Economic and Social Council, the International Court of Justice, and the Secretariat.

Connally was one of the prime drafters of the United Nations charter and in 1945, stepping down from his Foreign Relations chairmanship, became the first U.S. delegate to the UN General Assembly. He returned to the chairmanship in 1949 and retired from the Senate in 1953 at the age of seventy-six.

Most authorities agree that without Connally, his leadership, and the work of his subcommittee, the United States would not have taken the lead in forming the world organization and there would not have been a Dumbarton Oaks Conference, or a San Francisco Conference, or a United Nations.

The power of Henry Cabot Lodge, exercising a negative veto, had kept the United States out of the League of Nations in 1919. The power of the positive internationalism of Tom Connally, the right man in the right place, had put the United States at the head of the United Nations in 1945.

In the postwar era, Southern chairmen continued to guide the Congress. These chairmanships were interrupted in the Eightieth Congress (1947–48) and the Eighty-third (1953–54) by Republican majorities in the House and Senate. However, the Southerners returned in 1955.

The dean of the Senate was Walter George. He could have again become chairman of Finance. But committee importance fluctuates. Military Affairs becomes the most important during wars. Finance increases during times of depression or whenever there are to be important changes in the national debt or taxation laws. Foreign Relations waxes and wanes in proportion to the others and as America moves into or out of world affairs.

In 1955, George turned over the Finance chair to Harry Byrd of Virginia and returned to the Foreign Relations chair he had held in 1940. There he helped shape the Cold War policies of the 1950s.

"He is hand-in-glove with Secretary of State Dulles and the

President," reported *Time* magazine, "though sometimes his is the hand and theirs is the glove. And though the George hand is seemingly gentle, it can be steely."

George and Dulles were a team, and every Thursday, barring the Secretary of State's absence from the country, Dulles would have breakfast with George in the Mayflower Hotel and discuss policy and legislation.

On matters of foreign policy, it was through George, more than through Lyndon Johnson or any Republican, that the Eisenhower administration negotiated with the Democratic majority. George was not only Foreign Relations chairman, but also the most senior member on Finance, as well as president pro tem of the Senate.

In addition to those formal positions of power, he was the Congress' acknowledged tax expert and was well liked by Northern liberals. One of them, Mike Mansfield of Montana, he had carefully guided and schooled and made his protégé.

George's relations with Majority Leader Johnson, thirty years his junior, were close, even affectionate. And Johnson once said he would no more think of interfering in George's sphere of foreign policy than he would propose to try to tell a Texas uncle how to run a ranch.

In this period, George pushed through the Formosa resolution, the Paris [Vietnam] agreements, and the Southeast Asia Treaty Organization, all of which were designed to stabilize the Far East and did stabilize it for a decade.

His manner was casual. Because of the heavy work load in his own committees, he did not keep up with details in other fields. On a typical afternoon, George walked over to the junior senator from Georgia, Richard Russell, chairman of Armed Services. "Dick," he asked, "they tell me you've got a little bill coming up this afternoon. Now tell me about it." Russell spent two minutes outlining the main features. George nodded his agreement and later supported the measure. The "little bill" was a $750 million pay raise for servicemen.

At a nod from him, half a billion dollars would be spent. Treaties would be signed or rejected. Foreign trade could be expanded or shut off and whole nations could go into a depression if George shut off their trade agreements. The President courted him, and the Secretary of State was his 50–50 partner. He was, without competitor, the most important man in Congress, save possibly for House Speaker Sam Rayburn and Senator Richard Russell. Then he fell.

George's mistake was that he didn't attend to his home chores. In 1955, the son of Eugene Talmadge embarked on a two-year senatorial campaign to beat Walter George, the man who had defeated his father in 1938.

He was Herman Talmadge, outgoing governor of Georgia, forty-two years old and a self-labeled "country boy" with high intelligence and ability. Senator George's backers sent warning: "Do not underestimate Talmadge . . . he is able, very able . . . and dangerous."

Talmadge ran on a single main issue: "Walter is a fine man," he told the country folks, "but we don't see him much anymore." By the time George brought himself home for the 1957 elections, he found his financial sources had dried up. He retired without a fight and Herman Talmadge went into the Senate.

Walter George had forgotten a central fact about Southern politics: whether in Washington or electioneering back home, whether in the eighteenth century or the twentieth, everything is done on a personal basis.

The junior senator from Georgia in that era made no such mistakes. He was Richard Russell, chairman of Armed Services and a man who defused a potential World War III.

Russell was born country Southern and lived the old-time ways. His home, until he died in 1971 at age seventy-five, was Winder, Georgia, a red-clay farm town of about five thousand population. His family had lived in the deep South since Colonial times and in the Civil War his grandfather's cotton mill was burned by Sherman's troops.

Politics-as-career was built even more firmly into Russell than it was into other Southern legislators. His father had served in the state legislature, run unsuccessfully for both governor and U.S. senator, and eventually become chief justice of the Georgia Supreme Court.

Richard Brevard Russell's own rise was rapid. He was elected to the legislature at twenty-two and became the House speaker within six years. Three years later, in 1928, he was elected governor, the youngest in Georgia history. In 1932, he won his Senate seat, campaigning as a New Dealer, and within two years was a floor manager for New Deal legislation. Within ten years he was leader of the Southern bloc, chairman of Armed Services, second ranking member on Appropriations.

When Russell had come to Washington, he was a Southern agrarian Populist from the hard-times cotton country with typical Southern generosity and Southern flaws. He was far from the brutal passions of the Ku Klux Klan, yet he treasured the way of life which embraced white supremacy. In legislation he was progressive, being committed to rural electrification, farmers' loans, massive public educational aid. But he had no sympathy for the problems of the cities. In the 1950s and 1960s, he opposed civil rights legislation as an intolerable invasion of states' rights. Yet in 1935 the same man had said, "I trust and believe that the day is not far distant when the federal government will recognize its responsibility . . . and will provide funds to assist in the maintenance of [all] the public schools in this country."

In military matters, the chairman was again the epitome of the South. In 1954 he blocked President Eisenhower's attempt to send American bombers to aid the French at Dienbienphu. And in the 1960s he argued about the American interest in South Vietnam: "I don't buy this so-called domino theory. We don't have to have South Vietnam to hold back the hordes of communism." Yet, once engaged in Vietnam, he supported the effort with his fullest abilities. And during the Cuban missile crisis in 1962 he urged Kennedy to invade Cuba. Prestige, and imminent danger, could drive him to war, but generally he preferred out.

Russell was the patron of numerous younger senators, but his foremost protégé was Lyndon Johnson, whom he stumbled upon in 1938 when Johnson was a young Texas congressman interested in rural electrification.

"Every year the House cut REA funds and every year [Johnson] came to me to get the money restored in the Senate," Russell would recall. "He knew what he was talking about and I thought to myself, 'That boy's a good congressman.'"

Russell taught Johnson his legislative techniques and secured for him election as Senate minorities leader in 1953, when Johnson was not yet halfway through his freshman Senate term.

Throughout his career, Russell proved to be in the right place at the right time. The most historic of these occasions came in 1951 during the Korean War after President Truman had fired General Douglas MacArthur. General MacArthur, head of UN forces, had pushed the North Korean Army to the Chinese border. The Chinese hit him with a surprise attack and sent MacArthur's forces reeling back to the 38th parallel. He wanted to launch a counterattack into China. Truman said no. MacArthur said yes. Truman fired him.

The American public, experiencing its first frustrating war of containment in Asia, was weary of stalemate and furious at the firing. There was a public uproar for President Truman's scalp, and a hunger to rip into Communist China with everything up to and including atomic bombs. Republicans, who hadn't had a President since Hoover, were certain they could convert the unrest into the key issue of the upcoming presidential elections.

At the time it was uncertain who the Republican presidential nominee might be. Eisenhower was a possibility, as was Senator Robert Taft of Ohio. But the popular choice was Douglas MacArthur, the compelling orator who had announced in Korea, "There is no substitute for victory," who had returned home as a Caesar, an acclaimed hero waiting to be called.

The most likely scenario that could be foreseen at the time was that MacArthur would be handed the Republican nomination and would sweep into the presidency on a vow to end the war with victory by atomic weapons. Whether the Soviet Union would react was unknown, but the likelihood was that they would attack through Europe. In the spring of 1951, World War III was very much a possibility.

Just how close the United States was to the first all-atomic war was not revealed at the time. Subsequent events—recession, the Near East, Indochina, civil rights—moved so fast that the nation has never stopped to reflect on just how near it was then to nuclear holocaust.

Documents published by MacArthur and Eisenhower tell the story.

On December 2, 1952, less than a month after winning the presidential election, Eisenhower made a visit to Korea. He wrote: "My conclusion as I left Korea was that we could not stand forever on a static front and continue to accept casualties without any visible results. Small attacks on small hills would not end this war."

Two weeks later, Eisenhower, accompanied by John Foster Dulles, met in New York with Douglas MacArthur. The general handed the President-elect a "memorandum on ending the Korean War."

This remarkable document stated that the President should meet with Soviet Premier Stalin on neutral territory to end the war. And that:

". . . Such a conference [would] explore the world situation as a corollary to ending the Korean War.

"That we [would] insist that Germany and Korea be permitted to unite under forms of government to be popularly determined upon." There were other provisions for establishing a worldwide Soviet-American peace.

Should the Soviets not agree to the conference or the conditions, said MacArthur, then they should be informed "it would be our intention to clear North Korea of enemy forces. This could be accomplished through the atomic bombing of enemy military concentrations and installations in North Korea and the sowing of fields of suitable radioactive materials, the by-product of atomic manufacture, to close major lines of enemy supply and communication . . .

"The Soviet should be further informed that, in such eventuality [as the above], it would probably become necessary to neutralize Red China's capability to wage modern war . . . until such time as the communist government of China has fallen. This concept would become the great bargaining lever to induce the Soviet to agree upon honorable conditions toward international accord . . ."

Four months later, following his inauguration, Eisenhower decided he might use MacArthur's proposal for nuclear attack:

"A course of action other than a conventional ground attack in Korea was necessary," said the President. "To keep the attack from becoming overly costly, it was clear that we would have to use atomic weapons.

"This necessity was suggested to me by General MacArthur while I, as President-elect, was still living in New York. The Joint Chiefs of Staff were pessimistic about the feasibility of using tactical atomic weapons on front-line positions in view of the extensive underground fortifications which the Chinese Communists had been able to construct, but such weapons would obviously be effective for strategic targets in North Korea, Manchuria, and on the Chinese coast.

"If we decided upon a major, new type of offensive, the present policies would have to be changed and the new ones agreed to by our allies. Foremost would be the proposed use of atomic weapons. In this respect, American views have always differed somewhat from those of some of our allies. For the British, for example, the use of atomic weapons in war at that time would have been a decision of the gravest kind. My feeling was then, and still remains, that it would be impossible for the United States to maintain the military commitments which it now sustains around the world, without turning into a garrison state, did we not possess atomic weapons and the will to use them when necessary."[6]

Eisenhower, who was not an aggressive general was nevertheless captured by the frustration of the events and the mood of the times. He had decided upon atomic bombing of China—if the Chinese did not come to the peace table. Eisenhower's intentions were scary enough. MacArthur's plan had a qualitative difference. He wanted to issue a nuclear-backed ultimatum to the Soviet Union to guarantee a world peace, including unification of Germany and Korea under popularly elected governments. The implied alternative was World War III.

MacArthur's determination should not be doubted. He had built

[6] *Reminiscences* by Douglas MacArthur (New York: Fawcett Publications, 1965), page 467, and *Mandate for Change* by Dwight Eisenhower (Garden City, N.Y.: Doubleday & Company, Inc., 1963), pages 179–180. Just before Eisenhower began implementing the new policy, rumors were conveyed to the Chinese that the Americans were prepared to use atomic weapons. The Chinese did an abrupt about-face and agreed to peace talks.

a career on taking a position and enduring the risks, as was proved in his crushing of the Bonus Marchers in 1932, his return to the Philippines in World War II, and his imposition of constitutional government upon conquered Japan. He was hardly a man who wavered in the face of decision.

While Supreme Commander of UN forces in Korea, he had taken a stand challenging the civil government of the United States. And at the very height of his popularity, on the eve of his return as a national hero, there entered Richard Russell.

Before MacArthur arrived in the United States, Russell had sent him an invitation to testify before the Armed Services Committee. The general accepted.

MacArthur returned in April 1951 to speak immediately before a joint session of Congress, ending with his famous observation that "old soldiers never die, they just fade away."

An eyewitness was William S. White, author and journalist, who wrote:

"The scene was one that was quite indescribable without the reckless use of superlatives. If one may be pardoned such personal references as are necessary to make the point, the atmosphere was the most curiously emotional I had ever seen in service as a correspondent, including such matters as D-Day in Normandy, the liberation of Paris, and the death of Franklin Roosevelt.

"Sophisticated members of the assembled group of senators and representatives, including some of those opposed to MacArthur in principle and in policy, were observed openly to weep on the floor of the House . . . One of the most balanced and soundest public men I have ever known, a distinguished senator of great personal reserve, said to me as we walked back to the Senate chamber from the House: 'This is new to my experience; I have never feared more for the institutions of the country. I honestly felt back there that if the [general's] speech had gone on much longer there might have been a march on the White House.'"[7]

In this atmosphere, Russell set up his hearings. The men appointed were the elite of the institution, the combined memberships of Senate Foreign Relations and Armed Services. Russell

[7] *Citadel* by William S. White pages 244–45.

was chairman and also sitting were Connally of Texas, Walter George of Georgia, Fulbright of Arkansas, Sparkman of Alabama, Byrd of Virginia, Lyndon Johnson, John Stennis, and Russell Long.[8]

The Republicans proposed that MacArthur testify before a special joint House-Senate committee on how he was fired and how Truman "lost the war." The Democrats, under Russell's leadership, refused. There was some partisan motive in their action, although a very reserved one, to shield the Administration. On the whole, however, Russell was concerned with avoiding disclosures that would injure the national rather than the White House interest. The Republicans themselves conceded this pure motive after the hearings.

Russell next beat back an effort to have the hearings televised and broadcast. He announced they would be secret "for security reasons"—unless, and it was a big unless, MacArthur requested otherwise.

It was a gamble, but a shrewd one, based on Russell's assessment that MacArthur would not want to appear to be grabbing the spotlight. The gamble worked.

MacArthur agreed to secret hearings and thereby denied himself the chance to state, for days on end, his beliefs and position before what would undoubtedly have been the largest TV-radio audience in history.

Criticism of the closed hearings was at first heavy, especially from the press, but the method hit upon by the committee to give information was too fair for the criticism to endure. It was arranged to hand out from the hearing room each day a transcript of the whole proceedings, processed a page at a time, with only military information deleted that might have had a clear utility to hostile nations.

[8] Other Foreign Relations members were Democrats Theodore Green of Rhode Island, McMahon of Connecticut, Gillette of Iowa, and Republicans Wylie of Wisconsin, Smith of New Jersey, and Hickenlooper of Iowa, Lodge of Massachusetts, Tobey of New Hampshire, and Brewster of Maine. Other Armed Services members were Democrats Kefauver of Tennessee, Hunt of Wyoming, and Republicans Bridges of New Hampshire, Saltonstall of Massachusetts, Morse of Oregon, Knowland of California, Cain of Washington, and Flanders of Vermont.

The issue before the committee was whether any high policy, no matter how wrong, could in the end be settled by military rather than civilian officials.

Russell accorded the general all the honors due a hero of the Republic, treated him with elaborate courtesy and patience, but kept firm control of the hearings. He had promised MacArthur a fair and full hearing and gave him one. A full, fair, and very, very long hearing. The hearings began as the nation's biggest news story. By the time they ended, nearly two months later, cartoonists were picturing Russell and MacArthur with long white beards, and public interest had shifted to other arenas. The committee never issued a final report, no decision was ever made on the merits of the dismissal, and nobody seemed to notice.

The danger of the dictator-hero on the white horse, and the corollary plunge into World War III, had passed. The relatively orderly processes of government resumed. Russell had defused the bomb.

Richard Russell served in the Senate for twenty more years, until his death in 1971. His authority was based in part on his awesome institutional power. (In the 1960s, in addition to chairing Armed Services and heading the Southern caucus which voted as a bloc on issues of direct concern to the South, a bloc which included nine committee chairmen, Russell also was the de facto head of Senate Appropriations.) But to an equally large degree it was based on his character. Among his colleagues he was the "senator's senator."

Chapter 22
LEADERS II

Two important examples of congressional leadership in the 1940s through the 1960s are the Texans Sam Rayburn and Lyndon Johnson.

Lyndon Baines Johnson came to Washington as a congressman in 1937. He was not lonely for Texans. John Nance Garner of Red River County was Vice President. Sam Rayburn of Bonham County was House majority leader. Nine of the fifteen major House committee chairmen were Texans and for the next thirty years Texans would hold leadership roles in the nation.

During much of that time, the thirteen years embodied by the Eisenhower and Johnson administrations, Texans were the national leaders. They had an ability, said Lyndon Johnson, "to stick their heads up above the grass."

The demise of the era of Texans would have national consequences. Following Sam Rayburn's death in 1961 it became increasingly apparent there was no leadership in the House and following President Johnson's retirement in 1968 no leadership in the White House.

By 1973, former Senator Gene McCarthy was saying that lack of leadership was the central national problem.

"In the last two hundred years," said McCarthy, "we went from

George Washington to Richard Nixon, from John Adams to Spiro Agnew, from John Jay to John Mitchell, and from Alexander Hamilton to [Secretary of the Treasury] John Connally."

In the House, Speaker Rayburn had been succeeded by the do-nothing, inept John McCormack of Massachusetts, who was followed by the do-less and even more ineffectual Carl Albert of Oklahoma. In the Senate, Majority Leader Johnson had been succeeded by the intellectually aloof Mike Mansfield of Montana.

The absence of leadership seemed to extend across the American spectrum. In literature there was no Faulkner or Hemingway. (The most admired of their sucessors, Joseph Heller and Ralph Ellison had written no worthwhile sequels to their first works. Norman Mailer, Walker Percy, Eudora Welty, and John Gardner all worked brilliantly but so personally that they were in no way leaders of a school.) The finest plays produced in the 1960s and 1970s were the thirty-year-old masterpieces of Tennessee Williams, Arthur Miller, and Eugene O'Neill. In business there were no leaders, nor did science have an Einstein or a Fleming. In labor, George Meany had replaced Big Bill Haywood, John L. Lewis, and Walter Reuther. Even the black movement found itself adrift without a captain after the assassination of Martin Luther King, Jr.

In the absence of leadership, permissiveness became the condition. In politics, in religion, in business, in the judiciary, in the arts, and in social reform, the old rules evaporated. Who was present to insist on their value? They were not replaced by new rules. Anything went, in any field, if you could get away with it.

It is, of course, apparent that the old leadership had forfeited its powers because it had not kept abreast of rising social, political, and economical aspirations. Jefferson's declaration that "all men are created equal" had caught hold of the entire world. East challenged West, race challenged race, colonies challenged masters. Meanwhile, the means to achieve the new equality were being worked out in a million different experiments.

The condition of no leadership seemed, and probably was, unnatural. The millions of intelligent, fast-moving beings of the western world found themselves without direction, a whole galaxy of people gone out of their interlocking orbits and wandering into high-speed collisions. Nature had gone awry.

The world had experienced such episodes before. In western history, the most famous example was the era preceding, and culminating in, the Renaissance, when an entire new constellation of ideas burst into light. The West spent the next five hundred years, with leadership, working out those ideas.

The twentieth-century experience would likewise be temporary, but how temporary was unknown. Meanwhile, in the United States Congress, the last leaders had been the Texans.

Sam Rayburn served as House speaker from 1940 to 1961, more than twice as long as any speaker in House history.[1] His political skills were based on an astounding knowledge of parlimentary procedures, the various Southern institutions of seniority, committee appointment, protégés, and the Club, and a solid, down-home humanity. By general acknowledgment, he was the greatest of all House speakers.

The man who led the House from 1941 into the 1960s was born in Roane County, Tennessee, in the mountainous eastern part of the state on the Tennessee River in the heart of what would later be the Tennessee Valley Authority. He was the eighth of eleven children of a Confederate veteran and farmer, William Marion Rayburn, and his wife Martha.

The family moved to Texas in 1887, when Rayburn was five, and took up farming in the Red River Valley north of Dallas, where the soil was rich and black.

The log-cabin origins of many American leaders has become a cliché, but the cliché is frequently fact and Sam Rayburn was an example. He attended rural schools and led the life of a farm boy, working from sunrise to sunset in his family's cotton fields.

Rayburn's rise was typically Southern. He was twelve years old when he stood in the rain to hear then Representative Joe Bailey speak, and, he said, resolved then and there to become a congressman.[2] He swept floors, did other chores to work his way

[1] Republican majorities interrupted his speakership in 1947–48 and 1953–54.
[2] Democrat Bailey was a Texas congressman from 1891 to 1901 and U.S. senator from 1901 to 1913.

through East Texas Normal College, then spent three years teaching in country schools. He entered the state legislature at age twenty-four and spent his five dollars a day legislator's salary to finance law study at the University of Texas. At age twenty-nine he was chosen speaker of the Texas House, the youngest man ever chosen.

Rayburn was elected to the U. S. House in 1912, among the wave of Southerners who went in alongside Woodrow Wilson. He was appointed to the Interstate and Foreign Commerce Committee, of which he would become chairman in 1931.

His attack on corporate interests began almost immediately, as soon as it was proper for a freshman to speak out. In his first two years in the House, Rayburn sponsored a bill allowing the Interstate Commerce Commission power to regulate issuance of railway stocks and bonds.

In 1917, President Wilson gave Rayburn the job of sponsoring the War Insurance Act, which provided the first insurance ever for American soldiers and sailors, the first allotments for their families, and the first disability payments for wounded veterans.

During his chairmanship of Interstate and Foreign Commerce, Rayburn authored six major pieces of New Deal legislation. These included the Truth in Securities Act, the Railroad Holding Company bill, creation of the Securities and Exchange Commission (SEC), and creation of the Federal Communications Commission (FCC). In 1935 he wrote the Public Utilities Holding Company Act, which gave the Federal Power Commission Control of the manufacture, transmission, and sale of electric power in interstate commerce.

In 1936 he collaborated with another farm country liberal, the great Senator George Norris of Nebraska, to write and pass the Rural Electrification Act (REA), which brought electricity to a large part of the farm homes in the nation. Rayburn later said this was his finest achievement.

A stocky man, with shoulders like a Texas bull, Rayburn was already a pre-eminent member of Congress in 1931 when the Democrats seized a majority in the House as a prelude to the presidential victory two years later.

His closest friend was John Nance Garner, the Texan who had begun serving in the House in 1903 and became speaker in 1931. Rayburn was a regular at meetings of Garner's "bureau of education" where legislation and politics were discussed over bourbon.[3] Rayburn continued the practice, holding sessions in the late afternoon of his "board of education," which included congressmen of both parties and frequently senators.

Rayburn was Garner's campaign manager for the presidential nomination in 1932 and he also supported Garner for the presidency in 1940, although by then Garner had veered from Roosevelt's policies, which Rayburn strongly supported.

In the House leadership change of December 1936, Garner, then Vice President, backed Rayburn's successful bid for majority leader, following the election of former majority leader William Bankhead of Alabama to the speakership.

When Bankhead died in September 1940, Rayburn was elected House speaker, on motion of Republican Joseph Martin of Massachusetts, the minority leader. (Martin, during the Republican majorities of 1947 and 1953, would be the only other man to serve as speaker during the balance of Rayburn's lifetime.)

During 1940, Rayburn gave some counsel to a freshman that has since become virtually a part of the congressional oath.

"My advice to any new member who wants to stay here a long time," he said, "is to keep in mind that he has two constituencies: the people who sent him here and the colleagues with whom he must serve.

"You must please the people of your district if you want to stay here; and if you want to be in a position which enables you to help and please the people of your district, you must also please your colleagues in the House."

The House speakership was the peak of Rayburn's ambitions. Asked once why he never chose to run for the Senate, he replied: "I'd rather be speaker than ten senators."

[3] The "bureau of education" was a small room in the Capitol that was the unofficial meeting place of the House leadership, which occasionally included members of the Senate. Rayburn is usually given credit for inventing the institution, but in fact its originator was the Republican Nicholas Longworth (Ohio, 1903–31) when he was speaker from 1925 to 1931. Garner continued the practice, as did Rayburn.

He might have been President instead of Truman had he not withdrawn his name from consideration as his party's nominee for Vice President in the 1944 convention. When he withdrew, the convention chose Truman as Roosevelt's running mate.

Ironically, the man who in effect declined the vice presidency was with his close friend Truman on April 12, 1945, the day that Truman first received word of Roosevelt's death.

On that afternoon, Truman was presiding in the Senate. He received a message saying that Rayburn had called. Rayburn had "been in Texas," Truman remembered, "and he called and said there was a meeting of the Board of Education . . . so I went over, and before I could sit down, before I could even begin a conversation with the half a dozen fellows that were there, Sam told me that Steve Early [Roosevelt's press secretary] had called and wanted me to call right back. I did, and Early said to come right over to the White House and to come to the front entrance, and he said to come up to Mrs. Roosevelt's suite on the second floor. I didn't think much about it . . ."

Truman went to the White House expecting to be told that the President had returned from Georgia and wanted a conference. "Mrs. Roosevelt . . . she told me that . . . the President . . . was dead."[4]

The soft-spoken Rayburn presided over the House throughout World War II, passing the Roosevelt and Truman policies, many of which were highly contested. He single-handedly prevented the death of the Selective Service Act just four months before Pearl Harbor.

The draft had been authorized for only a year, and on the motion to extend it, the speaker stepped down from the rostrum to speak for the extension. It squeaked through by a single vote, 203 to 202. Before any member could waver and change his vote, Rayburn banged his gavel and announced the result. Had the measure been defeated, a million men would have been discharged from the Army, its strength at that time only 1.4 million.

Sam Rayburn's leadership directly affected four of the five crucial periods in American twentieth-century history. He was on

[4] *Plain Speaking* by Merle Miller (New York: Berkley Publishing Corp., 1974), pages 197–98.

board as a ranking committee member during the Wilson era, which saw a vast increase in presidential powers. He was a chairman and majority whip during the Roosevelt era, which further expanded the presidency but whose most significant effect was the mushrooming of bureaucratic power. And he was speaker during World War II and the Cold War era that followed. He was silent on the fifth crucial episode of his lifetime, the civil rights movement.

Rayburn was a traditional southern internationalist. President Truman credited Rayburn with passage of the Marshall Plan, which rescued the economy of postwar Europe.

Truman said that once he received the plan, his first step was to call in Rayburn. "He just wouldn't believe it," Truman recalled. "His first reaction was just like everybody else's. He said we couldn't afford it. He said, 'Mr. President, it will bust this country.'"

Truman argued that without the plan Europe would have the greatest depression in its history, "and I don't know how many hundreds of thousands of people will starve to death, and we don't want to have a thing like that on our consciences, not if it's something we can prevent, we don't."

Rayburn asked how much it would cost. Truman looked him in the eye and said sixteen billion dollars.

"His face got as white as a sheet, but I said to him, 'Now, Sam, I figure I saved the people of the United States about fifteen, sixteen billion dollars with that committee of mine, and you know that better than anyone else.

"'Now we're going to need that money, and we can save the world with it.'"

Rayburn looked at Truman and said, "Harry, I'll do my damndest."

"We went ahead and did what had to be done, and the Marshall Plan saved Europe," Truman recalled.[5]

Winston Churchill later called the Marshall Plan "the most unsordid act in history."

Sam Rayburn, so typical of the Southerners in his rise to power through the protégé-seniority-committee systems, in his ethics and

[5] *Plain Speaking,* Miller, pages 246–47.

manner, in his internationalism, was likewise typical in his racial attitudes. In 1949, after Truman and the Democratic party began moving toward civil rights reform for blacks, Rayburn appointed William Colmer of Mississippi, an extreme reactionary, to fill a vacancy on the House Rules Committee. It tipped the balance of the committee toward the Republican-Southern coalition and doomed much of Truman's legislative program.

Asked how the setback had occurred, a Truman aide replied, "What makes you think the speaker does what the President wants him to do on this or on a lot of other things?"

During the Eisenhower presidency, 1953–61, Rayburn, nearing his seventies, jogged contentedly along doing little to answer the rising aspirations of the underprivileged classes. He devoted considerable effort to promote the career of his protégé Lyndon Johnson, who became Senate majority leader. But in the House, he seemed to side more and more with the conservatives.

In reaction to this, the Democratic Study Group was created in the House. Organized in 1957 by eighty House liberals, and at first called "McCarthy's Mavericks" after founder Eugene McCarthy, then a congressman, the group began moving to overthrow the men such as Rayburn who were blocking liberal legislation.

During Rayburn's lifetime, the group did not move too aggressively. To do so, said McCarthy, "might be construed as a direct challenge to Rayburn," who, it was implied, would wreak punishment.

But following Rayburn's death in 1961, the group grew in influence, was joined in the 1970s by a caucus of black Democratic congressmen and freshmen Democrats, and in December 1974 comprised a majority of Democratic congressmen. With the strength of numbers, they seized the powers of committee appointment, overthrew the thirty-year custom of House seniority and deposed conservative Southern chairmen. Seniority was dead in the House and it was due directly to lack of citizen service during Rayburn's declining years and in the leadership vacuum that followed.

Rayburn had ultimately failed to follow his own advice. He had served at least the prejudices of his district, but he had not served his second constituency, his colleagues in the House who wanted liberal leadership.

Meanwhile, leadership in the Senate was alive and well. Lyndon Baines Johnson was far, far more receptive to the new aspirations.

It can be said that Sam Rayburn forfeited his leadership role in the House. Lyndon Johnson made no such forfeit—not in the Senate, nor in the presidency. He was one of the great innovators of social improvement. But neither his humane intentions nor his accomplishments could save him. In the end he fell, a victim, first, of the Vietnam War, and, second, to an almost equally large degree, of a renewed national prejudice against Southerners.

No President other than the unique, similarly homely and humane Lincoln was so viciously attacked in his appearance, his language, his pronunciation, and his very humanity. No President other than Lincoln was the object of such widespread revulsion.

It was Southern conservatives who first made a national sport out of mocking Lincoln. It was Northern liberals who did the job on Johnson. Johnson was a victim of Northern liberal prejudice, a prejudice which built up during the 1950s and extended toward all Southerners, particularly those in political life.

It was during the 1950s that Lyndon Johnson made his spectacular rise, being elected Democratic leader while still a freshman senator, and a senator who had won his district by a mere eighty-seven votes. Also during the 1950s it seemed to many that Lyndon Johnson, not Eisenhower, was the President. Johnson himself scoffed at the idea, saying the President was the sole national leader and all the Congress could do was "prod him into doing everything we can get him to do, and when he does something good we give him a twenty-one-gun salute."

Johnson, working with Rayburn, nevertheless did serve as a sort of prime minister in the Congress, working with Eisenhower with dispassionate professionalism, supporting or differing with him as he believed he should.

Johnson's career was very similar to Rayburn's. He was born in 1908 on a farm near Stonewall, Texas, graduated from a small college—Southwest Texas State Teachers—and taught school for two years.

Unlike most Southerners, and unlike Rayburn, he spent no time in the state legislature. His training instead began when he signed on as a secretary to a Texas congressman, Representative Richard Kleberg of the gigantic King ranch.

Johnson went to Washington in 1931 as Kleberg's aide and there he looked up an old family friend who had served in the Texas legislature with Lyndon Johnson's father. The family friend was Sam Rayburn.

Johnson's ambitions surfaced early. Older House members recall that he established himself as "speaker" of a "little Congress," a mock assembly made up of staff assistants.

In 1937 the congressman in Johnson's district died and Johnson won the election. During the campaigning he met President Roosevelt, and the President, always receptive to a friendly vote in the Congress, invited Johnson to return to Washington with him on the presidential train.

So Lyndon Johnson, freshman congressman, arrived in style, a guest of the President, close friend of committee chairman Rayburn, and a member of the New Deal team. Almost immediately he went over to the Senate, introduced himself to Richard Russell and asked for advice on rural electrification.

He was not a star in the House, indeed, rather a run-of-the-mill Southern moderate-to-liberal congressman. He voted New Deal on bread and butter issues, and he voted Southern on such matters as the poll tax, squashing of labor unions, and loose regulation of the oil and gas industry.

Johnson served on the prestigious Armed Services Committee but, all in all, stayed in the House longer than he wanted to. In 1941 he ran for the Senate against Pappy O'Daniel and lost by a narrow thirteen hundred votes. In 1948 he won over Coke Stevenson by an even slimmer margin—eighty-seven votes, out of one million cast.

Only five years later, he was elected minority leader in a Senate where the Republicans held only one seat more than the Democrats.

This magic elevation of Johnson came about when the Democratic minority leader, Ernest MacFarland, was defeated by a Republican, a Phoenix city councilman named Barry Goldwater.[6] Johnson, who had already made himself noticeable as a floor leader, was selected by the Democratic leadership because he was trustworthy and because he was a political centralist. But mostly because he was the hand-picked choice of Richard Russell. His role was to serve as a bridge between right-wingers such as Harry Byrd of Virginia and the Northern liberals. He was to the left of most Southern Democrats and to the right of Northern Democrats. Within two years, talk about Johnson for President had become so widespread that he had to formally deny it.

His rapid rise and opportunism might give a false impression that he was all ambition and no substance. Lyndon Johnson, to the contrary, had a deep feeling for humanity.

Life magazine writer David Nevin, in an interview at Johnson's Texas ranch, once showed him a collection of pictures emphasizing the beauty, hardness, and age-old virtues of Johnson's home country. Johnson, said Nevin, reacted with real anger.

"Fine, yes, very pretty—but where," the President asked, "are the farm-to-market roads all paved and properly shouldered? Where are the miles and miles of REA lines that run like silver laces through this country? How about the flood-control dams that have made a whole chain of lakes to the north? Do you know how many houses in Blanco County have hot water heaters?"[7]

Johnson reeled off some total figures. Ninety-nine-point something or the other. He knew. He was President of the United States and he knew how many people in his county had hot water heaters. And he knew about rural electrification and about the dams that ended the annual flooding, and the roads that let the people go to town to sell their produce and to participate in community life. As a congressman, he had had a good deal to do with the improvements.

[6] Until the Goldwater election of 1952, Arizona politics was dominated by Southern Democrats, a heritage that derived from the Southern origin of most of the early settlers, and was reinforced by the Mexican and Indian population, which felt affinity for Democratic party goals. The Goldwater election brought the Republicans into power and thereafter Arizona was a legitimate two-party state.

[7] *The Texans* by David Nevin (New York: William Morrow & Co., 1968), page 130.

There was a good deal of the Populist in Lyndon Johnson. When he first went to Washington, as an aide, his biggest hero was Huey Long. And running second to Long was Maury Maverick, the crusading congressman from the San Antonio district who had traveled the cities dressed as a bum to investigate the Depression. After Maverick came Roosevelt, who was a bit to the right of both Long and Maverick.

While a young congressman, and throughout his later career, Lyndon Johnson was secretly troubled by the racial problem and often maneuvered behind the scenes to secure economic benefits for blacks, Indians, and Mexican-Americans.

Such activity ran against the grain of many Johnson financial backers. Foremost among these was George Parr, the "Duke of Duval County." The "Duke" was the political boss of several counties in South Texas and the politics and the economy was based on keeping Mexican-American labor in serflike condition. Civil rights violations were regular features of the landscape. Yet Johnson, whether in the Senate or in the White House, never interfered with Parr's fief. And the term is not used hyperbolically. A fief was what Duval County was.

The reason for Johnson's benign neglect was that Parr had brought about his election to the Senate.

Johnson's opponent in the 1948 primary race was Coke Stevenson, a former Texas governor and onetime Parr favorite who had fallen from grace. The election was very tight and a count six days afterward showed that Stevenson had won by 113 votes out of almost one million cast. At that moment, one precinct, in Parr-bossed Jim Wells County, reported it had found 202 ballots which had not yet been counted. And 201 of the ballots were for Lyndon Johnson.

Recriminations flew, but the Democratic state executive committee upheld Johnson's nomination—and soon thereafter the last-minute ballots magically disappeared. Johnson went on to routinely win the general election.

Lyndon Johnson was Democratic leader in the Senate from 1953 through 1960. He was a great believer in persuasion, and this caused his friends to grouse that he treated his enemies better than his friends: gave them multiple chances, showered attention upon them.

Johnson dearly loved to quote the Prophet Isaiah—"Come, let us reason together"—and his famed laying on of hands—the touch, wink, smile, pat, tug—was a technique of persuasion. He once said "the only real power available to the leader is the power of persuasion. There is no patronage; no power to discipline; no authority to fire senators like a President can fire members of his Cabinet."

This was too modest. As leader, the Johnson style was to gather power. He was simultaneously (1) chairman of the Conference, (2) chairman of the Steering Committee, (3) chairman of the Policy Committee, and (4) leader. (The Republicans use four different men to fill the role of leader and the three other positions.) On the Steering Committee, Johnson handled committee transfers and assignments. On the Policy Committee, he had substantial control over legislative scheduling, which gave him not only power to help or hinder bills, but an unequaled knowledge of who wanted what, when, and why.

Another of his important powers was a tactical one. Johnson called it the "power of recognition," the right of the majority leader to be recognized first when he wanted the floor. Johnson exploited this right with great skill to initiate floor fights when and on the terms he wanted. All these helped greatly Johnson's desire for persuasion.

In the Senate, Lyndon Johnson passed the first civil rights legislation since Reconstruction.

As a congressman, he had never talked about civil rights, or the misery of blacks. He never had a solid political base in Texas until his presidency and it wasn't until he reached the Senate, with its larger constituency that he even risked talking about civil rights. He himself, after becoming leader, once criticized liberals on the matter of civil rights. He said they were obsessed with a question not then capable of resolution. "I want to run the Senate. I want to pass the bills that need to be passed . . . But all I ever hear from the liberals is Nigra, Nigra, Nigra."

In his personal life, he was not preoccupied with race. When he heard that the one funeral parlor in a small Texas town had refused to bury a Mexican-American killed in Korea, he arranged to have the youth buried in Arlington National Cemetery and went with the family to the funeral. He broke a Jim Crow rule at the Rice Hotel in Houston by refusing to attend a dinner there in his honor unless blacks were invited.

In the Senate, the Southerners who claimed him as their own, as he claimed them, were shocked when he refused to sign the Southern Manifesto protesting the Supreme Court's desegregation decision. (Back in Texas, some Johnson constituents burned a cross on the lawn of his ranch.)

And in 1957 he passed the first civil rights bill, a feat which required all of his political skills. To get the bill through, however, he had to accept compromises with the Southern bloc. For this he was fiercely denounced by liberal writers. One such described Johnson "as the modern Machiavelli in a Stetson hat and Texas boots who headed the civil rights forces off at the pass." Liberal Northern senators who had accepted the same compromises were not so denounced.

Johnson had expected the criticism, having even predicted beforehand that his actions would be regarded "cynically in some quarters and misunderstood in others." He nevertheless continued to press ahead with civil rights legislation.

His vision of equality and justice included not only racial minorities but that other group of scorned Americans, the white Southerners. That he included whites and blacks in his vision was indicated in numerous of his Senate speeches, including one which asked his colleagues to forswear prejudice: "Political ambition which feeds off hatred of the North or hatred of the South is doomed to frustration . . . There is a compelling need for a solution that will enable all Americans to live in dignity and in unity."

Johnson's bid for the presidency in 1960 was half-hearted. He never had much confidence he would beat Kennedy for the nomination. He had said in 1958, "I don't think anybody from the South will be nominated in my lifetime, if so, I don't think he'll be elected." Although there was a belief then that Kennedy's religion would defeat him, Johnson felt that a Southerner had less chance than a Catholic of being elected.

To everyone's surprise, including Sam Rayburn's, Johnson accepted the vice presidency and moved out of the Senate. Abruptly, the unique authority he had mustered as majority leader vanished. His former colleagues, as several made quite explicit, were not happy to allow him even the nominal privilege of presiding over the Democratic Conference. After this initial rebuff, he was noticeably withdrawn from activity in legislation.

Then came Dallas, November 22, 1963, and Johnson was President. He ran a strong presidency and passed an incredible amount of legislation and all this without much help. In the House, Sam Rayburn was dead. And of the Senate majority leader Mansfield, Johnson complained: "Why do I have to have a saint for Senate majority leader? Why can't I have a politician the way Eisenhower did?"

His vice president was worse. He once said: "You know the difference between Hubert and me? When Walter Reuther walks into the Oval Office and sits there with his hands in his pocket, telling Hubert that unless he puts more money into the Detroit ghettos they'll burn the city down, Hubert will sit in this rocker listening and smiling, but thinking all the time: how can he get Reuther to take his hand out of his pocket so he can shake it. When Reuther comes to me with a threat like that, I'm sitting in this rocker, listening and smiling; but thinking all the time: how can I get him to take his hand out of his pocket so I can cut his . . . off!"[8]

Johnson's main problem in the White House was credibility. He used television a lot and for some reason the medium made him look like a carnival-show swindle artist. The oratory that worked on a person-to-person basis came across on the tube as hypocrisy. And the more Johnson tried to appear sincere and truthful, the more grotesque and unbelievable he became. Compounding this appearance problem was a habit of exaggeration.

All politicians make promises, and in the South the contests usually come down to who can outpromise and outvilify the other man. Huey Long was a master at both promises and vilification. Johnson steered close to the Long style, but he made the mistake of conveying plans and intentions as matters already accomplished. This created the famed Johnson "credibility gap."

[8] "The Ambiance in LBJ's Oval Office" by Joseph Califano, *Washington Post*, May 30, 1974.

As the gap grew, he was criticized for even small lies. Once, while speaking before millions of South Koreans in Seoul, an unbelievably large crowd, Johnson was caught by the press proclaiming that his grandfather had fought at the Alamo, which was untrue, but also unimportant.

(Johnson was amused by the criticism. He laughed that if "Hugh Sidey [of *Time* magazine] ever had a crowd like that, he'd claim he was a great-grandson of George Washington.")

Johnson had three major areas of concern during his presidency. One was economic policy, which had been a primary concern of all Presidents since Hoover. The other two were special to Johnson: the Vietnam War and the civil rights–poverty programs. In all three cases, Johnson took the distinctly unpopular course. He fought inflation by raising corporate and personal income taxes. He pursued the war in Vietnam rather than simply abandoning it. And he went ahead on social legislation much faster than the nation was prepared to do.

The social legislation was mostly embodied in a program Johnson called "The War on Poverty." Though it fell short of complete victory, it did not fall short on vision and was perhaps the most determined commitment to social justice ever made by a President since Lincoln.

In the first hundred days of Johnson's assuming office after his 1965 inauguration, when he held office in his own right, Johnson passed more than three hundred Poverty Program acts. And many of them were landmark innovations dealing with education, health services, medical care, housing, welfare, urban and rural renewal, and the preservation of natural beauty.

He passed these without real leadership in either the House or the Senate. Johnson in effect became his own leader and Anthony Celebrezze, Secretary of Health, Education and Welfare, said that 70 per cent of the bills in his domain wouldn't have passed if Johnson had not intervened directly. Another HEW Secretary, Wilbur Cohen, said that the program was not comprehended by the public, the press, or the Congress. "It was too big, it was too much for them to swallow." Cohen added that it might take twenty years before the Johnson program would be appreciated, time for the historians to get around to evaluating it. The writer

Theodore White said that Johnson had designed a "legislative architecture" for the nation within which American life would "proceed for a generation."

And in the civil rights field, Johnson became the first President in history to publicly identify himself with the cause of the black. Johnson passed legislation and Johnson moved opinion. It was he, and it was probable that only a Southern President could have done it, who toured the South and asked for an end to the racial practices. "I know the troubles that the South has seen," said the President. "I know the ordeals that have tried the South through all of these years. And I want to see those burdens lifted off the South. I want the ordeals to end and the South to stand where it should stand as the full and honored part of a proud and united land."

Of Johnson, the black writer Ralph Ellison said: "When all of the returns are in, perhaps President Johnson will have to settle for being recognized as the greatest American President for the poor and the Negroes, but that, as I see it, is a very great honor indeed." And so said other black leaders, like Roy Wilkins, Whitney Young, Clarence Mitchell, and Charles Evers. A black man, Robert Weaver, HUD Secretary, summed it up: "I don't know when he got religion or how he got it, but he really understood what was bugging poor people and black people."

This was Lyndon Johnson, the man chased out of the White House like a wounded bear fleeing hounds.

Johnson, choosing not to run again, left office in early 1969 and retired to a brooding isolation at his ranch beside the Pedernales. He knew he had not received a fair judgment or hearing from the nation, that he had been hounded to political impotency by liberals and the press. He blamed this reaction on the fact of his Southern origin. It was because he was a Southerner that he had failed to get a hearing. It was because he was a Southerner that he was derided and mocked for his speech and ways and looks. It was in this period that he made his famous statement on "the disdain for the South that seems to be woven into the fabric of Northern experience."

In several interviews in this period, he reflected on the prejudice against Southerners and against Texans. How the Eastern journalists, especially the magazines, were always picking at the region. The very region and state that had done so much, so incredibly much, for the nation.

He knew the Texans had worth. When he went to Congress in 1937 nine of the fifteen major committees were chaired by Texans. Throughout his career Texans had been among the national leaders: Garner, Rayburn, Justice Tom Clark, Connally, himself.

And in one of the interviews, as David Nevin of *Life* listened and Johnson rocked on the porch overlooking the live oaks on the banks of the Pedernales, Johnson reflected on how Texans, because of the frontier harshness of their environment, were accustomed to risks and accustomed to making risky decisions. He felt the Texans had an ability to raise their heads up above the grass and look at the world. That this came in part from the frontier which bred courage and independence and tenacity. And that it came a good deal from breeding. "Texans believe breeding in cattle is important," Johnson thought. "And a lot of Texas bloodlines came down from Tennessee and Kentucky, good bloodlines infused with a love of freedom and a willingness to fight tyranny."

Chapter 23
POWER

When the first colonies began, Virginia and Massachusetts, the quarrel between North and South was laid down. The issue was not slavery. Slavery was only the most enduring of several propaganda tools—a cause, for and against, created by each side to rally its people. The true issue was economics. North versus South was and is still a collision between two economies. One based primarily on trade and industrialism, the other primarily on agriculture.

Such contests of economies last for generations and centuries. They bring into play vast ingenuities and powers that work in unforeseeable ways, each side working mightily against the other until one dominates the landscape, and the loser is left to scavenge on the periphery. The most myth-shrouded and ancient account of such a contest is that of Cain and Abel, the "first murder," where Cain the farmer slew Abel the nomadic shepherd.

In human experience, only the contests of religions rival the contests of economies in the arousing of powers, searing passions and awesome myths.

The United States has been the arena of such a contest for two hundred years. The most eloquent and influential spokesman of the Northern view was Alexander Hamilton. For the South, it was

Thomas Jefferson. Both were products of their time and, simultaneously, products of their heritage. In America, that heritage was already a century old when Hamilton and Jefferson entered public life.

Hamilton, the adopted New Yorker, gave industrialism its political philosophy. He believed that social stability could rest only on a firm alliance between government and business. The means to ensure this participation was by a large and powerful central government.

Jefferson, the Virginian, believed in a magic forest, each family secure on its own farm. He was revulsed by the cities, by factory workers, by industrialism. His dream was that America be kept free of the corruptions of industrialism: "Let us never wish to see our citizens occupied at a work-bench or twirling a distaff." Let America ship its materials to Europe for manufacture, rather than bring the workers to the new land "and with them their manners and principles."

"The mobs of great cities," he said not with scorn but with biased analysis, "add just so much to the support of pure government, as sores do to the strength of the human body."

To guarantee his Eden, he would allow only minimal powers to the government, and thereby to the industrial interests he always feared would dominate government. He insisted instead on maximum and specific prohibitions against government intrusion on individual liberties.

It had become a commonplace that Hamilton's view of America was the more accurate. Even as Jefferson assumed the presidency, it had become obvious that the realities of industrialism had overwhelmed his abstractions. He would say while President, and with a certain amazement, that the nation could only survive by striking a balance between agriculture, commerce, and manufacturing.

Because Hamilton prevailed is not to say that Jefferson was wrong. The two men were not arguing which course America would follow. They were not engaged in predictions. They were arguing advice of which course America *should* follow. The best avenue, not the probable avenue.

The struggle is not yet finished. The embattled South has indeed retreated to the periphery, driven there in part by its own devotion to the false propaganda of slavery and white supremacy, its strength and moral credit sapped by its own internal class struggle. But it still retains the power of its libertarian ideals. It continues to survive, battling for those ideals from its last redoubt, the U. S. Congress, and particularly within the walls of its Senate fortress. And, as in the instances of Tom Connally, Richard Russell, John Stennis, Lyndon Johnson, and Sam Ervin, its best ideals and values are of mighty service to the nation and the world.

As the power of federal government continues to increase, as liberties dwindle, as Hamiltonianism prevails, it would be wise to reconsider the warnings of Jefferson and the Virginians. Protection or liberty? Big government or small? Industrialism or nature?

If a reassertion of liberties is desired it will be at the cost of federal power. Protectionism, bureaucracies, and the doctrine of benign interference must be dismantled.

If it is possible at all, the key to such a reformation will be a renewed leadership in the Congress.

In 1883, Professor Woodrow Wilson wrote: "In a country which governs itself by means of a public meeting, a Congress or a Parliament, a country whose political life is representative, the only real leadership in governmental affairs must be legislative leadership—ascendancy in the public meeting which decides everything. The leaders, if there be any, must be those who suggest the opinions and rule the actions of the representative body."

In this, Wilson seemed to be wishing wistfully for something like the Senate Club, a phenomenon which was then temporarily absent, as Wilson observed:

"In this country we have no real leadership; because no man is allowed to direct the course of Congress, and there is no way of governing the country save through Congress, which is supreme." He commented that the chairmen of the era might possibly provide such leadership, but were not doing so.

He was particularly interested that the Senate ride herd on the growing powers of the President. The Senate, in Wilson's view, was the main check to executive power. "The President may tire the Senate by dogged persistence, but he can never deal with it upon a ground of real equality. He has no real presence in the Senate. His power does not extend beyond the most general suggestion. The Senate always has the last word . . ."

Seventeen years later, in the aftermath of the Spanish-American war, Wilson wrote that the executive powers had gone unchecked and ominously predicted the future course of national government.

"It may be that the new leadership of the Executive . . . will have a very far-reaching effect upon our whole method of government. It may give the heads of the executive departments a new influence upon the action of Congress. It may bring about, as a consequence, an integration which will substitute statesmanship for government by mass meeting."

Congress had actually begun surrendering its powers to the executive in 1794 when it granted President Washington general embargo powers when the Congress was not in session. Five years later it gave President Adams power to impose or suspend commercial restrictions against Republican France whenever "he shall deem it expedient and consistent with the interest of the United States."

Other delegations of congressional powers followed in a steady march, always designed to meet the expediency of the moment and seldom revoked. In 1824, Congress allowed the President the power to raise or lower duties at will in commerce with European nations. A number of Presidents, including John Quincy Adams, Jackson, Polk, Fillmore, Buchanan, Lincoln, Andrew Johnson, Grant, and Hayes made use of the power, though the Constitution specifically said: "The Congress shall have power to lay and collect taxes, duties, imposts and excises . . ."

The march of presidential power continued. Emergency powers were granted during the Civil War, the Spanish-American War, and World War I. And powers were granted in-between wars. The Fordney-Cumber Tariff Act of 1922 gave further tariff adjustment options to the President. Frequently these powers did not even meet the expediency they were designed to serve. In the 1922 act, for example, it was generally expected that the flexibility allowed the President would bring tariffs down. The opposite occurred.

There followed the numerous powers surrendered to the New

Deal to meet the Depression. The National Industrial Recovery Act (NRA) granted President Roosevelt enormous power to regulate industry. Power to minimize competition, raise prices, and restrict production. (The NRA was declared unconstitutional and led to Roosevelt's move to pack the Supreme Court.)

Such powers, often called "emergency powers," began as public necessities. But fairly quickly, the industrial interests and other vested interests began to bypass the Congress and persuade the President, through advisers, to use his powers for their benefit.

For instance, in 1959 President Eisenhower, acting under authority of previous amendments to the Trade Agreements Act, established quotas for oil imports on the basis of "national security needs." In fact, by keeping out low-cost foreign oil, the quotas acted as a price support for the domestic oil industry and kept prices artificially high. Competition was eliminated by presidential decree. It was subsequently estimated that the oil quotas cost American consumers $5 billion per year in higher prices through the 1960s.[1]

By 1975, any President of the United States, without prior consultation with the Congress, had the power to:

—Order a federal takeover of any aircraft plant or other defense-related industry.

—Declare such cities as Omaha and Colorado Springs to be military zones because of their sensitive defense facilities, and order the arrest of anyone entering or leaving those areas.

—Regulate radio and wire communications, including Western Union, and news agencies such as the Associated Press and United Press International.

—Close the New York Stock Exchange, suspend all currency trading, alter customs and import duties, and control shipping and rail transportation facilities.

—Place practically any person in the United States in military detention for up to one year. (This derived from section 1383 of title 18 of the U. S. Code which allowed the arrest of any person entering "a military zone prescribed under the authority of an executive order of the President . . ." Under the law, the President could declare the entire United States, or any portion thereof, a

[1] "Specific Instances of Congressional Delegation of Power," paper by G. A. Dean, General Research Division, Library of Congress, May 2, 1973.

military zone and put into detention any person he believed had violated the law.)

—Organize and control the means of production.

—Seize properties and commodities.

And so on.

In 1973, the Senate became alarmed at the increase in executive powers and created a Special Committee on Termination of the National Emergencies and Delegated Emergency Powers. With the help of an Air Force computer, the committee compiled a list of more than 470 federal statutes which could be activated in emergencies declared by the President. Some dated back to the 1800s.

Senator Frank Church of Idaho, co-chairman of the committee, likened the powers to "a loaded gun lying around the house . . . ready for use for purposes other than their original intention." His fellow chairman, Charles Mathias of Maryland, said only partly in jest, "This committee may have done a very dangerous thing. It has compiled all of these laws into a single volume, and it is now going to be very easy for any future officials to be well aware not only of its existence, but of its potential."

The groundwork had been laid for a potential dictatorship, and at the end of 1975, the powers had still not been revoked by the leaderless Congress.

Would the powers be used for cynical or destructive purposes?

They already have been. In 1970, in one of several instances, President Nixon declared a national emergency in response to a wildcat strike of postal employees in New York and Chicago. Two cities were translated into a "national emergency."

Nixon declared that adequate postal service was important to the well-being of the nation. The strike, he argued, could hinder the processing of men into the Armed Forces and impair tax collections and the distribution of social security and welfare payments. Following his statement, Nixon activated some Armed Forces reserve units to distribute the mail in New York.

And in the summer of 1974, as a debate on the Nixon impeachment got under way in the House, the Defense Department kept "unusually close control over lines of command." The Secretary of Defense, James Schlesinger, and the Joint Chiefs of Staff feared that Nixon, or one of his aides, might trigger a military takeover.

(A Pentagon spokesman said the fear was that President Nixon or one of his aides might get in touch "with some military units directly without going through the usual Pentagon chain of command and order that some action be taken to block the constitutional process.")[2]

It will be noticed that the Defense Department, a bureaucracy, acted in this instance independently of both the Congress and the President to preserve *its* view of the Constitution.

Indeed, the independence of bureaucracies became increasingly apparent as the Watergate scandals unfolded. The FBI, although its members were the source of the original Watergate tips to newsmen, had at its upper levels gone along with the White House in the coverup. The Central Intelligence Agency had mostly refused to go along. And the Internal Revenue Service had balked all the way along the line when the President tried to use it to intimidate and persecute political rivals and objectionable newsmen.

The "independence" of regulatory agencies, of cabinet departments, and other bureaucracies was saluted as public morality at its best. And in that regard, they had behaved in a responsible manner. But was the behavior "moral?"

To a degree. But in essence the bureaucracies were acting out of a sense of self-preservation. And if the power of the President had become glaringly clear during the 1970s, it was even more clear that the bureaucracies were semisovereign bodies. Governed by presidential appointees, approved by the Senate, who were in fact prisoners of the permanent staffs of the bureaucracies.

The power of the nation in the 1970s was mostly divided between the President and the bureaucracies, and the dominant partner was the bureaucracies.

Even President Nixon, in a speech at Camp David on November 27, 1972, worried aloud about the possibility of the federal bureaucracy running the government rather than the President controlling the bureaucracy.

The growth of bureaucracy was not envisioned by the drafters of the Constitution, and the Congress seems unable to handle the

2 *Washington Post*, August 24, 1974.

phenomenon. Even its control of the purse strings to fund bureau-cracies went out of its hands to a large degree in 1921 with the creation of the Bureau of the Budget. The new agency was the only central repository of information on who was spending what, when, and where. And the President and the Congress alike took their guidance from the bureau's recommendations.

All of this derives from the growth of government. Because of growth, Congress found it necessary to delegate powers to the executive. Because of growth, the Presidents subdelegated responsibilities to department heads.

The end result of this delegation of authority has been to allow non-elected administrators to make policy decisions for the nation. And it is little wonder that modern studies indicated that Americans were not voting in substantial numbers because they no longer believed that their vote had any effect on decision-making.

Apart from knowledge of their powers, the sheer existence of most of these bureaucracies is unknown to the public. Who has heard of the OSHA (the Department of Labor's Occupational Safety and Health Administration Agency)? Yet its power extends over virtually every businessman in the nation. An anonymous informant, even a business rival, may unleash OSHA agents to raid the business and seize its records. "Without delay, at any reasonable times," not necessarily during working hours, according to an OSHA pamphlet. No court order or search warrant is required, in OSHA's view, not even evidence of probable violations.

And then there is OPSR, a new Medicare and Medicaid monitoring agency. It can inspect and computerize the private medical records of any American resident treated by a doctor or admitted to a hospital.

There are of course better-known agencies. The Federal Bureau of Investigation began in the 1940s to compile, for its own survival, dossiers on the politics and social life of congressmen and other public figures.

And there are the regulatory agencies, designed ostensibly to protect the public property, the consumer, and the flow of commerce. They in fact to large degree serve industry. In the words of the chairman of the Federal Trade Commission, regulated industries are "federal protectorates, living in a cozy world of cost-plus, safely protected from the effects of competition, efficiency, and innovation." The chairman, Lewis Engman, estimated that such protection added $16 billion per year to the nation's transportation bill alone. "Our system of hidden regulatory subsidies makes welfare fraud look like petty larceny," Engman added.

The bureaucracies themselves are America's largest industry, or at least the largest payroll. The Department of Agriculture alone had, in 1975, 106,000 employes, one for every 26.6 farmers. Federal employes throughout the nation totaled 2.7 million, exclusive of military personnel. They were the single largest salaried group in the country, being exceptionally well-housed, well-vacationed and well-pensioned, far better off in these regards than their counterparts in the private sector.

The cost is astronomical. The Health, Education and Welfare Department's budget for 1976 topped $118 billion, more than one third of the total federal budget.

Such increase and size was not an aspect of "creeping socialism" or "share-the-wealth" programs. In fact, there had been no significant redistribution of wealth from rich to poor during the two decades of bureaucratic increase. Bureaucracies were growing simply because it is in the nature of social groups to grow, to grow in population and to grow in power.

In almost all instances, bureaucracies are created for a benign reason: to solve the social problems that arise from the inhabitation of a given area by more than one person. But whatever their design, their main social effect has been to provide a payroll. As problem solvers, they do not work as well as elected governments, for there is neither carrot nor stick. They do not need to please or fear a public constituency. The role of bureaucracies is simply to survive and grow, not serve.

Ingenuity and imagination are frowned upon. A radical innovation by a bureaucracy might endanger its existence. What they can do is quietly expand their powers and each expansion is at the cost of an individual liberty.

If a creature from another planet came to America, he would see on the one hand the television sets, the computers, the airliners and the farms and the space program, all the development of private enterprise. On the other hand, he would see the schools, the prisons, the garbage and the fires in the cities, the crime, and he might wonder why the system that developed the technology was not applied to the other problems. And why not? The bureaucracies have not worked. The private enterprise sector has worked. In agriculture alone the American private sector is a historical phenomenon. Could not the same private incentives be applied to other social problems? Under contract to the government, as in the space program?

What the problems of the cities and the problems of inequal distribution of wealth represent is the failure of the bureaucracies. It is time to look for alternatives:

A political solution seems in order: a return to Jefferson-style government.

The eighteenth-century Americans, and the Southerners more than others after that, have had a commitment to liberty, a respect for private property, and a belief in the efficiency and justice of a market economy.

That view arose from the theories of John Locke, among others, who believed that people are endowed with rights in government and in nature. Locke thought that no one should harm another "in his life, health, liberty or possessions." At the same time, men had a right to "order their actions and dispose of their possessions as they [see] fit."

He was not naïve. Like Jefferson, Locke accepted that man is an animal which devours his own kind. That in a state of no-government, people would naturally "transgress these bonds, invading others' rights . . . and doing hurt to one another." No person had a right to appropriate the only water hole in a desert and charge for access.

A minimal civil government was necessary. Jefferson recognized that even a minimal government, however, would attempt to expand its powers and encroach on the natural rights of the individual. So he wrote in constant safeguards against this.

Benign interference, as experienced in modern America, is a powerful attack on the natural liberties. The state should not coerce people to act for what it, the state takes to be their own good. The state should not engage in paternalistic activities.

Yet it continues to do so. And the road ahead seems to point toward a new serfdom, with each individual having some sort of property rights in his neighbor, a control over his conduct at home and in the community, from childhood to old age.

Such control is not desirable. The human being is at his best, and worst, when unfettered. At his best, he is magnificent and awesome, the creature who can gaze in wonder upward at an exploding universe of two billion galaxies, each with a hundred million suns, and wonder about them. And invent means to get there. He, a microbe on a speck of sand orbiting a minor sun in a medium-sized galaxy, is not intimidated by the heavens.

It cannot yet be argued successfully that the increasingly paternalistic government has failed. But it can be stated without dispute that it has already made major encroachments upon liberties. The question to be decided is whether to continue on the road to paternalism or to veer toward renewed liberties. This question should be decided by the body politic, not by one man in the White House, nor by anonymous bureaucrats. A reassertion of congressional leadership is due.

There is no reason to believe that a reformation cannot occur. The historical record shows vast human accomplishment. The past five thousand years have been virtually the only era of human liberty. Prior to then, and in much of the human experience during that time, men were chained and their necks held to the ground by environment and by the fear of creatures, including other men, around them.

But at different places and at different times, in the past five thousand years, social institutions including governments have been invented and evolved to increase liberties, and the ability to reflect and wonder.

Five thousand years ago, a man had the choice of being a toolmaker, a hunter, a farmer, or a shepherd, or an outlaw. A woman had the choice to be his mate and bear children. Since then, and only since then, the opportunity for human potential has increased geometrically a thousand times. The lands, the seas, the rivers and lakes and deserts and ice-capped poles, the arts and literature and all the aspects of commerce are open to human adventure and exploration. The very heavens themselves and the galaxies have been opened. And perhaps the species, in its invention of civilization five thousand years ago, was providing the opportunity for liberties and imagination so that ten thousand flowers of genius could blossom and carry the expansion of life and the human race to other worlds in the universe.

But whether the species is acting with cosmic aspiration is not to the point. What is to the point are liberties and the increase of human potential. They are brother to one another. And in 'this, America is more favored than all other nations in the world. Though it has restrictions on its citizens, and they are aggravating ones, there are nevertheless fewer restrictions and more guarantees for liberty than in any other state.

In America, with its political system and its social mobility, any individual can be what he wants to be. A communist, a bum, a President, a Holy Roller, a preacher, teacher, cook, tennis player, singer, astronaut, doctor, gardener, bricklayer, banker, street sweeper, or mayor. There has existed nothing like the American opportunity in human history. It is literally possible for anyone to be anything. It is easier for some, because of advantages of wealth, intelligence, physique, education, or social standing. But it is possible for all.

America is a noble thing. Forget the warts and pimples and scars and look at the whole being, the two-hundred-year-old nation and its place in world history. Nothing has ever existed like it in terms of human potential.

It is a legacy that should be preserved for future generations.

It may be suggested that the Western industrial world has been following a faulty path of paternalistic government. Like the old South following the false value of slavery, the direction has gone largely unquestioned by the members of the community. And it could end with equally miserable results.

A reformation of liberties probably can be achieved through the Congress. The alternatives seem to be status quo, rebellion, or a dictator President who would impose change. The safest solution for liberty is the Congress. As Jefferson said, "The basis of our government being the opinion of the people, the very first object should be to keep that right." Congress is the most direct representative institution of the people.

Liberty, as protected through the Congress. The most diligent guardians of that principle have been the best of the Southerners. It cannot be denied that they have wavered on that very principle, and that they have committed grievous errors and oppressed 40 per cent of their own population. But they have likewise, consistently over two hundred years, proven themselves capable of magnificent service to the nation.

Hamilton's vision of America has come true. But Jefferson's and the South's fears, too, have been realized. A massive government dominated by special interests—commercial, industrial, and, in an unforeseen development, bureaucratic. All this at a cost to liberties.

Perhaps it was inevitable—the machinery of economic determinism, with inexorable force, marching the nation to its Hamiltonian condition. But the Southerners have never agreed that it was inevitable. They have resisted every step of the way.

There will be more to come. Race has almost vanished as a political cause in the South and is being replaced by the equally traditional Southern politics of economic class against economic class. A more equitable distribution of wealth. A new populism is arising and it is being felt in the villages and towns.

These villages were the source of all the Southern leaders, from Jefferson to Randolph to Jeff Davis, the Bankheads, Huey Long, Tom Connally, Richard Russell, Sam Ervin, Lyndon Johnson. For two hundred years they poured forth from a single environment. Villages and towns large enough to be connected into the American information system, small enough to be bypassed in the national roll toward urbanization and industrialization.

There, sitting on the periphery, they were the products of a stable family system, with roots and a tradition of values.

In the beginning, in the frontier life of Virginia, the harsh realities forced the original families to work, to make decisions, and to be responsible for their own. As population grew, peer pressure duplicated and expanded the value system, being reinforced now in the schools and in the occasional communal contacts of farm families.

America speeded forward and these cultural enclaves were bypassed and largely forgotten. And a marvelous thing happened. They became sanctuaries for one part of the original America.

The sanctuaries were scattered across the nation, a sprinkling in the Northeast and Far West, quite a number of them in the Midwest. But by far the largest number of them were in the eleven states we call the South and the border states of Oklahoma and Kentucky.

North or South, the great population centers of America have produced strikingly few leaders of national quality. Only Boston has contributed anything like its proportionate share and virtually all of them came onto the national scene prior to 1800. Instead, for two centuries we have drawn our political leadership from the small-town sanctuaries. It is the small-town American who most often sits in the Congress, or the White House. And it is the small-towner who has most dramatically affected our political history.

Our finest Presidents, with the exception of the Roosevelts and Jack Kennedy, were the products of the sanctuary environments —Washington, Jefferson, Madison, Monroe, Polk, Lincoln, Wilson, Truman, Eisenhower, and Lyndon Johnson. All but the farm-raised Missourian Truman and the Kansan Eisenhower were from the South. As this is being written, it is likely that in at least one Southern town there is a boy or a girl preparing him- or herself for leadership. Perhaps there are hundreds of them. The best of the Southerners. Huey Longs marching with Martin Luther Kings.

Epilogue
POPULIST

The basic contribution made by America to the world's people is a *workable* system of political values. These values, discussed in earlier pages, are epitomized by two concepts: Jefferson's words that all men are created politically equal, and the Bill of Rights.

These values seem to have been most purely preserved in the small towns and rural areas of America, where they are reinforced by family, church, and community. They also are preserved in the often-dormant-but-never-dead political philosophy known as "populism."

In the year 1976 there arose from the rural South the unexpected phenomenon of Jimmy Carter, Populist. He was not the first Populist to run as the Democratic party's candidate, but he was the most sudden and the most successful.[1]

Carter's Scotch-Irish ancestors arrived in Georgia in the 1760s. He had roots and a strong family background with discipline and an emphasis on the rights of others. He has said, "I have a reservoir of self-assurance that comes from my own people."

His childhood was normal small-town. He was whipped by his father with a peach-tree switch for shooting his sister in the

[1] William Jennings Bryan was nominated by both the Democrats and the Populist parties in 1896, and by the Democrats in 1900 and 1908.

behind with an air rifle. He went skinny-dipping with the neighborhood boys and hid under a bridge when a wagon would pass. He had to milk cows before he went to school in the morning. His first-grade teacher, Eleanor Forest, kept him on the straight-and-narrow. "There wasn't a room big enough to hold me and a child who wouldn't mind," she said.

Carter's early relations with blacks were good. His next-door neighbor was a black bishop. Carter's father and the bishop held prayer meetings together. Another black neighbor was Henry Jackson, with whom Carter grew up as a boy. "I've been knowing Jimmy Carter since I was a child," Jackson told a magazine interviewer. "The Carters are a fine set of people. You see them today and you see them tomorrow and they're the same. Jimmy don't change. Way back there, when there was a difference in the black and the white, that didn't make any difference to them."

These values were passed on by Carter and his wife to their children. Said his son Chip, "We were taught at a very early age that everybody was equal. We had the only liberal parents in Plains, and I guess I suffered. I used to get in fights every day at school—I had to come home at lunch and change shirts."[2] His father and his grandmother were taking their lumps too, for trying to integrate the local Baptist Church.

During Chip Carter's adolescence, Plains, Georgia, changed. Racial demagoguery passed away. The town returned to the class consciousness of Populism.

Carter's introduction to politics came through his maternal grandfather, Jim Jack Gordy, an avid supporter of Georgia Populist Tom Watson. Carter went as a boy with his father and grandfather to Populist political rallies and apparently absorbed the ethic.

Carter wore a distinct Populist image when he ran for governor in 1970, campaigning against the "economic elite and the political power brokers." He pronounced himself a people's candidate, unwelcome in the banks and board rooms. One of his TV spots

[2] The interviews concerning Jimmy Carter's boyhood were made by Joyce Leviton of Atlanta and published in *People,* July 19, 1976.

showed Carter walking up to the door of a country club and having it slammed in his face.

In his inaugural as governor, Carter laid into "the powerful and privileged few." He called for "simple justice" for "the poor rural, weak, or black." In a speech at the University of Georgia in 1974 he lamented that "poor people . . . are the only ones who serve jail sentences." And when he announced his presidential candidacy the same year he damned tax inequities which allow a business executive to "charge off a $50 luncheon on a tax return and a truck driver who cannot deduct his $1.50 sandwich."[3]

His acceptance speech before the Democratic convention in 1976 resounded with Populist notes. He promised the poor he would seek jobs for "anyone able to work." He spoke of a "political and economic elite." He decried "unholy, self-perpetuating alliances that have been formed between money and politics." And again he declared he could "see no reason why big-shot crooks should go free and the poor ones go to jail." He repeated his endorsement of a national health system.

In that speech, and in subsequent ones, the general tone described a struggle between economic classes—of the deprived against the privileged. A more equitable distribution of wealth was needed. A new Populism was needed.

Carter later confirmed that his acceptance speech "was Populist in tone, at least I intended it to be." Asked if he considered himself a Populist, he replied, "I think so."

Carter's main political ally in his run for the presidency was also a Populist, a protégé of Martin Luther King, Jr. He was Congressman Andrew Young of Atlanta, formerly a chief aide to King, a man who marched with King in Selma, Montgomery, and Birmingham. And he marched with Carter in Florida, in Chicago and New York.

Of Carter, Young has said, "His childhood was with blacks. He knows the poverty of rural Southern people firsthand. We've had the kind of experience in Georgia that is practically unmatched anywhere else in the world. We have a black-white partnership

[3] *Time*, August 2, 1976.

in Atlanta. In the North, liberals want to solve problems *for* blacks."[4]

Andrew Young and Jimmy Carter, like Lyndon Johnson before them, have brooded upon the scorn heaped on the South by the North. In 1976, the black Georgian and the white Georgian declared their hope to remove it. Young said he and Carter seek the same goal of a rejuvenated South, restored to its proper importance in national politics.[5]

Carter and Young are heirs of a Populist tradition that precedes and spans their lifetime. In the presidential campaigns of 1892 and 1896, the Populists sought to form an alliance of the farmers of the West and South with the industrial workers of the North. They failed. In Huey Long and Martin Luther King, Jr., the Populists had two who sought not only a rural-urban alliance, but a black-white coalition. They died too early.

In 1976, however, it appeared that the time of the Populists had finally come.

[4] *Time*, July 26, 1976.
[5] Ibid.

INDEX

Abolition of slavery movement (abolitionists), 8, 31, 45, 47, 50–54, 66, 132, 142–43, 145–48. *See also* Antislavery movement; Emancipation movement

Adams, Charles, 129

Adams, Henry B., 26, 28n, 29–30, 37, 129

Adams, James Truslow, 25n

Adams, John, 19, 23, 32, 57–60, 66, 68, 70, 85, 89, 94–95, 106, 107–8, 114, 118, 359

Adams, Mrs. John, 108

Adams, John Quincy, 27, 96, 115n, 118, 119–20, 122, 134, 359

Adams, Samuel, 59, 60, 61, 73n

Adams family, 55, 56. *See also* individual members by name

African slave trade, 52, 53–54, 66, 146. *See also* Slavery (slave trade)

Agencies, regulatory. *See* Regulatory agencies, federal

Agnew, Spiro T., 301, 339

Agrarian South, the (agrarian democracy), 37, 39–40, 42, 43n, 46, 54, 63, 90, 114, 132, 150, 166, 187, 278, 285, 324, 373 (*see also* Agriculture; Planters; specific aspects, crops, developments, individuals); and North-South sectionalism, 37, 356–58, 373 (*see also* Sectionalism; specific developments, issues)

Agriculture, 37, 39–40, 42, 43n, 46, 114, 166, 278, 285, 324, 373 (*see also* Agrarian South, the; specific crops, developments, places); federal government and, 185, 189, 191, 192, 196–98, 201, 213–14, 229, 364, 365; and slavery, 46

Agriculture, U. S. Department of, 364

Agriculture Committee (U. S. Senate), 259

Alabama, 11, 99, 105, 122, 137, 151, 157, 159n

Albert, Carl, 339

Alien and Sedition Acts, 111–14, 315

Allen, James B., 13, 259n

Allen, O. K., 224–25

American Anti-Slavery Society, 142

American Revolution, 6, 10, 18, 19, 24, 33, 321; Virginia's role in, 55–71, 72–86

Ames, Fisher, 18, 21

Ames, Nathaniel, 21

Anderson, Clinton, 262n
Anderson, Robert, 161n
Antiballistic missile (ABM)
appropriation, 296
Antifederalists, 88–93, 94–97, 98,
101. *See also* Federalists;
Jeffersonians; specific
developments, events, individuals,
issues
Antislavery movement, 137, 142,
155, 160. *See also* Abolition of
slavery movement; Emancipation
movement
Antitrust legislation, 188–89, 278n
Appalachians, 99, 101, 191
Appropriations Committee (U. S.
Congress), 174, 179, 180, 183,
184; House, 259; Senate, 251,
259, 295, 337
Aristocracy (elite), 43, 75, 77, 82,
88, 95, 118–23, 129, 131, 158,
161, 168. *See also* Planters
(plantations), Southern
Arizona, 348
Arkansas, 230–33; congressmen, 11;
and secession, 159n
Armed Services Committee (U. S.
Congress), 180, 183, 184; House,
243, 259, 347; Senate, 251, 259,
262, 295–96, 329, 330, 335–36,
337
Articles of Confederation, 18, 55,
66, 72, 73–77, 78
Asian wars and treaties, Southern
leadership and, 320, 327–28, 329
Atlanta, Ga., 373
Atlanta *Journal*, 245n
Atomic (nuclear) weapons, Korean
War and, 332–34
Austin, Warren R., 327

Bailey, Joe, 202, 204–5
Balance of powers principle, 1, 72,
90–91, 95, 174, 358–69
Baldwin, Joseph G., 37–38, 39, 40,
41
Bankhead, John, 188, 201
Bankhead, William, 190, 201, 204,
322, 323, 342, 368
Bankheads, the, 368. *See also*
specific individuals by name

Bank of the United States, 90–91
Banks, Nathaniel P., 163
Banks and banking, 90–91, 270n;
federal government and regulation
of, 90–91, 185, 188, 189, 201,
225; Huey Long and, 222–24,
225–26
Baptists, Southern, 10
Barkley, Alben W., 175, 201, 203,
229
Barnes, Ben, 242
Barrett, William, 259
Bartlett, Josiah, 73n
Baton Rouge, La., 208, 209,
217–18, 219, 222, 224–25, 237
Batten, James, 307n
Bayh, Birch, 254
Beauregard, P. G. T., 161n
Benign interference principle,
federal government and, 277–80,
358, 364–69
Benton, Thomas H., 152
Bentsen, Lloyd M., Jr., 259n
Beyond the Ballots (Farley),
235–36
Bible, Alan, 262n
Bilbo, Theodore G., 122, 241, 268,
281, 284, 285; biography, political
activity, 287–91, 292, 297, 301,
303
Bill of Rights (U.S.), 1, 2–3, 56,
66–67, 72, 73, 80–82, 85, 98, 281,
370
Birth of a Nation, The (movie),
195
Black, Hugo L., 195
Black Caucus, 243
Black Codes, 167
Blacks (black Americans), 1, 2, 4,
7–10, 24–25, 30–37, 43, 44ff.,
122, 147–48, 155–57, 165ff., 167,
171–72, 209–10, 211, 243, 278,
289–91, 316–18, 339, 349, 354
(*see also* specific developments,
events, groups, individuals, issues,
movements, places); and civil
rights (*see* Civil rights); and Civil
War, 150, 155ff., 162–64ff. (*see
also* Civil War); FDR and New
Deal and, 202–3, 209; Klan and,

194–96; as office-holders, 6,
168–71, 284 (*see also* specific
individuals); and Reconstruction
era, 167ff.; and slavery (*see*
Slavery); and voting, 166, 167,
203, 211, 213, 316; and World
War I era, 192, 193–96
Blair, Frank, 149
Blount, Jacob, 102
Blount, Reading, 103
Blount, William, 98, 102–11, 118,
135, 312n
Bolling, Richard, 305
Bonus Marchers, 197, 335
Boone, Daniel, 100, 101
Booth, Mary Louise, 159n
Borah, William E. (Bill), 207, 221
Boston, Mass., 59, 61, 63, 83–84,
122n, 369; Tea Party, 55, 57, 65
Boulder Dam, 11
Bowen, Catherine Drinker, 24n
Breckinridge, John, 158
Brewster, Ralph O., 336n
Bridges, Styles, 336n
British, the. *See* Great Britain
(England, the British)
Brocato, James (Jim), 227n, 230n
Brooke, Edward W., 171, 284
Broussard, Edwin S., 220, 233–34
"Brown vs. Board of Education,"
303–4
Bruce, Blanche K., 11, 170–71, 284
Bryan, William Jennings, 187, 212,
245n, 370n
Buchanan, James, 154–55, 159, 359
Buckley, James L., 251
Buffalo, early Southerners and, 100
Bumpers, Dale, 270n
Bureaucracy (bureaucracies),
growth in size and power of, 243,
358, 363–69 (*see also under*
Federal government); New Deal
and, 201–2, 205, 277–80
Bureau of the Budget, 363
Burns, James MacGregor, 11, 180
Burr, Aaron, 94, 106, 114
Byers, James, 107
Byrd, Harry F., 200, 204, 259n,
263–64, 328, 336, 348
Byrd, Robert, 244–45, 259n, 262
Byrds (of Virginia), 241. *See also*

specific individuals by name
Byrnes, James F., 200, 202, 322,
327
Byrns, Joseph W., 201

Cain, Harry P., 336n
Caldwell, Erskine P., 2, 321
Calebrezze, Anthony, 353
Calhoun, John C., 10, 23, 25, 26,
28, 30, 115, 120, 123, 127, 130,
132, 152, 153, 154, 173, 177–78,
179, 184, 250, 253, 254, 256;
biography, political activity,
133–44, 148; and Concurrent
Majority doctrine, 141–42, 179;
and secession, 135–36, 138–40;
and slavery, 134–35, 137, 141–44
Califano, Joseph, 352n
California, 152
Camp, Lawrence, 325
Canada, 136
Cannon, Howard W., 259n, 262n
Cannon, Joseph G. (Joe), 180, 186,
253
Cape Cod, Mass., 41, 42
Capitals, United States (various,
listed), 87
Capone, Al, 229n
Caraway, Hattie, 202, 230–33
Caraway, Thaddeus, 230
Carey, James, 106, 107
Carlson, Frank, 310n
Carolinas, 42, 43, 99, 100, 106, 135,
136–39ff., 157, 306. *See also*
North Carolina; South Carolina
Carter, Chip, 371
Carter, Hodding, 165n, 285
Carter, Jimmy, 250n, 370–73; and
new Populism, 370–73
Case, Francis, 310n
Cass, Lewis, 152
Cavaliers, English, influence on
Southern character of, 38, 40, 41,
135
Central Intelligence Agency (CIA),
362
Centralized federal government,
357. *See also* Balance of powers
principle; Bureaucracy; Federal
government
Chafin, Eugene, 186n

Chairmanships, congressional
committees, Southern politics and
leadership and, 173, 181, 184,
199, 200–1, 295, 297, 298–305,
328ff. (*see also* specific
individuals by name); "dragon
chairman," 297, 298–305
Charleston, S.C., 43
Chase, Samuel, 56, 60
Cheves, Langdon, 135
China, and Korean War, 332, 333,
334
Christophe, and Haitian racial war,
50n
Church, Frank, 361
Churchill, Sir Winston, 344
Church of England (Episcopal
Church), 40, 41, 82
*Citadel: The Story of the U. S.
Senate* (White), 260, 261, 335n
Citizens' rights (*see also* Civil
rights): Jefferson and, 69–70
(*see also* "Free and equal"
doctrine; Jeffersonians)
Civilization (culture), Southern,
10–11, 23–25, 26, 36, 82, 85. *See
also* Community identification;
Group integrity; values (ideals);
specific aspects, developments,
events, individuals, issues, places
Civil rights (civil rights movement),
2, 7, 9, 54, 69–70, 132, 172, 174,
181, 303–5, 314–18, 344, 345; LBJ
and, 349, 350–51, 353, 354;
legislation, 264–65, 316, 345;
New Deal and, 203, 209;
Southern leadership and, 7, 9,
293–94, 299, 303–5, 308, 314–15,
316–18, 331 (*see also* specific
developments, individuals)
Civil rights acts (1957, 1960, 1964),
316
Civil War (Civil War era), 2–4, 66,
80, 148, 150–72, 184, 189, 292,
320, 321, 359 (*see also* specific
aspects, developments, events,
individuals, issues, movements,
places); difference between the
conduct of the North and the
South in, 2–4, 30; secessionist
doctrine and, 115–16, 139,
159–60, 164 (*see also* Secession)
Clancy, Paul, 310n, 314, 316n
Clark, Joseph S., 129, 261
Clark, Tom C., 355
Class (class consciousness, class
differences, class prejudice, class
structure, class struggle), 33,
43–44, 121–23, 141, 158, 190,
191–92, 358, 368, 371 (*see also*
specific classes, developments,
events, groups, individuals,
issues); Populism and, 190, 209,
211, 213, 237–38, 371–73 (*see
also* Populism); and race
problem, 147, 371
Clay, Henry, 27, 64, 96, 120, 130,
136, 254
Clayton Anti-Trust Act, 188
Clemenceau, Georges, 193
Cleveland, Grover, 185n, 245n
"Club," the (U. S. Senate), 251,
252, 253–73, 279–80, 281ff., 292,
297, 358 (*see also* specific
developments, individuals);
character and, 255, 268, 272;
defined, 254–55; influence of, 261,
279–80, 281ff.; makeup of, 254,
259n, 262n, 267–68, 279–80 (*see
also* specific individuals)
Coal mining, 191, 192
Cobb, David, 176
Cobb, Howell, 153
Cohen, Wilbur, 353
Cold War era, 328–37, 344
Colmer, William, 345
Colonial era (colonial America),
17ff., 36–54, 55–71, 72–86, 87ff.,
356–58, 359. *See also* specific
developments, places
Colonization Society, 54
Committee assignments (U. S.
Congress): chairman and (*see*
Chairmanships); and "power"
committees (*see* "Power"
committees); protégé system and,
244ff., 260 (*see also* Protégé
system); reforms in, 345–46;
Senate "Club" and, 260, 264–66,
269–70, 297 (*see also* "Club,"
the): seniority and (*see* Seniority
principle)

"Committee on Engrossed Bills, etc.," 177

Committees, U. S. Congress (congressional committee system), 73, 131, 135, 153, 154, 172, 173–84, 199, 200–1, 259–60, 279, 293, 297, 345–46; assignments to (*see* Committee assignments); chairmanships of (*see* Chairmanships); "conference," 178–79; creation of, 73; seniority and (*see* Seniority principle)

Communism, 69; McCarthy era and, 310, 313 (*see also* Cold War era)

Community identification (community sense), Southern, 4–5, 23–25, 26, 321. *See also* Civilization (culture), Southern; Values (ideals); specific aspects, developments, individuals, places

Concord, Battle of, 55, 57, 66

Concurrent Majority doctrine, 141–42, 179

Confederacy (Confederate States), the, 150, 160–65, 180 (*see also* Civil War); Confederate Congress, 161

"Conference committees," 178–79

Congress, U. S., 1, 2, 7, 11–13, 17ff., 57, 65, 77–80, 98–111, 155, 187, 319ff., 358 (*see also* House of Representatives, U. S.; Senate, U. S.; specific committees, developments, events, individuals, issues, legislation); blacks in, 168–71 (*see also* specific individuals by name); in Civil War era, 139–40, 150, 152ff.; committees of (*see* Committees, U. S. Congress); Continental (*see* Continental Congress); and growth of bureaucracy and executive powers, 358–69; meetings listed (1790–present), 87; need for new leadership in, 358ff., 366–69; origin and organization of, 73, 77–80; and protégé system, 239, 240–52; and sectionalism (1790s), 98–116;

Senate "Club" and (*see* "Club," the); Southern leadership and, 11–13, 201, 279–80, 281ff., 319ff. (*see also* Leadership; specific developments, individuals)

Congressional Government (Wilson), 186

Connally, John, 339

Connally, Tom, 13, 204, 228, 240, 266, 279, 320, 322, 326–27, 336, 355, 358, 368; background, political activity, 326–28; and Senate Foreign Relations Committee, 326–28; and United Nations, 279, 320, 327–28

Connecticut, 113

Connecticut Compromise, 79

Conservatives, 278, 281; formation of coalition in Congress, 205, 345

Constitution, Virginia's, 56, 66, 76

Constitutional Government (Wilson), 186

Constitutional Union party, 158

Constitution of the United States, 1, 4, 5, 8, 11, 17, 18, 20–21, 26, 39, 55, 56, 60–71, 72–86, 90–91, 119, 121, 127; adoption of, 76–85; and balance of powers principle, 90–91, 95, 359, 362–63; and Bill of Rights (*see* Bill of Rights); Constitutional Convention and debates on, 7, 9, 17–23, 75, 76–85, 103, 119, 121, 127, 255; FDR and the Supreme Court and, 204–5; federalists and, 88, 90–91; and implied powers doctrine, 90–91, 95; nullification and secession and, 112, 127, 138–39; Senate "Club" and, 257, 261, 273; and slavery, 52, 61, 68, 74, 79–80; Southern leadership and, 76–85, 278, 282, 314–18; strict interpretation of, 30, 95, 132; Virginia's role and, 56, 66, 76–85 (*see also* specific individuals); and World War I, 189, 190

Continental Congress, 17ff., 57ff., 103; First, 57ff., 65ff., 72ff.; meetings (listed), 87; Second, 66–71, 72ff., 87; Virginia and organization of, 55–56

Coolidge, Calvin, 219–20
Coppola, Frank, 230n
Cornwallis, General, surrender of, 75
Costello, Frank, 229, 230n
Cotton, 52, 136, 189, 192, 201, 278
Cotton gin, invention and use of, 52, 136
Coughlin, Father, 235
County agent program, 189
Crawford, William, 120
Creek Indians, 102, 105
Creoles, Louisiana, 147, 156
Cromwell, Lord, 38, 41, 82
Cuba, 153, 154; missile crisis, 331
Cumberland, Earl of, 26
Cyr, Paul, 218, 219

"Damned Yankees," origin and dating of term, 24n
Dartmouth College, 6
Davis, Jefferson, 3–4, 10, 26, 100n, 130, 132, 149, 150, 151, 170, 368; biography, political activity, 151–55, 159–60; as President of the Confederate States, 160–61, 164–65
Davis, Jimmie, 248n
Deadlock of Democracy, The (Burns), 180
Dean, G. A., 360n
Dean, John, 5n
Debs, Eugene, 186, 214
Debts (indebtedness), federal, 90–91, 95–96, 114, 326
Declaration of Independence, 1, 18, 49, 112; Jefferson and, 24, 56, 57, 60, 62–71; Virginia and, 56, 58, 60, 62–71
Defense Department, U. S., 361, 362
DeKalb, Miss., 282, 291, 294–95, 297
Delaware, 146
Demagogues (demagoguery), 118, 121–23, 148–49, 166, 238, 268, 303, 325. *See also* specific individuals, issues, movements
Democracy, Jeffersonian. *See* Jeffersonians (Jeffersonian democracy, Jeffersonian principles and values)
Democracy in America (Tocqueville), 50–51, 52, 53, 54
Democratic National Convention (1948), 97
Democratic party (Democrats), 12–13, 27, 89, 91–92, 95–98, 106–16, 117–19ff., 133ff., 341 (*see also* Congress, U. S.; specific developments, events, individuals); caucus, 299; Civil War era, 110–11, 152–72 *passim;* creation of, 73, 86; and FDR and New Deal era, 199–206, 277ff.; and Populism, 370–73 (*see also* Populism; specific individuals); and protégé system, 240–52; and Radical Republicans (1854–76), 110–11; and Senate "Club," 253–73; and slavery issue, 148–49; Southern wing, 11, 12–13, 97, 180, 193, 205, 278, 341; and World War I and Wilson era, 185–96ff.
Democratic-Republican party, 73n, 89, 91–92
Democratic Steering Committee, 250, 260, 327, 350
Democratic Study Group, 345
Depression era (Great Depression), 196–98, 199, 360; FDR and New Deal and, 199–206, 209–11, 277–80, 360; Huey Long and, 209–11, 223, 237
DePriest, Oscar, 171
Dickinson, John, 73, 78
Dies, Martin, 190
Dirksen Everett M., 262n, 266, 312
District of Columbia (*see also* Washington, D.C.): establishment of, 87n
Dixie Democrats (Dixiecrats), 133
Dodd (Thomas J.) case, 282–83, 293
Douglas, Paul H., 258, 267, 269, 270
Douglas, Stephen A., 158
"Dragon chairman," 297, 298–305
Drayton, William Henry, 74–75
Dred Scott case. 155

Driscoll, Alfred E., 268
Dulles, John Foster, 328–29, 333
Dumbarton Oaks Conference
(1944), 327, 328
Dunmore, Lord, 145
Duties (tariffs). *See* Tariffs

Early, Steve, 343
Eastland, James O., 174–75, 241,
255, 280–82, 295, 299–305;
biography, political activity,
281–82, 297, 299–305; as "dragon
chairman," 297, 298–305; and
Senate Judiciary Committee, 297,
304–5
Economy (economic developments
and issues), 13, 39–40, 42, 43–44,
45–54, 75, 84, 196ff., 278, 353,
368 (*see also* Agrarian South;
Banks and banking; Class;
Industry; Poor, the; Working class;
specific aspects, developments,
events, groups, individuals, issues,
movements); class and (*see*
Class); FDR and New Deal and,
199–206, 207ff.; growth in size
and power of bureaucracy and
executive branch of government
and, 359–61, 365, 368; and
North-South sectionalism, 13,
36ff., 42, 43–44ff., 75, 135–42,
356–58, 368 (*see also* specific
aspects, developments, groups,
events); Populism and, 211–14
(*see also* Populism); and slavery
and Civil War, 45–54, 155ff., 164
(*see also* Slavery); Southern
blacks and, 147–48, 155, 171;
Southern leadership in foreign
affairs and, 321, 329; World War
I and Wilson era, 185, 187,
188–94, 196
Education, 189; free blacks and,
157, 158, 165–66; Huey Long
and, 210, 211, 217, 225; school
desegregation and, 294, 303–4
Edwards, Edwin, 248, 249
Ehrlichman, John D., 258, 283
Eisenhower, Dwight D., 295n, 329,
331, 332, 333–34, 338, 345, 352,
361, 369

Electoral College, 20–21, 77, 94,
114, 115n
Elizabethan England, influence on
Southern character of, 41, 82,
191, 306
Ellender, Allen J., 182, 208, 233,
248–49, 262n
Ellison, Ralph, 339, 354
Ellsworth, Oliver, 18
Emancipation movement, 23, 24–25,
33–35. *See also* Abolition of
slavery movement; Antislavery
movement
"Emergency powers," executive,
360–62
Emigration. *See* Immigration
(immigrants)
Engerman, Stanley L., 45n, 46
England. *See* Great Britain
(England, the British)
Engman, Lewis, 364
Episcopal Church (Church of
England), 40, 82
Ervin, Sam J., Jr., 5, 11, 132, 246,
250, 252, 253, 254, 257, 262n,
266, 279, 284, 302–3, 306–18,
358, 368; biography, political
activity, 306–18; and civil rights
issue, 314–18; and Joe McCarthy,
279, 293, 309–14; and Nixon,
283, 308–10, 315–16
Ethiopian Regiment (1775), 145
Europe, Marshall Plan and, 279,
344
Evans, Hiram, 209–10
Evers, Charles, 354
Every Man a King (Long), 215
Executive branch, balance of
powers and. *See* Balance of
powers principle; Federal
government; Presidency
(presidents)

Fair Housing Bill, 315
Farley, James, 7, 200, 202, 225,
235–36
Farming *See* Agrarian South, the;
Agriculture; specific committees,
developments, individuals, kinds,
legislation, places
Faulkner, William, 2, 285, 339

"Favorite son" candidates, 200
Federal Bureau of Investigation (FBI), 362, 363
Federal Communications Commission (FCC), 341
Federal government (*see also* specific agencies, branches, developments, events, groups, individuals, issues, movements): and balance of powers (*see* Balance of powers principle); and benign interference policy, 277–80, 358, 364–69; growth in size and power of bureaucracy and, 185–94, 197–98, 199–206, 243, 277–80, 358–69; and need for new leadership, 358, 366–69; and paternalism, 366–69; states' rights and, 88, 95–96 (*see also* States' rights)
Federal Hall (N.Y.C.), 17–23, 87–88
Federalists (Federalist party), 88–93, 94–97, 98, 101, 104–6, 107–16, 118, 120, 135, 136, 154, 176, 184, 256, 356–58, 368. *See also* specific individuals, issues
Federal Trade Commission, 363; creation of, 188
Felton, Rebecca Latimer, 212
Few, William, 18
Filibuster (s) and filibustering, 2, 27, 131–32, 141, 184, 264–65, 268; Huey Long and, 226–29; John Randolph and, 27–28; Rule 22 (cloture) and, 264–65
Fillmore, Millard, 359
Finance Committee (U. S. Congress), 180, 183, 184; Senate, 251, 259, 295, 324, 325, 328, 329
Finch, Robert, 294n
Finlay (frontiersman), 100, 101
Fiscal policies, 7. *See also* Banks and banking
Flanders, Ralph E., 336n
Florida, 106, 136, 153; congressmen, 11; and secession, 159n
Fogel, Robert William, 45n, 46
Foote, Shelby, 285
Force Bills, 205

Fordney-Cumber Tariff Act (1922), 359
Foreign affairs (foreign policy, foreign relations), 7, 12, 117, 128, 130 (*see also* specific aspects, committees, developments, events, individuals, issues, movements); federalists and antifederalists and, 88, 91–92, 136; Southern leadership and, 128, 189–93, 279, 295–96, 320–37 (*see also* Interventionism
Foreign Relations Committee (U. S. Congress), 180, 183, 184; Senate, 295, 298, 320–21, 322, 324, 325–30, 335–36
Forest, Eleanor, 371
Formosa resolution, 329
Forrest, Nathan, 194
Fort Sumter, S.C., 161
France (the French), 21, 49, 69, 91–92, 102, 321, 322, 359
Frankfort (Pa.) meeting, 57–66, 85
Franklin, Benjamin, 56, 61, 67n
"Free and equal" doctrine, Jefferson and, 9, 56, 69, 339. *See also* Jeffersonians (Jeffersonian democracy, Jeffersonian principles and values)
Free blacks, 147, 148, 155–56, 165ff.
Freedmen's Bureau, 165–66, 167
Frémont, John C., 154
French Revolution, 69, 91–92
"Freshmen's Revolt" (1974), 259
Fritchey, Clayton, 261–62
Frontier (frontiersmen), 93, 98ff., 119, 122; and Southern values, 355, 368
Fulbright, J. William, 179, 267, 270, 295, 298, 299, 336

Gardner, John, 339
Garner, John Nance, 128, 200, 205, 224, 227, 240–41, 339, 342, 355
Garrison, William Lloyd, 142, 149
George, Walter, 132, 203, 204, 320, 323–26, 328–30, 336; biography, political activity, 323–26, 328–30
George II, King, 43
George III, King, 20, 57, 61, 64, 68

Georgia, 11, 43, 122, 137, 146, 241, 245, 323, 324–25, 330–31, 370–73 (*see also* specific places); Klan and, 195; and secession, 159n
Germany, 333 (*see also* Nazis); immigrants from, 148; and World War II, 320, 321–23
Gerry, Elbridge, 18
Gillette, Guy M., 336n
Gilman, John, 18
Gladstone, William E., 131
Glass, Carter, 193, 204, 205, 222, 226, 321, 323, 327
Goldwater, Barry, 261, 296, 348
Gordon, Mrs. Mattie Lena, 290n
Gordy, Jim Jack, 371
Government, federal. *See* Federal government; specific agencies, branches
Grant, Ulysses S., 163, 164, 170, 290, 359
Graves, John Temple, 320n
Great Britain (England, the British), 21, 31, 36, 38, 39, 40, 41, 42, 43, 49, 56, 57, 61, 64, 65–66, 67, 75, 77, 82, 88, 91–93, 101, 102, 106, 107, 108, 119, 136, 153n; and World War II, 321, 322–23, 326
Great Depression. *See* Depression era (Great Depression)
Great Society, LBJ and, 2
Greeley, Horace, 164
Green, Theodore, 336n
Green Brier (river), 99
Grosjean, Alice Lee, 219
Group integrity, Southern patriotism and, 321
Gwinnett, Button, 73n

Haldeman, Bob, 283
Hamilton, Alexander, 77–78, 80–81, 85, 89, 140, 176, 206, 339; and Bank of the United States, 90–91; and conflict with Jefferson, 81, 90–93, 94–96, 111, 112–13, 115n, 357, 368 (*see also* Jeffersonians); and Federalists, 89, 90–93, 94–96, 111, 112–13, 115n, 136, 356–58, 368
Hamilton, James, 138, 139

Hancock, John, 56
Hansen, Clifford P., 259n
Harlan County, Ky., 191
Harper, S. J., 215–16
Harrison, Benjamin, 62, 153
Harrison, Henry, 96
Harrison, Pat, 201–2, 284, 301, 326
Harrodsburg, Ky., 100
Harvard University, 6
Hatfield, Mark O., 283
Hayden, Carl T., 262n, 266, 295
Hayes, Rutherford B., 359
Haywood, Big Bill, 339
Health, Education and Welfare, U. S. Department of, 364
Hebert, F. Edward, 175
Heflin, Thomas, 188, 189
Heller, Joseph, 339
Henrico County, Va., 145
Henry, John, 62
Henry, Patrick, 25, 32, 58, 62, 64–65, 83, 84, 88, 104, 113–14, 145; and Declaration of Rights, 81, 82
Hewes, Joseph, 73n
Hickenlooper, Bourke B., 262n, 336n
"Hideaway" offices (U. S. Congress), 182
Hill, Lister, 183, 262n
History of the Negro Race in America from 1619 to 1880 (Williams), 162–63, 165–66
History of the Province of New York (Smith), 51
Hitler, Adolf, 320, 321, 323
Hoey, Clyde, 309
Holland, Spessard, 262n
Hoover, Herbert, 175, 197, 219, 221, 234–35
Hopkins, Stephen, 73n
Hopkinson, Francis, 73n
House of Burgesses, Virginia, 63n, 64, 65
House of Representatives, U. S., 20–21, 22, 87–88, 91, 92, 94, 95, 97, 114, 120, 127, 128, 130, 134–35ff., 187, 338–55 *passim* (*see also* Congress, U. S.; specific committees, developments, individuals); blacks in, 168–71 (*see also* specific individuals by

name); committee chairmen, 299;
described, powers, 77–80, 127,
128, 170; end of seniority system
in, 345–46; lack of leadership in,
338ff.; organization of, 77–80;
and power committees, 259; and
protégé system, 240–47; senority-
committee system in, 173–77,
178–84, 345–46; Southern
political strength in, 127, 128,
278, 338ff. (*see also* specific
committees, developments,
individuals)
Hruska, Roman L., 259n, 262n, 316
Huey Long (Williams), 229–30n
Hughes, Charles Evans, 204
Huitt, Ralph, 268n, 269
Hull, Cordell, 188, 199, 200
Human rights. *See* Citizens' rights;
Civil rights; "Free and equal"
doctrine
Humphrey, Hubert H., 261, 263–64,
352
Hunt, Lester C., 336n
Hunter, R. M. T., 153
Huntington, Samuel, 18

Illegitimate children, slavery and,
48
Immigration (immigrants), 84,
122n, 148; and Democratic party,
111
"Implied" powers doctrine, 90–91,
95
Income tax, first, 188
Indentured servants, 10, 39, 49, 144
Independence, American (*see also*
American Revolution): Virginia
and Southern role in, 55–85 (*see
also under* Virginia)
"Indian Bill of Rights," 315
Indians, American, 99, 100, 101,
102, 105–6, 119, 151, 315, 348n,
349
Industry (industrialism, industrial
North), 4, 42, 52, 54, 90, 114,
132, 136–37, 141 (*see also*
Economy; specific aspects,
developments); and growth in size
and power of bureaucracy and
federal government, 185, 191,
194, 359–60, 363, 367, 368 (*see
also* specific developments, events,
individuals); and North-South
sectionalism, 4, 42, 114, 356–58,
368, 373
Internal Revenue Service, 362
Interstate and Foreign Commerce
Committee, 341
Interstate Commerce Commission,
341
Interventionism (internationalism),
Southern leadership in foreign
affairs and, 320–23, 326–27,
331–37, 344–45. See also under
Foreign affairs
Irish immigrants, 148
Isolationism, Southern, 322

Jackson, Andrew, 7, 97, 102n,
105, 109, 110, 115n, 119, 133,
136, 178, 207, 208, 217, 238, 359;
as President, 117–18, 119–23, 136,
139–40
Jackson, Henry, 371
Jackson, Henry M., 183, 259n, 260,
262n
Jackson, Thomas J. (Stonewall),
163
Jamestown, Va., 22, 41, 44, 63
Japan, and World War II, 320, 321,
335
Jay, John, 52, 93, 339
Jay Treaty, 11, 92, 93, 98, 100n,
107, 111
Jefferson, Peter, 62
Jefferson, Thomas, 6, 7, 9, 11, 23,
25, 36, 62–71, 81, 83, 112, 118,
119, 133, 138, 140, 185, 186, 238,
292, 339, 365, 368, 369;
background, described, 62–71, 98;
and blacks and slavery, 8, 24–25,
65, 66, 67, 142; and creation of
Democratic party, 73; and
Declaration of Independence, 24,
56, 57, 62–71; and "free and
equal" doctrine, 9, 56, 339 (*see
also* Jeffersonians); and Hamilton,
81, 90–93, 94–96, 111, 112–13,
114, 115n, 357–58, 368 (*see also*
Federalists); and John Marshall,
6, 7, 11; and John Randolph, 26,

27, 35; as President, 117, 118, 153; and secession, 112, 116, 135, 138; as Secretary of State, 89, 92–94; as Vice President, 108, 109, 110; and "Virginia and Kentucky Resolves," 112
Jefferson family, 62. *See also* specific individuals by name
Jeffersonians (Jeffersonian democracy, Jeffersonian principles and values), 9, 56, 62, 90, 91, 95–98, 106, 111, 112–13, 114ff., 121, 132, 136ff., 185, 188, 197 206, 211, 278, 279, 339, 357–58, 368, 370; and "free and equal" doctrine, 9, 56, 339
Jim Crow era and laws, 171–72, 194–97, 206, 278
Johnson, Andrew, 12, 153, 164, 166, 186, 359
Johnson, Edwin, 310n, 311, 312
Johnson, Hugh, 235
Johnson, Lyndon B., 2, 7, 10–11, 12, 30, 128, 149, 181n, 182, 183, 293, 314, 329, 336, 338–39, 345, 346–55, 358, 368, 369, 373; biography, political activity, 338–39, 346–55; and "credibility gap," 352–53; and persuasion technique, 349–50; as President, 348, 351–55; and protégé system, 241, 242, 243, 244, 293, 331–32; and Senate "Club," 254, 258, 261, 264–65, 266, 267, 269–70, 310
Johnston, J. Bennett, Jr., 247–51, 254, 259n, 260
Johnston, Olin D., 203, 316
Joint Chiefs of Staff, 361
Jordan, B. Everett, 259n, 262n
Jordan, Barbara, 241–45
Journalists. *See* Newspapers (the press)
Judicial review concept, 1
Judiciary Committee (U. S. Congress), 180, 184; House, 242–43; Senate, 251n, 254, 259, 295, 297, 304–5
Just a Country Lawyer (Clancy), 310n, 314, 316n

Kefauver, Estes, 261, 336n

Kennedy, Edward M. (Ted), 260, 296
Kennedy, John F., 258, 261, 267, 293, 295n, 299, 331, 351, 352, 369
Kennedy, Robert F., 258
Kentucky, 5, 93, 99, 100–1, 111–14, 355, 369
Kerr, Robert S. (Bob), 258, 265, 298
Key, V. O., 285
King, Martin Luther, Jr., 11, 149, 172, 238, 339, 369, 372, 373
King, Rufus, 118
Kleberg, Richard, 347
Kleindienst, Richard G., 302
Knowland, William F., 336n
Knox, Henry, 89
Kohler, Walter, 268
Korean War, 321, 332–37
Ku Klux Klan, 2, 172, 194–96, 209–10

Labor (*see also* Working class): slave, 44–54 (*see also* Indentured servants; Slavery)
LaFollette, Robert M. (Bob), 254
Laird, Melvin R., 294n
Land acquisitions. *See* Territorial acquisitions, Southerners and
Lanterns on the Levee (Percy), 287n
Latrobe, Benjamin Henry, 99n
Laussat, Pierre Clément de, 101–2
Lawyers (trial lawyers), Southern politicians and practice as, 246
Leadership (leaders), Southern, 4, 5, 132, 134ff., 173ff., 200–1, 253–73 *passim*, 278–80, 281ff., 306–18, 319–37, 338–35 (*see also* specific aspects, developments, events, issues, individuals, movements); absence of, 338–40, 358ff.; growth in size and power of bureaucracy and federal government and need for new, 358ff., 366–69; values of small Southern towns and development of, 45 (*see also* Values)
League of Nations, 193, 322
Lee, Henry ("Light Horse" Harry

Lee), 23, 36, 102
Lee, Launcelot, 22
Lee, Richard Henry, 22–23, 25, 56, 57, 58, 60, 67, 70, 71, 72, 273
Lee, Robert E., 23n, 36, 163, 164
Lee, S. S., 161n
Lees, the, 10, 22, 23, 64, 65, 83. *See also* specific individuals by name
Legislature (*see also* Congress, U. S.; House of Representatives, U. S.; Senate, U. S.; specific places): balance of powers and, 1 (*see also* Balance of powers principle); two-house, organization of, 18
L'Enfant, Pierre Charles, 87
Lever Food Control Act, 192
Leviton, Joyce, 370n
Lewis, John L., 339
Lewis and Clark expedition, 117
Lexington, Battle of, 55, 57, 66
Liberals (liberal legislation), 202–3, 293, 345–46, 350, 351, 353–54, 373 (*see also* specific developments, individuals, issues, legislation); FDR and New Deal and, 202–3; LBJ and, 345–46
Liberator (newspaper), 142
Liberia, 53–54, 290, 324
Liberty, government interference and, 365–69. *See also* Bureaucracy
Lincoln, Abraham, 2, 10, 12, 100n, 149, 153, 158–59, 161, 164, 214, 290, 359, 369
Livingston, Robert R., 56, 67n, 73n
Locke, John, 43n, 365
Lodge, Henry Cabot, 328, 332, 336n
Long, Earl K., 209n, 247n, 289
Long, Gillis, 259
Long, Huey P., 7, 12, 13, 30, 122, 202, 206–11, 240, 241, 244, 247n, 248, 250, 267, 271, 349, 352, 368, 369, 373; assassination of, 203, 237, 238; background, described, political activity, 207–8, 210, 214–15, 218–19, 224, 236, 238–39; and blacks, 206, 209–10, 211, 234, 237; and FDR and New Deal, 200, 202, 224, 225–26,

229n, 230, 234–37; and Populism, 207, 211–14ff., 238; and Share-the-Wealth program, 207–11, 216, 220–21, 232, 236–38; and use of filibuster, 226–29
Long, James, 214
Long, John, 214–15
Long, Rose McConnell, 250n
Long, Russell, 208, 230n, 250, 251, 252, 254, 259, 262n, 295, 336
Longworth, Nicholas, 342n
"Lords Proprietors," 43
Louis XV, King (France), 49
Louis XVI, King (France), 91
Louisiana, 11, 115, 122, 146, 151, 159, 169, 200, 210–11, 214–20, 221, 222, 240, 247–51, 285 (*see also* specific places); blacks in, 146, 147, 156, 157, 209; Huey Long and, 207–11, 214–20, 221, 222, 229, 235, 236–37; Purchase, 11–12, 117, 153, 174; territory, 11–12, 101, 105, 106, 117, 153, 174
Lowndes, William, 135
Luciano, Lucky, 229
Lyell, Sir Charles, 47–49, 148, 157
Lynchings, 194, 291

MacArthur, Douglas A., 197, 332–37; address to joint session of Congress by, 335; Russell and, 332–37
Macaulay, Wilkes, 282
McCarthy, Eugene J., 254, 258, 338–39, 345; on lack of leadership as central national problem, 338–39
McCarthy, Joseph R. (Joe), 268, 279, 293, 304, 309–14; Eastland and, 304; Ervin and, 279, 293, 309–14; Stennis and, 293
McClellan, John, 174, 259, 262n, 265
McCormack, John W., 339
MacFarland, Ernest W., 348
McKean, Thomas, 73n
McKeithen, John J., 247, 248–49
McKellar, Kenneth D., 228
Maclay, William, 18

McMahon, Brien, 336n
McNamara, Robert S., 293
Madison, James, 7, 11, 25, 64, 72, 73, 77, 81, 82, 83, 91, 92, 107, 109, 112, 116, 127, 133, 138, 140, 175, 176, 177n, 369; as President, 117, 118, 136, 153, 189, 211, 238, 256
Maestri, Robert S. (Bob), 229n
Mafia, the, Huey Long and, 207, 229n, 237
Magnuson, Warren G., 258, 259n, 262n
Mahon, George H., 175
Mahon, John, 316
Mailer, Norman, 339
Malcolm, Samuel, 107
Manhattan (N.Y.C.), 17, 44. See also New York City
Mansfield, Mike, 183, 262n, 296, 298, 329, 339, 352
Marshall, George C., 279
Marshall, Humphrey, 93
Marshall, John, 6, 8, 36, 62, 64, 83
Marshall Plan, 279, 344
Martin, Joseph W., Jr., 342
Marx, Karl, 141, 143
Maryland, 42, 43, 75, 99, 146
Mason, George, 56, 64, 78, 88, 104
Massachusetts, 5, 38, 41, 42, 55, 56, 59, 84, 113, 356. See also specific places
Mathias, Charles, 361
Maverick, Maury, 197–98, 349
Mayfield, Earle B., 195
Meany, George, 339
Mellon, Andrew W., 197
Mencken, H. L., 10
Methodists, 10
Mexican-Americans, 348n, 349, 350–51
Mexico, 152, 154
Mifflin, Thomas, 58, 59
Military, the: Joe McCarthy and, 310–11; Southern leadership and, 295–96, 320–23
Military Affairs Committee, U. S. Senate, 173, 328
Miller, Arthur, 339
Miller, Merle, 271, 343n
Mills, John, 270

Mills, Wilbur D., 175, 243
Mining, coal, 191, 192
Minority veto doctrine, 141–42
Miscegenation, 34, 46, 48, 147
Mississippi, 11, 99, 105, 106, 122, 135, 137, 146, 150–53, 241, 281–97, 298–305; Black Codes, 167; black office-holders, 169, 170, 284; and Civil War era, 159, 162–63, 164–65, 169; free blacks in, 157; politics in, 285ff.; and secession, 159, 164–65; senators from, 169, 281–97, 298–305 (see also specific individuals by name)
Mississippi River, 100, 102, 106, 117, 128, 151
Missouri, 122
Missouri Compromise, 155
Mitchell, Clarence M., Jr., 354
Mitchell, John N., 258, 283, 294n, 339
Monroe, James, 62, 64, 83, 118, 133, 369; as President, 117, 118, 119, 121–23, 153
Montgomery, Ala., 160–61
Moray, Alexander, 42
Morison, Samuel Eliot, 85
Morris, Gouverneur, 79
Morris, Robert, 18
Morse, Wayne L., 267, 269, 270, 336n
Morton, Thruston B., 262n
Mount Vernon, Va., home of George Washington in, 18, 20, 21–22, 104–5
Mulattoes, 48
Mundt, Karl E., 262n
Murray, William H. ("Alfalfa Bill"), 200
Murrow, Edward R., 303
Muskie, Edmund S., 262n, 264–66, 267, 269

Nashville, Tenn., 103, 105, 151
Natchez Trace, 151
National bank, 90–91
National Democratic party, 158
"National emergencies," growth of executive powers and, 360–62
National Industrial Recovery Act (NRA), 360; legislation, 304

National Republicans, 96–97, 120
Nazis: Klan compared to, 195, 196; and World War II, 321–22 (*see also under* Germany)
Nelson, Thomas, 73n
Nero, Alfred, 320
Nevin, David, 348, 355
New Deal era, 2, 7, 97, 174, 199–206, 207ff., 224, 225–26, 234–39, 277–80, 323, 324, 325, 341, 342, 347, 359–60
New England (New Englanders), 6, 7, 18, 23, 36n, 51, 95, 99, 113, 115, 191, 211, 256 (*see also* specific events, individuals, places); Southern role in American Revolution and, 55, 56ff.; and Virginia compared, 37ff., 55ff., 82, 83–86
New Freedom, Woodrow Wilson and, 2, 186, 193–94, 196
New Jersey Plan, 77, 78
New Mexico, 152
New Orleans, La., 46–47, 106, 145, 147, 148, 151, 156, 191, 246–47; Battle of, 119; *Daily Picayune,* 156; Huey Long and, 209, 210, 222–24, 233
Newspapers (the press), 3, 5, 6, 109, 110, 111 (*see also* individual publications); and Northern prejudice against the South, 5, 6, 109, 110, 111, 354–55; Southern, 195–96
New York City, 44, 63, 122n, 159; congresses in, 17–23, 87ff.
New York State, 57, 85; and slavery, 51–53, 54
Nicholson, Francis, 63
Niles, Hezekiah, 28–29
Nixon, Richard M., 5, 129, 243, 244, 252, 257, 258, 294, 296, 302, 339, 362; Ervin and, 308–10, 315–16; and "national emergency" powers, 360–61; resignation of, 279, 283–84, 296, 301, 308–9
Noblesse oblige tradition, 122, 131
Norfolk, Va., 191
Norris, George W., 207, 221, 253, 341

North Carolina, 11, 100, 102, 103–5, 137, 146, 307, 317–18 (*see also* Carolinas); free blacks in, 157; and secession, 159
NRA. *See* National Industrial Recovery Act (NRA)
Nuclear weapons, use of. *See* Atomic (nuclear) weapons, Korean War and
Nullification doctrine and issue, 111–14, 127, 137–40, 141
Nunn, Sam, 250n, 259n, 260

O'Daniel, W. Lee (Pappy), 347
Office-holders, black, 6, 167–71, 284. *See also* specific individuals by name, places
Oglethorpe, James, 43
Oil and gas companies and interests, 347, 360; Huey Long and, 216, 218
Oklahoma, 5, 122, 369
O'Neill, Eugene, 339
Opinion-shapers, Northern, 5–6
Opium Exclusion Act (1909), 278n
OPSR, 363
Oregon, 101, 153n, 154
Osgood, Samuel, 89
OSHA, 363
Otis, James, 61
Overton, John H., 233–34

Parks, Mrs. Rosa, 172
Parliamentary techniques, use by Southern politicians of, 86. *See also* Politics; specific devices, individuals, issues, kinds
Parr, George, 349
Party affiliation, Senate "Club" and, 254
Pastore, John O., 259n, 261, 262n
Paternalism, federal government and, 366–69. *See also* Benign interference principle; Protectionism
Paterson, William, 77
Patman, Wright, 175, 197
Patriotism, Southern, 321
Peace Movement of Ethiopia, 290n
Peltier, Harvey, 233
Pendergast, Tom, 272

Pennsylvania, 56, 57, 85. *See also* specific places
People (magazine), 370
Pepper, Claude D., 200, 322–23
Percy, LeRoy, 286–89
Percy, Walker, 285, 287n, 339
Percy, William Alexander, 284, 287–89
Perez, Leander, 304
Peters, Phillis Wheatley, 51–52
Philadelphia, Pa., 18, 57, 58, 59, 63; Constitutional Convention (1787), 75; First Continental Congress, 65
Pickering, Timothy, 58–59, 68, 107, 108
Pierce, Franklin, 153
Pike, James Shepherd, 167–69
Pilgrims, 41, 42, 44, 82
Pinchbeck, P. B. S., 169
Pinckney, Charles, 76–77, 79, 81, 132, 253, 256
Pinckney, Thomas, 94, 95
Pinckney Plan, 77, 256
Plains, Ga., 371
Plain Speaking (Miller), 271n, 343n
Planters (plantations), Southern, 37, 39–40, 43n, 122–23, 161. *See also* Agrarian South; Agriculture; Aristocracy (elite); specific developments, places
Plymouth colony, 42
Poage, W. R., 175
Pocahontas, 26
Poland, and World War II, 322
Political parties (party politics), creation and evolution of, 2, 72, 73, 86, 88–97, 98–116, 117–23, 127ff. *See also* Politics; specific developments, individuals, issues, parties
Politics (political power, system, and tradition), Southern politicians and, 1–2, 4–13, 22–23, 36ff., 86, 97, 122–23, 127–32, 133ff. (*see also* specific aspects, developments, devices, individuals, issues, places); and contributions to the nation, 1–2, 279–80, 281ff. (*see also* specific developments, individuals); FDR

and New Deal era and, 199–206, 277–80; and leadership (*see* Leadership); and new Populism, 13, 368–69, 372–73 (*see also* Populism; specific individuals, movements); post-Civil War, 166–72; and protégé system, 239, 240–52 (*see also* Protégé system); and Senate "Club," 253–73 (*see also* "Club," the); and seniority-committee system, 172, 173–84; and U. S. Senate as Southern bastion of strength, 123, 127–32, 134ff., 200–1, 218–19, 256–57, 278, 281ff. (*see also* specific individuals); Virginia's role, 82–86 (*see also under* Virginia); World War I and Wilson era, 185ff.
Polk, James, 7, 153, 154, 359, 369
Poor, the (poverty), 95; class and (*see* Class; Working class; specific groups); FDR and New Deal (*see* Roosevelt, Franklin Delano; New Deal era); Huey Long and, 211–14ff., 216, 220–21, 232, 236–38, 364, 365; Jimmy Carter and, 372–73; LBJ and, 353; populist movement and, 207, 211–14ff., 285, 372–73 (*see also* Populism; specific individuals); redistribution of wealth and (*see* Wealth, redistribution of)
Populism (populist movement), 122, 190, 207, 211–14ff., 285, 286; Barbara Jordan and, 243–44; Huey Long and, 207, 211–14ff., 238; Jimmy Carter and, 372–73; LBJ and, 349; as new Southern politics, 13, 368–69, 372–73; and Southern values, 368–69, 370–73; Tom Watson and (*see* Watson, Tom)
Port Hudson, Miss., 162–63
Poverty Program, LBJ and, 353
Powell, Lazarus, 160
"Power" committees, U. S. Congress, 175–76, 184, 249–50, 251, 254, 259–60, 272, 273
Power in the Senate (Ripley), 293n
Powhatan, 26n

Presidency (Presidents), 2, 88, 94, 132 (*see also* specific developments, individuals by name); balance of powers and (*see* Balance of powers principle); growth in power of bureaucracy and, 277–80, 358–69 (*see also* Bureaucracy; specific developments, individuals); need for leadership and, 362–69; and seniority-committee system and control of Congress, 173–74, 175, 178; Southern, 7, 12, 117–23, 354–55 (*see also* specific individuals by name)
Press, the. *See* Newspapers (the press)
Progressivism, 213–14
Prostrate State: South Carolina Under Negro Government, The (Pike), 168, 169
Protectionism, federal government and, 358. *See also* Benign interference principle; Paternalism, federal government and
"Protégé" system, 239, 240–52, 260, 292–93, 297
Provost marshals, use in Civil War era of, 3
Proxmire, William, 268–70, 315–16
Pryor, Roger, 161n
Public Utilities Holding Company Act, 341
Puritans (Puritan Yankees), 82, 85

Quincy, Josiah, III, 115
Quincy, Josiah, IV, 32

Race (racial attitudes, issues, policies, and relations), 6, 8–10, 12, 13, 24, 32–33, 44–53, 54, 147, 171–72, 279 (*see also* Blacks; Civil rights; Slavery; specific aspects, developments, events, groups, individuals, issues, movements, places); and Civil War era, 155ff., 166–72 (*see also* Civil War); class and, 147, 371; FDR and New Deal era and, 205, 206, 277, 278; Huey Long and, 209–10, 234; Jimmy Carter and, 371, 372–73; Klan and, 194–96; LBJ and, 340, 349, 350–51, 353, 354; Southern leaders and, 289–91, 293–94, 297, 302–5, 314–15, 316–18, 341, 349 (*see also* specific developments, individuals, issues, places)
Radical Reconstruction era, post-Civil War, 168–72
Radical Republicans (1854–76), 110–11, 158, 159, 161, 167–72
Rainey, Henry, 201
Rainey, Joseph Hayne, 11, 170
Ralph Nader Congress Report (1972), 258
Randolph, Edmund, 19, 27, 36, 76, 81, 83, 89, 128, 132
Randolph, John (of Roanoke), 18–19, 25–35, 36–37, 130, 173, 177, 189, 211, 227, 238, 256, 306, 309, 368; biography, political activity, 18–19, 25–35, 36–37, 73, 114, 127, 136–37, 173, 177, 189, 227; and use of filibuster, 26–35, 238
Randolph, Mary Isham, 36
Randolph, Peyton, 36
Randolph, Richard, 19, 31
Randolph, William, 36
Randolphs, the, 10, 25, 36, 64, 83. *See also* specific individuals by name
Ransdell, Joseph E., 218–19
Rapallo, Treaty of, 322n
Rape (s), incidence of, 43, 45
Rayburn, Sam, 11, 30, 181n, 182, 200, 201, 241, 320, 323, 338, 339, 340–46, 352, 355; biography, political activity, 340–46, 347
Rayburn, William Marion, 340
REA. *See* Rural Electrification Act (REA)
Reconstruction Act, 167
Reconstruction era, post-Civil War, 166–72
"Red-necks" ("crackers"), 43, 285, 286, 301
Reed, Roy, 247n
Regulatory agencies, federal, growth

in size and power of bureaucracy and, 362–64
Republican party (Republicans), 12, 38, 73n, 96–97, 149, 332, 336, 342, 345, 350 (*see also* Congress, U. S.; specific developments, individuals, issues); Civil War era, 154, 158–59, 161, 167–72 (*see also* Radical Republicans); FDR and New Deal era and, 203, 205; origin and evolution of, 96–97, 149; and seniority system, 178–84; and Wilson and World War I era, 185ff.
Reuther, Walter P., 339, 352
Revels, Hiram R., 11, 149, 150, 170, 171, 284
Revolutionary War, American. *See* American Revolution
Revolutions, 7, 69–70. *See also* specific aspects, events, places, wars
Reynolds, Robert R., 323
Rhode Island, 57
Richmond, Va., 45
Ripley, Randall B., 293n
Robertson, A. Willis, 265
Robinson, Joseph T. (Joe), 201, 204, 205, 221, 228, 231, 253
Rodney, Caesar, 56
Rolfe, John, 26, 27n
Roosevelt, Eleanor, 226, 343
Roosevelt, Franklin Delano, 2, 7, 12, 118n, 182, 195n, 198, 199–206, 234–37, 240, 253, 259, 335, 343, 369; and Eastland, 303; and Huey Long, 200, 202, 224, 225–26, 229n, 230, 234–37; and LBJ, 347, 349; and New Deal, 199–206, 224, 225–26, 234–37, 277, 303, 342, 344, 360; and Southern leadership and World War II, 320, 322–23, 324–26; and Supreme Court, 204–5, 360; and Truman, 271–72; Walter George and, 324–26
Roosevelt, Theodore, 185–86, 369
Roper, Dan, 200
Roundheads, 38, 41, 135
Rules Committee (U. S. Congress), 259, 299
Rule 22 (U. S. Senate), 264–65

Rural Electrification Act (REA), 201, 324, 331, 341, 348
Rush, Benjamin, 59
Russell, Richard B., 13, 132, 183, 250n, 253–54, 258, 260, 262–63, 266, 267, 279, 295, 298, 330–37, 358, 368; biography, political activity, 330–37; and foreign affairs, 320, 331–37; and LBJ, 347, 348; and MacArthur, 332–37; and Stennis, 292–93, 295
Russia. *See* Soviet Union (Russia)
Rutledge, Edward, 56, 58, 73n

St. Clair, Arthur, 103
Saltonstall, Leverett, 336n
San Francisco Conference (1945), 328
Schlesinger, James R., 361
School desegregation, 294, 303–4; Stennis and, 294
Schwellenbach, Lewis B., 272
Scott, Hugh, 259
Scott, Winfield, 152
Seabury, Paul, 320n
Secession, 2, 7, 111, 112, 114–16, 135–36, 138–40; Calhoun and, 135–36, 138–40
Second Visit to the United States, A (Lyell), 47–49
Sectionalism, North-South, 2–4, 7–10, 23ff., 36–54, 57ff. (*see also* specific aspects, developments, events, individuals, issues, movements, political parties); and Civil War (*see* Civil War); economic issues and (*see* Economy); and evolution of political parties, 89–93, 94–97, 117–23, 127–32, 135ff.; 1790s, 93, 95, 97, 98–116; slavery and, 137, 142–49 (*see also* Slavery); tariffs and, 136–37, 142; Wilson and World War I era, 185ff.
Securities and Exchange Commission (SEC), 341
Segregation system, 45, 171–72, 194–96, 294, 303. *See also* Civil rights; Race; specific aspects, groups, individuals, movements, places
Selective Service Act. 343

Senate, U. S., 1, 6–7, 20–21, 22, 89, 127–32, 134ff. (*see also* Congress, U. S.; specific developments, events, individuals, issues); blacks in, 170–71 (*see also* specific individuals by name); and Civil War, 152ff., 170; "Club," 251, 252, 253–73, 281ff., 358 (*see also* "Club," the); committees (*see* Committees, U. S. Congress; specific committees); establishment in, 129; and growth of bureaucracy and executive power, 358–69; history, powers, and tradition, 78–79, 127–32; need for leadership in, 358ff.; organization of, 78–79; "power" committees, 259–60 (*see also* "Power" committees); and "protégé system," 247–52 (*see also* "Protégé system"); and sectionalism (1790s), 93, 95, 97, 107–16; seniority system and, 172, 173ff., 177–84, 200–1; Southern political leadership and strength in, 123, 127–32, 134ff., 200–1, 218–19, 256–57, 278, 281ff. (*see also* specific developments, individuals, issues); and Wilson and World War I era, 187, 193

Seniority principle (U. S. Congress), 2, 131, 172, 173–84, 200–1, 259–60, 272, 273, 279, 293, 297, 300, 345–46

Separation of powers doctrine, 72. *See also* Balance of powers principle

Servants, indentured. *See* Indentured servants

Sevier, Ambrose H., 178

Seward, William H., 153

Sharecroppers (tenant farmers), 10, 192, 285

Share-the-wealth programs, 207–11, 216, 220–21, 224, 232, 236–38, 364, 365, 368. *See also* Populism; specific individuals

Shay, Daniel, rebellion led by, 76

Sherman, Roger, 56, 67, 73n, 78, 79

Sherman, William Tecumseh, 10, 161–62, 189

Sidey, Hugh, 353

Simmons, William, 195

Slave codes, 146–47

Slave laws, 49

Slavery (slave trade), 6, 7–8, 9, 10, 11, 24–25, 27, 30, 31–35, 39–40, 41–42, 43, 44–54, 66, 80, 134–35, 137, 141–49, 158, 356, 358 (*see also* Blacks; specific developments, events, individuals, movements, places); abolition movement and (*see* Abolition of slavery movement); Calhoun and, 134–35, 137, 141, 142–44; as cause of Civil War, 2; and Civil War, 2, 151–54, 155ff. (*see also* Civil War); Constitution and, 52, 61, 68, 74, 79–80; and history and condition of slaves in the South 44–54; Jefferson and, 8, 24–25, 65, 66, 142; rebellions and, 144–46, 147; and sectionalism, 137, 142–49, 154; trading banned, 146

Slavocracy, 158

Small towns, Southern values and ideals and, 4–5, 368–69, 370–73. *See also* Community identification; Values (ideals), Southern

Smathers, George A., 262n

Smith, Al, 199

Smith, H. Alexander, 336n

Smith, Hoke, 189, 214, 255

Smith, Judge Hoke, III, 245–47

Smith, Howard, 299, 305

Smith, John, 26n, 42

Smith, William, 51, 177n

"Solid South," 97

South Carolina, 25, 133–40, 144, 146, 169–70 (*see also* Carolinas); free blacks in, 157; and secession, 159

Southeast Asia Treaty Organization, 329

Southern bloc, 73, 337, 351

"Southern Manifesto," 303, 351

Southern Politics (Key), 285n

Southwest Territory, 104–6

Soviet Union (Russia), 298, 332, 333

Spain, 101, 102, 105, 106, 119, 128, 319

Spanish-American War, 359
Sparkman, John J., 175, 252, 262, 270, 336
Special Committee on Termination of Natural Emergencies and Delegated Emergency Powers, U. S. Senate, 361
Special interests, federal government and, 368
Spoils system, 121
Stalin, Joseph, 333
Stamp Act, 59, 64–65; Congress, 89, 175
Standard Oil, 217, 218
Standing committees (U. S. Congress), 173, 176, 177ff., 181, 183
States' rights, 7, 30, 34, 74, 88, 95–96, 97, 120, 132, 188, 317 (*see also* specific aspects, developments, events, issues); FDR and New Deal era and, 205, 206; nullification and secession and, 112–14, 137–40 (*see also* Secession); tariffs and, 137–40; Wilson and World War I era, 188, 190
States' Rights party (1948), 97
Stennis, John C., 11, 13, 132, 149, 250, 252, 253, 259, 262, 279, 291–97, 298, 302–3, 358; and Armed Services Committee, 295–96; biography, political activity, 281–84, 291–97, 310, 336; and Dodd case, 282–83, 293; and Senator Joseph McCarthy, 293
Stevenson, Adlai E., 261, 262
Stevenson, Coke R., 347, 349
Stone, Thomas, 73n
Stowe, Harriet Beecher, 6, 66, 166n
Strong, Caleb, 18
Subversive Activities Control Board (SACB), 315–16
Sugar production, 52
"Summary View of the Rights of British America, A" (Jefferson), 65–66
Supreme Court of the United States, 6, 18, 130, 174, 303–4; FDR and, 204–5, 360
Swanson, Claude A., 200

Swanstrom, Roy, 93n
Symington, Stuart, 183, 259, 262

Taft, Robert A., 254, 291, 332
Taft, William Howard, 186
Talmadge, Eugene, 122, 241, 325, 330
Talmadge, Herman, 13, 246, 257–58, 259, 279–80, 283, 330
Talmadges, the, 241. *See also* specific individual by name
Tammany Society (N.Y.C.), 115n
Tariffs (duties), 11, 96, 136–40, 152n, 359; reforms, 188; wars, 75
Taxes, 7, 20, 21, 64–65, 91, 96, 188, 206, 217, 218, 225, 359. *See also* specific kinds, taxes
Taylor, Zachary, 12, 151, 152
Tazewell, Henry, 108
Tea Party (Boston, Mass.), 55, 57, 65
Technology, 365
Tenant farmers (sharecroppers), 10, 192, 285
Tennessee, 11, 103, 105, 106, 108, 109, 110, 122, 135, 151, 340, 355; free blacks in, 157; and secession, 159n
Tennessee Valley Authority (TVA), 324, 340
Territorial acquisitions, Southerners and, 153, 154. *See also* specific individuals, issues, places
Texans, The (Nevin), 348n
Texas, 11, 122, 152, 159n, 197, 240–45, 338–55; and leadership in U. S. Congress, 338–55 (*see also* specific individuals by name)
Textile industry, 191
Thomas, Elbert D., 320, 327
Thompson, William A. (Big Bill), 229–30n
Thurmond, J. Strom, 97, 270, 293, 304
Time on the Cross (Fogel and Engerman), 45–46
Tindall, George, 191, 322
Tobacco, 39, 40, 52, 82, 83, 136, 201
Tobacco Control Act, 201
Tobey, Charles W., 336n

Tocqueville, Alexis de, 10, 49–51, 52, 53, 54, 140–41, 211

Touro, Joseph, 227

Towns, Southern values and ideals and. *See* Small towns, Southern values and ideals and

Trade Agreements Act, 360

Treaty-making power, U. S. Senate and, 128

Treen, David C., 248n

Truman, Harry S., 182, 270–72, 343, 344, 345, 369; and General MacArthur, 332, 336; and Marshall Plan, 344

Trusts, government regulation of, 188–89, 278n

Tuscaloosa, Ala., 157

TVA. *See* Tennessee Valley Authority

Two-party system, evolution of, 2, 89–97. *See also* Political parties; specific individuals, issues, parties

Tydings, Joseph D., 258

Udall, Morris K., 181–82

Uncle Tom's Cabin, 6

Underwood, Oscar, 132, 188, 195

Union, the, Civil War and, 159–65. *See also* Civil War

United Nations, 2, 12, 49; and Korean War, 332, 335; Tom Connally and beginning of, 279, 320, 327–28

United States of America: capitals (various) listed, 87; naming of, 73; Southern role in creation of, 1ff., 18, 23ff., 36ff., 55–86 (*see also* specific developments, events, individuals)

Universities (*see also* specific institutions by name): Northern, 2, 5, 6; Southern, 6

Values (ideals), Southern, 4–5, 10–11, 23ff., 36ff., 355, 358, 365–69, 370–73 (*see also* Community identification; Group integrity; Jeffersonians; Leadership; Patriotism; specific aspects, developments, individuals, issues, movements, places); small towns and frontier areas and, 4–5,

355, 368–69, 370–73

Van Every, Dale, 101n

Vantage Point, The (Johnson), 11n

Vardaman, James K., 188, 290, 241, 284, 285, 286–89, 303

Versailles Treaty, 193, 322

Veterans' bonuses, 197, 335

Veto: Andrew Jackson and, 121; minority, 141–42

Vietnam War, 295, 320, 321, 329, 331, 353

Violence (violent crime), Southerners and incidence of, 43–44n

Virginia (Virginians), 5, 6, 11, 22–23, 25, 27n, 31, 36ff., 73, 90, 91, 99, 113, 118, 122, 135–36, 137, 139, 150–51, 159, 241n, 356, 358 (*see also* specific events, individuals, places); and Bill of Rights, 56, 73, 85; character and creativity of, 25ff., 83–86 (*see also* specific developments, individuals, places); and Constitution, 56, 66, 76–85; and New England and New Englanders compared, 37ff., 55ff., 82, 83–86; politics in, 25, 122–23; role in American Revolution of, 55–71, 72–86 (*see also* specific developments, individuals); and slavery, 44–54, 146, 157; and "Virginia and Kentucky Resolves," 111–12; and Virginia Plan, 72, 76–80, 85, 104, 256

Volstead Act (1919), 278n

Voting rights, 79, 80, 95, 316; blacks and, 166, 167, 169, 203, 211, 213, 316

Voting Rights Act (1965), 316

Walker, Clifford, 195

Wallace, George C., 304

War Department, 3

"War Hawks," 136

War Insurance Act (World War I), 341

War of 1812, 136

War of Independence. *See* American Revolution

"War on Poverty," 353–54

Wars, foreign, Southern political

leadership and support of,
320–23, 325–27, 329, 331–37
Washington, D.C., 117. *See also*
District of Columbia
Washington, George, 18, 56, 57,
58n, 60, 62, 64, 65, 66, 75, 77, 81,
83, 85, 87n, 89–90, 104–5, 114,
327n, 339, 359; as President,
20–22, 23, 25, 27n, 36, 87n,
89–90, 92, 93, 94, 118
Watergate affair, 5, 13, 246, 258,
283–84, 307, 362
Watkins, Arthur V., 310n, 311, 312
Watson, Tom, 122, 190, 212–13,
245n, 324, 370
Wayne, Anthony, 104
Ways and Means Committee:
House, 173, 175n, 176–77, 243,
259; Senate, 173, 175, 176–77,
259
Wealth, redistribution of, 207–11,
216, 220–21, 224, 232, 236–38,
364, 365, 368 (*see also* Poor,
the; Populism)
Weaver, James B., 213
Weaver, Robert C., 354
Webster, Daniel, 96, 129, 130, 152,
254, 290
Weiss, Carl Austin, 237
Welty, Eudora, 285, 339
Wheeler, Burton K., 207
Whig party (Whigs), 96, 97, 152,
154, 158
Whiskey tax, 96, 111
White, Edward Douglass, 187
White, George H., 171
White, Theodore, 354
White, William S., 252, 260, 261,
335
White Citizens' Councils, 172
White supremacy, 132, 137, 149,
174, 206, 331, 358
Whitney, Eli, 136
Wigfall, Louis T., 161n
Wilkins, Roy, 354
William and Mary College
(Williamsburg, Va.), 62, 63, 83
Williams, Edward Bennett, 310
Williams, George Washington,

162–63, 165–66
Williams, John Sharp, 193
Williams, T. Harry, 208, 229–30n,
234
Williams, Tennessee, 285, 339
Williamsburg, Va., 40, 62–64,
83–85; creative and intellectual
community in, 62, 83–85
Willkie, Wendell L., 237
Wilson, Woodrow, 2, 7, 12, 152,
173, 184–90, 192–94, 199, 200,
203, 205, 212, 213, 253, 256, 320,
341, 344, 358–59, 369; and New
Freedom, 186, 193–94; and
World War I and fourteen-point
program, 192–93, 322
Wingate, Paine, 18
Winn Parish, La., 214–15
Wisconsin, 208–20
Wise, Henry A., 153
Wood, Fernando, 159n
Working class, 118, 121, 207–11
(*see also* Class; Labor; Poor, the;
Slavery; specific developments,
individuals, issues, movements,
places); FDR and New Deal and,
199–206; Populism and (*see*
Populism); Southern blacks and,
147–48, 166–67, 171 (*see also*
Blacks); World War I and Wilson
era, 188, 189, 191
World War I, 189–93, 194, 215–16,
320–21, 322, 341, 344, 359
World War II, 320–23, 325–27, 335,
343, 344
Wright, Jonathan Jasper, 169–70
Wright, Richard, 285
Wylie, Alexander, 336n
Wynkoop, Henry, 22
Wythe, George, 62, 64, 76, 81, 83

Yale University, 6
Young, Andrew, 372–73
Young, Milton R., 259n
Young, Whitney, 354

Zemurray, Sam, 218
Zwicker, Ralph, 310–11